The Subject of Elizabeth

The Subject of Elizabeth

Authority, Gender, and Representation

⌒ LOUIS MONTROSE ⌒

The University of Chicago Press
Chicago and London

Louis Montrose is professor of literature at the University of California at San Diego. He is the author of *The Purpose of Playing: Shakespeare and the Cultural Politics of the Elizabethan Theatre*, also published by the University of Chicago Press.

The University of Chicago Press, Chicago 60637
The University of Chicago Press, Ltd., London
© 2006 by The University of Chicago
All rights reserved. Published 2006
Printed in the United States of America

15 14 13 12 11 10 09 08 07 06   1 2 3 4 5

ISBN: 0-226-53473-1 (cloth)
ISBN: 0-226-53475-8 (paper)

Library of Congress Cataloging-in-Publication Data

Montrose, Louis Adrian.
    The subject of Elizabeth : authority, gender, and representation / Louis Montrose.
        p.   cm.
    Includes bibliographical references and index.
    ISBN 0-226-53473-1 (alk. paper)—ISBN 0-226-53475-8 (pbk. : alk. paper)
    1. Great Britain—History—Elizabeth, 1558–1603—Historiography.   2. English literature—Early modern, 1500–1700—History and criticism.   3. Elizabeth I, Queen of England, 1533–1603—Public opinion.   4. Elizabeth I, Queen of England, 1533–1603—In literature.   5. Queens—Great Britain—Biography—History and criticism.   6. Public opinion—Great Britain—History—16th century.
    7. Authority in literature.   8. Sex role in literature.   9. Queens in literature.
    I. Title.
    DA355.M66   2006
    942.05′5′092—dc22

                                                                    2005023695

In loving memory of my parents

Contents

⌒ PART 5 ⌒ Time's Subject

Illustrations

Acknowledgments

The subject of Elizabeth has been central to my research and writing since the beginning of my academic career. During that long time, I have benefited from the specialized knowledge of many other scholars, from the generous material assistance of several institutions, and from the interest and advice of colleagues, all of which I wish gratefully to acknowledge here.

Although much of the research and most of the writing for this book have been done relatively recently, it builds upon and in places briefly incorporates material from essays of mine published over the past twenty-five years. These essays are mentioned in the notes and listed in the bibliography. Substantial portions of two recent essays appear here in revised form: "Idols of the Queen: Policy, Gender, and the Picturing of Elizabeth I," *Representations* 68 (Fall 1999): 106–61; and "Elizabeth hinter dem Spiegel: Die Ein-Bildung der zwei Körper der Königin," in *Der Körper der Königin: Geschlecht und Herrschaft in der höfischen Welt seit 1500*, edited by Regina Schulte (Frankfurt: Campus Verlag, 2002), 67–98. I am grateful to the editors of *Representations* and the University of California Press and to Campus Verlag for permission to reprint this material.

At various stages of my research and writing on the subject of Elizabeth, I have been fortunate to receive fellowship support, for which I am deeply grateful to the Stanford Humanities Center, the National Endowment for the Humanities, the John Simon Guggenheim Memorial Foundation, and the University of California. On several occasions, the Committee on Research of the UC San Diego Academic Senate has funded travel and research in connection with this project; and the librarians and staff of the UC San Diego library and its interlibrary loan department have been unstinting in the provision of assistance. One of my greatest professional satisfactions has been to teach the subject of Elizabeth to several generations of graduate students at UC San Diego, and to learn from them in return.

During the course of my work, I have benefited from the assistance, criticism, and encouragement of many individual scholars, graduate assistants, archivists, curators, and owners of artworks. Some particular debts are acknowledged elsewhere; here I wish to extend my sincere gratitude to all of those who contributed in ways large or small to the making of this book. At the University of Chicago Press, Alan Thomas remained supportive of the project during its long gestation, Randolph Petilos helpfully facilitated the permissions process, and an anonymous reader generously offered detailed queries and suggestions from which I have benefited in making my final revisions; to all of them, my thanks. Those errors of fact or lapses of judgment that may remain in the following pages are poor things but my own.

Last and foremost, I want to express my loving thanks to my wife, Caroline Ding, who has had nothing and everything to do with the completion of this book.

A Note on Quotations from Early Modern Texts

My quotations from early modern texts come from a wide range of sources, including sixteenth-century printed books and manuscripts as well as later editions. I have made no attempt to modify spelling and punctuation in order to make all quotations conform to a single standard. Rather, with a few duly noted exceptions, I have preferred to quote these texts as I found them. The general exception, made for ease of reading, is that I have silently modernized the usages of *i* and *j*, *u* and *v*, and have expanded obsolete typographical contractions.

Introduction: Foundations and Trajectories

This book is not about the person of Queen Elizabeth but rather about the field of cultural meanings that were personified in her. In other words, it is about the projection of power and the contestation of authority in Elizabethan society, as these were manifested in the production, circulation, and appropriation of the royal image. In sixteenth-century Europe, public authority was invested in positions normally occupied by men, in their roles as fathers, husbands, masters, teachers, clerics, magistrates, or lords. The body politic of kingship with which she was endowed at her coronation rendered Queen Elizabeth a spectacular exception to this rule. Nevertheless, she remained a woman in her body natural, and therefore subject to those pervasive cultural perceptions of female weakness and disability that called into question the propriety and effectiveness of her authority. The feminine gender of the ruler had a profound impact upon the relations of power and upon their representation. Such representations, however, not merely were consequences of the ruler's gender but were themselves particular constructions of it. As the governor of both church and state, the monarch occupied the central place in the hierarchical and homological system within which her subjects' identities were fashioned; in theory, if not always in practice, her office and person not only compelled their collective subjection but also guaranteed their particular subjectivities. At the same time, because she was the ruler of a society that was pervasively patriarchal in its organization and distribution of authority, both public and domestic, she embodied an anomaly at the very center of that system, a challenge to the homology between hierarchies of rule and gender. This was a cognitive dissonance with both political and affective consequences. A range of strategies was generated by means of which this contradiction in the cultural logic could be variously articulated and obfuscated, contained and exploited—not only by the sovereign but also by her subjects and by interested parties abroad. Such strategies are the focus of my book.

The period during which I have been working on the subject of Elizabeth has produced a large body of fruitful scholarship about Queen Elizabeth and Elizabethan political culture, as well as about many other aspects of Elizabethan culture and society that bear directly upon the issues in this book.[1] Much recent work on Queen Elizabeth I in biographical and literary studies has been engaged in constructing a heroic narrative that celebrates the triumph of an extraordinary woman's will and intellect over perilous circumstances and tenacious adversaries. This has frequently proved to be a compelling and enlightening project, and it is one from which my own work has benefited, but it is not the project I pursue here. My study focuses instead upon the complex and diverse, the contradictory and contestatory processes that shaped the collective discourse about Queen Elizabeth and subjected it to myriad individual and collective appropriations. The discourse of Elizabethan power personified in "the Queen" was traversed by multiple and potentially antagonistic strategies. Herself a gendered and historical situated subject, Elizabeth Tudor was a privileged agent in the production of the royal image, but she was not its master. Her power to shape her own strategies was itself shaped—at once enabled and constrained—by the repertoire of values, institutions, and practices (including the pictorial and literary conventions) available to her for appropriation and innovation. She demonstrated an extraordinary capacity to work the available terms in order to serve her own needs and interests; and, by the same token, her subjects and others often reworked those terms to serve theirs. The vast majority of those who have left records of that cultural work are men—for reasons that follow from both the masculinist biases of early modern culture and from the perceived challenge to those biases that was personified in Queen Elizabeth.[2] Accordingly, in this book, the ways in which masculine subjects of the Elizabethan state negotiated their agency are as interesting to me as the ways in which Queen Elizabeth negotiated hers; and most interesting of all are the ways in which these two processes constantly interacted and frequently clashed.

At a fundamental level, all Elizabethan subjects may be said to have participated in a ceaseless and casual process of producing and reproducing "the Queen" in their daily practices—in their prayers and oaths, their gossip and their fantasies. But she was also rather more consciously and systematically fashioned by those Elizabethan subjects who were engaged in producing the texts, pictures, and performances in which the Queen was variously represented to her people, to her court, to foreign powers, and to Elizabeth herself. Over the course of a long reign, many subjects of various statuses, skills, and interests were engaged in sponsoring, designing, executing, or subverting representations of royal authority, and many either profited or suffered as a consequence of that engagement. From this perspective, the ruler and the ruled are construable as subjects differentially shaped within a shared conjuncture of cultural forms and social relations, who jointly reshaped that conjuncture in the continuous process of performing, speaking, picturing, and writing it. Thus, the term "subject" in my title is intentionally ambiguous. In *The Subject of Elizabeth*, I mean to suggest both the Queen as a historical agent—Elizabeth Tudor—and also the Queen as a subject in the discourse of her subjects, and thus as subjected to her subjects through representation.[3] Queen Elizabeth was as much the creature of the Elizabethan image as she was its creator.

Like some of my other work, both published and in progress, this book seeks to illuminate the gendering of Elizabethan political culture by analyzing the work of the Elizabethan imaginary.[4] I use this term to designate the collective corpus of images, tropes, and other verbal and iconic resources that provided a growing and changing matrix for the varied and sharply contested processes of royal representation. The chapters of this book analyze some representative examples of this Elizabethan imaginary at work, each chapter focusing upon a particular occasion or issue. Seventeen chapters are disposed into five parts; the latter are organized and ordered according to a combination of thematic and chronological considerations that are outlined in the framing introduction to each part. These may be summarized as follows. Part one contextualizes the representation of Elizabeth within the traditions of Tudor dynastic portraiture, focusing upon issues of legitimacy and succession and upon the marking of gender difference within the framework of dynastic continuity. Part two explores ideological conflicts and affinities between the Reformation castigation of Catholic religious practice as idolatry and the Elizabethan regime's encouragement of what John Bossy has called *monarcholatry*—the symbolic sacralization of the monarch as head of both church and state.[5] Part three studies the symbolic territorialization and manipulation of the royal body by supporters and enemies of the Elizabethan regime, both domestic and foreign. This gender-coded and frequently sexualized discourse made Queen Elizabeth the representational medium for religious and geopolitical negotiations and conflicts on an international scale. Part four addresses some cultural manifestations of the sectarian and popular dissention that was endemic in Elizabethan England and Ireland and was manifested in attacks upon royal symbols and defamatory remarks about the Queen's person. The emphasis here is upon Catholic resistance during the last two decades of the reign. Part five considers some of the ways in which Elizabeth's advancing age intensified problems in representation of the Queen's two bodies, destabilized elements of the reigning iconography, and provided new occasions for misogynistically coded subversions of royal charisma. The cultural texts and topics studied in these five parts follow a roughly chronological order, one that suggests the shifting priorities and problems of royal representation during the course of Elizabeth's reign and her lifecycle.

I am formally a literary scholar, and much of my published work during the past quarter-century has focused on poetic and dramatic aspects of the subject of Elizabeth.[6] Relatively little of that work reappears in the present volume, however, and what does has been significantly recontextualized. In this book, I am concerned neither with canonical works of literature nor with the topics and vocabularies of contemporary literary theory but rather with forms of cultural production that are usually the focus of study in other disciplines. These forms include iconic images of the Queen and textual descriptions of Elizabethan visual culture, as well as prescriptive and descriptive texts of the sort that make up the documentary archive of social and political history, such as letters, diplomatic dispatches, speeches, memoirs, treatises, polemical pamphlets, depositions and legal records, statutes, and policy papers.

In sixteenth-century Europe, polities that were monarchical in form gave iconic representation to the state by means of the royal portrait. At its most hieratic and formulaic, the royal image appeared on coins of the realm, as initial illuminations on government rolls and royal charters, and on impressions of the various royal seals borne by official decrees, orders, patents, and correspondence. These signs of royal authority and prerogative were at once the most common icons of Tudor monarchs and the ones that most tangibly manifested their unique power and status within the realm, their incarnation of the state. Of all royal portraits, these official ones presumably drew least attention to themselves *as* portraits. Patriotic portraits of Queen Elizabeth, designed to elicit and display the personal loyalty and devotion of her subjects, were made for popular consumption in the form of woodcuts and engravings. On the evidence of government attempts to regulate them, many of these would seem to have been relatively crude and ephemeral; most of those that survive are actually from late in the reign, and some are the work of manifestly skilled engravers. Also extant from the beginning to the end of the reign are a large number of woodcuts and engravings of the Queen that served as frontispieces or illustrations in printed Elizabethan books and pamphlets on a wide range of topics. Many of these images are marked by traditional religious and political iconography, although frequently put to new uses as dictated by the gender and religio-political policies of the sovereign. Images of the Queen also appeared on medals struck to mark various occasions of national significance, and were worked into cameos and other forms of jewelry to be worn or given as gifts by members of the court and aristocracy. Portraits of the Queen—frequently, watercolor miniatures but also panel paintings in oils—played a significant part in the culture of courtship by which the Queen's most eminent subjects manifested their devotion and maintained her favor. They were also essential items in the conduct of marriage negotiations with foreign princes; and, more generally, in the maintenance of cordial relations with the rulers of other states. In the course of this book, I shall at least touch upon examples of the royal image produced in all of these media.

Roy Strong has written that, during the sixteenth century, "portraiture was one aspect of [the] massive expansion of the Idea of Monarchy, involving the dissemination [of] a ruler's image in paint, stone, print and metal throughout the realm on a scale unheard of since Classical antiquity."[7] Indeed, the proliferation of images of Habsburg, Valois, and Tudor princes provides compelling visual evidence for the consolidation of the powers of the dynastic state, and for the highly personalized nature of political identity and affiliation, during the early modern period. And if the image of the dynastic early modern state was personified in the royal portrait, it was also thereby gendered. Both in theory and in practice, a normative precondition for sovereignty was masculinity. Thus, the visual representation of royal authority in the person of a woman— not merely a royal consort, nor even a regent, but a prince regnant—entailed distinctive imaginative challenges and opportunities both to those who sponsored and produced such representations and to those who sought to subvert them.

In my treatment of visual images, I am broadly concerned with powers ascribed to the Elizabethan royal image and powers addressed against it; with its deployment by a variety of agents in order to serve interests that sometimes coincided with and sometimes opposed those of the Elizabethan regime itself. The kinds of cultural production I analyze include not only iconic representations of the Queen but also textual descriptions of such representations and anecdotal accounts of actions and attitudes that they aroused in some of those who beheld them. These texts take two general forms: those actually made a part of particular pictures—inscribed upon the frame, within a cartouche, or across the picture plane itself; and those in which pictures and other visual forms, images, and spectacles are described or mentioned. Some of the pictures I discuss incorporate texts that were apparently intended to guide and delimit the beholders' "reading" of the dominant visual images—although, as I shall suggest, such textual inscriptions never adequately translate the picture, and are sometimes actually at odds with it.[8] The visual and the verbal are radically distinct representational media, with differing resources and limitations; and in the highly sensitive project of royal representation, those formal differences might well be put to the service of differing interests.

Not only texts incorporated within pictures but also diaries, diplomatic dispatches, proclamations, treatises, and texts in various other genres provide some indication of how visual representations were discursively perceived, judged, and appropriated within a range of socio-political, diplomatic, and religious milieux. Celebratory court portraits in oils or watercolors have by now become synonymous with the Elizabethan royal image. However, I am concerned to put these dominant media of representation into dialogue with contemporaneous popular and dissident practices of royal representation. There can be legitimate scholarly reasons for making analytical separations between fine art and popular imagery, just as there can for distinguishing the study of pictures from the study of texts about pictures. However, my method here aims to demonstrate the value of studying them in conjunction, for these visual and textual, popular and courtly, practices of royal representation occupy different situations within a shared cultural field, and their significance is generated relationally.

Although my analyses of specific pictures often attend to iconography and other topics traditionally of concern to art historians, it will be clear that I am not working within the traditional disciplinary paradigm of art history. Instead, I am seeking to practice an interdisciplinary and dialogical approach to the study of sixteenth-century visual and verbal cultures. I remain mindful that pictorial signification lies primarily in the complex organization and interplay of line and shape, texture and color, light and shadow, and only tangentially in terms of words or concepts. Nevertheless, what makes icons of Elizabeth and other Tudor dynasts rewarding subjects for cultural analysis is not only the specific formal qualities of individual pictures but also the historical dynamics at work in the process of representation itself: the relative status, interests, and influence of the people who commissioned, executed, and viewed such objects; the social spaces, occasions, and transactions that framed their display and beholding; the formulation and enforcement of regulations for their making, distribution, and use; the ways and means by which the royal image was appropriated and defaced—by whom, for what reason, and to what effect. In all of these senses, the object of my critical attention throughout this book is not the canon of Elizabethan royal portraits but rather the politics of Elizabethan visual culture, as these are preserved in two related but distinct archives—that of iconic images and that of written texts.

Much of the textual material I interpret is anecdotal in nature. It has sometimes been charged that such evidence tends to be selected for its sensational content rather than for its cultural representativeness, and that historical arguments made upon the basis of such anecdotal evidence are therefore arbitrary or illegitimate. In making my own selection and interpretation of anecdotal evidence, I have borne these sometimes justifiable charges in mind. Some of the anecdotes recounted here will perhaps be considered unrepresentative, in the sense that there are relatively few extant and known similar instances. However, that does not necessarily render them cultural anomalies, radically at odds with the normative and quotidian experiences, practices, and beliefs of their time and place. On the contrary, such anecdotes may also justifiably be considered as representative, in the distinct but crucial sense that they bring into convergence, and intensify for scrutiny, significant and even central historical concerns that are otherwise dispersed into more fragmentary, oblique, or diffuse articulations throughout the varied discourses of Elizabethan culture. Of course, such representativeness requires demonstration. And this is accomplished not merely by the provision of "context" or by the citation of other, similar instances but by the analytical exfoliation of the anecdote itself, by a discovery or showing forth of its status as a site for the meaningful convergence of various active social forces and cultural narratives. In order for us to apprehend the original capacity of the local instance to generate immediate affect and a wider cultural resonance, scholarship must labor to elucidate the ideological motifs or *ideologemes* that are embedded in the narrative particularities of the anecdote.[9] Working by means of dilation or digression, this probing of connections in the cultural logic may disrupt the development of a linear argument; it may also negate the frisson achieved by rhetorical performances that maximize the anecdote's strangeness. For such losses, analysis may offer the intellectual compensation of historical understanding. If anecdotes employed in ostensibly historical arguments are to be more than sensational flourishes, they must derive their legitimacy from the demonstration of their unrepresentative representativeness.

My choice of images, texts, and topics is to some degree idiosyncratic and serendipitous—as such choices usually are. However, I read individual images, small gestures, particular events, passing remarks, and the patterns that they form, as historically significant markers of broader cultural understandings and beliefs, as local sites at which major ideological forces converge, collide, and interact. The chronological and generic range of the texts and images discussed is intended to provide an evidentiary basis for my claim that the Elizabethan imaginary is characterized by affectively charged appropriations of the royal body, and that these appropriations gender and personalize relations of power and claims to authority. Here I emphasize the subjective, affective, and fantasy-based elements that subliminally shape and impel agents, events, and ideologies. Such cultural texts are the object of my attention here not because they are factually correct but rather because they are telling indicators of shared attitudes and perceptions; it is their status as clues to what was imaginable that confers upon them their claim to historical significance.

Much of this book addresses cultural materials that are normally within the purview of social, political, and art historians, but it addresses those materials with the analytical methods and interpretive strategies characteristic of literary studies. By working against the grain in this cross-disciplinary way, I hope to have produced a study that early modernists in all of these disciplines will find illuminating rather than merely eccentric. The conviction underwriting my critical practice is that the way literary scholars can most effectively study the workings of the Elizabethan imaginary is to provide close readings of the complex operations by which figurative discourse produces knowledge and power, and by which it shapes experience and belief. Central to this endeavor is attention to a wide range of surviving textual and iconic materials, so that now-canonical literary works are not privileged in a way that gives them a wholly anachronistic importance relative to the rest of the historical archive. I do not propose to elide the real differences among these various kinds of cultural texts. Rather, I am seeking to demonstrate that such materials are amenable to, and reward, that close attention to the formal and figurative generation of meaning which is the hallmark of literary studies but which literary scholars normally reserve for the study of canonical literary works. In principle, early modernists from within the discipline of literary studies should be concerned not merely with a delimited and privileged body of "literary" texts but with any and all of the kinds of early modern culture that are recoverable in legible form, with their varying generic norms and their almost unlimited capacity for generic hybridity. In other words, as an early modern *literary* scholar, my primary concern is not to study a particular class of writings but rather to practice a particular mode of cultural analysis, one that contributes to a collective and interdisciplinary study of early modern culture. In *The Subject of Elizabeth*, I hope to have advanced that goal.

Dynasty and Difference

Throughout part one, my concern is with the variety of ways in which acts of writing, picturing, and performing gave imaginative shape to those particularities of Elizabeth Tudor's personal history that conditioned her rule, and thus had collective consequences for her subjects. Here I focus upon issues of legitimacy and succession, in all of the intertwined familial, legal, and political senses of those terms; and upon the marking of gender *difference* within the framework of dynastic *continuity*. I consider how these issues are both articulated and obfuscated in various genres of verbal and visual culture; my emphasis, however, is upon the pictorial representation of legitimacy and succession in selected group and individual portraits of the Tudor dynasts. Here I organize and analyze key portraits of members of the Tudor dynasty in such a way as to fashion a brief history-through-images—a diachronic Tudor family portrait—that can serve as this book's introduction to the vexed and central issues of legitimacy, succession, gender, and religion that faced the Elizabethan regime. In chapter one I discuss the interwined problems of legitimacy faced by Elizabeth at her accession: that occasioned by the circumstances of her parents' history, and that conditioned by contemporary debates about women's nature and women's "regiment," or ability to rule. Chapter two studies the theme of filial emulation in Tudor dynastic portraiture and pageantry, and its inflection by gender difference. Chapter three discusses the comparative performance and representation of Tudor queenship in the frequently contrasting but also sometimes parallel reigns of Mary and Elizabeth Tudor. With particular reference to family portraits, chapter four focuses upon the Elizabethan construction of Tudor dynastic legitimacy in terms of continuity in the agenda of religious reform.

Contested Legitimacies

In order to situate the interplay of dynasty and difference in Tudor England, I begin not with a monumental Elizabethan state portrait but rather with an ephemeral Henrician text: a letter describing an event in which a crude picture of Elizabeth's royal father was appropriated and subjected to popular mockery. In 1533, the year in which Elizabeth Tudor was born, a secretary to the Company of Merchant Adventurers wrote to Thomas Cromwell, Henry VIII's principal minister, with intelligence from the Low Countries. He reported the scandalous action of a market vendor from Antwerp, who had

> Images and Pictures in cloth to sell: among the which clothes he had the Picture of our soveraigne Lord the Kyng.... And this day settyng up the same Picture upon the Burse to sell, he pynned upon the body of the said Picture a Wenche made in cloth, holdyng a paier of balance in her hands; in th'one balance was fygured too hands to geder, and in th'other balance a fether, with a scripture over her head, saiyng that Love was lighter then a fether, whereat the Spanyards and other of the Duche nacion had greate pleasure in deridyng, jestyng, and laughyng therat, and spekyng sondry opprobrious words ayest his moost noble Grace and moost gracious Quene his bedfelowe.[1]

Thomas Cromwell's scandalized informer provides us with a brief but intriguing glimpse into an impromptu act of popular satire against the high and mighty, one that is firmly placed within its religious, geopolitical, and commercial milieux. What the letter describes is not merely the hawking of King Henry's picture in the marketplace but a kind of political street theatre in which that picture is subjected to further appropriation of a more explicitly subversive sort. It seems that the King was being derided for his unseemly treatment of his wife of many years, the much admired Catherine of Aragon, and for his open cohabitation with Anne Boleyn. Henry had clandestinely married Anne on 25 January 1533, after the discovery of her pregnancy, and some four months before the date of the letter to Cromwell. On the day following the date of the letter, the King's marriage to Queen Catherine was declared null and void; and a week after that, the visibly pregnant Anne was honored with a lavish royal entry into London and was crowned as Queen in Catherine's stead.

The derision, jesting, and opprobrious words directed against the King of England in the streets of Antwerp had been catalyzed by the improvised addition to Henry's portrait. However, such responses were undoubtedly rooted in wider and deeper concerns: most obviously, in sectarian and national antipathies; but apparently also in abiding communal values regarding the sacrament of marriage and the lusts of the flesh, values that may have transcended differences between papists and reformers, Spaniards and Englishmen. There is substantial evidence that not only "Spanyards and other of the Duche nacion" but significant numbers of the King's own English subjects sympathized with their Spanish-born Queen Catherine, defamed Anne Boleyn, and disapproved of the King's actions. It was also in 1533 that a parson in Lancashire responded to the proclamation of Anne's accession by declaring, "I will have none for queen but Queen Catherine; who the devil made Nan Bullen, that whore, queen?" And in the same year, another was reported to have said that "the King is but a knave and liveth in avowtry [adultery], and is an heretic and liveth not after the laws of God.... I set not by the King's crown, and if I had it here, I would play at football with it."[2] King Henry justified his divorce upon the scruples of his conscience. Nevertheless, at least some of his subjects saw his actions as an offense against the sacramental view of wedlock that was espoused in such popular works as *De institutione feminae christianae*, which praised marriage as "a bande and couplyng of love, benyvolence, frendshippe, and charite, comprehendynge with in hit all names of goodnes, swetenes, and amyte." Written by the Spanish Humanist Juan Luis Vives and dedicated to Queen Catherine, this influential work had appeared in print in English as early as 1529.[3]

If foreign ambassadorial reports are to be believed, some Londoners walked out of church when called upon to pray for their new, English-born Queen Anne; and at an earlier point in the royal affair, some had actually rioted against her:

> It is said that more than seven weeks ago a mob of from seven to eight thousand women of London went out of the town to seize Boleyn's daughter, the sweetheart of the king of England, who was supping at a villa ... on a river; the king

not being with her; and having received notice of this she escaped by crossing the river in a boat. The women had intended to kill her, and amongst the mob were many men disguised as women; nor has any great demonstration been made about this, because it was a thing done by women.[4]

Although the reported numbers are surely inflated, this account does suggest some sort of popular collective action that subjected the King's affairs to the moral standards of the local community.[5] This performance was thus an assimilation of high politics to the rites of popular culture; at the same time, however, it was also an improvisation of such rites for the purposes of political protest: In other words, the genre of the reported event combined elements of charivari or "rough music" with those of popular riot; and the female community's traditional regulation of wayward women was appropriated by those subjects—including cross-dressed men—who dared, however indirectly, to vent their disapprobation of the personal conduct of their king.[6] In the Antwerp market, "Spanyards and other of the Duche nacion" were unconstrained in their mockery of the English king, and their actions, too, partook of the spirit of charivari.

Simon Thurley has specified the historical conditions that transformed the official image of Henry VIII into that of an imperial ruler with supremacy over the church: "The momentous parliamentary acts of 1529–1539 radically altered the nature of Kingship in England. Not only was the traditional relationship between the king and the Pope rejected, but the nature of the king's civil powers was altered to accommodate and enforce his new spiritual position. The consolidation of this new position was achieved by a carefully orchestrated and skilfully executed image-making operation."[7] It would be mistaken, however, to assume either that the Tudor regime consistently pursued coherent long-term policies or that it was consistently effective in translating its policies into visual—or verbal—imagery. As the foregoing discussion has illustrated, it was beyond the powers of the Henrician regime to control the foreign production, dissemination, and appropriation of crude pictures of the King; and, even within the realm, what Thurley calls the Henrician regime's "image-making operation" appears to have been limited in its scope and of uncertain efficacy among the King's own subjects.

Whatever their degree of technical skill or formal innovation, neither image makers nor the images that they fashioned were merely transparent instruments of an omniscient and omnipotent royal will. And, indeed, the history of royal representation in the early modern period is as much a history of appropriation and degradation as it is a history of regulation and celebration. In practices of picturing, as in practices of writing and performing, the power of the state to control the signifying process was both limited in its means and uncertain in its effects. And just as the ideological forces operative in the pictorial field were not monolithic, neither were they neatly polarized into an opposition of dominance and resistance, the monarch and the monarchomach. Tudor royal images were employed in a wide range of cultural work, which included enhancing and subverting the charisma of the monarch; legitimating and resisting the authority of his or her regime; seeking to influence royal sympathies and policies in matters religious, civic, and military; and pursuing personal advantage in the competition for courtly favor and reward. Various interests, including rivalrous and opposed ones, were at work in the production and apprehension of visual representations of the monarch. And the same holds true for the many written accounts of royal icons and spectacles, both printed and unprinted, which collectively constitute a distinctive early modern genre of political *ekphrasis*. The commissioning and shaping, the perception and promotion, of the royal image were components of a dynamic and unstable process. In its motives and in its impact, this process was just as likely to be hortatory or contestatory as it was to be panegyrical.

As will become evident in the course of my analyses, my caveats regarding the Henrician regime's "carefully orchestrated and skilfully executed image-making operation" apply perhaps even more clearly to the image-making activities promoted and policed by the Elizabethan regime. Indeed, the Flemish incident reported to have taken place in 1533 could be claimed to be the earliest instance of image appropriation involving Elizabeth herself. After all, although she was as yet unborn, Elizabeth was already visibly growing within the womb of "Nan Bullen, that whore." Thus, she was the manifest incarnation of the tainted royal union that had prompted the jesting, derision, and opprobrium—the rough music—performed in the streets of Antwerp. Throughout most of the lifetime of Elizabeth Tudor, the courtships, marital prospects, and sexual conduct of the monarch would continue to be both an urgent matter of state and an endless subject of gossip within and beyond the realm; and she would spend much of her reign dealing with the religious, legal, political, and diplomatic consequences of the sensational events that had occasioned her own birth.

Henry VIII's single-minded quest to secure a direct and legitimate masculine succession generated a tangled chain of momentous actions and unintended consequences. These included the King's assumption of royal supremacy over the church; his divorce from Queen Catherine, on the grounds that her prior espousal to his deceased brother made their own marriage incestuous; Henry's marriage to Anne Boleyn, the sister (and, according to some, also the daughter) of a former royal mistress; Anne's subsequent execution on grounds of adultery with several men, including her own brother; and Henry's formal bastardization of his daughter, Elizabeth. The reigns of Henry and his offspring were marked not only by the establishment of the royal supremacy in matters spiritual as well as temporal but also by wider upheavals in popular religious belief and practice; as a consequence, dynastic issues now converged with ideological ones. This peculiarly Tudor convergence of religious with family values received a comprehensively hostile formulation from the Catholic polemicist Nicholas Sander:

> The hypocrisy of the king, pretending the fear of God when he put Catherine away; the incestuous marriage with Anne Boleyn, I say incestuous marriage of Henry, for if Anne was not his own child, she was the child of his mistress; the incest also of Anne Boleyn with her own brother; the ecclesiastical supremacy of the king, which Henry was the first to assume, are the foundations on which that religion is built and stands, which England held and professed under Henry, Edward, and Elizabeth.

As Sander later summarized it, "Now, all English Protestants . . . honour the incestuous marriage of Henry and Anne Boleyn as the wellspring of their gospel, the mother of their Church, and the source of their belief."[8] The progress of the Protestant Reformation—or, depending upon one's allegiances, the spread of the Protestant heresy—was understood to be intimately tied to the personal beliefs and policies of the reigning monarch, and thus to be conditional upon continuities and changes within the fragile Tudor succession.

Succession was an especially vexed issue in Tudor England. The first sentence of Francis Bacon's unfinished *History of Great Britain* tersely records the demise of the Tudor dynasty, framing it as the enabling condition for the birth of Great Britain in the accession of King James VI of Scotland to the English throne: "By the decease of Elizabeth, Queen of England, the issues of King Henry the Eight failed; being spent in one generation and three successions." In an earlier letter discussing his projected history, Bacon wrote of the offspring of Henry VIII as "these barren princes," and remarked upon the anomalous dynastic history of the later Tudors: "the strangest variety that in like number of successions of any hereditary monarchy hath ever been known. The reign of a child; the offer of an usurpation . . . the reign of a lady married to a foreign Prince; and the reign of a lady solitary and unmarried."[9] When Elizabeth came to the throne at the age of twenty-five—indeed, as a condition of her accession—she was without surviving close male kin. She was also without a husband; and despite both the persistent importunings of the men who served her and the marriage negotiations that she conducted almost continuously throughout the first two decades of her reign, Elizabeth remained unmarried until her death. In his shrewd appreciation of his late queen, Bacon observed that

> the reigns of women are commonly obscured by marriage; their praises and actions passing to the credit of their husbands; whereas those that continue unmarried have their glory entire and proper to themselves. In her case this was more especially so; inasmuch as she had no helps to lean upon in her government, except such as she had herself provided; no own brother, no uncle, no kinsman of the royal family, to share her cares and support her authority. And even those whom she herself raised to honour she so kept in hand and mingled one with another, that while she infused into each the greatest solicitude to please her she was herself ever her own mistress.[10]

In his second sentence, Bacon suggests that Elizabeth's deprivation of family was seriously disadvantageous to her rule; in his third sentence, however, he affirms it to have been a precondition for her autonomous authority. This paradox illuminates both the gender-specific expectations that handicapped Elizabeth at her accession and the unconventional strategies by which she sought to turn those liabilities to advantage during the course of her reign.

The liabilities of gynecocracy had been definitively anatomized in the ill-timed blast "against the monstrous regiment of women" written by the Scottish reformer John Knox and published shortly before Elizabeth's accession. Knox's polemic opened with the declaration that "to promote a Woman to beare rule, superioritie, dominion, or empire above any Realme, Nation, or Citie, is repugnant to Nature; contumelie to God, a thing most contrarious to his reveled will and approved ordinance; and finallie, it is the subversion of good Order, of all equity and justice."[11] Knox based his antigynecratic jeremiad upon the scriptural principle of female subjection:

> God hath subjected Womankinde to man, by the ordre of his creation, and by the curse that he hath pronounced against her.... Besides these, he hath set before our eyes two other Mirrors and glasses, in whiche he will that we shulde behold the ordre which he hath appointed and established in nature: The one is the naturall bodie of man; the other is the politik or civile body of that common welth, in which God by his own Word hath apointed an ordre. (390)

And just as that body is "a monstre, where there was no head eminent above the rest ..., no lesse monstruous is the bodie of that Common welth where a Woman beareth empire" (391). Knox's intended targets were the Catholic queens regnant and female regents of mid-sixteenth-century Europe: Mary Stuart, Marie de Guise, and, in particular, Mary Tudor—"that horrible

monstre Jesabel of England" (420)—who had resubjected Reformation England to the Church of Rome. And in pursuing his attack, Knox argued strenu-
ously against the invocation of Debora as a legitimating biblical precedent for
these demonic latter-day instances of female regiment: "In these of our ages,
we finde crueltie, falshed, pride, covetousnes, deceit, and oppression.... the
spirit of Jesabel and Athalia.... How unlike our mischevous Maryes be unto
Debora" (404). Knox's misogynistic rhetoric served the radical religio-political
argument that it was "the dutie of the Nobilitie, Judges, Rulers and People of
England not only to have resisted and againstanded Marie, that Jesebel, whome
they call their Queen, but also to have punished her to the death, with all the
sort of her idolatrous Preestes, together with all such as should have assisted
her" in furthering the apostasy of the English nation and the persecution of
the godly.[12]

On 17 November 1558, "Marie, that Jesebel"—England's Catholic ruler and
its first queen regnant—died after a brief but contentious reign of five years and
five months. On the same day, at the instruction of the Lords in Parliament,
the heralds proclaimed Mary's presumptively Protestant half-sister, Elizabeth
Tudor, as England's second queen regnant.[13] In response to the noxious blast
that Knox had aimed in part at the new queen's late sister, the Marian exile
John Aylmer wrote a guarded defense of the legitimacy of Elizabeth's accession.
Aylmer sought to exempt Elizabeth, whom Protestants hoped would champion religious reform, from his coreligionist's otherwise congenial judgments
about the monstrous regiment of women. Aylmer shared Knox's moral denunciation of Queen Mary Tudor and his argument for the divinely sanctioned
subordination of women in general. Again like Knox, Aylmer endorsed the
subordination of married women to their husbands in a patriarchal domestic
domain, and he also affirmed in principle their exclusion from the political
nation. Unlike Knox, however, Aylmer made an exception to the latter condition in those rare cases—such as that of Elizabeth Tudor—in which women
are called to rule by the hand of divine providence. Having so badly timed
his blast against queenship, Knox subsequently granted a similar exception
for England's new Protestant queen; nevertheless, this grudging concession
hardly mollified the infuriated Elizabeth.[14]

In meeting the challenge to mount a limited defense of female regiment,
Aylmer turned to an Old Testament exemplar; in order to efface the all too
fresh precedent of Elizabeth's Catholic half-sister, Aylmer, like Knox, invoked
Debora:

> Deborah judged and that lawfully, which cam not to it by enheritaunce, but
> by extraordinarye callinge. Much more may she that to Gods callinge hathe

joygned thordinarie meanes of enheritaunce, her commons consent, and confirmacio[n] of lawes. To Saynt Austen and all the rest, which wolde have women in the subjection of their husbandes, is to be answered as before: that their meaning and speaking was, of every private woman in the bonds of mariage: And not of those which God by birth hath called to the governments of realmes.[15]

Like most others in 1558, Aylmer fully expected Elizabeth to marry and to conform to wifely subjection when she did so; at the same time, however, he claimed that when she did marry, her political sovereignty would suffer no diminution: "I graunte that, so farre as perteineth to the bandes of mariage, and the offices of a wife, she muste be subjecte: but as a Magistrate she maye be her husbandes heade.... Whie may not the woman be the husbandes inferiour in matters of wedlock, and his head in the guiding of the commonwealth" (C4v). However difficult such an arrangement might prove in practice, in his theoretical defense of Elizabeth's regiment, Aylmer was willing to go so far as to dissolve the familiar homology between the gendered hierarchies of household and commonwealth.

Aylmer's unusual argument was driven not by any protofeminist impulse but rather by unquestioning obedience to the mysterious ways of God:

I would not in dede that any woman should stand in the election, but men only.... the male is by all lykelihod meter to rule, then the woman in many respectes.... But when it standeth in no mans election, but in his hande that shapeth male or female.... Then hath mans voyce no authoritie, by cause he hath gyven over his right in chusing, by comon consent unto God. That he according to his inscrutable wysdome, may chuse and dispose, as he pleaseth. (I1r)

Although their political and religious allegiances were radically different, Aylmer would no doubt have concurred in principle with the assessment of the Spanish ambassador in London, writing to the Emperor Ferdinand in 1559, that "Her Highness is after all a woman ... and very susceptible to passions."[16] Thus, at the same time that he justified the accession of Elizabeth Tudor as providentially sanctioned, Aylmer also inscribed her authority within a conciliar paradigm that in practice constrained her royal prerogative:

The regiment of Englande is not a mere Monarchie ... nor an Oligarchie, nor Democratie, but a rule mixte of all these, wherein ech one of these have or shoulde have like authoritie. Thimage whereof ... is to be sene in the parliament house, wherin you shall find these 3 estats. The King or Quene, which representeth the Monarche. The noble men, which be the Aristocratie. And the Burgesses and Knights the Democratie. (H3r)

Because of this provision, he continued,

> It is not to England so daungerous a matter, to have a woman ruler, as men take
> it to be. For first it is not she that ruleth but the lawes, the executors whereof be
> her judges.... 2. She maketh no statutes or lawes, but the honerable court of
> Parliament.... 3. If she shuld judge in capitall crimes: what daunger were there
> in her womannish nature? none at all. For the verdict is the 12. mennes. (H3v)

He concluded that "If to be short she wer a mere monark, and not a mixte
ruler, you might peradventure make me to feare the matter the more, and the
les to defend the cause" (H4r).

For Aylmer, then, the legitimacy of Elizabeth's rule depended upon its being
a divinely sanctioned anomaly, which was in practice to be limited and shared
by a masculine political nation. And, indeed, his tract was as much a defense
of limited monarchy and parliamentary prerogative as it was a defense of Elizabeth's sovereignty.[17] The fact that Aylmer's was the most substantial defense
of Elizabeth's cause to have been printed at the time of her accession makes
its circumspection all the more striking. The highly conditional nature of his
defense of Elizabeth's regiment—including his predication of the legitimacy
of gynecocracy upon the constitutional principle of mixed monarchy—may
be taken as representative of the thinking of those members of the Protestant
elite who were among the new queen's strongest supporters. In this sense, *An
Harborowe for Faithfull and Trewe Subjectes* is an index to the cultural framework of ideas and attitudes that Elizabeth faced—and, presumably, at least
partially internalized—when she ascended the throne.[18]

My concern with the problems of legitimation facing Elizabeth Tudor
and her regime is focused upon two perceived needs. One was to affirm her
untainted descent from Henry VIII, in the face of the formal charges of incest,
bastardy, and adultery that surrounded her birth. The other was to justify
her kingly authority, in the face of venerable and pervasive cultural beliefs in
female inferiority as well as the intense and learned sixteenth-century attacks
on gynecocracy that were rooted in those beliefs. These were intertwined
consequences of Elizabeth's gender: For her, legitimacy was simultaneously
a condition of daughterhood and of queenship. Whatever impact they may
have had upon her personal psychology, both the prevailing ideology of gender
and her own tumultuous family history shaped not only the problems that
Elizabeth Tudor confronted as queen but also her resources for dealing with
them; and this dynamic profoundly affected not only the political and religious
landscape of sixteenth-century English society but also the configuration of
the collective Elizabethan imaginary.

Filial Emulation

A number of recent writers on Queen Elizabeth have claimed that, when she received visitors in the Privy Chamber at Whitehall, she liked to stage herself before the imposing image of her father that dominated Holbein's great wall painting of the Tudor dynasty. I am unaware of any Elizabethan source for this claim; nevertheless, it is both attractive and plausible.[1] After all, the very theme of Holbein's painting was the succession and filial emulation of the Tudor dynasty; and this celebrated work continued to adorn the wall of the Privy Chamber at Whitehall throughout Elizabeth's reign. It was there that she frequently entertained ambassadors and others whom she sought to impress with her regal authority and to honor with her special favor. Elizabeth did explicitly employ rhetorical strategies of identification with her father—as, for example, in her address to a joint delegation of lords and commons during the notably outspoken Parliament of 1566. In the course of her angry response to pressuring that she marry and secure the succession, she asserted that "thowghe I be a woman yet I have as good a coreage awnswerable to mye place as evere my fathere hade."[2] As suggested here by Elizabeth's conditional clause— "Thowghe I be a woman"—such strategies of identification were double-edged. They risked emphasizing precisely the condition that she wished to neutralize: namely, the radical difference between the Queen and her father, a difference that was culturally grounded in the assumed innate inferiority of Elizabeth's gender, in her naturally deficient female body, and in all of the attitudes, practices, and policies that flowed from that perceived difference.

Henry VIII's kingly image had as one of its hallmarks the display of masculine prowess—martial, chivalric, and erotic.[3] Such displays were especially conspicuous in the earlier years of the reign, when Henry performed his princely *virtù* in the tournament lists and upon the battlefield. These feats

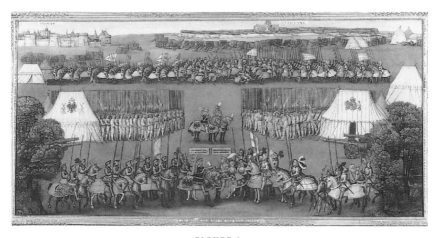

FIGURE 1

The meeting of Henry VIII and the Emperor Maximilian I in 1513. Artist unknown; ca. 1545. Oil on panel.
The Royal Collection © 2005, Her Majesty Queen Elizabeth II.

were celebrated and inflated in Revels Office accounts; in Edward Hall's influential chronicle; and in monumental pictures such as "The meeting of
Henry VIII and the Emperor Maximilian I" (fig. 1), which memorialized the
King's youthful military and diplomatic triumphs.[4] The various elements of
Henry's regal virility are combined early in the reign in a spectacle that was
performed at Westminster on 12–13 February 1511. The birth of a son to Henry
and Catherine of Aragon was the great occasion for this dynastic celebration, which involved a magnificent tournament, pageant, and masking. (The
celebration was premature, for the newborn prince died ten days later.) *The
Great Tournament Roll of Westminster*, a richly illuminated visual account of
the events, represents the King in his allegorical disguise as the knight *Ceure
loyall*, jousting before the Queen and her ladies (fig. 2).[5]

Holbein's monumental wall painting for the Privy Chamber at Whitehall dates from some three decades after the accession of Henry VIII, and it
wholly eschews the imagery of martial and amorous chivalry that was associated with the young king. Nevertheless, it projects more powerfully than
any other Henrician icon the gender-specific resonance of the royal body. In
this work—of which only part of the original cartoon survives—the painter
vividly portrays the power of the reigning monarch as manifest in the size,
strength, and carriage of his body (fig. 3).[6] Extant seventeenth-century copies
of the painting, made before its loss in the 1698 fire that destroyed Whitehall,
indicate that in the final version Holbein presented his image of Henry VIII in
a fully frontal pose (fig. 4). Of the four royal figures represented, only the king
regnant looks directly at the viewer. There is an emphatic contrast between his

thrusting pose and the self-contained demeanor of his deceased father, Henry VII, the founder of the Tudor dynasty, who stands behind him. The royal consorts, Elizabeth of York and Jane Seymour, are positioned on the left hand of the two kings. Neither queen engages the viewer's gaze; each demurely clasps her hands together, a chaste and obedient female instrument of the Tudor dynastic imperative. The graphic contrast between the figures of Henry VIII and Henry VII parallels the Latin inscription on the central tablet, in which the regal accomplishments of the son, who had routed the Pope and restored an English *imperium*, surpass those of the father, who had healed internecine strife by uniting the houses of Lancaster and York.[7] Holbein's regal conception befits the claims to temporal and spiritual dominion made by the first two Tudor monarchs against the powers of the ancient nobility, on the one hand, and against those of the papacy, on the other.

Karel van Mander, writing at the beginning of the seventeenth century, remarked of Holbein's likeness of Henry VIII that "the King as he stood there, majestic in his splendour, was so lifelike that the spectator felt abashed, annihilated in his presence." This was surely the response that the royal icon was intended to elicit.[8] How much more awesome, then, must the effect have been when the King was physically present and in state in the Privy Chamber.

FIGURE 2
King Henry VIII as *Ceure loyall*, tilting before Queen Catherine (of Aragon) and her ladies. Artist unknown; 1511. *The Great Tournament Roll of Westminster*, membranes 25–26. Illuminated manuscript on vellum. College of Arms, London.

FIGURE 3

Henry VII and Henry VIII. Fragment from the cartoon for the Whitehall
Privy Chamber Mural by Hans Holbein the Younger; 1537. Ink and
watercolor on paper, mounted on canvas. National Portrait Gallery,
London.

FIGURE 4

Copy by Remigius van Leemput, 1667, after the now lost Whitehall Privy Chamber Mural by Hans Holbein the Younger. Oil on canvas. The Royal Collection © 2005, Her Majesty Queen Elizabeth II.

In a memoir composed upon the death of Queen Elizabeth, John Clapham remarked of her father that "the greatness of his personage seem[ed] to carry a kind of proportion with the greatness of his state. And surely among other outward gifts of nature, the stature and lineaments of body are not least to be respected, specially in such princes as appear themselves in person at solemn interviews and public assemblies, as this king ofttimes did."[9] In the real presence of the king—who was, as the Henrician Bishop Gardiner put it, "the image of God upon earth"—Holbein's icon was made flesh; a mysterious incarnation of the Tudor state was effected.[10] Likewise, since none of Henry VIII's progeny were actually represented in Holbein's painting, the spectacle of the living Queen Elizabeth standing or seated before the images of her late father and grandfather could have presented a powerful visual assertion of her legitimate succession to the body politic of Tudor kingship. However, if she did indeed pose herself before this painting, Elizabeth would also have foregrounded the anomalous condition of her rule. Neither king nor queen consort but queen regnant and (as Bacon later put it) "a lady solitary and unmarried," Elizabeth Tudor strove throughout her reign to employ all of the resources at her command to make the greatness of her personage appear proportional to the greatness of her state.

Although none of Henry VIII's children were represented in the Whitehall wall painting, it nevertheless projected its dynastic theme beyond past and present. The year in which it was painted, 1537, also saw the birth of Prince Edward—a blessed event that promised to secure, at last, the continuity of the Tudors in the male line.[11] Thus, the prominence and ample proportions of the king's codpiece would seem to be especially appropriate to the dynastic theme of this particular painting. The same holds true for the large canvas of the King and his family, produced by an unknown artist within a decade of the Holbein group portrait (fig. 5). This icon was apparently intended for the more public Presence Chamber at Whitehall, where it was recorded as being displayed during the reign of Elizabeth.[12] Roy Strong observes that the composition "derives ultimately from that of a Virgin and Child enthroned flanked by standing saints."[13] This is a suggestive remark, for it implies that the King himself here incarnates the inspiriting Godhead, his patriarchal image having literally displaced the maternal figure at the center of the composition; at the same time, the association of the King with the divine will reinforces a link to the imperial iconography of Holbein's wall painting. Holbein's influence is palpable in the likeness of the deceased queen as well as in that of the living king, whose massive form and conspicuous codpiece are now at the center of the composition. In closest proximity to the king's body is that of Prince Edward, his son and heir. The father's right hand is upon the son's shoulder; and Edward, alone among the flanking figures, shares King Henry's fully frontal

FIGURE 5
The family of Henry VIII. Artist unknown; ca. 1543–47. Oil on canvas. The Royal Collection © 2005, Her Majesty Queen Elizabeth II.

gaze. As the vessel through whom the King has produced his legitimate male offspring, Jane Seymour has earned her subsidiary place in the central group, on the king's left hand. As Shakespeare's King Leontes enthuses upon meeting Florizel, the son and heir of King Polixenes, "Your mother was most true to wedlock, prince, / For she did print thy royal father off, / Conceiving you."[14]

In the wings, isolated by columns, are the royal daughters: Mary, the eldest born, on the king's right hand, and Elizabeth on his left. The latter figure is believed to be the earliest extant portrait of Elizabeth Tudor. The prior bastardizations of both of Henry's daughters had been confirmed by the Second Succession Act of 1536. Produced shortly thereafter, Holbein's wall painting for the Privy Chamber excludes any reference to either of the princesses or to their respective mothers, Catherine of Aragon and Anne Boleyn. In 1543, shortly before the composition of the anonymous painting for the Presence Chamber, the Third Succession Act placed Mary and Elizabeth into the entail following the lawful issue, male or female, of their father and half-brother; neither daughter, however, was explicitly restored to legitimacy.[15] However contingent their places in the succession, Mary and Elizabeth were now guaranteed their places in the picture, their presence within the chamber, and their position upon the same plane as the central group. These two royal daughters had starkly different maternal lineages and religious upbringings; nevertheless, both were female and retroactively bastardized, and that shared status presumably justified their common exclusion from the central frame. Masculine authority, legitimacy, and succession are gloriously affirmed under the canopy of state; and the flanking figures of Mary and Elizabeth are oriented toward that cynosure. However, their skirts trail toward the archways that lead away from the Presence Chamber. Positioned outdoors, just beyond the archways, are the ruder figures of a maidservant and a jester (identifiable as Henry's court Fool, Will Sommers) who bears a monkey; beyond these are the gardens and buildings of Whitehall Palace, decorated with grotesques and statuary of heraldic beasts. Thus, each daughter occupies a space that is mediatory between the hieratic royal body at the center of the painting and the base and hybrid figures at the margins.

In their representations of the gendered royal body, both Whitehall portraits of Henry VIII manifest the inseparability of sexual and political potency, virility and rule; and both celebrate masculine succession as the triumphant legitimation and fruition of Henry's kingship. The historical record suggests that the King was driven by an urgent need to realize such ideas. The same themes are conspicuous in representations of King Henry's male heir, commencing in Edward's infancy with Holbein's delightful portrait of the crown prince at between one and two years of age (fig. 6). In this New Year's gift

to the King, the infant heir grasps a gilded rattle as if it were a scepter: Here,
indeed, is His Majesty the Baby. The portrait includes a tablet that reconstrues
the themes of dynastic continuity and filial emulation that had been inscribed
upon the Whitehall wall painting of Henry VIII and *his* father:

> Little one, emulate thy father and be the heir of his virtue; the world contains
> nothing greater. Heaven and earth could scarcely produce a son whose glory

would surpass that of such a father. Do thou but only equal the deeds of thy parent and men can ask no more. Shouldst thou surpass him, thou hast outstript, nor shall any surpass thee in ages to come.[16]

In this case, as in the earlier one, the actual subject of the panegyric remains Henry VIII—the king regnant, and the painter's patron.

The sense that this father might be emulated but not surpassed is also conveyed in subsequent portraits of the youthful Edward, in which the son's pose is a pale imitation of Henry VIII's in Holbein's Whitehall icon. Perhaps the best executed of these pictures, and certainly the most germane to my subject, is a three-quarter-length one (fig. 7) that pairs with a portrait of Edward's half-sister Elizabeth (fig. 8). These apparently companion portraits are from about the same date (ca. 1546–47), and both have been attributed to William Scrots.[17] Edward is placed within a rich interior, dominated by a classical column with an equestrian figure carved in a roundel; the room is lit from a large window, also decorated with antique carvings, that opens onto an expansive park. Edward's pose, garments, and accoutrements all mirror his father's. The beholder's attention is drawn by the directness of his gaze; by the jeweled insignia of the Prince of Wales that rests upon his chest; and by his codpiece, where his right hand and the ornamental hilt of his dagger meet in a gesture of virility that is also, perhaps, a promise of dynastic continuity. The details of the painting meld elements of both the active and the contemplative lives with those of princely magnificence.

The background of Elizabeth's portrait is a relatively dark and heavily curtained interior, an enclosed space. In place of the open window is an open book upon a lectern. This folio, presumably a Bible, is the most conspicuous object in the room; its white pages constitute the largest area of brightness other than the face and shoulders of Elizabeth herself. She is dressed richly but without ostentation. Her hands are positioned similarly to those of her brother, but they are holding a small book—presumably, a devotional work— over the place on her dress that is equivalent to the place where Edward wears his codpiece. Not only is a ribbon visible, marking a place in the book that Elizabeth holds, but the tip of her right index finger is between the pages. This small but telling detail conveys the suggestion not that the book has been thrust into her hands as a mere prop but rather that she has been interrupted in the act of reading. Throughout the sixteenth century, it was most common for portraits of learned and godly men to represent them as holding, reading from, or gesturing toward a sacred book—as, for example, in the portrait

FIGURE 7
Edward VI when a prince, attributed to William Scrots; ca. 1546–47. Oil on panel. The Royal Collection
© 2005, Her Majesty Queen Elizabeth II.

of Archbishop Thomas Cranmer (fig. 9) that is contemporaneous with that
of the young Lady Elizabeth. A measure of the gendered piety, learning, and
authority inscribed in Cranmer's portrait is being appropriated to enhance
the portrait of his goddaughter.[18]

It is the virtuous, studious, and accomplished royal pupil represented in
young Elizabeth's portrait that Roger Ascham was describing in a letter to John

FIGURE 8
Elizabeth I when a princess, attributed to William Scrots; ca. 1546–47. Oil on panel. The Royal Collection
© 2005, Her Majesty Queen Elizabeth II.

Sturm in 1550. Having briefly praised the accomplishments of the young King
Edward, Ascham goes on at considerable length in his praise of Elizabeth:

> I have no difficulty in finding subject for writing in her praise, but only in setting
> bounds to what I write. I will write nothing however which I have not myself
> witnessed. She had me for her tutor in Greek and Latin two years.... It is

difficult to say whether the gifts of nature or of fortune are most to be admired in that illustrious lady. The praise which Aristotle gives wholly centres in her—beauty, stature, prudence, and industry. She has just passed her sixteenth birthday, and shows such dignity and gentleness as are wonderful at her age and in her rank. Her study of true religion and learning is most energetic. Her mind has no womanly weakness, her perseverance is equal to that of a man.... She reminds one of Hippolyte rather than of Phaedra.[19]

FIGURE 9
Archbishop Thomas Cranmer, by Gerlach Flicke; 1545 or 1546. Oil on panel. National Portrait Gallery, London.

What higher compliment could a humanist scholar pay to an adolescent girl than to compare her to a chastely virtuous male youth while contrasting her to a wantonly passionate matron? The paired portraits of Edward and Elizabeth are strongly gender-coded: the open and enclosed ambient spaces, the hand upon the dagger and the finger within the book, the suggestions of prospective virile kingship and pious womanhood. However, the portrait of Elizabeth not only emphasizes maidenly modesty, piety, and restraint but also suggests the opportunities for intellectual accomplishment and moral authority that a Christian humanist education made possible for the daughter of a king—even one who had been legally rendered illegitimate and was thus officially denied the title of princess. These were opportunities of which the Lady Elizabeth evidently took full advantage.

There is extant an affectionate and deferential letter from Elizabeth to Edward, written sometime between the execution of the portrait under discussion and the writing of Ascham's letter to Sturm. In fulfilling Edward's request for her portrait (perhaps the present one, but more likely a miniature by Levina Teerlinc), the young Lady Elizabeth wrote that

> for the face, I grant, I might well blush to offer, but the mind I shall never be ashamed to present. But though from the grace of the picture the colors may fade by time, may give by weather, may be spotted by chance, yet the other nor time with her swift wings shall overtake, nor the misty clouds with their lowerings may darken, nor chance with her slippery foot may overthrow.[20]

The youthful Elizabeth takes the occasion to meditate upon the contrast between transient physical beauty and the enduring virtues of the mind. She presents herself to her younger half-brother (possibly now the King) as an exemplar of Constancy and Fortitude who stands unwaveringly against that slippery female, Fortune. Here we can observe Ascham's well-tutored pupil, beginning to formulate the sententious humanist tropes that she would continue to develop, vary, and reiterate throughout her own reign, particularly when she addressed herself to such accomplished masculine audiences as ambassadors, parliaments, and university scholars.

A dozen years after the Ascham letter previously quoted, he wrote again to Sturm in praise of his former pupil, now his Queen:

> The glory she derives from herself, and the adornments of talent and learning that she possesses, I have described to you in another letter. I will now only state in addition, that neither at court, nor in the universities, nor among our heads of church or state, are there four of our countrymen who understand Greek better than the Queen herself.... All her own subjects, and very many foreigners, are

witnesses to her proficiency in other languages. I was one day present, when she replied at the same time to three ambassadors ... in three languages.[21]

Elizabeth took conspicuous pride in her skill in languages and her learning in both classical and patristic authors, and these accomplishments were often admiringly noted by those whom she had sought to impress.[22] She herself eschewed false modesty when, speaking at the close of her fifth parliament in 1585, she allowed that "I am supposed to have many stoodies, but most philosophicall. I must yelde this to be trewe: that I suppose fewe (that be no professors) have reade more."[23] Such accomplishments constituted a mark of distinction and a source of authority for a monarch whose gender excluded her from opportunities for martial or chivalric prowess. In his 1562 letter to Sturm, Ascham recalled that in his 1550 letter he had "stated, that in her whole manner of life she more resembled Hippolyte than Phaedra. Which observation I then referred, not to the graces of her person, but wholly to the chastity of her mind" (66). The central gesture in the portrait of the adolescent Lady Elizabeth—that of the book held against the lower torso, with a finger inserted between the leaves—strikes me as an apt biblio-genital visual metaphor for that chaste intellectual power of which Ascham writes.

Well before the painting of her bookish portrait, Elizabeth was already busy making pious books as well as reading them. As a New Year's gift for 1544/45—that is, at about the time she was included in the group portrait of Henry VIII and his children (fig. 5)—Elizabeth had presented to her stepmother Katherine Parr a neatly handwritten copy of her own translation of Marguerite de Navarre's *Le miroir de l'âme pécheresse*, bound and covered with her own embroidery. For the following New Year, she presented as a gift to her father a volume containing her translations into French, Italian, and Latin of her stepmother's own pious composition, *Prayers, or Meditations*. In Elizabeth's prefatory epistle—which constitutes her only known letter to her father, the King—she writes that this "composition by a queen as a subject for her king" has been translated "by me, your daughter. May I, by this means, be indebted to you not as an imitator of your virtues but indeed as an inheritor of them."[24] Here a bastard daughter seizes the opportunity to declare her work an act of filial emulation and, furthermore, to assert boldly that her own piety and learning manifest her royal legitimacy.

Elizabeth prefaced her earlier translation of *Le miroir de l'âme pécheresse* with an epistle to her stepmother; in it, she provided her own summary of Marguerite's mystical method for experiencing and representing in familial terms the encounters between the soul and the Godhead: "She (beholding and contemplating what she is) doth perceive how of herself and of her own strength she can do nothing that good is, or prevaileth for her salvation, unless it be through the grace of God, whose mother, daughter, sister, and wife by the scriptures she proveth herself to be."[25] As Anne Lake Prescott has demonstrated, the "relatively few errors and somewhat more frequent omissions" in Princess Elizabeth's translation of Marguerite's text "often concern this set of relationships" and may be read as symptomatic of deeply vexed feelings toward the royal father, who had declared her a bastard and had executed her mother. For example, where Marguerite writes of paternal love for a daughter, Elizabeth mistranslates "père" as "mother," and she omits Marguerite's similitude between divine mercy and paternal forgiveness.[26] It may well be that the eleven-year-old Elizabeth's work on this project stood her in good stead when, following the deaths of her father and half-siblings, she herself finally assumed the body politic of Tudor kingship. An essential element in the statecraft by which Elizabeth Tudor sought to establish and maintain a congenial authority over her subjects was to figure it in parental and conjugal metaphors: by herself and by some of her subjects, she was variously represented not only as a wife or mother but also as a father or husband to her people.[27] Bacon's "solitary and unmarried" queen constructed her political relationships upon the grid of familial bonds; and this construction can be seen to constitute a creative recoding of the sinful soul's relationship to God.[28]

A rather different project of appropriation appears to be at work in the subsequent printing history of what had originally been the Lady Elizabeth's private gift to her stepmother. In 1548—shortly after the death of Henry VIII, and as he prepared to return from continental exile to the more congenially reformist England of Edward VI, Protector Somerset, and the dowager Queen Katherine—John Bale edited Elizabeth's englishing of Marguerite de Navarre and saw it into print as *A Godly Medytacyon of the Christen Sowle*. The volume includes an Epistle Dedicatory "To the right virtuous and Christianly learned young Lady Elizabeth, the noble daughter of our late sovereign King Henry the Eighth" (Shell, *Elizabeth's Glass*, 83), and it is illustrated with a woodcut representing Elizabeth kneeling before Christ with a pious book or bible in her hand (fig. 10). In his Epistle, Bale attacks "the Romish clergy" and opposes to it the spiritual nobility of Elizabeth and "many other noble women and maidens more in this blessed age," who evince regard for "the pure doctrine and faith" (86). In a Conclusion that follows Elizabeth's text, Bale compiles a catalogue of "noble women, which in this land of Britain or realm of England have excelled in beauty, wit, wisdom, science, languages, liberality, policies, heroical force, and such other notable virtues, and by reason of them done

A Godly Medytaty on of the christen sowle, concerninge a loue towardes God and hys Christe, compyled in frenche by lady Margarete quene of Nauerre, and aptely translated into Englysh by the ryght vertuouse lady Elyzabeth doughter to our late soverayne Kynge Henri the.viij.

Inclita filia, sereniſſimi olim Anglorum Regis Henrici octaui Elizabeta, tam Græcæ quam latine fœliciter in Chriſto erudita.

FIGURE 10

The Lady Elizabeth holding a religious book and kneeling before Christ. Artist unknown. Title page of *A godly medytacyon of the Christen sowle concerninge a love towardes God and hys Christe, compiled in Frenche by Lady Margaret queene of Navere and aptely translated into Englysh by the ryght vertuous lady Elyzabeth doughter to Kynge Henri the viii* (Wesel, 1548). STC 17320. Woodcut. By permission of the Folger Shakespeare Library, Washington, DC.

feats wonderful" (100). This catalogue culminates in the heroic example of the Henrician Protestant martyr, Anne Askew, who "as Christ's mighty member, hath strongly trodden down the head of the serpent and gone hence with most noble victory over the pestiferous seed of that viperous worm of Rome" (101).

By means of the Epistle and Conclusion with which he frames Elizabeth's translation of Marguerite, Bale inscribes her within the discourse and agenda of Protestant reform: His gynephilic celebration of women worthies is subordinated to this end, as is his refashioning of what Patrick Collinson characterizes as the "quasi-Lutheran, proto-Protestant, Augustinian limits" of the Christian beliefs actually manifested in Elizabeth's translation of Marguerite's text.[29] In their address to and representation of the Lady Elizabeth, Bale's texts combine panegyrical, didactic, and admonitory motives. And in the strategies by which he seeks to enlist her in the cause of a religious ideology for which she had not openly declared herself, he adumbrates the repeated attempts later made by some of Queen Elizabeth's godly subjects to flatter or to shame her into emulating in practice the exemplary images of reform which they set before her in numerous sermons, speeches, and pictures. Like other contemporaneous and subsequent religious reformers, Bale was hostile to the notions of sacred kingship that had been so powerfully reasserted in Henry VIII's version of the Reformation, and codified in the Act in Restraint of Appeals (1533) and other legislation. Bale attempted to recruit the Lady Elizabeth to the party of Anne Askew; nevertheless, Queen Elizabeth would prove herself to be her father's daughter by her tenacious maintenance of the royal supremacy and her consummate cultivation of the aura of sacred kingship.

It is hard to imagine that the young Lady Elizabeth's feelings about her seldom-seen father were anything other than profoundly ambivalent. Nevertheless, she seems to have cultivated her paternal identification actively during the reign of her half-sister, undoubtedly spurred on by Queen Mary's calculated slights and barely contained resentments. In a lengthy, shrewd, and revealing dispatch about the state of England that he sent to the Doge in 1557, the Venetian ambassador Michiel wrote that Queen Mary was consumed by inconsolable and remediless distress, arising "from two causes, or rather from two contrary effects, viz., from love and hate." The former effect proceded from Mary's "violent love" for her husband, King Philip, who was largely absent from England. (Indeed, Philip's virtual abandonment caused Mary to vent her "violent love" upon his portrait: "The Queen, on hearing that the King would not return to England for a long time, was in a rage, and caused his picture to be carried out of the Privy Chamber.")[30] The latter effect of

Mary's distress—her hatred—was "owing to her evil disposition . . . towards her sister my Lady Elizabeth, which although dissembled, it cannot be denied that she displays in many ways the scorn and ill will . . . she bears her." Michiel explains that the complex reasons for this hatred included Anne Boleyn's responsibility for the suffering of Mary's mother, Catherine of Aragon, and for Mary's own ignominious treatment during Anne's brief reign; the loyalty and sympathy inspired by the vulnerable but politic Elizabeth among Mary's own Protestant subjects; and the prospect that this "illegitimate child of a criminal who was punished as a public strumpet [was] on the point of inheriting the throne with better fortune than herself, whose descent [was] rightful, legitimate, and regal."[31] A comment reported by a follower of Jane Dormer, Queen Mary's closest companion, is consistent with Michiel's observations: "We see how different were the mothers of these two queens, and of the latter the father might be doubted, for Queen Mary would never call her sister, nor be persuaded she was her father's daughter. She would say she had the face and countenance of Mark Sweton, who was a very handsome man."[32] According to this account, Mary not only insisted that Elizabeth was the illegitimate offspring of her mother's adultery; adding insult to injury, she assigned paternity to the lowest in rank of the five men who were executed as Anne's lovers: the court musician Mark Smeaton, who had reportedly confessed his guilt under torture.

Queen Anne was executed for purported acts of adultery and incest that constituted high treason against her sovereign. However, although Elizabeth was declared illegitimate shortly before her mother's execution and was no longer styled as "Princess," the King did not formally repudiate his own paternity. Both before and after her accession, Elizabeth's Catholic adversaries vehemently maintained that Elizabeth was the bastard offspring of Henry and his whore. As already suggested, some went further, claiming that Anne's mother had also been Henry's mistress, that Anne herself was the illegitimate offspring of their adultery, and thus that Elizabeth was the incestuous offspring of the King and his own illegitimate daughter. Alternatively, it was reasoned that because of her mother's treasonous infidelity to the King and the confession of Mark Smeaton, Elizabeth was a bastard fathered by one of Anne's base lovers and therefore not of the blood royal at all. Even if Elizabeth were considered to be the natural child of King Henry, her legitimacy was still seen to be tainted by incest and illegitimacy, because her mother's elder sister had earlier also been the King's mistress. This was a family romance befitting the House of Atreus.

Few English monarchs can have ascended the throne with a more questionable, lurid, and violent pedigree than did Elizabeth Tudor. And it continued to provide choice material for opponents of the Elizabethan regime and its policies until late in her reign. Thus, when continental Catholics with a literary bent wanted to condemn the execution of Mary, Queen of Scots, in 1587, they could contribute to *De Jezebelis Anglae*, a collection of French and Latin poems reviling Queen Elizabeth, whom one of the included sonnets addressed as "bastarde incestueuse . . . et fille de ta soeur."[33] And in the incendiary pamphlet that he wrote to prepare the ideological ground for the Armada in 1588, England's cardinal-in-exile, William Allen, sought to remind Elizabeth's subjects that this "wicked Jesabell" was

> an incestuous bastard, begotten and borne in sinne, of an infamous courtesan Anne Bullen, afterwarde executed for aduotery [*sic*], treason, heresie and inceste, amongst others with her owne naturall brother, which Anne, her said supposed father kepte by pretensed marriage, in the life of his lawfull wife, the most renonmed and blessed ladie Queen Katherine . . . as he did before unnaturally knowe and kepe bothe the said Annes mother and sister.

In excoriating Elizabeth "not onely for injust intrusions and usurpations, but also for . . . followinge her said supposed fathers waies (who was *radix peccati* of our daies)," Allen is trying to have it both ways—simultaneously questioning her royal paternity and declaring that the very nature and depth of her wickedness affirm her affinity with King Henry.[34]

An acute analyst of the interplay among religious, political, and emotional forces at the Marian court, the Venetian ambassador observed of the Lady Elizabeth that

> She is proud and haughty, as although she knows that she was born of such a mother, she nevertheless does not consider herself of inferior degree to the Queen, whom she equals in self-esteem; nor does she believe herself less legitimate than her Majesty. . . . She prides herself on her father and glories in him; everybody saying that she also resembles him more than the Queen does; and he therefore always liked her and had her brought up . . . in the same way as the Queen.[35]

In November 1558, when Queen Mary was near death, the Count of Feria reported to King Philip of Spain on his interview with Elizabeth, the heir presumptive: "She is a very vain and clever woman. She must have been thoroughly schooled in the manner in which her father conducted his affairs. . . . She is determined to be governed by no one."[36] Shortly thereafter, Elizabeth became queen; and Feria confirmed to King Philip his earlier assessment: "She seems to me incomparably more feared than her sister and gives her orders and has her way as absolutely as her father did."[37] A half-century later, Sir John Harington would remember his recently deceased godmother in similar terms: "Surely she did plaie well hir tables to gain obedience thus wythout constraint: again, she coude pute forthe suche alteracions, when obedience was lackinge, as lefte no doubtynges whose daughter she was."[38]

The first pageant that Elizabeth encountered after her ceremonial entry into London on the day before her coronation had as its theme legitimacy and lineal descent, and thus an orderly transition that preserved social harmony. A pamphlet recording, describing, and interpreting this civic spectacle of royal initiation was in print within ten days of the actual performance. The pamphlet describes the pageant scaffold as follows: "Upon the lowest stage . . . wer placed two personages representing kynge Henrie the seventh and Elizabeth hys wyfe," enclosed in red and white dynastic roses, respectively. Out of these two roses

> sprang two braunches gathered into one, which wer directed upward to the second stage or degree, wherin was placed one, representing the valiant & noble prynce king Henrie theight which sprong out of the former stocke, crowned with a crowne imperiall, & by him sate one representing the right worthie ladie quene Anne, wife to the said king Henrie theyght, & mother to our most soveraign ladie quene Elizabeth that now is. . . . From their seate also proceaded upwardes one braunche directed to the third and uppermost stage or degree, wherin lykewyse was planted a seate royall, in the whiche was sette one representynge the Quene's most excellent majestie Elizabeth nowe our most dradde soveraygne Ladie.[39]

Elizabeth's coronation entry staged a heraldic *tableau vivant* of Tudor genealogy that conveniently leaped over both King Edward VI and the recently deceased Queen Mary in order to impress upon the spectators an image of Elizabeth as the destined fruit of the seed of Henry VIII and Henry VII.

At the conclusion of its narrative and its description of the pageants encountered by Elizabeth, the pamphlet appends "Certain notes of the quene's majestie's great mercie, clemencie, and wisdom used in this passage." This supplementary collection of Elizabethan human-interest stories functions to show the new queen engaged in face-to-face interactions with her common subjects, and as already practicing the royal virtues abstracted and allegorized in the pageants. For example,

> In Cheapeside her grace smyled, and being therof demaunded the cause, answered, for that she had heard one say, Remember old king Henry theight. A naturall child, which at the verie remembraunce of her fathers name toke so great a joy, that all men may well thinke, that she rejoysed at his name whom this realme doth holde of so woorthie memorie: so in her doinges she will resemble the same. (61)

This example demonstrates an interesting and innovative generic modulation within the pamphlet, a modulation of symbolic narrative into exemplary anecdote, of textualized ceremony into textualized improvisation. The printed pamphlet supplements and reinforces the heraldic genealogy of the pageant with an application of the common touch—an unusually solicitous appeal to the loyalties of the humblest of the new queen's subjects. At the same time, it moves its readers from the pageant's abstract assertion of Elizabeth's legitimacy to vivid proofs of her filiation in her bearing, speech, and conduct.

A year after Elizabeth's accession, Sir Thomas Chaloner presented as a New Year's gift to the young queen a long Latin poem he had written in praise of Henry VIII. At its conclusion, the poem turns to "Elizabeth, whose imperial eye and brow shine forth and recall so well the face of her thrice-great father":

> O maiden, blessed in so resembling your parent, blessed in dominions, and blessed in the divine gifts of genius and of form, there remains yet one thing. You, who are so blessed in your own person, dare at some time (having already too much delayed) to bestow the bonds of your modesty on a husband—a man who will be blessed and more than blessed. For then a little Henry will play in the palace for us, a handsome child who happily will bring to mind his grandfather, than whom no man was ever more handsome or more outstanding for handsome deeds.[40]

At the end of his panegyric for Henry VIII, Chaloner appears to embrace his new sovereign's own strategies of legitimation by emphasizing that not only her physical appearance but also her intellect and her temperament are a direct inheritance from her father. At the same time, however, in its final modulation from encomium into exhortation, Chaloner's poem registers the limited willingness or ability of the new Elizabethan political nation fully to embrace the prospect of gynecocracy. In urging marriage and motherhood upon Elizabeth, and in its prospect of "a little Henry . . . who will bring to mind his grandfather," the poem's final rhetorical gesture is to subsume the queen regnant within a fundamentally masculinist vision of filial emulation, dynastic succession, and imperial kingship.

The Tudor Sisterhood

"The Quene's Majestie's passage through the citie of London to westminster the daye before her coronacion" was a rite of passage for the new sovereign. As reconstructed in the officially sanctioned printed account, the stations of the journey occasioned a coherent program of allegorical pageants that confirmed the royal succession, affirmed principles of good government and reformed religion, and encouraged the young, unmarried woman who was now queen with demonstrations of popular support and citations of biblical precedent for female magistracy—most notably, that of "Debora with her estates, consulting for the good government of Israel."[1] Of course, Elizabeth and her new subjects had a far more pertinent precedent immediately to hand in their newly deceased sovereign, Queen Mary. In a prayer upon her accession, Elizabeth was hailed as a

> Prince . . . of no mingled blood, of Spaniard or straunger, but borne mere Englishe here amongst us, and therfore most naturall unto us. Of education, brought up and instruct in al vertuous qualitees and Godly learnynge, specially . . . in the sincere knowlege and folowing of Gods holly woord. . . . Of wisedome so ware, as she maie shun the inconveniences and follies that her sister fell in.[2]

In terms of her personal virtues and natural sympathies—her mercy and wisdom, her Englishness, and her Protestantism—the new queen is here constructed as an antithesis and an antidote to her predecessor. The enduring caricatures of Bloody Mary and Good Queen Bess—still active in popular biography and historiography—perpetuate a dual representation deeply rooted in Elizabethan Protestant propaganda.

At the accession of Elizabeth, the militantly Protestant position was by no means representative of the religious beliefs and practices of English men and women at large. Of those who had newly become Elizabethan subjects, many remained Catholic by commitment or by habit, and many more were doubtless indifferent in matters of religion.[3] Among those who held to the old faith and had been loyal Marian subjects, the accession of Elizabeth may have been regarded with reserve or even with apprehension. This profoundly unsettled state of affairs is at once acknowledged and neutralized in one of the "notes of the quene's majestie's great mercie, clemencie, and wisdom" that is rehearsed in Mulcaster's account of Elizabeth's coronation entry:

> One of the knyghtes about her grace had espied an auncient citizen, which wepte, and turned his head backe.... How may it be interpreted that he so doth, for sorowe, or for gladness? The queens majestie said, I warrant you it is for gladnes. A gracious interpretation of a noble courage, which wold turne the douteful to the best. And yet it was well known that as her grace did confirme the same, the parties cheare was moved for very pure gladnes for the sight of her majesties person, at ye beholding wherof, he tooke such comfort that with teares he expressed the same.[4]

The "auncient citizen, which wepte, and turned his head backe" might well stand as an emblematic personification of residual Marian loyalism, of resistance to the new political order and to the unwelcome prospect of religious change. The Queen's gentleman reads the old man's gesture as "doutetful"; and, following the rhetorical practice of Puttenham, we might view this "auncient citizen" as an embodied trope who performs "*Amphibologia ... the ambiguous*, or figure of sence incertaine.*" Puttenham explicitly links this rhetorical figure to equivocal sayings and prophecies, by which "many insurrections and rebellions have bene stirred up in this Realme."[5] Nevertheless, the Queen generously chooses to read the sign *in bono* rather than *in malo*. Such is the efficacy of royal grace—or so Mulcaster implies—that the old man's ambiguous gesture is immediately clarified as a gesture of love toward his new sovereign. The old man who weeps does not speak his meaning; an ambiguous figure interpreted by others, he is produced and effaced in Mulcaster's text in order to promote the new queen's magnanimity and to inculcate loyalty to her regime.

In a poem made on the occasion of the succession by George Cavendish, we can hear an interesting countervoice to that of Protestant triumphalism. This poem is not a paean to the advent of Elizabeth but rather "An Ephitaphe of our / late queen Marye."[6] Cavendish focuses upon the life and virtues of the late queen: her piety, restoration of "the right Religion / And faythe of ffathers" (2349–50), and suppression of heresy and iconoclasm; her lineage, "bloode and parentage / In all Europea. / no prynces equall" (2328–29); her political legitimacy, and her military triumphs over the Northumberland coup and the Wyatt rebellion; her marital alliance with Philip of Spain, "the Roos and pomgranatt / joined in oon" (2307). Cavendish emphasizes Mary's status as a virgin queen, one who married only for the welfare of her subjects:

> To a virgyns lyfe / whiche lyked the best
> Profest was thyn hart / when moved with zele /
> And teeres of Subjectes / expressyng request
> Ffor no lust but love for the comen weale
> Virginites vowe / thou diddest repelle
> Knytt with a kyng Coequall in valoure
> Thyn estate to conserve / as quene of honoure /
> (2300–2306)

Finally, when he addresses his new queen, "Elizabethe excellent / of God elect," and bids her to "make for your myrror / Mary thye sister / late quene of honor" (2363, 2368–69), Cavendish is exhorting Elizabeth to emulate rather than to repudiate the Marian paradigm.

The biographical and historiographical tradition has often discounted the importance of the Marian precedent in the Elizabethan construction of queenship; or, when sensitive to issues of gender and rule, it has tended to pair Mary and Elizabeth as mirroring opposites, respectively disastrous and dazzling in their queenship.[7] It would be a mistake, however, simply to conclude that Elizabeth drew only negative exempla from the reign of Mary. Elizabeth also seems to have found elements in her sister's queenly self-fashioning that she could seize upon and refashion as her own—at the same time that she and her supporters sought to project the Elizabethan image as an antithesis to the Marian one. Mary was England's first anointed queen regnant; and, at the time of her accession, she was still unmarried. The accession of Elizabeth raised vexatious issues regarding the authority of a queen regnant and how that authority might be affected by her marriage either to a subject or a to foreign prince. Many of the same issues had already been raised and debated at length following the accession of her sister, and the Marian experience must have deeply impressed itself upon both Elizabeth and the Elizabethan political nation.

On 3 August 1553, when Mary first entered London after the collapse of Northumberland's attempted coup in favor of Lady Jane Grey, she asserted her legitimate authority through a spectacular public display of royal power.

One estimate at the time put the size of her entourage at ten thousand; of those many, the personage who immediately followed the new queen in the entry procession was the Lady Elizabeth.[8] This may well have been one of those instances, during the course of her short and unhappy reign, in which Mary provided her shrewdly observant half-sister with a model for emulation in the art of queenship. Within a few months after this event, Queen Mary's intention to marry the Spanish and Catholic Prince Philip had precipitated the Wyatt Rebellion; and with her throne endangered, Mary attempted to secure the loyalty of London's citizens in an address at the Guildhall. Here is John Foxe's report of her speech:

> Now, loving subjects...I am your queen, to whom at my coronation, when I was wedded to the realm and laws of the same (the spousal ring whereof I have on my finger, which never hitherto was, nor hereafter shall be left off), you promised your allegiance and obedience unto me. And that I am the right and true inheritor of the crown of this realm of England, I take all Christendom to witness. My father, as ye all know, possessed the same regal state, which now rightly is descended unto me.... And I say to you, on the word of a prince, I cannot tell how naturally the mother loveth the child, for I was never the mother of any; but certainly, if a prince and governor may as naturally and earnestly love her subjects, as the mother doth love the child, then assure yourselves, that I, being your lady and mistress, do as earnestly and tenderly love and favour you....
>
> As concerning the marriage...I assure you, I am not so bent to my will, neither so precise, nor affectionate, that either for mine own pleasure I would choose where I lust, or that I am so desirous, as needs I would have one. For God, I thank him, to whom be the praise therefore, I have hitherto lived a virgin, and doubt nothing, but with God's grace, I am able so to live still. But if, as my progenitors have done before, it might please God that I might leave some fruit of my body behind me, to be your governor, I trust you would not only rejoice thereat, but also I know that it would be to your great comfort.[9]

Within this passage, we can observe Mary strategically deploying a battery of tropes which Elizabeth would quickly adopt as her own when she inherited Mary's crown: the metaphorical marriage to her subjects; her inheritance of the body politic of kingship from her father, Henry VIII; the similitude comparing her love for her subjects with that of a mother for her children; the valorization of her status as a virgin; her willingness, nevertheless, to forgo the blessings of the single life and to marry for the sake of her subjects' collective welfare. Over the course of a reign many times longer than Mary's, and as occasion required, Elizabeth would continue to elaborate upon this same rhetorical repertoire.

Two months after Mary's speech at the Guildhall, Parliament passed an "Acte declaring that the Regall Power of this Realme is in the Quenes Majestie as fully and absolutely as ever it was in any of her mostc noble Progenitours Kinges of this Realme." Because regal power in England had previously been attributed solely to kings, it was now necessary explicitly to confer such power upon England's first queen regnant. This was the rationale for the statute, although there is some evidence that it was actually designed by the Lord Chancellor, Archbishop Gardiner, to forestall arguments that the Queen's power was absolute precisely because she was not bound by the laws that restrained the kings of the realm.[10] A passage in *The Mirror for Magistrates* that was written during the reign of Mary and Philip made the following strategic defense of gynecocracy:

> And although some Realmes more carefull than wise, have entailed their crowne to the heire male thinking it not meete for the feminine sexe to beare the royall office: yet if they consyder all the circumstaunces, and the chiefest uses of a Prince in a realme, they shall se howe they are deceived: for princes are gods lieutenauntes or deputies, to se gods lawes executed among theyr subjectes, not to rule according to their owne lustes or devyses.... And as for wysedome and pollicie, seing it consisteth in following the counsayle of many godly, learned, & long experienced heades, it were better to have a woman, who consideringe her owne weaknes and inabilitye, shoulde be ruled thereby, than a man which presuming upon his owne fond brayne, wil heare no advise save his owne.[11]

In order to defend the cause of limited monarchy against a potential threat of tyranny, this writer argued not merely for the legitimacy but for the desirability of female regiment, and did so precisely on the basis of perceived female weakness. Another of the statutes crafted by the Marian parliament declared

> that youre majestye as our onely Quene, shal and may, solye and as a sole quene use, have, and enjoye the Crowne and Soveraynte, of, and over your Realmes, Dominions, and Subjectes ... in suche sole and onelye estate, and in as large and ample maner and fourme ... after the solemnisation of the sayde maryage, and at all tymes durynge the same as your grace hath had, used, exercised and enjoyed ... before the solemnization of the sayde mariage.[12]

The motivation for such legislation was not enthusiasm for the principle of female rule but rather an urgent need to assert that the legitimate inheritrix of the English crown would have precedence over her foreign consort, *despite* the inferiority of her gender. Implicit in such a position was the expectation that the influence of her foreign husband upon the Queen's rule would be tempered by the counsel of already known and trusted men who were her natural subjects. Such constitutional arguments conjure up a dramatic scenario in which the English Queen's native counselors engage her foreign husband in a masculine rivalry for control of her body politic.

That Mary's status as queen would be fundamentally unaffected by her marriage to Philip had already been stipulated in the marriage treaties, the terms of which had been confirmed by Parliament and disseminated to the whole realm by means of a royal proclamation. However, Philip's own royal status was not envisioned as that of a mere consort, as would have been the case had the genders been reversed; rather, his status seems to have been construed as that of a co-monarch for the duration of his marriage to the Queen. According to the proclamation, "Prince Philip shall for so long as the matrimony endureth be allowed to have and enjoy jointly together with the same most noble Queen his wife the style, honor, and kingly name of the realms and dominions unto the said most noble Queen appertaining, and shall aid the same most noble Queen his wife in the prosperous administration of her realms and dominions."[13] The practice of such principles depended in large measure upon the personal interplay between Philip and Mary as King and Queen, husband and wife. And pervasive cultural perceptions that the inherently weak, inconstant, and impassioned nature of womankind made them unfit to rule were doubtless reinforced by Mary's well-documented devotion and deference to her largely absent husband.[14] When his sometime sister-in-law Elizabeth succeeded his deceased wife Mary as Queen of England, Philip wrote that "it would be better for herself and her Kingdom, if she would take a consort who might relieve her of those labours which are only fit for men."[15] There can be no doubt that he had held the same opinion while he was King of England; and, indeed, he gave serious consideration to extending his tour of duty by marrying Elizabeth, too.[16]

The marriage of a queen regnant to a foreign prince was unprecedented in England; and the English elites had a vested interest in ensuring that an implicit contradiction between the hegemonic domestic paradigm of husbandly authority and the anomalous political circumstance of female rule would not lead to an erosion of English sovereignty, thereby endangering the security and privileges of the Queen's natural subjects. This concern was acute to many members of the English polity, regardless of their religious affiliation, in particular because their prospective king was heir to the Spanish throne and a scion of the Habsburg dynasty. That such concerns had some foundation is suggested by the proclamation of the new regnal style, which gave precedence to Philip; by the Privy Council's instructions that state papers be recorded in Latin or Spanish for the King's comprehension, and that the King and Queen be joint signatories to royal documents; and also by the iconography of the

FIGURE 11
Philip and Mary silver sixpence, obverse
("PHILIP Z MARIA D G REX Z REGINA ANG"),
1557. Ashmolean Museum, Oxford.

FIGURE 12
The Great Seal of Philip and Mary, 1554–58. By
permission of the British Library (Seal 84, C.33).

most widely disseminated official images of the reign—its coins, seals and charters.[17] As in the examples illustrated here (figs. 11, 12, and 13), these represented Philip and Mary as joint sovereigns, with a single crown suspended between them. In two of the three, Queen Mary occupies the position of consort, on the viewer's right.

The gratuitous embroiling of England in the Franco-Habsburg war in 1557, with the consequent loss of Calais, the last remnant of England's French conquests, was precisely the kind of negative consequence of a foreign alliance that the marriage treaties of Philip and Mary had been intended to forestall. This national indignity faced Elizabeth immediately upon her accession, and the lesson was obviously not lost on her. In the speech with which he opened

FIGURE 13

King Philip and Queen Mary. Artist unknown. Plea roll, King's Bench; Easter 1556. Polychrome
illumination. The National Archives (PRO), UK: ref. KB27/1178 (2).

the first Elizabethan parliament in January 1559, Lord Keeper Sir Nicholas
Bacon praised his new queen as one

> that is not, nor never meaneth to be, so wedded to hir owne will and fantasie
> that for the satisfaction thereof she will doe any thinge that were likely to bring
> any bondage or servitude to her people. . . . a princesse that never meaneth nor

intendeth for any private affection to advaunce the cause or quarrell of any
forreigne power or potentate to the destruccion of her subjectes, to the losse
of any her domynions, or the impoverishing of her realmes.[18]

He did not invoke the names of Philip and Mary, nor did he need to do so.

Despite the brevity of her reign, there are extant a number of portraits of Mary
Tudor as a queen regnant.[19] Conspicuously absent from the repertoire of Marian images, however, is the Tudor succession picture. Whether on coins, seals,
or charters, or in portraits, Mary chose to be represented individually or with
her Spanish, Catholic, and Habsburg consort (fig. 14). Two celebrated portraits of Queen Mary were painted in 1554, those by Hans Eworth (fig. 15) and
Antonis Mor (fig. 16).[20] Although both painters were from the Low Countries,
Mor was in service to the Habsburg family, whereas Eworth was patronized by
the Tudor court. Despite their shared date and similarities in details of dress
and jewelry, these two portraits manifest significant differences in style and
composition, differences which may in part be attributable to the divergent
sources of their patronage. Eworth's work is closer to the native style in its relative lack of depth, its smooth surfaces and fondness for abstract patterning,
its relative idealization and softening of the Queen's features, and its posing of
the figure standing and with her hands clasped. It has a general affinity with
such examples from the prior decade as the female figures in the Henrician
family group (fig. 5) and the portrait of the young Lady Elizabeth (fig. 8). Mor's
work evinces a greater illusion of volume and depth, and a more pronounced
use of chiaroscuro; the Queen appears close to the viewer, her pose is more
naturalistic and animated, and her strongly lit face vividly reveals the signs of
aging and irregularities of complexion that are suppressed in Eworth's image.

The apparent naturalism of Mor's work must have been at the behest, or at
least with the approval, of his patrons. These were the Emperor Charles V, who
had arranged the marriage of Queen Mary to his son and heir in order to further his dynastic interests, and who had originally commissioned the portrait
of his new daughter-in-law; and Philip himself, who was newly married to
Mary and at the English court when the portrait was painted, and who adopted
Mor as his own court painter in 1554 and promptly pensioned him. A decade
later, during Queen Elizabeth's own Habsburg courtship maneuvers, she told
the Emperor Maximilian's envoy of her determination that "she would take
no man whom she had not seen. . . . She knew very well how the King of Spain
had cursed the painters and envoys when he first beheld Queen Mary, and she
would not give the Archduke Charles cause to curse."[21] It has been suggested

FIGURE 14

Mary I and Philip of Spain. Artist unknown; 1557. Woburn Abbey. By kind permission of His Grace the Duke of Bedford and the Trustees of the Bedford Estates.

that Mor's likeness is a response to, or a compensation for, such flattering portraits, of which Eworth's could perhaps serve as an example.[22] In both portraits, Mary wears a large and splendid pendant jewel that was a Habsburg wedding gift. In Mor's painting, the pious Queen grasps a red rose, an emblem not only of the Tudor dynasty but also of her sacred namesake—and,

FIGURE 15
Mary I, by Hans Eworth; 1554. Oil on panel. The Society of Antiquaries of London.

FIGURE 16
Mary I, by Antonis Mor; 1554. Oil on panel. Museo Nacional Del Prado, Madrid.

perhaps, evocative of her supposed pregnancy, which was rumored very soon after the marriage. If Mary's pregnancy had been genuine, and had succeeded in producing an heir, a likely political consequence would have been England's absorption within the European hegemony of the Habsburg dynasty and the entrenchment of its recent official return to the Catholic Church. There would have been no Elizabethan Age. Thus, while Mor represents Mary in state, a queen regnant seated upon her throne, other aspects of the painting's style and composition, as well as the circumstances and agents of its commission, suggest that both Mary and her throne were being valued as potential Habsburg possessions and as instruments of a dynastic statecraft that was neither Tudor nor indigenously English. Indeed, Karen Hearn has suggested that "the broader iconography of the portrait . . . characterises the Queen as a Habsburg consort, rather than an English sovereign."[23] In its circumscription of Queen Mary within the political agendas and artistic tastes of the Habsburg dynasty, Mor's portrait makes visually manifest Philip's comprehensive intent to control Mary's royal image, her body, and her state.[24]

For those whose visual image of Queen Elizabeth has been formed by the striking allegorical portraits of her later years, the extant portraits from the first decade of her reign are conspicuous only for their relatively understated treatment of their regal subject. They eschew the elaborate iconography of monarchy and the overt personal symbolism that are characteristic of many such later royal portraits.[25] Iconic allegory makes a discreet entrance into Elizabethan royal portraiture in the two finely drawn and brilliantly colored oil portraits attributed to the young Nicholas Hilliard and painted in the early 1570s. In each of these pictures, the Queen wears a large jewel suspended from a necklace: one, the image of a life-rendering pelican, tearing its breast in order to succour its young with its blood (fig. 17); the other, the image of the singular and self-renewing phoenix upon its burning pyre (fig. 18).[26] Each jewel gives symbolic form to a royal trope that would be elaborated in word and image throughout the rest of the reign: the Pelican, that of the Queen as a nurse and mother to her people, willing to sacrifice herself for their welfare; the Phoenix, that of the Queen as a unique and self-sufficient being, whose constancy was given verbal form in her motto, *semper eadem*.[27]

It could be said that the paired icons of the Pelican and the Phoenix provide a matrix for much of the work of the Elizabethan imaginary. In combination, the Pelican and the Phoenix may be understood as symbolic responses—or mythical solutions—to the all too tangible Elizabethan political quandaries of royal marriage and succession. Within the symbolic economy of the Elizabethan imaginary, the Phoenix was associated with the quasi-mystical powers inhering in the Queen's virginity. The prominence of this image and its associated motto in the later years of the reign suggests that the perceived succession crisis was being given imaginary resolution in a fantasy of the Queen's perpetual self-renewal. The Pelican is associated with the Queen's displacement of her maternity from her offspring to her subjects—a trope that was initiated by Elizabeth herself in a speech to her second Parliament in 1563: "I assure yow all that though after my death yow may have many stepdames, yet shall

FIGURE 17
Elizabeth I (the "Pelican" portrait), attributed to Nicholas Hilliard; ca. 1572–76. Oil on panel. Walker Art Gallery, Liverpool.

yow never have any a more naturall mother then I meane to be unto you all."[28] As noted above, Elizabeth's maternal metaphor appropriated and improved upon Mary's similitude: "If a prince and governor may as naturally and earnestly love her subjects, as the mother doth love the child, then assure yourselves, that I, being your lady and mistress, do as earnestly and tenderly love and favour you."[29] There is also evidence that such maternal

FIGURE 18

Elizabeth I (the "Phoenix" portrait), attributed to Nicholas Hilliard; ca. 1572–76. Oil on panel. National Portrait Gallery, London.

tropes had been turned against Elizabeth's hapless predecessor: According to David Loades, Mary's reign had witnessed the circulation of "crude wood-cuts of *Maria Ruyna Anglia* which portrayed a many-breasted queen suckling bishops, priests and Spaniards." John Knox provided a caption for such images when, in his "Faithful Admonition to the Professors of God's Truth in Eng-land" (1554), he wrote of Mary that "she, in all her doynges, declareth moste

manyfestlye, that under an English name she beareth a Spaniardes herte."[30]
Elizabeth was doubtless aware of such anti-Marian polemics, which often emphasized that Mary was half Spanish and had a Spanish husband: In her 1563
parliamentary speech, then, Elizabeth was making emphatically clear that her
own maternal care and sacrifice would be for her "natural" subjects rather
than for Jesuits or Spaniards.

   In her royal image, as in every other aspect of her rule, Mary's queenship
proffered to Elizabeth a uniquely relevant precedent, whether the Elizabethan
response was to appropriate or to repudiate the Marian example. The bejeweled *imprese* worn as pendants by Elizabeth in the Pelican and Phoenix portraits make the strongest possible iconographic contrast with the Habsburg
wedding present worn by Mary in her portraits. Equally strong, and of
like political resonance, is the stylistic contrast between Mor's work and
those attributed to Hilliard that were painted perhaps two decades later. The
Elizabethan portraits are in the highly decorative native English style, and display an affinity with the jewel-like art of the limner or watercolor miniaturist;
stylistically, the Marian portrait is a continental renaissance painting in the
tradition of Raphael and Titian. This emphatic contrast of cultural styles subtly underlines the contrast between the "mere English" Elizabeth, on the one
hand, and her half-Spanish half-sister and the latter's Habsburg consort, on
the other. Thus, both in style and in iconography, Mor's fine portrait of Mary
subtly affirms precisely those likely consequences of a dynastic marriage that
Elizabeth worked so assiduously to avoid, at the same time that she sought
to extract maximum political and diplomatic advantage from her erstwhile
availability.

The Protestant Succession

The Elizabethan chronicler Raphael Holinshed undoubtedly expressed an understanding shared by many of his Protestant contemporaries when he represented the circumstances of Mary's death and Elizabeth's accession as evidence of God's handiwork: "It so pleased the heavenlie majestie of almightie God, when no other remedie would serve, by death to cut hir off, which in hir life so little regarded the life of others: giving hir throne, which she abused to the destruction of Christs church and people, to another who more temperatlie and quietlie could guide the same."[1] The compelling issues of social stability, religious reform, and political legitimacy here raised by Holinshed are given iconic form in the largest of the Tudor dynastic allegories painted during the reign of Elizabeth (fig. 19). This painting is convincingly attributed to Lucas de Heere and ascribed to the early 1570s. It was given new life and a significantly wider potential spectatorship in the 1590s, when a copy updating the Queen's costume was painted, and an engraving by William Rogers (fig. 20) was printed that included verses different from and more extensive than those incorporated into the original work.[2] The original frame of de Heere's painting bears the following explanatory verses:

> A face of muche nobillitye loe in a litle roome,
> Fowr states with theyr conditions heare shadowed in a showe
> A father more than valyant. A rare and vertuus soon.
> A zealus daughter in her kynd what els the world dothe knowe
> And last of all a vyrgin queen to Englands joy we see,
> Successyvely to hold the right and vertues of the three.

This description of the painting as a "showe" suggests the perception of its generic affinity with royal spectacle, such as that of "The Quenes Majesties

FIGURE 19

Allegory of the Tudor Dynasty, attributed to Lucas de Heere; ca. 1572. Oil on panel. Amgueddfa ac
Orielau Cenedlaethol Cymru/National Museums & Galleries of Wales.

Passage through the Citie of London to Westminster the Day before her Coronacion." Like the pageants of the Coronation entry, the painting includes
within the same representational space both historical and allegorical personages, both visual tableaux and written texts; and, again like the 1559 pageants,
the painting is concerned with themes of succession and legitimacy, right religion and good goverment. In word and image, this painting articulates a
vision of Elizabeth as a champion of European Protestantism; and it does so
through a revision of the Henrician succession picture (fig. 5), which was still
conspicuously displayed in the Presence Chamber of the Queen's residence at
Whitehall.[3]

The inscription along the bottom of the original panel reads, "THE QVENE
TO WALSINGHAM THIS TABLET SENTE / MARK OF HER PEOPLES AND HER OWNE
CONTENTE." Apparently, then, the painting was a personal gift from the Queen
to her indispensable servant, Sir Francis Walsingham, at that time her emissary
to France and subsequently her Secretary of State. Under these circumstances,
we may infer that she had a more direct role than was usual in shaping the
representation—or, at least, in approving it after the fact. De Heere was a Dutch
Protestant exile, and Walsingham was one of the most zealous advocates of
the international Protestant cause within the government—a position that

FIGURE 20

Allegory of the Tudor Dynasty, after the painting attributed to Lucas de Heere, by William Rogers; ca. 1590–95. Engraving. © The Trustees of The British Museum.

oftentimes put him at odds with his royal mistress. Combining these connections with the painting's representation of Elizabeth as protectress of religious reform and harbinger of peace, Roy Strong has identified the occasion of the painting as a commemoration of the Anglo-French Treaty of Blois in April 1572, which Walsingham had helped to negotiate. While entirely plausible, this local reading does not exhaust the painting's significance. A larger political, religious, and diplomatic context for the Protestant dynastic allegory is provided by other momentous events that occurred around this time: These included, in 1569, the eruption and successful suppression of the Northern Rising, which had been led by Catholic peers; and, in 1570, the promulgation of the Papal Bull, *Regnans in excelsis*, which declared Elizabeth a usurper, a criminal, and a heretic; excommunicated her; and released all of her subjects from obedience to her commands and statutes.[4]

The painting identifies Elizabeth with Henry VIII and Edward VI and opposes her to Mary and Philip. Elizabeth's legitimacy, her temporal and spiritual powers within her kingdom, and her pivotal role in the international Protestant cause are thus affirmed by various markers of gender, filiation, and alliance. In its conspicuous allusion to, and revision of, the Henrician painting of Henry VIII and his family (fig. 5), the Elizabethan work seeks to

confer upon the reigning Queen the mantle of temporal and spiritual authority that Henrician dynastic strategies had conferred upon Prince Edward. In
the course of doing so, it bends those originally Henrician strategies in the
more rigorously Protestant direction that had been initiated during Edward's
own reign, and accommodates them to a differently gendered iconography of
royal power. For the most part, the later painting retains the earlier painting's
disposition of the principle figures across the pictorial surface; at the same
time, however, it effects a radical shift in the figures' relative placement from
front to back within the represented space. Equally striking is the change from
isolated groupings of hieratically posed figures to a dynamic interplay among
figures in movement.

Mary now occupies the most recessed plane and is yoked to her husband,
the Catholic and Spanish King Philip II; rushing in behind them, armed and
menacing, is the god of war. Behind Mary and Philip is painted a cityscape,
possibly that of Rome, represented in a state of decay; behind Elizabeth and
her attendants is a well-ordered and flourishing garden. These background
scenes suggest an allegorical opposition on the model of the Marian *Ruinosa
respublica* and the Elizabethan *Respublica bene instituta*, a pageant presented
to Elizabeth "at the litle conduit in Cheape" during her entry into London
on the day before her coronation.[5] Whereas the Henrician dynastic painting
differentiated between the youthful Mary and Elizabeth only in terms of their
age and stature, the Elizabethan painting creates an opposition between negative and positive types of female regiment. Religious and marital choices have
emerged as fundamental and intertwined markers of difference; and, paradoxically, it is the Protestant *virgin* who triumphs over the Catholic *matron*.
In comparison to the neutral Henrician family portrait, here Mary's position
on the beholder's left has taken on an appropriately sinister resonance; her
decisive linkage to the embodiment of the alien and hostile Habsburg dynasty
emphasizes her own half-Spanish identity, her Catholicism, and her fealty to
the Pope. Thus, the pairing of Philip and Mary in this painting recalls the
official iconography of the Marian reign, but now seen through Elizabethan
Protestant eyes: As Anne Hooper had written to Heinrich Bullinger in 1555,
regarding the paired royal images on the new Marian coinage (fig. 11), these
are "the effigies of Ahab and Jezebel."[6]

The royal patriarch and architect of an imperial English monarchy remains at the center of the composition. However, he has lost his overbearing
Holbeinian demeanor and posture (and his conspicuous codpiece), and now
turns his head and inclines his body toward his second daughter. The figure of Edward has been transferred from the left side to the right side of the

composition in order to serve as a mediator between Henry and Elizabeth in a representation of the Protestant succession. As he receives a sword from his father—presumably "the sworde of ye Spirit, which is the worde of God" (Ephesians 6:17)[7]—Edward turns his head and his glance toward Elizabeth. Elizabeth now occupies the forwardmost plane; and she holds by the hand the figure of Peace, who treads upon the flaming sword of war. Plenty, with bared breast and cornucopia, stands behind them, thus completing a triad of maidenly Graces. The marginal servants and grotesques of the Whitehall painting have been transformed into antithetical, gender-coded moral allegories: the masculine, malevolently martial; and the feminine, bountifully irenic. At the same time, these flanking figures have undergone a stylistic metamorphosis: in the Elizabethan painting, the native style of the historical figures contrasts with the mannerist treatment of the classically inspired allegories who accompany them.[8] The linkage of Philip and Mary with Mars, in the left background, constitutes a baleful antithesis to the triad of Elizabeth with Peace and Plenty, in the right foreground. The picture frames the Marian triad within it as a papistical antitype of everything for which the Tudor Protestant succession is being celebrated.

This Tudor group portrait—like Holbein's (figs. 3 and 4)—decenters the image of the reigning monarch; nevertheless, the eyes of the other figures are upon her. As the only living member of the Tudor dynasty, the figure of Elizabeth is positioned in the foreground of the pictorial space, closest to the spectator, and thus in the historical present. She alone looks directly at the beholder, as she gestures toward the peace and prosperity that have followed in the wake of her accession. Here we should recall the inscription upon the painting's frame, which in turn recalls both the inscription on Holbein's wall painting in the Privy Chamber at Whitehall (fig. 4) and that on his portrait of the infant Prince Edward (fig. 6). The theme of dynastic succession and filial emulation is once again invoked, but now within a context that has been enlarged to include siblings and daughters. Elizabeth is said to incorporate her father's valor, her brother's virtue, and her sister's zeal. It is worthy of note that the text inscribed upon the frame seeks to extract something positive from the Marian example, which is not evident in the picture itself. That the verbal representation of Mary is equivocal rather than explicitly denunciatory may well be due to the tempering influence of the conservative Queen Elizabeth herself. In other words, there is a tonal discrepancy between the pictorial image and the expository text, and this may suggest that the latter medium was more easily subjected to royal attention, direction, or control than was the former. Certainly, in the public, popular, and reproduceable medium of

FIGURE 21

Henry VIII, Edward VI, and the Pope: An allegory of the English Reformation. Artist unknown; ca.
1570(?). Oil on panel. National Portrait Gallery, London.

William Rogers' later engraving (fig. 20), the revised text is more explicitly
anti-Marian, and more attuned to the tone of the pictorial image.[9]

Conspicuous by her absence from this Elizabethan version of the Tudor Protestant succession is the Queen's own mother. This is an omission that becomes
more pointed if we recall the presence of Jane Seymour, Edward's mother and
Anne Boleyn's successor, in both of the Henrician pictures, which continued
to be displayed in the palace of Whitehall throughout Elizabeth's reign. There
were Elizabethan writers with strong Protestant credentials who made a point
of lauding Queen Anne for her own pivotal role in the English Reformation;
and part of their mission in doing so seems to have been to spur her insufficiently zealous daughter to emulation. The familiar Tudor painting of "Henry
VIII, Edward VI, and the Pope" was apparently intended to serve a related
purpose (fig. 21). In the case of this painting, however, it is Elizabeth herself
who is conspicuous by her absence. The painting celebrates Henry VIII and
Edward VI as the royal champions of ecclesiastical reform, and Edward in
particular as an iconoclast and vanquisher of papal iniquity. It was long assumed to be an Edwardian work, but Margaret Aston has now convincingly
demonstrated that much of the painting's iconography is indebted to pictorial

sources originating in the Low Countries in the 1560s, and thus that it must be redated to the period around 1570. In other words, it is contemporaneous with the Elizabethan picture of the Tudor succession (fig. 20). This was perceived by the godly to be a critical moment in the history of the Reformation in England; and Aston interprets Henry's dying gesture toward the enthroned Edward and the exclusion of any representation of Elizabeth as implying that the work is intended to admonish the religiously conservative Queen to emulate the reforming zeal of her late brother. Thus, "Henry VIII, Edward VI, and the Pope" must take its place among the other Tudor group portraits that defined the Protestant succession—and, too, among those hortatory addresses to the Queen that began as early as Bale's edition of the Lady Elizabeth's *Glasse of the synnefull soule*.[10]

In his defense of Elizabeth's accession against Knox's untimely *First Blast of the Trumpet*, John Aylmer posed this rhetorical question: "Was not Quene Anne the mother of this blessed woman, the chief, first, and only cause of banyshing the beast of Rome, with all his beggerly baggage? was there ever in Englande a greater feate wrought by any man then this was by a woman?" As Aylmer succinctly put it, at a later point in his tract, "who brought in the light of gods worde into Englande? a woman, who lighteth now again the candle after it was put oute? a woman."[11] Also in 1559, Alexander Ales, a Scottish Protestant divine who had been at court in 1536 and in contact with the King and Cromwell, wrote for the newly crowned Queen Elizabeth a narrative of her own mother's fall. Ales was "persuaded that the true and chief cause of the hatred, the treachery, and the false accusations laid to the charge of that most holy Queen, your most pious mother, was this, that she persuaded the King to send an embassy into Germany to the Princes who had embraced the Gospel." This conspiracy of papists and venal politicians intended, "along with her, to bury true religion in England and thus to restore impiety and idolatry." Ales relates to Elizabeth that, at the very time that the King's Council was debating the Queen's fate, he himself was an eyewitness to the following scene of royal pathos: "Never shall I forget the sorrow which I felt when I saw the most serene Queen, your most religious mother, carrying you, still a little baby, in her arms and entreating the most serene King, your father, in Greenwich Palace, from the open window of which he was looking into the courtyard, when she brought you to him."[12] Very shortly thereafter, Queen Anne was committed to prison within the Tower. Ales is strikingly frank in relating to the new Queen not only her royal father's consuming desire for a male heir but also his wantoning with Jane Seymour and his callous indifference to the fate of Elizabeth's innocent mother. Whatever personal impact such stories may have had upon Elizabeth—and she can hardly have been indifferent to them—they seem to have had little effect upon the public strategies through which she fashioned her filial bonds.

Sometime in the first half of Elizabeth's reign, William Latymer wrote a Protestant hagiography of Anne Boleyn which he dedicated to the Queen. Latymer had been one of Anne's chaplains, and was subsequently a chaplain to Elizabeth herself. In his dedicatory epistle to the Queen, he presented his work as "a myrror or glasse" wherein she might behold "the moste godly and princely ornamentes of your moste gracious and naturall mother; not a litill to your highnes comforte . . . by like example . . . to mayntayne Christes true, pure and syncere religion, to the honour of your crowne, to the comforte of your moste humble subjectes, and to the enlarging of your realme."[13] After she ascended the throne, Queen Mary made a thoroughgoing effort to rehabilitate and suitably honor her deceased mother, Catherine of Aragon, to whom she had always remained openly, even defiantly, loyal. As Queen, Elizabeth did nothing comparable in regard to her own mother. Although she rewarded and advanced Boleyn relatives and her mother's loyal servants and supporters, she made no significant public gestures aimed at the rehabilitation of her mother's deeply ambivalent reputation.[14] Given the apparent provenance of the Elizabethan picture of the Tudor succession as a gift from the Queen, we may assume that its iconography represented her own wishes. If so, it suggests that Elizabeth promoted her identification with the masculine body of Protestant kingship rather than her membership in the community of pious women reformers; that she sought to assert her unalloyed succession from and identification with King Henry and his forebears, in both natural and mystical senses.

These thematic elements of the Tudor Protestant succession receive perhaps their final iconic form in a late Elizabethan painting of the Queen with her father and brother, unsigned and unattributed but dated 1597 (fig. 22).[15] This painting bears the following inscription: "PROFESSORS AND DEFENDORS OF THE TRVE CATHOLICKE FAYTHE." Although belated in its subject, simplified in its iconography, and relatively crude in its style, this work bears an instructive relationship to its more distinguished predecessors. The painting restores to the dynastic group portrait the Holbeinian image of King Henry, which had continued to be the model for numerous full-length individual portraits of the King painted during the reign of Elizabeth.[16] With its massive proportions, fully frontal pose, and prominent codpiece, the figure of Henry VIII fills the left half and the most forward plane of the panel. Nevertheless, the figure of Queen Elizabeth—who, at the date of the painting, had been on the English

FIGURE 22

Henry VIII, Edward VI, and Elizabeth I as "Professors and defendours of the trve catholicke faythe."
Artist unknown; 1597. Oil on panel. Art Institute of Chicago. Photograph © The Art Institute of Chicago.

throne for four decades—is placed in relative parity with that of her father. Her far more modestly proportioned body is filled out by her wide farthingale, puffed sleeves, expansive ruff and veil, and high crown. The Queen's hands are positioned similarly to those of her father, although her right hand grasps a fan rather than a sword. The figure of Queen Mary and any allusion to the unfortunate Marian interlude have now been expunged from the iconic record. As the inscription implies, there is no place here for any ecumenical gesture: The zealous Mary had professed and defended the patently false Catholic faith of papistry. Occupying the center of the field but also the most recessed plane of the painting, the slight and youthful figure of King Edward VI serves as a chronological mediator between the dominant figures of his father and sister. This aspect of the composition resembles, then, the earlier Elizabethan dynastic painting (fig. 19). At the same time, Edward's pose is congruent with that of his sister and successor, both figures being turned slightly in the direction of their progenitor.

In this Tudor family portrait, a strangely destabilizing effect is created by the youthfulness of Edward's diminutive figure and its spatial subordination to the mature and matched couple in the foreground. There is a compositional equivocation in the nature of the relationships among the figures. And, from the perspective of my subject, this equivocation centers upon the relationship betweeen the female figure and the two male figures: The representation of Elizabeth equivocates between the positions of daughter and sister, on the one hand, and those of wife and mother, on the other. In other words, the 1597 dynastic painting represents Elizabeth as much like King Henry's consort as like his offspring—as is also suggested by her position on Henry's left hand. Likewise, Elizabeth's long deceased younger half-brother now also appears equivocally as if he were the mature Queen's child—a diminutive and youthful figure placed between the mature pair, yet posed behind rather than in front of them. Here Edward is the once and future male heir of the Tudor dynasty, resolutely English and Protestant, who was so long and so fervently wished for by the men of the Elizabethan political nation. In this context it may be relevant that popular rumors of King Edward VI's survival and prophecies of his return—as well as the occasional appearance of imposters claiming to be Edward—occurred during the reigns of both Mary and Elizabeth, and that such rumors were especially conspicuous in the 1580s and 1590s, as the Queen grew old and the succession remained unsettled.[17]

In the spatial configuration of this family portrait, we may see an after-image of the reputed father-daughter incest between Henry and Anne that Catholic polemicists claimed to be Elizabeth's own origin. Both Henry and Elizabeth had been tainted by such claims of his incest and her illegitimacy. Of course, no subversive intent can reasonably be ascribed to this late Elizabethan dynastic painting, which is manifestly motivated by religious fervor and political loyalty. Rather, I suggest that here the political transcoding of the young Elizabeth's familial tropes appears to have come full circle. The painting registers the troubled awareness of many Elizabethan subjects at century's end that the aged and barren Elizabeth Tudor was the last of her line and had stedfastly refused to name a successor. In this sense, the belated family portrait addresses itself to the Elizabethan problematic of dynastic succession. Obliquely registered in the manifest subject of the 1597 painting is a matter of state that preoccupied many late Elizabethans but about which they were forbidden by statute to speculate. Writing after the Queen's demise, Bacon captured vividly this late Elizabethan mood of collective apprehension:

> Queen Elizabeth . . . knowing the declaration of a successor mought in point of safety be disputable, but in point of admiration and respect assuredly to her disadvantage, had from the beginning set it down for a maxim of estate to impose a silence touching succession. Neither was it only reserved as a secret of estate, but restrained by severe laws, that no man should presume to give

opinion or maintain argument touching the same; so though the evidence of right drew all the subjects of the land to think one thing, yet the fear of danger of law made no man privy to other's thoughts.[18]

At the same time that the painting explicitly celebrates the Tudor dynasts as "PROFESSORS AND DEFENDORS OF THE TRVE CATHOLICKE FAYTHE," it also poses an implicit rhetorical question about the uncertain post-Tudor future of the English Protestant commonwealth. Within the context of such simultaneously collective and subjective anxieties, the formal equivocation of the painting between representations of two distinct family formations suggests a sublimation of the incest motif into a visual fantasy—a fantasy that transforms the imminence of dynastic extinction into a prospect of dynastic renewal, and the apprehension of religious rupture into an affirmation of religious continuity.

PART TWO

Idolatries

Of the sermons or homilies prepared and printed by the Elizabethan regime to be preached regularly at religious services, by far the longest was the "Homily against Peril of Idolatry and Superfluous Decking of Churches." Copious scriptural and historical examples buttressed the homily's conclusion that "as well by the origin and nature of idols and images themselves, as by the proneness and inclination of man's corrupt nature to idolatry, it is evident, that neither images, if they be publicly set up, can be separated, nor men, if they see images in temples and churches, can be stayed and kept, from idolatry."[1] Idolatry was a seduction, an infection, to which mankind was inherently vulnerable. This firm belief in the rooted weakness of the flesh must have given ardent reformers a perspective from which to comprehend how so many of their fellow countrymen could so obstinately persist in the old faith and its ritual practices. It was where traditional Catholic spirituality experienced the sacred made visible and tangible in the material world, in holy acts, objects, and places, that the reformers discovered evidence of human depravity.[2]

In part two, I explore the ideological tension between this Reformation repudiation of idolatry, which Protestants indelibly associated with Roman Catholic belief and practice, and the active promotion by the Elizabethan political establishment of discourses and practices that extolled the person of the Queen and inculcated attitudes of adoration toward the royal image. John Bossy has described this phenomenon as one of those "migrations of the holy" that manifested a "geological shift in Christian conceptions of the relation between the sacred and the body social or politic" during the sixteenth century. In Elizabethan England, one central impetus to what he dubs "monarcholatry" was the concerted effort of committed Protestants to advance and secure a godly commonwealth, to meld reformed religion with English national identity.[3] To this end, they cast their conservative and politic sovereign in a messianic role, hoping thereby to woo or to coerce her into performing it.[4] Another such impetus, emerging later in the reign, was the promotion of paeans to the Queen's inviolable virginity by that faction which sought to obstruct her proposed marriage alliance with the French Catholic François, duc d'Anjou. Mixing material self-interest with reformist zeal and xenophobia, they sought to forestall what they were sure would be the catastrophic consequences of such a match for the Queen's natural subjects and for the native political institutions that constrained the royal prerogative. In each of these interrelated projects, men of the Elizabethan political nation sought to construct the royal image in such as way as to serve what they took to be the greater interests of the godly English commonwealth. Insinuating critique and exhortation into encomium, they worked to appropriate "the Queen" through the very process of celebrating her. Thus, when criticized for flattering Queen Elizabeth in his court sermons, Alexander Nowell responded that "he had no other way to instruct the queen what she should be but by commending her."[5] Queen Elizabeth responded to these ostensibly flattering attempts to constrain her personal will and to challenge her royal prerogative sometimes by resisting them and sometimes by seeking to make them her own. The quasi-idolatrous "cult of the Virgin Queen" may have had its origins in a symbolic resistance to the royal will; nevertheless, in its exorbitant final phase, this resonant nexus of images was instrumental to the interests of the monarch and her increasingly authoritarian and isolated regime. In other words, it became a feature of what historians of political culture are now calling "the second reign of Elizabeth I."[6]

As demonstrated by each of the significant developments I have outlined here, the relationship between iconoclastic and idolatrous Elizabethan cultural attitudes was complex and contradictory both in its means and in its motives; and it is upon such complexities and contradictions that I shall focus in what follows. In chapter five, I briefly survey the range of perspectives, both religious and secular, that Elizabethan subjects manifested toward monarcholatry. Chapter six explores the oscillation between opposed and conflated representations of Elizabeth and the Virgin Mary, focusing upon Richard Topcliffe's account of Queen Elizabeth's discovery of a Marian "idol" during the royal progress of 1578. Chapter seven focuses upon Sir Walter Ralegh's varied practices of royal courtship both at court and in the New World, in which he made a strategic appropriation of idolatry. Chapter eight addresses a number of texts, performances, and pictures manifestly adulatory of the Queen, in order to probe the mixture of interests driving those who invented and sponsored them, and it concludes with some general reflections upon the nature and dynamics of the cultural discourse that some scholars have characterized as the Cult of Elizabeth.

Imagery, Policy, and Belief

In 1559, the new Elizabethan regime proclaimed religious injunctions that were intended to undo the policies of the preceding Marian regime and to resume the interrupted work of reformation. Included were orders that "to the intent that all superstition and hypocrisy crept into divers men's hearts may vanish away, they shall not set forth or extol the dignity of any images, relics, or miracles"; and that "they shall take away, utterly extinct, and destroy all shrines . . . pictures, paintings, and all other monuments of feigned miracles, pilgrimages, idolatry, and superstition."[1] Within a few months of this proclamation, however, another was issued that commanded

> all manner of persons hereafter to forbear the breaking or defacing of any parcel of any monument, or tomb, or grave, or other inscription and memory of any person deceased being in any manner of place, or to break any image of Kings, princes, or noble estates of this realm, or of any other that have been in times past erected and set up for the only memory of them to their posterity in common churches and not for any religious honor.[2]

The Elizabethan government seems to have realized very quickly that the iconophobic program of religious reform could easily mutate into an attack upon the dynastic and genealogical symbols of monarchical, aristocratic, and gentry authority, and that this in turn could threaten the very foundation of the established socio-political hierarchy. Here was an intimation of an underlying contradiction between reformation from above and reformation from below. The Elizabethan regime had to find ways to channel and delimit popular iconoclasm and to check the unpredictable impulses and momentum of religious reform if the symbols and images through which its own authority was manifested were to remain untainted and efficacious.

The second of the 1559 proclamations indicates an attempt to chart a distinction between sacred and profane images and the kinds of honor due to them: The former were pernicious because they were conducive to idolatrous worship, whereas the latter inculcated due respect for civic authority and dynastic lineage. Protestant reformers ignored the niceties of Catholic theology that discriminated the veneration (*dulia*) due to the Saints from the veneration (*hyperdulia*) due to the Virgin, and discriminated both from the adoration (*latria*) due to the Trinity—distinctions that were, in any case, probably a good deal clearer in doctrinal texts than they were in the quotidian spiritual practices of many lay Catholics.[3] But if Protestant polemicists refused to recognize the varying modalities within Catholic worship, their Catholic counterparts were prepared to respond in kind to those of the new state religion. In the *Injunctions* that he published in 1571, Archbishop Grindal ordered that "some convenient crest"—in practice, the royal arms—replace the cross upon the rood beams of the churches under his authority. The Catholic controversialist Nicholas Sander wrote in reaction to such initiatives as Grindal's that

> in place of the cross of Christ, which they threw down, they put up the arms of the king of England.... It was like a declaration on their part that they were worshippers, not of our Lord, whose image they had contemptuously thrown aside, but of an earthly king, whose armorial bearings they had substituted for it.[4]

Similar charges were used by William Allen, Elizabethan England's preeminent Catholic cleric-in-exile, in his 1588 pamphlet justifying the Spanish Armada and inciting a domestic rebellion to overthrow the Queen:

> She impiouslie spoiled all sanctified places of their holye Images, Relikes, memories, and monuments of Christe our Saviour, and of his blessed mother and Saintes, her owne detestable cognisaunce and other prophane portraitures and paintings exalted in theire places.[5]

In defending such Anglican innovations against charges of monarcholatry, the Elizabethan apologist Thomas Bilson raised as many problems as he answered when he insisted that the reverence paid to the royal arms or to princely images "is accepted as rendered to their owne persons, when they cannot otherwise be present in the place to receive it but by a substitute, or a signe that shal represent their state."[6] Nicholas Sander sought to exploit what Catholics perceived to be the ideological vulnerability of the new state church when he mockingly issued his own iconoclastic challenge: "Breake if you dare the Image of the Queenes Majestie, or Armes of the Realme."[7] Arguments about whether or not royal images and symbols were idols were thus part of a larger ideological struggle over the nature and legitimacy of the royal supremacy.

The establishment of the Anglican state religion was marked by the work of cultural appropriation and substitution in matters of church liturgy and decoration; furthermore, from at least the early 1570s, elements of Catholic symbolism and ritual were adapted to the project of honoring—indeed, of glorifying—the monarch. Sacred forms and practices were absorbed into the nominally secular discourses of civic and courtly pageantry in praise of the Queen; and by this indirect symbolic means, she was endowed with an aura and resonance of the sacred. The process was at its most highly articulated in the festivities that came to mark observances of the Queen's Accession Day, 17 November: in the towns, bonfires, bell-ringing, and sermonizing; and in the court, jousting and extravagant pageantry.[8] Cardinal Allen did not fail to excoriate such observances in his 1588 Armada pamphlet:

> She hathe caused the annuall daie of her coronation in all partes of the realme to be sacredly kepte and sollemnised, with ringinge, singinge, shewes & ceremonies, & farr more vacation from all servile labors then any day either of our blessed lorde or ladie, & which ys more abhominable, havinge abolished the solemne feaste of our blessed ladies nativity, she hathe caused her owne impure birthe day to be solemnlie celebrated, and put in to the kalender the verie eve of the said holie feaste and put out the name of an other sainte the 17. of November, to place the memory of her Coronation.[9]

In a panegyrical poem in honor of Accession Day in the previous year, 1587, Maurice Kyffin had enjoined his fellow subjects to "Adore Novembers sacred Sev'nteenth Day, / Wherein our Second Sunne began her Shine."[10] Such effusions were grist to the mill of Catholic polemic.

The failure of the Armada, widely interpreted among loyal and godly Elizabethans as a sign of divine favor toward reformed England and its Queen, only further escalated the hyperbole of the Accession Day rites. The court painter and herald Sir William Segar gives the following partial description of the celebrations that were performed before Elizabeth in the tiltyard at Westminster on 17 November 1590:

> Her Majesty beholding these armed Knights coming toward her, did suddenly heare a musicke so sweete and secret, as every one thereat greatly marveiled. And hearkening to that excellent melodie, the earth as it were opening, there appeared a Pavilion, made of white Taffata . . . like unto the sacred Temple of the Virgins Vestall. This Temple seemed to consist upon pillars of Pourferry, arched like unto a Church, within it were many Lampes burning. Also, on the one side there stood an Altar covered with cloth of gold, and thereupon

> two waxe candles burning in rich candlesticks, upon the Altar also were layd
> certaine Princely presents, which after by three Virgins were presented unto
> her Majestie.[11]

It should be noted that in Segar's description, the iconography of the royal English virgin melds the church with the temple, the Catholic cult of Mary with
the Roman cult of Vesta. Such syncretism enhanced the assertion of imperial monarchy, while diluting the incipiently blasphemous Marian references
with classical and pagan ones. Thus, even in its most exorbitant phase, the
iconography of the "cult" of Elizabeth tended to be more nuanced and more
oblique in its appropriation of specifically Marian and other sacred Christian
symbolism than is suggested by the invective of its Catholic antagonists. At the
same time, of course, the allusive linkage of the royal cult to both the discred-
ited Catholic cult of the Virgin and the pagan cults of classical antiquity could
only reinforce the perceptions of those disposed to find such royal celebrations inherently idolatrous. The process of Elizabethan royal representation
was always ideologically fraught and vexed by contradiction—and never more
so than when it was celebrating the cult of Elizabeth.

Those who enforced Queen Elizabeth's imperium in matters temporal
and spiritual—and, too, those who invented the visual and verbal forms in
which that imperium was manifested—found themselves having to defend the
imagery and pageantry of state against Catholic polemicists who denounced as
idolatrous the reverence shown by Elizabethan subjects toward royal images,
symbols, and holidays. But it was not only the adherents of the old religion
who found the new rituals of state to be offensive. The official position of the
Elizabethan regime remained ambiguous, a subject of debate, and a source
of tension even within Protestant circles. For example, a Puritan preacher
named Robert Wright, who was in trouble with the authorities in the 1580s,
had initially aroused their ire when he spoke "against the keeping of the queen's
day. Which, he said *was to make her an idol.*"[12] In his *First Blast of the Trumpet
against the Monstrous Regiment of Women*, John Knox had already declared
that

> Monstruous is the bodie of that Common welth where a Woman beareth
> empire; for either doth it lack a laufull heade (as in very dede it doth), or els
> there is an idol exalted in the place of the true head. An idol I call that which
> hath the forme and appearance, but lacketh the vertue and strength which the
> name and proportion do resemble and promise.

Thus, as far as Knox was concerned, to be a queen regnant was, ipso facto, to
be an idol.[13]

It is not clear if Archbishop Whitgift was responding to Catholic or to Puritan criticism of Accession Day observances when in an Accession Day sermon he reproved "those fantasticall spirits . . . which dissalow and mislike this manner of yerelie celebrating this day . . . as though wee did it supersititiouslie, or dedicated the day unto her, as to some Sainct, whereas in deede wee doe but our duetie, and that which is most lawfull for us to doe."[14] Certainly, the tone of defenses of Accession Day printed toward the end of the reign implies the existence of strongly dissenting attitudes toward the institution. For example, in 1601, Thomas Holland felt compelled to defend "the Accession Day triumphs at court" and other "signes of joy that day usually exhibited by the people of the land," against charges that they are "foolish, ridiculous, meere heathenish, and actions that savoure of nothinge else but meere flatteries"; and also to defend the church services in honor of that holiday against charges that they were "materially foolish, meere parasiticall, and spiced with flattery, which reduce men backe again to the fearfull abomination of heathenish Idolatrie."[15] In a 1602 Accession Day sermon, John Howson denounced nonconformists as co-conspirators with Catholics against the institutions of the state church.[16] In the rhetoric of Howson's sermon, the monarcholatrous tendencies of Accession Day become a fully fledged doctrine of royal absolutism: "God honoreth Princes with his owne name, so that they are called *Gods* . . . and furnisheth them with divine and supernatural qualities. . . . They have power absolute without limitation accountable only to God for their actions."[17] It is not surprising that this sermon stirred controversy. As John Chamberlain reported in a letter to Dudley Carleton, "Doctor Howson vicechauncellour of Oxford made a sermon there on the Quenes day that is accused of false doctrine, and hath bred much brabling."[18]

There were also those within the ambience of the court for whom the cult of Elizabeth was a phenomenon not to be understood primarily in sectarian terms—whether Catholic, Anglican, or Puritan—but rather in terms of statecraft. Most extant evidence of such a perspective tends to be from the very end of the reign or from the immediately post-Elizabethan period. For example, in a diary entry in April 1603, John Manningham recorded a friend's conversation as follows: "Wee worshipt noe saintes, but wee prayed to ladyes, in the Q[ueenes] tyme. . . . This superstition shall be abolished, we hope, in our kinges raigne."[19] What makes this quip notable is that it so pithily performs a conversion of the whole discourse of idolatry from the domain of religious ideology into that of gender politics: The fundamental distinction here is not between Catholic and Protestant practices of worship but rather between Elizabethan and Jacobean styles of courtship. In a political culture focused upon a virgin queen regnant, enlightened self-interest had compelled gentlemen to adopt a gynephilic courtly style, one that conflated religious with amorous discourses. With the advent of a king had come the welcome prospect of an end to the need for such performances, which were apparently perceived by the performers to be frivolous and uxorious, and demeaning to manly virtue.

The observations of John Clapham—who, like Manningham, was writing very shortly after the Queen's demise and the King's accession—evidence a related perspective of critical distance from the cult of Elizabeth. À propos of public reaction to the Queen's passing, he writes that

> [t]he people began to talk diversely, many seeming to marvel even at vain and ordinary things, as namely that living and dying a virgin she was born on the vigil of that feast, which was yearly kept in remembrance of the birth of our Lady the Virgin, and that she died on the vigil of the Feast of the Annunciation of our Lady. . . .
> But among men of better understanding the accounts of her life and the manner of her government was called to mind and censured.[20]

The popular vanities to which Clapham refers appear to have been widely disseminated, for they are also found in print in 1603 in Thomas Dekker's pamphlet *The Wonderful Year*.[21] Writing in emulation of Tacitus, Clapham prefaces his memoir with a statement of principle: "He that will write truly the lives and actions of great personages ought to have his mind free as well from fear as partiality; the one forbearing ofttimes to utter the truth of things for giving cause of offense, and the other misreporting them, either upon malice or for desire to please."[22] Clapham's observations repudiate the providentialist and occult discourses characteristic of Elizabethan monarcholatry, and are instead characterized by a tone that is distinctly rationalist and skeptical.

Before the increasingly authoritarian last decade of the Elizabethan reign, perspectives like Clapham's are not much in evidence in the textual record. By then, however, what Patrick Collinson has characterized as a "suppressed, critical neo-stoicist republicanism" had become conspicuous in the writings and actions of alienated younger courtiers and scholars.[23] In the 1590s, as the glorification of the Queen became both more exorbitant and more hollow, the criticism of her regime became more pointed. The Queen's death presented Clapham with the occasion to make a dispassionate judgment regarding her rule, a frank assessment of her political virtues and vices. Even so, Clapham chose not to circulate his memoir, let alone to publish it, perhaps because he was more inclined to censure his late sovereign than to praise her. Among the political vices that Clapham ascribes to Elizabeth, those that concern him most and to which he repeatedly makes reference, are her vanity and her vulnerability to flattery by her courtiers and favorites:

> As for flatterers, it is certain that she had many too near her, and was well contented to hear them. Howbeit, though it be a great fault in princes...yet it is more tolerable in them to be flattered and praised sometimes for such virtues as they have not than to be hated and despised for known vices.[24]

The kind of flattery Clapham had in mind is manifest in the advice solicited from Edward Dyer by Sir Christopher Hatton, who was anxious to preserve his own status as royal favorite against the competition of his rivals: "Acknowledge your duty," counseled Dyer, "declaring the reverence which in your heart you bear, and never seem deeply to condemn her frailities, but rather joyfully to commend such things as should be in her, as though they were in her indeed."[25] A protégé of Lord Burleigh, Clapham was neither a zealous railer against Elizabethan idolatries nor a calculating worshiper of the Virgin Queen but rather a prudent observer of the mysteries of state.

Iconomachy

In his continuation of Nicholas Sander's widely read polemical history of the English Reformation, *The Rise and Growth of the Anglican Schism*, Edward Rishton wrote with manifest outrage that,

> to show the greater contempt for our Blessed Lady, they keep the birthday of queen Elizabeth in the most solemn way on the 7th day of September, which is the eve of the feast of the Mother of God, whose nativity they mark in their calendar in small and black letters, while that of Elizabeth is marked in letters both large and red. And, what is hardly credible ... the praises of Elizabeth are said to be sung at the end of the public prayers, as the Antiphon of our Lady was sung in former days.[1]

Rishton's claim is that the Elizabethan regime and its official church had systematically sought to substitute the Queen of England for the Queen of Heaven, thus making an idol of Elizabeth and idolators of her loyal Protestant subjects.

The thesis that underlies the shared sectarian agenda of Sander, Rishton, and Allen is that the establishment and empowerment of the Elizabethan regime and the Anglican church were accomplished by means of a concerted appropriation of Catholic—and, specifically, Marian—symbolism and ritual. Shorn of its sectarian agenda, this thesis has been given new life in the influential modern studies of Frances Yates and Roy Strong.[2] These scholars argue for the programmatic fashioning of a "cult of Elizabeth" that functioned as a substitute or compensation for the world of sacramental rituals and sacred images that the Elizabethans had lost by virtue of the Reformation and its attendant iconoclasm. For example, in her seminal work on the imperial iconography of Queen Elizabeth, Frances Yates writes suggestively that the bejeweled and painted images of the Virgin Mary had been cast out of the churches and monasteries, but another bejeweled and painted image was set up at court, and went in progress through the land for her worshippers to adore. The cult of the Virgin was regarded as one of the chief abuses of the unreformed church, but it would be, perhaps, extravagant to suggest that, in a Christian country, the worship of the state Virgo was deliberately intended to take its place.[3]

The coy phrasing of the last sentence seems both to advance and to retract the "perhaps, extravagant" claim for a pseudo-Marian cult of Elizabeth. Although it may not have been her intended point, Yates's equivocation in fact captures well the rhetorical, affective, and ideological ambiguity that marked the attitudes of Elizabethans themselves toward the royal "cult," a cultural discourse that they collectively sustained, elaborated, and appropriated to their own ends during the course of the reign.

Here I explore the dynamics of this ambiguity by looking at a complex instance of the cultural confrontation between Marian and Elizabethan cults. This was one of those occasions when (as Yates puts it) the Queen "went in progress through the land for her worshippers to adore," and in the course of which she herself cast out a Marian idol. The summer progress of 1578 took the itinerant Elizabethan court through much of Norfolk and Suffolk. The highlights included the week-long pageantry that honored and entertained the Queen on her visit to Norwich, then England's second city, as well as the spectacular iconoclastic rite which she personally supervised at the modest Suffolk estate of an unfortunate recusant gentleman named Edward Rookwood.

The festivities at Norwich were quickly memorialized in print in two lengthy accounts. For our knowledge of the latter event, however, we are reliant upon the intelligence of Richard Topcliffe, subsequently a notorious pursuer of Catholic priests and those who harbored them. In a letter to one of his patrons, the Earl of Shrewsbury, Topcliffe reported the goings-on at Euston as follows:

> This Rookewoode is a Papyste of kynde newly crept out of his layt wardeshipp. Her Majesty, by some meanes I know not, was lodged at his house, Ewston, farre unmeet for her Highnes, but fitter for the blacke garde; nevertheless (the gentilman brought into her Majesty's presence by lyke device) her excellent Majesty gave to Rookewoode ordenary thanks for his badd house, and her fayre hand to kysse; after which it was brayved at: But my Lord Chamberlayn, noblye and gravely understandinge that Rookewoode was excommunicated for Papistrie, cawled him before him; demanded of him how he durst presume to attempt her reall presence, he, unfytt to accumpany any Chrystyan person; forthewith

sayd he was fytter for a payre of stocks; commanded him out of the Coort, and
yet to attende her Counsell's pleasure; and at Norwyche he was comytted. And,
to dissyffer the gent. to the full; a peyce of plaite being missed in the Coorte,
and serched for in his hay house, in the hay rycke suche an immaydge of our
Lady was ther fownd, as for greatnes, for gayness, and woorkemanshipp, I did
never see a matche; and, after a sort of cuntree daunces ended, in her Majesty's
sighte the idoll was sett behinde the people, who avoided: She rather seemed
a beast, raysed upon a sudden from hell by conjewringe, than the picture for
whome it hadd bene so often and long abused. Her Majesty comanded it to the
fyer, which in her sight by the cuntrie folks was quickly done, to her content,
and unspeakable joy of every one but some one or two who had sucked of the
idoll's poysoned mylke.[4]

This intriguing narrative is characterized throughout by a disorienting oscillation between the categorical opposition and the ambiguous conflation of
Marian and Elizabethan images, of Catholic rituals and Protestant counter-
rituals, of idolatrous and iconoclastic impulses. Furthermore, Topcliffe insin-
uates that the whole event was actually a kind of sting operation, designed
to entrap, expose, and discredit the Queen's host and the old religion. At the
same time, however, his account remains opaque as to the nature and extent
of the Queen's collaboration: Was she actually in control of these events, or
was she merely playing her assigned role in a drama scripted by others and
devised for her own edification?

Queen Elizabeth's consignment of the Marian "idol" to the fire was an action that conformed to a rite of Protestant iconoclasm already well established
in Tudor England. Like the 1559 proclamation with which I began the previous
chapter, this counterritual was based upon the injunctions of Deuteronomy
7:5: "Ye shal overthrowe their altars, and breake downe their pillers, and ye
shall cut downe their groves, & burne their graven images with fire." Purgative
fire symbolically cleansed the Christian community of polluting elements,
whether these were idolatrous statues, pictures, vestments, and texts, or human bodies possessed by demoniacal heresies. Two decades before the event
at Euston Hall, the accession of Queen Elizabeth and the expectation of a
resumption of religious reform had triggered an extended period of iconoclastic fervor in London, where statues of the Virgin and saints, rood lofts and
crosses, books and altar cloths in large numbers were destroyed in great public
bonfires. And, as Margaret Aston has noted, "the instrument of the bonfire
long continued to serve a useful purpose in places where local diehards were
discovered harbouring images, resistant to reform."[5] In such instances, officials supervising the ritual conflagration deemed it vital that members of
the local parish bear witness to and participate in the process by which the

vestiges of the old religion were cast away and the social body was cleansed and made whole. Thus, however curious the particulars of Topcliffe's account, the reported events at Euston Hall conformed in outline to a familiar iconoclastic ritual of reformation by fire.

In the scenario outlined by Topcliffe, a decision was made ("by some meanes, I know not"), to house the Queen in the conspicuously inadequate accommodations available at Rookwood's modest estate. When ("by lyke device") Rookwood was brought in to kiss the royal hand, he was denounced as a papist by the Lord Chamberlain—at that date, the Earl of Sussex. The Lord Chamberlain then challenged the Queen's host for presuming "to attempt her reall presence," and forthwith commanded him "out of the Coort": In other words, Rookwood was being evicted from the place that had been his own home until Queen Elizabeth had come to visit. Now, however, by virtue of the Queen's "real presence," Rookwood's modest house had become the royal court, of which the Lord Chamberlain was the chief household officer, having control over both the allocation of lodgings at court and the organization of royal progresses.[6] Topcliffe's phrase "reall presence" constitutes a particularly pointed example of the monarcholatrous migration of the sacred: By punningly equivocating between the charismatic "*royal* presence" and the sacramental "*real* presence," it activates the theological controversy regarding the status of the host that was at the heart of sixteenth-century sectarian strife, and it appropriates that sacramental status to the person of the Queen. In what sounds suspiciously like a set-up, designed "to dissyffer the gent. to the full," a missing piece of royal plate became the pretext for searching Rookwood's hay house, where the incriminating idol was conveniently discovered. In a scenario of Spenserian vividness and resonance, the false image of holiness is confronted and unmasked by the true. In the "reall presence" of the Queen, the sensuously seductive Marian idol ("for greatnes, for gayness, and woorkemanshipp, I did never see a matche") is revealed as the devil's own handiwork: "She rather seemed a beast, raysde upon a sudden from hell by conjewringe, than the picture for whome it hadd bene so often and long abused." As someone who was to become a consummate manager of such discoveries, Topcliffe writes appreciatively of the performance that was conjured up by the righteous enemies of Rookwood and his ilk and impressed with such force upon the imaginations of the local witnesses. He implies that in this confrontation, the corrupting popish idol has been separated out from the true image of Marian spiritual purity, and that the latter is now manifested in the real presence of Her Majesty the Queen.

Euston was the last stop in Suffolk on the Queen's itinerary; from there she processed into Norfolk and on to Norwich. Her only significant stop between Euston and Norwich was at Kenninghall Place. This great house had been the center of the Howard estates in East Anglia, and home of Thomas Howard, fourth Duke of Norfolk, who had been executed for high treason a decade earlier on the disputed charge that he was a closet Catholic who had conspired to dethrone Elizabeth and put Mary Stuart in her place. By choosing to spend three nights there, the Queen was making a powerful point about the Crown's resolve to compel the obedience of its mightiest subjects. The intended recipient of the lesson was presumably the Queen's reluctant host at Kenninghall Place, Philip Howard, Earl of Surrey and subsequently Earl of Arundel, who was the attainted duke's eldest son. Within five years of the Queen's summer visit, Philip Howard would find himself in circumstances not unlike Rookwood's: in 1583, Elizabeth invited herself to dinner at Arundel House in London; after having lavishly entertained her there, Howard was summarily confined to house arrest and subsequently imprisoned for months while his Catholic connections were investigated.[7] A decade after the 1578 progress, and like his father before him, Arundel was attainted for high treason; he would die in prison in 1595 as a condemned traitor—and also as a Catholic martyr, who was finally canonized in 1970. On the occasion of the Queen's 1578 visit, his only punishment would be the crushing debt he assumed for the privilege of entertaining his dearest dread and her huge entourage. The 1578 summer progress and other such periodic peregrinations of the court through large areas of England were a symbolic means whereby a regime with limited and unreliable financial, military, and technical resources might affirm its hegemony over an unruly and localized society. For a state that inhered in its sovereign, a state in which the delegation of royal power could be either dangerous or ineffectual, it was of some importance that the Queen physically possess her domains and that she be seen to do so. These were occasions during which the monarch could engage in staged demonstrations of reciprocal affection with her common subjects, and could also submit to inspection in their own estates the landed elites who were her most powerful and potentially her most dangerous subjects. Like Philip Howard, many of the latter remained Catholic in their religious convictions; and no matter how fervently they protested their loyalty to the Queen and her regime, they were never above suspicion.

The seminary founded at Douai by William Allen had been training and ordaining English Catholic priests and secretly sending them back into England since 1574. The first trial and execution of one of these priests for treason had already taken place in 1577. A succession of increasingly harsh anti-Catholic proclamations and statutes followed the sensational trial and execution of Edmund Campion and several other Jesuit missionary priests in 1581. The Elizabethan regime's new campaign was aimcd not only against the mission itself but also against the recusant Catholic laity in England who were its flock, its abettors, and its recruits. Harsher legislation and prosecution was complemented by the amplification of a discourse that shaped an Elizabethan antipapist imaginary in terms of those secret spaces within the home and within the heart where treason resided.[8] One pamphleteer fantasized a chillingly original solution to this problem of hidden truth:

> If a window were framed in the brests of these discontented catholikes, that her Majestie and the state-guiding counsell and all true friends to the kingdom might know their secret intentions: . . . many false hearts would be found lurking under painted hoods, and cakes of foule cancred malice under meale mouthed protestations.[9]

The rhetoric of the 1578 progress is proleptic of the intensified antipapist campaign to come. In the pious and extravagant professions of loyalty that are conspicuous in the civic pageantry and orations addressed to the Queen in Norwich, there may be an implied contrast of its prosperous merchant oligarchy to the suspect Catholic nobility and gentry, like Howard and Rookwood, upon whom the Queen imposed herself during the same progress. The account by Bernard Garter, which was in print within eight days of the Queen's departure from Norwich, records an official emphasis upon the unfeigned devotion of her Majesty's subjects there. In his oration of greeting (as englished by Garter), the Lord Mayor averred that "We would account nothing more pretious (most Royall Prince) than that the bright beame of your most chast eye, which doth so chere us, might penetrate the secret strait corners of our hartes: then surely should you see how great joyes are dispersed there . . . in beholding thee the light of this Realme" (*Records of Early English Drama*, 251). And in his oration to the Queen, the public schoolmaster reiterated this collective wish for surveillance by the royal gaze in terms of a paradoxical desire for bodily penetration by the beam of her virgin eye: "I would to God you coulde pearce these our breasts with your eyes, and throughly viewe the hidden and covered creekes of our mindes: then undoubtedly shoulde you beholde an infinite heape of good will closely shutt upp within" (270). The Queen could rest assured that there was no treasonous papistry secreted within the closets or within the hearts of the godly citizens of Norwich.

On the evidence of Garter's text, the Norwich pageantry also repeatedly impressed upon the minds of the Queen and her subjects a maternal figuration of her imperium: The "personage representing the Cittie of Norwich" told the

Queen in greeting, "Thou are my joy next God, I have no other, / My princess and my peerlesse Queene, my loving nurse and mother" (257); in his oration, "The minister of the Duch Church" praised her as "most excellent Queene, the nourse of Christ his church.... O thou most faithfull nourse of the churche of God" (264, 266); upon Elizabeth's departure, Garter himself publicly bid her "Farewell oh Queene, farewell oh Mother deere, let JACOBS GOD thy sacred body guarde" (277); the Lord Mayor concluded his own farewell oration by hailing her as "Thou Nurce of religion, Mother of the Comon Wealth, Beautie of Princes, Solace of thy Subjectes" (280). Although the oration prepared for the Queen's departure by Mr. Limbert, the schoolteacher, was not delivered because of a change in the royal schedule, his extravagant variant upon the maternal theme was almost immediately available in print for the edification of the pamphlet's readers:

> How lamentable a thing is it, to pul away sucking babes from the breastes and bosomes of thir most loving mothers?... Nature hath not ingendered in any man such large love, and so great good will, no not towarde them whom they have begotten, or of whom they themselves have bene begotten, as is the love and goodwill wherewith we advaunce, obey, and reverence your Majestie, being the mother and nurse of this whole Common welth, and Countrie. (284)

These godly speakers were drawing upon a scriptural passage that was a favorite of sixteenth-century reformers: "And Kings shalbe thy nourcing fathers, and Quenes shalbe thy nources" (Isaiah 49:23), glossed in the Geneva Bible as "meaning, ye Kings shalbe converted to ye Gospel and bestow their power, & autoritie for the preservation of the Church."

Within the field of meanings constituted by the 1578 progress, the metaphors of nurture employed by Topclifffe and by the citizens of Norwich signified in a relationship of antithesis. When Topcliffe wrote that "Her Majesty comanded it to the fyer, which in her sight by the cuntrie folks was quickly done, to her content, and unspeakable joy of every one but some one or two who had sucked of the idoll's poysoned mylke," he was making it clear that he was not excoriating the sacred personage of the Virgin Mary but rather what he viewed as the idolatrous Marian cult through which the false doctrines and noxious practices of the Catholic church were so perniciously disseminated. Indeed, he may well have been echoing the language of the Elizabethan *Homily against peril of Idolatry*, which averred that "the rabblement of the popish church ... have from their childhood been brought up amongst images and idols, and have drunk in idolatry almost with their mother's milk."[10] What we have in Topcliffe's letter and in the contemporaneous Norwich pamphlets are antithetically inflected versions of a core metaphor of the Elizabethan

Protestant imaginary, drawn from scripture and ultimately grounded in the materiality of maternal nurture, and thus of heightened rhetorical propriety and affective charge in the case of a virgin queen who declared herself the supreme governor of the church and the mother of her people.

There is evidence that the itinerary of the progress through Norfolk and Suffolk was hastily arranged among those at the highest level of the court who were especially sympathetic to the reformist cause, and in particular by the Earl of Leicester. Its agenda was to curtail the attempted suppression of Puritan activity in the Norwich diocese by the conservative Bishop Freke and to discredit the recusant and crypto-Catholic gentry who were his allies, thereby strengthening the position of committed Protestant gentry in county affairs and enfranchising godly preachers.[11] As Sir Thomas Heneage wrote to Sir Francis Walsingham after the event, the progress had been intended as much for the Queen's edification as for the benefit of her subjects: "By good meanes her Majesty is brought to believe right and intreate well dyvers most zealous and loyall gentlemen of Suffolk and Norfolk whome the foolysh Bisshoppe has malysiously complayned of to her Majesty."[12] As Topcliffe reports the outcome in his letter,

> Shortly after, a great sort of good preachers, who hadd beene longe comaunded to silence for a lytell nycenes, were licensed, and again commanded to preache, a greater and more universall joye to the cuntrees, and to most of the Coort, then the disgrace of the Papists; and the gentilmen of those partts, being great and hotte Protestants (almost before by pollycye discreddyted and disgraysed) were greatly countenanced. (189)

By the conclusion of the progress, not only Edward Rookwood but twenty-two other prominent Catholic gentlemen from the two counties had been forced to appear before the Privy Council at Norwich; when all but one refused to conform, they were subjected to fines and confinement. At the same time, a number of leading local Protestant gentlemen were knighted, and the Puritan preachers who had been subjected to censorship and intimidation were now unmuzzled.

As I have already suggested, from one perspective the whole enterprise seems a dress rehearsal for the full-scale campaign against the priests of the clandestine Jesuit mission and the Catholic flock who harbored them—a campaign in which Richard Topcliffe would come to play so a notorious a part.[13] That campaign would very shortly begin in earnest, with the capture, torture, show trial, and execution of Campion and other Jesuits in 1581. There is

evidence that the Jesuit mission that commenced in 1580 was initiated during the late 1570s at the urging of English recusant gentry as well as clerical
exiles like William Allen. They saw an opportunity in the Queen's prospective marriage to the Duc d'Anjou and in the crisis it had provoked within
the Protestant political nation.[14] The convergence of agendas in the Norwich
progress suggests that the Protestant elites also understood the nature of the
relationship and the threat that it posed to them.

As they had sought to do frequently from the very beginning of the reign,
during this progress the Queen's councilors were seeking to mold her will to
their designs by entertaining her with political theatre, by putting on a series
of shows in which she was both the privileged performer and the intended
audience. The scenarios of praise and counsel performed at Norwich drew
upon classical as well as scriptural sources. As recorded in Garter's pamphlet,
for example, a pageant featuring addresses by Debora, Judith, and Hester
was followed by a song celebrating the Queen's embodiment of the various
virtues of Juno, Venus, Diana, Pallas and other classical goddesses (256–61).
The goddesses subsequently appeared to Elizabeth in their own persons, Venus
addressing her as "an other VENUS" and presenting "a whyte Dove" (273), Pallas addressing her as "thou Goddesse" and presenting "a Booke of Wisedome"
(274), Diana addressing her as "my Virgin Queene" and presenting "a Bowe and
Arrowes nocked and headed with silver" (275). This familiar transformation
of the Judgment of Paris into a trope of royal encomium was reiterated in public oratory: "These sundry giftes of Goddesses three, Elizabeth possesseth.…
This Lady mayst thou Goddesse call, for she deserves the same" (288). In his
pamphlet advertising the pageantry in Norwich, Churchyard records a show of
his own devising for which he was personally commended by the Queen. In this
device, wandering Cupid encountered "Dame Chastitie and hir maydes, called
Modestie, Temperance, Good exercise, and Shamefastnesse," who set upon
him and drove him off. Taking from him his bow and quiver of arrows, Chastity
presented these as gifts to the Queen, "bycause (sayd Chastitie) that the Queene
had chosen the best life, she gave ye Queene CUPIDS bow, to learn to shoote at
whome she pleased, since none coulde wounde hir highnesse hart" (304–5).
In the Queen's entourage during the course of this progress were the French
ambassador, de Mauvissière, and the special emissaries of the Duc d'Anjou,
brother of Henri III, who had come to press a newly reopened initiative for an
Anglo-French marriage alliance. De Mauvissière was also at that time encour-
aging the Earl of Oxford and other disaffected Catholic and crypto-Catholic
English peers like Philip Howard, who hoped for a considerable improvement
in their personal fortunes and in their co-religionists' circumstances should
the royal marriage come to pass. Churchyard's device appears to have been

intended as an intervention into this fraught negotiation, made on behalf of the Protestant party in the Council, led by Leicester and Walsingham.[15]

The collective goodwill of the Queen's subjects in Norwich manifested itself in a series of orations and pageants that resonated sympathetically with the agenda of those privy councillors, parliamentarians, and members of the political nation who wished to preserve and strengthen the progress of religious reform against what they perceived to be entrenched domestic resistance and a calamitous royal marital alliance with Catholic France. As the monarch and several hundred members of her itinerant court processed through much of East Anglia over the course of several weeks, the variously scripted and improvised events and interactions of the progress combined to constitute a vast social drama. Its guiding aim appears to have been to promote the collective interests of the English Protestant commonwealth against the forces of Catholicism on both domestic and international fronts; and its ground plot was the triumph of the Virgin Queen over false idols and popish conspiracies, entangling alliances and fleshly perturbations. In the records of the 1578 progress, we can witness several already extant royal tropes beginning to coalesce into the panegyrical discourse of sovereignty that would come to dominate the later years of the reign. This discourse appropriated and sought to synthesize Catholic and classical elements, thereby generating a multiform image of Elizabeth as a providential Virgin Queen, a nurturing mother to her people and their reformed church, a chaste and self-possessed goddess of love and beauty. In pursuit of this religio-political agenda and of their own material advancement, many Elizabethan subjects contributed their talents to the collective fashioning of that richly figurative and ideologically unstable discourse which we have come to recognize as the cult of Elizabeth.

Instrumental Adoration

Sir Walter Ralegh offers a compelling example of a court figure who sought, with spectacular if fragile success, to turn the collective process of Elizabethan cult-formation to the pursuit of his own material, intellectual, and geopolitical concerns. In stark contrast to such royal favorites as the earls of Leicester and Essex—both scions of the Elizabethan aristocracy—Ralegh was a younger son from the minor provincial gentry. Ralegh's rapid acquisition of status, wealth, and honor was wholly a consequence of his personal relationship with his sovereign; and any prospect of its continuance and increase depended upon his successful maintenance of her attention and favor. Accordingly, he boldly and self-consciously fashioned an idiosyncratic style of royal veneration, which is given a concise iconic form in the handsome portrait (fig. 23) dated 1588, the Armada year. Here Ralegh's figure is clothed in black and white, the Queen's colors; and it is profusely adorned with pearls, a conventional symbol of chastity that was also her signature jewel. In the upper left-hand corner of the canvas is inscribed Ralegh's personal motto, *Amor et virtute*, surmounted by a crescent moon, emblematic of the Queen as Cynthia-Diana. In this context, it may be that the motto both affirms the subject's chaste and obedient courtship of his virgin queen and also asserts the compatibility of that service with the gentleman's pursuit of his masculine honor.[1]

A native of the west country, Walter Ralegh was a mariner whom the Queen had nicknamed "Water." In his extended and hyperbolical lyrical complaint, *The Ocean to Cynthia*, such biographical data feed into the cosmological conceit of the Queen's attractive and distracting powers upon him—like those of the moon upon the waters:

FIGURE 23
Sir Walter Ralegh. Artist unknown; 1588. Oil on panel. National Portrait Gallery, London.

When shee did well, what did ther elce amiss?
When shee did ill what empires could have pleased?
No other poure effectinge wo, or bliss
Shee gave, shee tooke, shee wounded, shee appeased.[2]

Here, all compact, are the lunatic, the lover, and the poet. Ralegh's portrait is
an iconic equivalent for his own extravagant courtly verse; it suggests that in
his very appearance, as well as in his conduct and his discourse, Ralegh fuses

FIGURE 24
Elizabeth I, with arrows and crescent moon in her hair, by Nicholas Hilliard; ca. 1586–87. Watercolor
miniature on vellum, mounted on card. Victoria & Albert Museum, London; V&A Images.

the courtship of the Queen's patronage with the courtship of her person. Although manifestly a portrait of Ralegh himself, in its every detail the painting
evokes the absent presence of another: the Mistress/Queen/Goddess whose
votary he is. Those of Ralegh's contemporaries who scorned his ambition,
arrogance, and pride doubtless would have regarded such devotions as cynically self-serving; others, the devout of either Catholic or Puritan persuasion,
might have been inclined to regard Ralegh's 1588 portrait as the picture of an
idolator.

    As Margaret Aston has recently pointed out in another context, "to a
good many of Queen Elizabeth's subjects—those well-versed in scriptural
priorities—Diana was *the* idol of the New Testament, whose ill-fame radiated
from Acts 19." As Aston goes on to remind us, Acts 19 "describes the uproar
caused by the craftsmen of Ephesus, who feared for the loss of their trade, making silver shrines for Diana, as a result of St. Paul's preaching that the great
goddess was a mere man-made idol whose magnificent worship ought to be
destroyed."[3] Scripture unequivocally condemned the Ephesian artisans for
their materially self-interested perpetuation of the idolatrous cult of Diana;
nevertheless, the avowedly Christian makers of later Elizabethan pageantry

and poetry kept busy turning out panegyrical identifications of Elizabeth with Diana, the virgin goddess of the hunt, or with Cynthia, the Artemisian moon goddess. In *iconic* representations, if not necessarily in *textual* ones, this identification tended to be made obliquely—as, for example, in the crescent moon jewel adorning Elizabeth's hair in one of Nicholas Hilliard's miniatures (fig. 24), or in the one fixed upon the Queen's crown in the celebrated "Rainbow" portrait (fig. 25), or in the crescent moon *impresa* included in Ralegh's

FIGURE 25

Elizabeth I (the "Rainbow" portrait). Artist unknown; ca. 1600–1603. Oil on canvas. Hatfield House, Hertfordshire. Courtesy of the Marquess of Salisbury.

FIGURE 26

The Goddess Diana, attributed to Frans Floris, ca. 1560. Oil on panel. Hatfield House, Hertfordshire.
Courtesy of the Marquess of Salisbury. Photograph: Photographic Survey, Courtauld Institute of Art.

1588 portrait. A similar crescent moon ornament crowns the image of the
goddess Diana in a half-length allegorical portrait (fig. 26) that was probably
once owned by William Cecil, Lord Burghley, or by his son Robert. In this
image, the virgin huntress grips a bow in her hand, bears a quiver full of arrows
upon her back, and holds a hound by a leash. Unsurprisingly, its subject has
sometimes been identified as Queen Elizabeth-as-Diana. Although there is

no conclusive evidence for this identification, the display of such a picture of the virgin goddess at the home of the Queen's most valued and powerful servants would have been a gracefully oblique compliment to the Virgin Queen.[4] The circumspect handling of such classical identifications in Elizabethan royal portraiture was likely a consequence of anxieties regarding the taint of pagan idolatry—and, too, anxieties regarding an iconoclastic response to idolatry that had a precedent in scripture.

In 1596, the year following his fortune-hunting voyage to the Caribbean and Orinoco, Ralegh published *A Discoverie of the large, rich, and beautifull Empire of Guiana*. If we are to believe his own account, Ralegh carried the royal icon with him beyond the seas, to the very margins of the known world. Whether or not he actually did so, his discourse reveals personal strategies of iconic appropriation at work within the manifest collective process of cultural imperialism; and it is upon these that I wish to focus here.[5] Ralegh presents to his noble patrons and gentle readers the following account of his *modus operandi* among the indigenous peoples of Guiana:

> I did not in any sort make my desire for gold knowen, because I had neither time, nor power to have a greater quantity. I gave among them manie more peeces of gold, then I received, of the new money of 20 shillings with her Majesties picture to wear, with promise that they would become her servants thencefoorth.[6]

This passage exemplifies the subtlety and guilefulness of Ralegh's rhetoric of address to his readers. Here he seeks to gain the confidence of his fellow countrymen by sharing with them what he claims to have withheld from the Indians. In practical terms, however, all that he had to share amounted to little more than excuses for having returned empty-handed from the land of El Dorado. Indeed, thanks in part to his disbursement of those golden coins, he was returning home to England with less gold than he had possessed when he left.

The "peeces of gold ... of the new money of 20 shillings with her Majesties picture" that Ralegh gave to the Indians to wear were presumably the 20 shilling coins minted during the last decade of the reign. This coin bore on the obverse a bust of the queen in profile, with ruff and imperial crown; on the reverse was the crowned shield of the royal arms flanked by "E R" and surrounded by a legend of Pauline (and Spenserian) resonance: "SCVTVM FIDEI PROTEGET EAM" ("The shield of faith shall protect her") (fig. 27). Coins of the realm bore what were the most widely disseminated of royal images; yet

FIGURE 27
Elizabeth I gold pound of 20 shillings, obverse and reverse; 1583–1603. Ashmolean
Museum, Oxford.

it was precisely their formality, ubiquity, and utilitarian purpose that would
have rendered such images unremarkable to those who daily handled them.
Obviously, a halfpenny of base metal would have been treated very differently
from a gold coin of twenty shillings, but that would have been because of
the enormous difference in their material worth and relative exchange values.
What Ralegh implies is that in the New World context, European norms
of value have been reversed: The (purported) ubiquity of gold and golden
artifacts in Guiana neutralizes the twenty-shilling coin's exchange value there.
It is not the material substance of the coin but rather the symbolic value of
the royal image impressed upon it that is all-important in Ralegh's exchanges
with the natives.

To put Ralegh's strategy anagrammatically, his narrative reconstitutes *coin*
as *icon*: In function, the twenty-shilling piece is now equivalent to a medal,
cameo, or locket miniature of the Queen. Such an object is the so-called
Drake Jewel, which Queen Elizabeth purportedly presented to Sir Francis
Drake on the occasion of the defeat of the Armada. This precious object
contains a miniature of the Queen painted by Nicholas Hilliard around 1586–
87, again showing her with a crescent moon and arrows as hair ornaments,
and on the inside of the lid, a painting of Queen's Phoenix emblem. The
miniature is encased in an enameled gold locket, set with jewels and bearing
on its cover a sardonyx cameo into which the profiles of a black emperor
and a white lady are carved (fig. 28). On at least two occasions, Drake had his
portrait painted in three-quarter length, proudly wearing this jewel suspended
from a chain around his waist.[7] Such wearing of emblems of personal loyalty
to the sovereign had become popular in England in the mid 1580s; and, in
turn, the practice seems to have spawned a subgenre of Elizabethan courtly
portraiture, in which the painting's subject bears a miniature image of the
Queen as a token of reciprocal favor and devotion. Another such example

is the portrait of Sir Christopher Hatton, the Lord Chancellor and another
royal favorite, who holds a jeweled cameo of the Queen in a panel painting
dated 1589 (fig. 29). The fashion may have been a response to numerous real
and rumored Catholic assassination plots against Elizabeth, plots promoted
by Spain, the Papacy, and English Catholic exiles, and inspired by the Queen

FIGURE 28
Elizabeth I, by Nicholas Hilliard; ca. 1586–87. Watercolor miniature in
a jeweled locket (the "Drake" jewel). Anon. loan, Victoria & Albert
Museum, London; V&A Images.

FIGURE 29
Sir Christopher Hatton, holding a cameo of Queen Elizabeth. Artist unknown; ca. 1589. Oil on panel.
National Portrait Gallery, London.

of Scots.[8] Thus, Ralegh's speaking picture of the New World natives wearing the image of Queen Elizabeth suggested to his English readers that Protestant England had bested Catholic Spain in the struggle for the Indians' hearts and minds; and this happy thought carried the enticing prospect that the Indians' gold and their land would surely follow. The very acceptance of Ralegh's dissembled gifts by the naturals of Guiana betokened their subjection to the Queen whose image they bore, and thus their uncomprehending entry into

the circulations of England's nascent imperial economy—an economy that
was to be fueled, in the future, by their own gold.

Ralegh relates that earlier in his voyage he had conferred with the native
chieftains on Trinidad, following his burning of a Spanish settlement there:

> I made them understand that I was the servant of a Queene, who was the
> great Casique of the North, and a virgine ... that shee was an enemie to the
> Castellani in respect of their tyrannie and oppression, and that she delivered
> all such nations about her, as were by them oppressed. ... I shewed them her
> Majesties picture which they so admired and honoured, as it had bene easie to
> have brought them idolatrous thereof.
>
> The like and a more large discourse I made to the rest of the nations both
> in my passing to Guiana, and to those of the borders, so as in that part of the
> world her Majestie is very famous and admirable, whom they now call Ezrabeta
> Cassipuna Aquerewana, which is as much as Elizabeth, the great princesse or
> greatest commander. (353–54)

It is highly unlikely that the picture of Her Majesty that Ralegh revealed to the
Indians would have been a panel painting, but it could well have been a miniature that he carried upon his person. If so, it was perhaps similar to the one
limned by Nicholas Hilliard in the later 1580s (fig. 24), which represents the
Queen with a jeweled moon and arrows in her hair. As already suggested, in its
allusion to the Queen as Cynthia-Diana, this particular miniature has an affinity with the lunar *impresa* in Ralegh's own 1588 portrait. Whatever its medium
and provenance, the reported effect of the royal icon upon the Trinidadians is
most suggestive: "I shewed them her Majesties picture which they so admired
and honoured, as it had bene easie to have brought them idolatrous thereof."
The evangelizing Ralegh claims that in the New World, he displayed the royal
icon in order to evoke wonder and worship in the Queen's prospective subjects.
Equally suggestive is the way in which Ralegh foregrounds his production of
that effect for the benefit of his English readership—a readership that the text
constructs as including the Queen, her counselors, her courtiers, and prospective investors.[9] Ralegh's invocation of Elizabeth in the high astounding terms
of the Indians' own language was obviously calculated to impress the English
naturals and, in particular, their great *Casique*. Of course, without Ralegh's
mediation, "Ezrabeta Cassipuna Aquerewana" would never have resounded
among the nations of America, nor would it have been intelligible to his fellow
English.

Ralegh's *Discoverie* is a printed tract promoting colonial enterprise that eschews explicit appeals to religious conversion as a motivation or a pretext for
conquest. The absence of a religious mission from the *Discoverie* becomes more

conspicuous when it is compared to a policy paper entitled "Of the Voyage for Guiana," probably composed following Ralegh's 1595 voyage and apparently intended to promote a full-scale invasion. This anonymous manuscript proposes as its primary justification for subduing and annexing Guiana "to the Crowne Imperiall . . . of England," that "by this meanes infinite nombers of soules may be brought from theyr idolatry, bloody sacrifices, ignoraunce, and incivility to the worshipping of the true God aright to civill conversation, and also theyr bodyes freed from the intollerable tiranny of the Spaniards."[10] Ralegh's emphasis is decidedly more on bodies than on souls, more on geopolitics than on theology, and his great enemy is the King of Spain rather than the Catholic religion as such. In his *Discoverie*, Ralegh represents himself as spreading the gospel of England's Elizabeth to the imagined corners of the earth. This virgin warrior who delivers the world's nations from the tyranny and cruel oppression of the evil Spaniards (or "Castellani") has absorbed attributes of both Christ and Mary—a process of appropriation, or "cult" formation, that would have been evident to Ralegh's English readers, even if not to his putative American interlocutors.

The practice of idolatry, and the perpetuation of ignorance, superstition, and moral indolence among the people, were among the direst of the charges that the Protestant reformers hurled against the edifice of the Roman church. And, as I have suggested, those charges were also occasionally turned back upon the Elizabethan political and religious establishment by some of its own opponents, whether Papist or Puritan. In their encounters with the indigenous inhabitants of the Americas, Elizabethans, like other sixteenth-century Europeans, tended to categorize their hosts as pagans and as idolators. Thus, in his personal narrative of the first Elizabethan expedition to "the Countrey, now called Virginia," which was carried out in 1584 under the auspices and control of Ralegh, Arthur Barlowe writes of the Algonkians that "when they goe to the warres, they carry with them their Idoll, of whome they aske counsell, as the Romanes were woont of the Oracle of Apollo"; and he flatly asserts that this "Idoll . . . is nothing else, but a meere illusion of the Devill."[11] An engraving of this so-called idol was published in the 1590 edition of Thomas Harriot's *A Briefe and true report of the new found land of Virginia*, a promotional account of the second (1585) expedition to Virginia under Ralegh's sponsorship (fig. 30). An authority on mathematics, navigation, astronomy, and natural philosophy, Harriot was Ralegh's client and adviser, and the most observant and reflective member of this expedition. He wrote that the native priests "are notable enchaunters," and he contrasted the "subtilty" of the chiefs and priests to "the common and simple sort of people." Harriot observed that the credulity of the latter concerning the indigenous eschatology "maketh them

Ther Idol Kivvaſa.   XXI.

He people of this cuntrie haue an Idol, which th ey call K I w a s a : yt is carued of woode in lengthe 4. foote whoſe headeis like the heades of the people of Florida, the face is of a fleſh colour, the breſt white, the reſt is all blacke, the thighes are alſo ſpottet with whitte. He hath a chayne abowt his necke of white beades, betweene which are other Rownde beades of copper which they eſteeme more then golde or ſiluer. This Idol is placed in the temple of the towne of Secotam, as the keper of the kings dead corpſes. Somtyme they haue two of thes idoles in theyr churches, and ſomtine 3. but neuer aboue, which they place in a darke corner wher they ſhew tetrible. Thes poore ſoules haue none other knowledge of god although I thinke them verye Deſirous to know the truthe. For when as wee kneeled downe on our knees to make our prayers vnto god, they went abowt to imitate vs, and when they ſaw we moued our lipps, they alſo dyd the like. Wherfore that is verye like that they might eaſelye be brongt to the knowledge of the goſpel. God of his mercie grant them this grace.

D 2

FIGURE 30

"Ther Idol Kiwasa," engraved by Theodor de Bry after a drawing by John White. Printed in Thomas Harriot, *A Briefe and true report of the new found land of Virginia* (Frankfurt, 1590), plate XXI. By permission of the Folger Shakespeare Library, Washington, DC.

have great respect to their Governours, and also great care what they do, to avoid torment after death, and to enjoy blisse."[12] Here Ralegh would have found much food for thought.

When Ralegh came to write of his own firsthand encounter with the natives of Guiana, and made the striking claim that it would have been easy for him to have led them into idolatry by means of the Queen's picture, he was conjuring with an image of himself as priestly manipulator of the royal idol. Rather than pursue a proselytizing mission that would lift the pagan savages out of their benighted spiritual condition, the agent of Christian civilization entertained the prospect of enchanting them. Ralegh's turn of phrase suggests that possession of the power to lead the ignorant and superstitious into idolatry was a prospect that intrigued him—and, perhaps, even tempted him. As is well known, there were those among his enemies who branded Ralegh an atheist, and aligned him with the kind of heterodox thinking that was being flaunted in the "atheist lecture" that Richard Baines had attributed to Christopher Marlowe: "That the first beginning of Religioun was only to keep men in awe. . . . That it was an easy matter for Moyses being brought up in all the artes of the Egiptians to abuse the Jewes being a rude & grosse people." Indeed, in the same note, Baines attributed to Marlowe the opinion "that Moyses was but a Jugler & that one Heriots [i.e., Thomas Harriot] being Sir W Raleighs man Can do more then he."[13]

Doubtless, Baines's Marlowe would have found little to distinguish the uses of religion among the natives of Virginia or Guiana from those among the Israelites or the English. In writing coyly that "it had been easie to have brought them idolatrous" of the Queen's picture, Ralegh fleetingly disrupts the habitual Elizabethan insistence that Protestant England constituted a moral and spiritual antithesis to Catholic Spain. However, any intimation that the English had malign intentions toward the Indians is immediately recuperated in Ralegh's reaffirmation of his own magnanimity, and his Queen's. By contrast, the Baines note attributes to Marlowe a remorselessly cynical perspective upon the supposed moral distinction between the two churches: "That if there be any god or any good Religion, then it is in the papistes because the service of god is performed with more Cerimonies, as Elevation of the mass, organs, singing men, Shaven Crownes & cta. That all protestantes are Hypocritical asses." Here the finer points of theological controversy are laughed to scorn. Baines's Marlowe has it that all institutionalized religions are ideological mystifications that promote the idleness, idolatry, and fear, which function "to keep men in awe." On this Machiavellian understanding, papistry proves the more effective mystification, and it does so for precisely those reasons for which the Protestant iconoclasts had excoriated it: namely, the spectacular display and sensuous appeal that it had in common with the popular theatre for which Marlowe wrote and which Protestant reformers habitually vilified as an idolatrous inheritance from heathens and papists. By claiming that he could easily have brought the natives into idolatry at the sight of the Queen's picture but that he chose not to do so, Ralegh harnesses a potentially transgressive energy that he employs simultaneously to several ends, all of which advance his own interests: By means of this rhetorical strategy, he flatters his sovereign with a testimonial to the power of her virtue and beauty; he suggests the pliancy of the Indians, and thus the ease with which they will be conquered; and he advertises his own loyalty, faith, and temperance. At the Elizabethan court, where he was a devotee of the Queen in her manifestation as Cynthia-Diana, Ralegh himself performed the role of an idolator. In the text of his *Discoverie*, however, he removes the operative site of this royal cult image from England to Guiana: There, he represents himself as Elizabeth's apostle to the Americans, producing, disseminating, and controlling the Queen's charismatic power over others. As a consequence of Ralegh's self-representation as mediator of the Elizabeth cult, the operations of the royal talisman are demystified. However, the final effect of this demystification is not a flagrant "subversion" of royal authority but rather a shrewd and subtle foregrounding of the politic subject's agency in sustaining that authority—that power "to keep men in awe"—and to do so to the mutual benefit of his sovereign and himself.

A Cult of Elizabeth?

At the beginning of chapter six, I quoted a passage in which Frances Yates describes the pseudo-Marian "bejeweled and painted image" of Elizabeth that was "set up at court, and went in progress through the land for her worshippers to adore." In that passage, Yates's specific reference is to a late Elizabethan picture that shows the Queen in procession, under a canopy of state, and surrounded by the members of her court (fig. 31).[1] Yates characterizes the picture's iconography as appropriating the late medieval cult of the Virgin Mary: "the worship of 'diva Elizabetta,' the imperial virgin, in place of that of the Queen of Heaven, gorgeously arrayed through street and countryside." By contrast, Roy Strong identifies the painting's iconography as pagan and classical: "What we are looking at is an Elizabethan version of a Roman imperial triumph."[2] Rather than adjudicate between these claims, I would stress that together they help to make the point that the iconography of the Elizabeth cult was not a unified and coherent system but rather was hybrid and improvisatory—therefore unstable and potentially contradictory—and that it drew upon various sources in varying combinations at different moments in the reign, to suit the tactical circumstances of particular occasions.

Strong has convincingly shown that the figure occupying the center foreground of this painting, standing immediately below and in front of the Queen, is Edward Somerset, fourth Earl of Worcester. In 1601, Worcester succeeded the Earl of Essex as Master of the Horse, and he may well have commissioned this painting to celebrate that new royal honor. Strong makes the uncontroversial point that "the celebration of Worcester is . . . subservient to that of Elizabeth." Of course, it was requisite that the celebration of the Queen should take precedence. Perhaps less obvious and more significant, however,

FIGURE 31

Elizabeth I in procession, attributed to Robert Peake; ca. 1600. Oil on canvas. Private collection.
Photograph by Percy Hennell, courtesy of Sherborne Castle Estates.

is that this splendidly festive image of the Elizabeth cult is made the occasion
and the means to commemorate the honor and worship of one of Elizabeth's
noble followers. By means of this oblique displacement, the Queen remains
the nominal subject of the painting, but its real subject becomes the Earl of
Worcester in his relationship to the Queen.

By this alteration of focus, I mean to suggest that those Elizabethan subjects who commissioned and paid for portraits of the Queen, either for their
own use or as gifts to her or to others, were likely to have been motivated
not only by devotional impulses but also by self-interested strategies—even
if such impure motives sometimes amounted to no more than a desire to enhance their own prestige by basking in the Queen's reflected glory. The images,
texts, and performances of royal panegyric were also subject to the material
and ideological motives of those who fashioned them, and to their powers
of synthesis and invention; to the representational resources and limitations
of the particular media in which they were realized; and to the specific occasions and audiences for which they were devised. The aim of this chapter
is to examine two representative instances of impure motives at work in the
production of the cult of Elizabeth—as manifested by the Earl of Leicester, one
of its prominent sponsors, and by Thomas Churchyard, one of its prominent

makers—and to offer some summary conclusions based upon these instances and upon the material in the preceding chapters of part two.

෧ මු

In Roy Strong's invaluable study of royal portraiture and pageantry, *The Cult of Elizabeth*, there are passages in which he makes claims similar to those made by Frances Yates, in regard to what she characterizes as "the worship of the state Virgo"; unlike Yates, however, Strong makes those claims in unequivocal terms: "The cult of Gloriana was skilfully created . . . deliberately to replace the pre-Reformation externals of religion, the cult of the Virgin and saints with their attendant images, processions, ceremonies and secular rejoicing."[3] These claims are given specificity in the following discussion of the celebrated "Rainbow" portrait of Queen Elizabeth (fig. 25):

> If I had to suggest the occasion which evoked this extraordinary votive image I would turn to the last spectacle of the reign, Elizabeth's visit to Robert Cecil in December 1602. For this [John] Davies composed a re-statement of his Eliza mythology in a courtly contention between a wife, and widow and a maid. These three meet en route to "Astraea's shrine," upon which tapers are burning in honour of this "saint" "to whom all hearts devotion owe." Is it too fantastic to suggest that this shrine centred on the Rainbow Portrait? No other setting seems to provide a context better suited to the religious overtones of this sacred icon in which Royal Astraea is unambiguously presented as an object of worship.[4]

If we take Strong's terms in their strong sense, the historical and artistic implications are quite extraordinary. He "unambiguously" asserts that the "Rainbow" portrait was treated as a sacred icon within a quasi-liturgical setting in which the Queen was an object of worship by her preeminent privy councillor. As I have suggested above, in making this claim Strong adopts an interpretive perspective similar to that of the Elizabethan regime's Catholic adversaries. To Cardinal Allen, Elizabethan monarcholatry was a compulsory yielding to the Queen, "most servilly as to our household and home God, and as to a verie nationall idol, subjection bothe of bodie and soule."[5] Of course, in Strong's analysis there is no trace of the theologically based moral outrage and censure that permeate the writings of Allen; nevertheless, the setting he describes for the commissioning, execution, and original display of the portrait would surely have been recognized by any devout Elizabethan—whether Protestant or Catholic—as flagrantly idolatrous.

There is certainly much evidence that concerted efforts were made to elicit powerful affects of devotion toward the royal virgin, and that their purpose was to strengthen the hold of both the Anglican church and the Elizabethan regime upon the loyalties of Elizabethan subjects in a perilous period of ideological conflict and social change. And, certainly, Catholic critics like Sander, Rishton, and Allen denounced such strategic appropriations of traditional religious symbols and practices because they perceived them to be blasphemous and conducive to idolatry. Nevertheless, despite the extravagant metaphorical language that some of her adherents employed, I remain skeptical that any avowedly Protestant Elizabethan literally worshiped the Queen or adopted a flatly idolatrous attitude toward her image.

In order to arrive at an interpretation such as Strong's, it seems to me that one must discount the nuanced and coy performativity at the heart of Elizabethan courtly culture. For example, compare Strong's hypothetical scene of Elizabeth worship with one actually scripted and presumably performed before the Queen when she was entertained by the Earl of Leicester at his Wanstead estate in 1578. Written by Leicester's nephew, Philip Sidney, the entertainment has come down to us as *The Lady of May*. What concerns me here is the epilogue to the entertainment, addressed to the Queen and spoken by Rhombus, a schoolmaster, as he presents to her the gift of an agate necklace. The relevant passage is as follows:

> But to you, Juno, Venus, Pallas *et profecto plus*, I have to ostend a mellifluous fruit of my fidelity. *Sic est*, so it is, that in this our city we have a certain neighbour, they call him Master Robert of Wanstead. He is counted an honest man, and one that loves us doctified men *pro vita*; and when he comes to his aedicle he distributes *oves, boves et pecora campi* largely among the *populorum*. But so stays the case, that he is foully commaculated with the papistical enormity, *O heu Aedipus Aecaster*. The *bonus vir* is a huge *catholicam*, wherewith my conscience being replenished, could no longer refrain it from you, *proba dominus doctor, probo inveni*. I have found *unum par*, a pair, *papisticorum bedorus*, of Papistian beads, *cum quis*, with the which, *omnium dierum*, every day, next after his pater noster he semper suits "and Elizabeth," as many lines as there be beads on this string.[6]

The passage begins with the comic pedant putting a tedious Latinate spin on the panegyrical trope of the three goddesses. This particular trope was also deployed to entertain the Queen in Norwich in that same year, and would shortly be used by George Peele for the climax of his court play *The Araygnement of Paris* (1582).[7] Rhombus then reveals to the Queen that her noble host is "foully commaculated with the papistical enormity"; and the ocular proof of Leicester's closet Catholicism is the string of "Papistian beads" upon which he says his *pater noster*. Yet the Earl's idolatrous devotions are of an idiosyncratic sort, for in the daily bidding of his beads, he follows his *Pater Noster* not with an *Ave Maria* but with an *Ave* Elizabeth.

The scholarly consensus is that this entertainment was performed before the Queen when she visited Wanstead in May 1578. That visit marked the final stop on a relatively brief and informal progress that was a prelude to the grand perambulation of East Anglia which consumed most of the subsequent summer. This latter was the progress that took her to Norwich, and to the estate of the unfortunate Master Edward Rookwood of Euston. As I have noted, the Earl of Leicester seems to have had a hand in arranging that progress and the events with which the Queen was edified during its course; and he was a member of the Queen's itinerant court throughout the progress, only departing a few days before its conclusion in order to prepare to receive her once again at Wanstead. As reported by Thomas Churchyard, it was at Wanstead in late September that the summer progress officially ended, "and to knit up all, the good chere was revived . . . with making a great feast to the Queene."[8] Perhaps it is not a coincidence that the unique manuscript in which Rombus's final speech appears was found at Helmingham Hall in Suffolk, close to the route of the Queen's 1578 progress.

The comically idolatrous epilogue to *The Lady of May* seems playfully to counterpoint the serious ideological agenda of the 1578 progress—whether it was performed at Wanstead in May (as seems most fitting) or, perhaps, in September, either as a prelude or as a postlude to the summer's campaign to root out papistry. By the conclusion of the progress, the recusant gentlemen of Norfolk and Suffolk stood revealed as duplicitous and disloyal subjects and as secret idolators; and they had already been duly punished for their transgressions. The performance at Wanstead discovered the Queen's host to be the antithesis of Rookwood and his ilk: within the secret closet of his heart, the Queen's trusted councillor and favorite, Robert Dudley, prayed only to the true God and to His anointed handmaiden. This, then, was an idiosyncratic and intimate variant upon the loyal sentiments expressed by the Earl's friends and clients in Norwich: As the Lord Mayor put it there, "We would account nothing more pretious (most Royall Prince) than that the bright beame of your most chast eye, which doth so chere us, might penetrate the secret strait corners of our hartes: then surely should you see how great joyes are dispersed there." Leicester, however, intended that the Queen penetrate only selected corners of his heart. At the same time that he arranged this mock discovery of his purported secret devotions to the Queen, he was also earnestly arranging to conceal from her another performance of devotion that had the force of law: shortly before Elizabeth's return to Wanstead to celebrate the end of the summer progress, Leicester privately married there Lettice, dowager

Countess of Essex and daughter of Sir Francis Knollys. When the secret was
maliciously revealed to the Queen several months later, at the height of the
Anjou courtship crisis, the bride and groom were hastily banished from court.
During this perilous period—perhaps more urgently than at any other point
during Elizabeth's reign—Leicester had good reason to want to make public
testimonials of his faithfulness to his sovereign mistress.

As I have already suggested, in evaluating the productions of Elizabethan
royal pageantry and panegyric, we need to take account not only of those
who sponsored them but also of those who made them, and of their skills,
circumstances, and motives. Although the paucity of documentary evidence
makes this difficult to do, we may gain some insight into these issues from
various passages in the publications of Thomas Churchyard. Churchyard had
a central role in the scripting and performance of the Norwich celebrations,
among others, and was an assiduous producer of royal panegyric throughout
his precarious career as a professional writer. At the beginning of his "Discourse of The Queenes Majesties entertainments in Suffolk and Norffolk,"
Churchyard states that

> the Shewes and purposed matter penned out by me . . . I thoughte it conveniente
> to printe . . . in order, as they were invented: for I was the fyrste that was called,
> and came to Norwiche about that businesse, and remained there three long
> weekes before the Courte came thither, devising and studying the best I coulde
> for the Citie, albeit other Gentlemen . . . dyd steppe in after, and broughte to
> passe that alreadye is sette in Print in a Booke.[9]

Bernard Garter's "The Joyfull Receyving of the Queenes most excellent
Majestie into hir Highesse Citie of Norwich" was entered into the Station-
ers' Register only eight days after the conclusion of the Queen's visit and three
weeks before the entry of Churchyard's pamphlet. Although he had been
beaten into print, Churchyard used his own publication to advertise both the
chronological primacy and the seriousness of purpose of his contribution, and
to record it for posterity unmixed with the baser matter of others' inventions.
As he put it proudly at the conclusion of his account, "Thus have you truly
hearde the reporte of mine owne workes and inventions, with the which did
no any one deale but my selfe" (328).

The printed account also allowed the author to rescue from oblivion those
of his inventions that had not been performed due to rain or a royal change
of mind. As Churchyard's Mercury points out to the Queen during one of the
pageants, "Thus you see, a Shew in the open fielde is alwayes subject to the

suddayne change of weather, and a number of more inconveniences than I expresse" (317). Churchyard expands upon these "inconveniences" in a later passage: "The Courte upon remove, the Citie troubled with many causes, and some seeking to do service like my selfe, moved me to doe somewhat of my selfe, bycause myne aydes (as many times they were before) were drawen from me, each one about his owne businesse, and I lefte to mine owne inventions and policie" (327). The foregoing quotations highlight the complex nature of the relationship between such retrospective accounts as Churchyard's and the events that they purport to record.[10] The printed text does not merely transcribe what was spoken or was intended to be spoken within the formal presentation; it also embeds the quoted speeches within a narrative that both describes and interprets the dynamics of the actual performance, its circumstances, and its setting. Such accounts constitute a distinctive genre of the early modern printed book; and considered generically, they have a formal tendency to draw attention away from the manifest encomiastic content of the royal pageantry they describe, foregrounding instead the interplay between intention and contingency in the process of performance and reception.

Churchyard's panegyrical texts characteristically register not only inclement weather or changes of schedule and other incidental inconveniences but also the author's literary performance anxiety, his apprehension of a competition in the marketplace of poetical devices so fierce that it jeopardizes his bid for patronage. He offers an unusually candid picture of this anxiety in the Epistle Dedicatory "To the Queenes Most Excellent Majesty" that prefaced a collection of his royal encomia printed in 1592:

> If hope of your princely favor did not carry me beyond the compasse of my ordinary judgement, I had long agoe surceased the common course of writing in verse to your Majestie, but a sweete and comfortable conceite of your gracious goodness towards me, ever and at all times commanded my muse, my pen, and uttermost power, to goe about no other earthly felicity then the serving and pleasing of the onely Phoenix of this world, my betters farre have beene ful of that fortunate humor, and thriven well thereby.... Now in this quenchles desire of mine that encreaseth a continuall thirst to do well, there riseth a restles cogitation, making me think, that verse, or that booke, or that peece of service ... will be happely accepted. But beholding ... a multitude of people as well desposed as my selfe, that are running and preasing apace before me, some with rare inventions and some with deep devices to the honouring of your Majestie. I feare they have carried cleane away so much knowledge from me, that there is left no device, nor matter to study on, such is the bounty of our time, & forwardnes of their wittes which are learned, that all fine inventions

are smoothly reaped from my reach, & cunningly raked away from my use or commoditie. Then am I forced, to search what substance or slender stuffe of poetrie lyes cowching in mine owne shallow head.[11]

Churchyard might well have been reflecting here upon the circumstances in which he had found himself back in 1578, when his own efforts to entertain and impress the Queen, the city fathers of Norwich, and his gentle readers faced direct competition from others of equal or greater facility. But the larger implication of Churchyard's confession to the Queen is that the hyperbolic Elizabethan rhetoric of royal praise was impelled by a kind of mimetic desire— that it was at least as much about emulating and overgoing the conceits of one's rivals as it was about finding a means of representation adequate to the Queen's manifest virtues.[12]

With the perspective of this Dedicatory Epistle in mind, let us consider a passage from another of Churchyard's poems in praise of the Queen, this one appended to "A discourse of the joy good subjectes have when they see our Phenix abroad," and published in the following year, 1593:

> A peerelesse paragon, in whom such gladsome gifts remaine,
> Whose seemly shape wroght as out of wax wer made ye mold
> By fine devise of thought, like shrined Saint in beaten gold.[13]

Churchyard's simile of the Queen "like shrined Saint in beaten gold" resonates with the "immaydge of our Lady" that was discovered in Rookwood's hayloft, of which Topcliffe wrote, "for greatnes, for gayness, and woorkemanshipp I did never see a matche"; and, too, with Frances Yates's description of the pseudo-Marian "bejeweled and painted image" of Elizabeth that was "set up at court, and went in progress through the land for her worshippers to adore." In striving to invent a vivid figure for the Queen's virtue and beauty, Churchyard courts the hyperbolic force of idolatry; at the same time, he seeks to neutralize the danger of such contamination by the tactical rhetorical choice of simile rather than metaphor, and by foregrounding the status of his similitude as poetic invention, "wroght as out of wax wer made ye mold / By fine devise of thought."

If scholars of Elizabethan visual, verbal, and performance culture take the overripe tropes of royal panegyric as if they were testaments of faith or acts of worship, they risk exaggerating the extent, consistency, and sincerity of this royal cult of personality, and they fail to give due weight to the pragmatic calculations that were at work in its invention and elaboration. In a sharp reaction against work like that of Yates and Strong, Sydney Anglo has written that

> the whole panoply of panegyric was aimed upward to please the monarch, not downward to persuade doubting courtiers of the rectitude of the regime.... If compliments addressed to the Queen were largely matters of form, venal, or part of a courtly game, then the term *Cult*—which implies worship, devotion and sincerity—is too highly coloured and tendentious.[14]

Anglo's skepticism is salutary; but he overcompensates for the "cultist" perspective by reducing the bulk of courtly panegyric, pageantry, and symbolism to mere flattery—unequivocal, undialectical, and ineffectual. Anglo obviously intends the phrase "courtly game" to be deprecatory, to imply trivial or inconsequential activity. However, as I have sought to demonstrate throughout the foregoing analyses, the structure and dynamics of Elizabethan court culture conferred an instrumental efficacy upon such manifestly otiose activities. In Puttenham's memorable formulations, the "profession of a very Courtier ... is in plaine termes, cunningly to be able to dissemble," and his modus operandi is to "busily negotiate by coulor of otiation." It is on this understanding that Puttenham englishes and personifies the rhetorical figure of *allegoria* as "The Courtier,"

> which is when we speake one thing and thinke another, and that our wordes and our meanings meete not. The use of this figure is so large, and its vertue of so great efficacie as it is supposed no man can pleasantly utter and perswade without it, but in effect is sure never or very seldome to thrive and prosper in the world, that cannot skilfully put in [use], in somuch as not onely every common Courtier, but also the gravest Counsellour, yea and the most noble and wisest Prince of them all are many times enforced to use it.[15]

Thus, the nuanced performance of what Anglo calls "courtly game" was the sanctioned medium through which court society manifested its collective ethos, and the channel through which those within the orbit of the court pursued and negotiated their individual and common interests.

The larger point here is not that royal panegyric was aimed either upward toward the monarch or downward toward her courtiers but that it was a discourse both shared and contested by the monarch and her courtiers, by the state and its subjects.[16] The Queen herself was an avid player in this courtly game, and the stakes were frequently high. The antithetical accounts of Strong and Anglo appear equally indifferent to that strategic ambiguity which allowed the Elizabethan court to parody sacred discourses and practices, and thus to pursue its politic purposes by playing the wittily ostentatious game of royal flattery. I construe the cultural phenomenon of Elizabethan royal pageantry and iconography primarily as an ideological apparatus operated by those who constituted the political nation: the Queen, her court and council and their clients, the members of parliament and the civic elites. Through this symbolic medium, these individuals and groups negotiated their complex interrelationships; and, at the same time, they sought collectively to catalyze the common people's loyalty to the regime and to secure their submission to those social arrangements which sustained it. In other words, I construe the cult of Elizabeth neither as a quasi-mystical object of belief nor as a mere courtly game but rather as a core component of Elizabethan statecraft, one within which elements of devotion, diversion, and duplicity were inextricably mixed.

PART THREE

Queen and Country

Queen Elizabeth was a subject of representation in a variety of media; and those multifarious representations collectively constituted a medium for political and religious polemic, both within and beyond the realm. From Elizabeth's accession until her death, the circumstantial fact that the body politic of English kingship was incarnated in the natural body of an unmarried woman ensured that gender and sexuality were foregrounded in representing the Elizabethan state and in articulating its relations with other states and with its own subjects. In this sense, the Elizabethan image was an important resource for the geopolitical imaginary of the later sixteenth century; and the scope of this geopolitical resourcefulness is the subject of part three.

The mystical body of English kingship was an artificial body, a political fiction: "a Body that cannot be seen or handled, consisting of Policy and Government . . . utterly devoid of . . . natural Defects and Imbecilities, which the Body natural is subject to."[1] The "body natural" of Elizabeth Tudor, in which this "body politic" inhered, was material in a way that the body politic was not. At the same time, however, it was also an ideological construct, in which human anatomical and physiological features signified in historically specific ways, as constituents of an early modern cultural system of sex and gender. As Mary Douglas has written in a cross-cultural study of bodily metaphors paradoxically entitled *Natural Symbols*, "systems of symbols, though based on bodily processes, get their meaning from social experience. . . . There are no natural symbols." She posits a homology between the ideology of the body and the organization of society, in which "the symbols based on the human body are used to express different social experiences" of the relationship between the individual and the collective.[2] From this perspective, Elizabethan somatic symbolism is culture-specific in two fundamental and interrelated ways: If dominant structures of thought and belief privilege the Prince's body in relation to the subject's, they also privilege the male body in relation to the female. The version of Woman produced in Tudor discourses on medicine, law, religion, and domestic economy was almost invariably an imperfect and inherently unstable version of Man.[3] Following Tyndale's 1526 englishing of the New Testament, Woman was ubiquitously conceived of as "the weaker vessel" (Peter 3:7); and it was a commonplace that such feminine frailty was corporeally most manifest and most dangerous at the orifices—in particular, in women's speech and in their sexual conduct.[4] Chastity, silence, and obedience were the oft repeated orthodox ideals of both maidenly and matronly comportment. At the same time, the patriarchal imperative of this cultural paradigm was that these always incipiently wayward women be under the guidance and control of men in positions of authority—primarily their husbands, but also variously their fathers, masters, ministers, and magistrates.

The paradoxically doubled body of Queen Elizabeth provides an idiosyncratic and privileged illustration of Douglas's cross-cultural thesis that "the body is a model which can stand for any bounded system. Its boundaries can represent any boundaries which are threatened or precarious." She adds that "all margins are dangerous. . . . We should expect the orifices of the body to symbolize its specially vulnerable points. . . . Each culture has its own special risks and problems. To which particular bodily margins its beliefs attribute power depends on what situation the body is mirroring."[5] As an unmarried queen regnant, ruling an island country that was of increasing strategic consequence in a world racked by religious and geopolitical strife, Elizabeth herself was frequently made the representational medium for religious controversy, patriotic fervor, and xenophobic diatribe. In such cases, the discourse was almost invariably gender-coded, and it made meaning through symbolic manipulations of the royal body. In particular, those symbolic manipulations focused upon the sexual purity or pollution of the Queen's body, upon the integral strength or the dangerous permeability of its contours and orifices. This discourse was worked not only by the Queen and by the agents of her regime but also, with equal assiduousness and ingenuity, by her supportive and her resistant subjects at home, her sympathetic clients and her implacable enemies abroad. In representing Queen Elizabeth, the image makers of later sixteenth-century Europe were also articulating particular positions at the intersection of religious, national, and gender identities.

In the following chapters, I study some domestic and foreign instances of the Elizabethan geopolitical imaginary at work, intending thereby to suggest something of both its ideological diversity and its affective range. In chapter nine I consider three geopolitically inflected courtly representations of the

Queen, from different moments in the reign, which together provide a foil for the materials of the subsequent chapters. Chapter ten explores the interplay of hostile and encomiastic continental appropriations of the royal image. Such representations were devised as interventions into the geopolitical and religious struggles of the 1580s—a theatre of war and diplomacy engaging England, France, and Spain, and focused upon the Low Countries. Chapter eleven examines verbal and visual images that gave a vividly personalized shape to the conflict between England and the forces of Spain and the Papacy, a conflict which reached a climax at the end of the 1580s in the Armada.

The Geopolitical Imaginary

At the court of Elizabeth, it was a tradition on New Year's Day for the nobility, attendant courtiers, and household officers to present gifts to the Queen, which she reciprocated with precisely graduated quantities of gilt plate or with other, more modest remunerations to her servants.[1] These exchanges were meticulously inventoried on great rolls bearing the flamboyant royal signature. The Queen's gifts came from magnates and from menials; they ranged from jewels and rich furnishings to finely bound books and fanciful constructions in marzipan. Each gave according to his or her ability: For example, at New Year's 1579—a particularly dissonant moment in Elizabethan politics—Robert Dudley, Earl of Leicester and Master of the Horse, gave "a very fair jewel of gold, being a clock garnished fully with diamonds and rubies," while John Dudley, Sergeant of the Pastry, gave "a very fair pye of quynces."[2] The subject's vital personal relationship to the sovereign could be renewed symbolically by an exchange of gifts at the threshold between the old court year and the new.

Such ritualized acts of prestation and the artifacts that they bestowed could also be made occasions for the coded public display of positions regarding matters of policy. This was one of those means by which courtiers, councillors, and foreign ambassadors at the Elizabethan court might "busily negotiate by coulor of otiation."[3] Thus, in 1571 the Earl of Leicester "made a new year's present to the Queen consisting of a jewel containing a painting in which the Queen was represented on a great throne with the queen of Scotland in chains at her feet, begging for mercy, whilst the neighboring countries of Spain and France were as if covered by the waves of the sea, and Neptune and the rest of them bowing to this Queen."[4] The vast and complex subject described here, fusing portraiture with cartography and political allegory, might seem more appropriate to the representational resources of a monumental fresco or oil painting than to a watercolor miniature encased in a jewel. However, as this report by the Spanish ambassador suggests, it is precisely the inverse relationship between the diminutive size and the fragility of the limned portrait, on the one hand, and the geopolitical scope and belligerent tone of its subject, on the other, that gives this act of prestation its paradoxical capacity both to stir powerful affects and to facilitate their display.

Through the offices of de Quadra, the Spanish ambassador, and his own brother-in-law, Henry Sidney, Sir Robert Dudley had been in secret negotiations with King Philip of Spain during the early 1560s; his hope was to secure Habsburg support for his quest to become Elizabeth's consort in return for a conciliatory English policy toward the Catholic Church.[5] The plan came to nothing; and shortly thereafter, with questionable seriousness, Elizabeth was proposing Dudley as a consort for Mary, Queen of Scots. It was this royal matchmaking that served as an occasion to raise Dudley to the peerage as Earl of Leicester.[6] By the time of Leicester's 1571 New Year's prestation, Mary was Elizabeth's enforced guest in England, and would remain so until her execution in 1587. At the same time, Elizabeth herself was in convoluted marriage negotiations with the heir to the French throne, the Catholic duc d'Anjou—an initiative that may well have given Leicester reason to feel that his own special relationship with his sovereign mistress was under threat. The bejeweled miniature that he gave as his New Year's gift was another small gesture in the extravagant and rewarding courtship of his sovereign that he had assiduously pursued since her accession. The Spanish ambassador had reported to King Philip as early as 1566 that Dudley continued to keep up the game of courtship in order that "the *Queen* should not be led to think that he relinquished his suit of distaste for it and so turn her regard into anger and enmity against him which might cause her, *womanlike*, to undo him."[7] The ambassador's remark about the Queen's potential to be womanlike instances a pattern widespread in the recorded conversation and correspondence of Elizabeth's male contemporaries. In this misogynistically inflected variant upon the trope of the Queen's Two Bodies, the inherent contradiction between sovereign authority and gender inferiority makes for a dangerous instability in the monarch's disposition, and thus presents an ever-present personal danger to those male subjects who are her closest advisers and her favorites.

The provocatively patriotic and imperialist theme of Leicester's New Year's gift registered his loyal opposition to the Queen's French match, and added for good measure a menacing gesture toward the King of Spain, his own erstwhile patron and the international champion of the Catholic cause. Leicester's prestation was, then, a courtly performance projecting a complex of significations and insinuations, addressed not only to the Queen but to those personal rivals and foreign enemies who might witness or hear of it. The latter included King Philip himself, to whose obviously attentive ambassador we owe the report that I have quoted here. For my purposes, what is perhaps most significant about the anecdote is the medium of the message: Leicester chose to pursue his strategic interests and to display both his loyalties and his antipathies by the ostentatious public presentation of a painted miniature in a jeweled setting. Whether the Queen herself was their subject, their possessor, or their recipient, pictures, jewels, poems, masques and other cultural productions could play a significant role in the mediation of the court's internal dynamics and in the regime's conduct of policy, both foreign and domestic.

One of the more compelling iconic examples of this process at work is the series of royal portraits painted during the culmination of the Queen's marriage negotiations with François, duc d'Anjou, during the late 1570s and early 1580s. This courtship turned out to be the highly charged final act of the serio-comic Elizabethan marriage play that had commenced at her accession.[8] After two decades during which the Queen deferred satisfaction of her subjects' importunings that she marry, in 1579 it seemed quite likely that she would finally meet their request by marrying a French, Catholic prince. Ironically, this prospect provoked not relief but rather anguish among members of the godly political nation of English Protestants. Among the Queen's subjects, the most notorious public reaction against the match was John Stubbs's pamphlet, *The Discoverie of a Gaping Gulf Whereinto England in Like to Be Swallowed by an other French mariage* (1579). The visceral imagery of ingestion and absorption conveyed by Stubbs's title is complemented at the opening of his text by an image of penetration and invasion: "The French . . . have sent us hither, not Satan in body of a serpent, but the old serpent in shape of a man, whose sting is in his mouth, and who doth his endeavor to seduce our Eve, that she and we may lose this English paradise."[9] Like the title, the text explicitly homologizes Queen and Country. Stubbs argues that Elizabeth is putting the satisfaction of her (misguided) personal desires before her duty to protect the collective welfare of "her body politic or commonweal body, which is her body of majesty"; in effect, he is engaged in a rhetorical struggle against the royal prerogative for control of the metaphor of the Queen's Two Bodies.[10] Stubbs had the temerity to offer rudely forthright and unsolicited counsel to his prince, and in the process to defame the royalty of France—and to do all this within the public medium of print, in a concerted effort to shape public opinion. For his efforts, the loyal and patriotic Stubbs had his right hand chopped off with a cleaver in the marketplace at Westminster.

The political reasoning underlying the Queen's unusually ferocious response to Stubbs's book is clear in the royal proclamation that was occasioned by its writing, printing, and dissemination:

> No person which hath regard to [the Queen's] honor should esteem of the said seditious book or the maintainers or spreaders thereof otherwise than of a traitorous device to discredit her majesty, both with other princes and with her good subjects, and to prepare their minds to sedition, offering to every most meanest person of judgment by these kind of popular libels authority to argue and determine in every blind corner at their several wills of the affairs of public estate, a thing most pernicious in any estate.[11]

What the regime deemed to be seditious was not merely the specific content of Stubbs's tract but its underlying assumption of a right and duty to debate policy: The specter of "every most meanest person of judgment," arrogating to him or herself the "authority to argue and determine in every blind corner at their several wills of the affairs of public estate" suggests that what the Queen found most alarming and abhorrent about the affair was the regime's inability to shape and control public opinion. Although Queen Elizabeth might sometimes seek the counsel of her privy councillors and favorites, she would not tolerate unsolicited advice even from them, particularly on such sensitive issues as her marriage and the succession. And within the confines of the House of Commons during parliamentary sessions, "free speech" remained a fragile and narrowly circumscribed liberty, only grudgingly granted by the sovereign. In theory, the authoritarian Elizabethan regime made no allowance for an open public sphere; and in practice, it did its best to monitor and constrain its subjects' speculations, opinions, and judgments concerning matters of state. Nevertheless, the offering of unsolicited public advice to the monarch was widely disseminated in printed sermons and tracts, and—in more oblique and coded form—in pageants, plays, poems, and pictures.

However recklessly aired, Stubbs's opinions were by no means extreme; on the contrary, they represented the sentiments of many in the Elizabethan political establishment who were themselves too prudent to publish their thoughts. Others, also adverse to the prospect of a royal marital alliance with an alien prince, found means more congenially elegant and oblique by which to make their point. During this tumultuous period, a number of royal portraits were painted that gave a new iconographic complexity and a mystical resonance to the gendered royal body and to the politics of Elizabethan royal chastity. In each of these portraits, the Queen is represented as holding a riddle, or sieve. The version that interests me here may be the earliest of these; it is dated 1579 and is attributed to George Gower (fig. 32).[12] Near the upper left-hand corner

FIGURE 32
Elizabeth I (the Plimpton "sieve" portrait), by George Gower; 1579. Oil on panel. By permission of the
Folger Shakespeare Library, Washington, DC.

of this painting, behind the Queen, a luminous globe is visible against the dark
background; and this imperial motif is repeated, elaborated, and made more
prominent in subsequent versions, including the celebrated one now in the
Pinacoteca Nazionale di Siena (fig. 33).[13] In Gower's "sieve" portrait, however,
the iconographic focus of attention is upon the sieve itself, the circular form
in the very foreground of the painting. Here Elizabeth holds the allegorical
instrument close to her body—indeed, it appears to be attached to the Queen's

FIGURE 33

Elizabeth I (the Siena "sieve" portrait). Artist unknown; ca. 1580–83. Oil on canvas. Pinacoteca Nazionale, Siena. Su concessione del Ministero per i Beni e le attività culturali. Foto Soprintendeza PSAD Siena & Grosseto.

dress by means of a thick ribbon that is passed through a clasp on the front of her skirt. By this means, the painter makes a tangible connection between the Queen's physical anatomy and the resonant symbolism of the mundane object that she holds in her hand. The sieve constitutes a displacement of the Queen's sexuality. The interpretive question concerns how that sexuality is being symbolized in the sieve.

Roy Strong has established the presence of two iconographic traditions for the sieve represented in this group of portraits. One of these is the iconography of virginity, deriving from the tradition of "the Roman Vestal Virgin, Tuccia, who, on being accused of impurity, filled a sieve with water from the River Tiber and carried it without spilling one drop to the Temple."[14] The other tradition is that of the emblem book, in which the sieve represents the power of discernment, the ability to sift the good from the bad—or, as Geffrey Whitney put it in his version of the emblem, "to purge the seedes, / From chaffe" (fig. 34).[15] William Camden reported that the most common of Queen Elizabeth's many "heroicall devises" was "a Sive without a Motte."[16] However, the sieve in this and other such portraits does carry a motto upon its rim: *A terra il ben mal dimora insella* (literally, "to earth the good bad remains in the saddle"). This not altogether coherent motto appears to allude to the emblematic interpretive tradition, that of discernment; on the other hand, its obscurity and individuality of reference remind us that here the universal applicability of the *emblem* is being subordinated to the elite and recondite tradition of the *impresa*.[17] The confluence of the two discrete iconographic traditions in these portraits produces a logically contradictory icon, one that must represent the properties of impermeability and (selective) permeability simultaneously. It is perhaps for this reason that the sieve as pictured does not conform to either tradition. The Queen is shown neither winnowing grain nor carrying water. Instead, she holds an empty sieve in a vertical position that emphasizes its circular form and thus its analogical relationship both to her own female anatomy and to the globe that appears in the background. The visual argument that connects the sieve both to the Queen's sexuality and to England's imperial destiny is grounded in this formal equivalence. If the image of the sieve in this painting invokes two conventional and mutually exclusive iconographic frameworks, it also visually subverts them in the interests of a paradoxical "heroicall devise" uniquely appropriate to a virgin queen whose realm is an empire.

The painting's iconographic ambiguity extends to the identification of Elizabeth with Tuccia. Acceptance of this identification implies that the Queen, too, had been subject to charges or rumors of unchastity and was in need of vindication; and, indeed, there is much documentary evidence that this was the case. For example, during the course of the 1571 Anglo-French royal marriage negotiations, Catherine de' Medici, dowager Queen of France, remarked to Elizabeth's ambassadors that "it is all the hurt that evil men can do to Noble Women and Princes, to spread abroad lies and dishonourable tales of them, and . . . we of all Princes that be women, are subject to be slandered wrongfully of them that be our adversaries." She was speaking of her son's prospective

To THO. STVTVILE *Eſquier.*

I N fruictefull feilde amid the goodlie croppe,
The hurtfull tares, and dernell ofte doe growe,
And many times, doe mounte aboue the toppe
Of higheſt corne: But ſkilfull man doth knowe,
     When graine is ripe, with fiue to purge the ſeedes,
     From chaffe, and duſte, and all the other weedes.

Ouid. 5. Triſt. 4.
Viue ſine inuidia, mol-
léſque inglorius annos
Exige, amicitiaſ &
tibi iunge pares.

By which is ment, ſith wicked men abounde,
That harde it is, the good from bad to trie:
The prudent forte, ſhoulde haue ſuche iudgement ſounde,
That ſtill the good they ſhoulde from bad deſcrie:
     And ſifte the good, and to diſcerne their deedes,
     And weye the bad, noe better then the weedes.

                                  Interiora

FIGURE 34
"Sic discerne," in Geffrey Whitney, *A Choice of Emblemes* (Leyden, 1586), 68. By permission of the Folger Shakespeare Library, Washington, DC.

bride, and alluding to those rumors of Elizabeth's promiscuity—in particular, her intimacy with Dudley—that had circulated widely among the Queen's common and gentle subjects and throughout the courts of Europe since the very beginning of the reign.[18] International gossipmongering about Elizabeth's sexual conduct and appetites was particularly rife during the first two decades of the reign, when she was the top prize on the European marriage market and used that position as a central instrument of her foreign policy. Ambiguity of sexual reference also extends to the sieve itself, both because the agrarian purpose of this humble tool—the material basis of the emblem—was to allow passage to what Whitney calls "seedes," while barring passage to "chaffe," and because the inscription's equation of the sieve with a saddle reinforces an allusion to sexual activity.[19]

An answer to the riddle of the sieve may lie obscured in the topical context of the Anjou courtship, as Doris Adler has suggested.[20] Nevertheless, the portrait does not merely celebrate the Queen's virginity but puts it into semiotic play: In the very process of exalting Elizabeth's chastity, the painting glances at the persistent rumors of her unchastity and at those eroticized elements of her personal style and conduct which had fed such rumors; and in the very process of celebrating the Queen's powers of discernment and her autonomy, it perpetuates that erotic style and so sustains the politics of desire whereby her suitors strove to possess her favor and her councillors sought to constrain her will. Queen Elizabeth's courtships—her shrewd deployment of her ambiguous status as both a virgin ruler and a prospective royal bride—were of central importance to the geopolitical aims and strategies of her regime; and this centrality is underlined by the conspicuous presence of the globe in each of the "sieve" portraits. The iconographic ambiguities in these pictures give visual form to the courtship dynamics that were a hallmark of Elizabethan statecraft. The "sieve" portraits are not merely celebrations of royal chastity; they are compelling icons of Elizabethan eroto-politics, as these were played out both within the ambiance of the court and upon the global stage.

My final example comes from the beginning of the last decade of the reign. The so-called Ditchley portrait of the Queen was painted in the early 1590s by Marcus Gheeraerts the Younger (fig. 35). By this time, marriage negotiations were no longer a viable instrument of Elizabethan diplomacy; and, among Elizabethan subjects, growing signs of alienation from their aged and barren Queen impelled the promotion of her image as a virgin mother to her people. The painting takes its modern title from the placement of Elizabeth's feet in Oxfordshire, in the vicinity of Ditchley, which was the estate of Sir Henry Lee.

FIGURE 35

Elizabeth I (the "Ditchley" portrait), by Marcus Gheeraerts the Younger; ca. 1592. Oil on canvas. National Portrait Gallery, London.

Lee was a central figure in the development of the Accession Day tournaments that are a hallmark of the Elizabeth cult, and was the Queen's champion until his retirement from the tilt in 1590. In a poem commemorating the 1590 tilts and the occasion of Lee's retirement, George Peele created a contemporaneous literary analogue to the visual rhetoric of the Ditchley portrait. Here he lauded the Queen as

> Elizabeth great empress of the world,
> Britanias Atlas, Star of Englands globe,
> That swaies the massie scepter of her land,
> And holdes the royall raynes of Albion.[21]

Elizabeth visited Lee at Ditchley during her progress of 1592, and it has been surmised that the picture commemorated or was originally a part of her entertainment there.[22] Certainly, the Ditchley portrait has a special place in the collective project of royal adulation that Lee had done so much to establish and sustain. The visual hyperbole of this painting makes it emblematic of the cult of Elizabeth in its post-Armada phase: Here is the glorious and beneficent public image of an increasingly isolated monarch and her authoritarian regime.

The figure of Elizabeth in the Ditchley portrait is exquisitely clothed in a richly embroidered and bejeweled gown of maidenly white silk with silver thread; the matching hanging sleeves extend to the ground, creating an appearance of angel's wings. The cosmic background divides into sunlight and storm. According to the now-fragmentary sonnet inscribed on the canvas, these signify, respectively, the heavenly glory and divine power of which the Queen is the earthly mirror. The sonnet form of the inscription, and its still partially legible images and tropes, link it to the hybrid Petrarchan and Neoplatonic royal panegyrics that were the currency of court poetry and pageantry in the 1590s. The sonnet's opening sentence—which reads simply "The prince of light"—announces the visual image as an apotheosis of Queen Elizabeth. In John Bossy's terms, the Ditchley portrait seems intended to situate its beholders in a condition of monarcholatry. The sonnet functions as an appropriate title of address to the mortal deity who, as God's anointed substitute, embodies the sun that shines upon England. That the Queen is also heralded by storm and lightning is a reminder that power coexists with grace in the royal demeanor, and thus that she simultaneously inspires both love and fear. As Sir John Harington put it in an epistolary recollection of his late Queen and godmother, "When she smiled, it was a pure sun-shine, that every one did chuse to baske in, if they could; but anon came a storm from a sudden gathering of clouds, and the thunder fell in wondrous manner on all alike."[23]

Gheeraert's splendid painting, the largest known portrait of Queen Elizabeth, represents her like some great goddess or a transfigured Virgin Mary, standing with her feet upon the surface of the globe and her head amidst the heavens. Much of the monarch's island nation is enclosed by the hem of her gown and hanging sleeves, a compositional feature perhaps recalling the iconography of the *Madonna della misericordia*, which was widely disseminated in England during the fourteenth and fifteenth centuries and represented Mary as Our Lady of Mercy, spreading her cloak over the mortal suppliants gathered at her feet.[24] In 1601, in what was to be her final parliamentary address, Queen Elizabeth described herself as "a taper of trewe virgin waxe to wast my self and spend my life that I might give light and comfort to those that lived under me." Similarly, upon the death of the Queen, Thomas Dekker played upon this Elizabethan appropriation of Marian imagery, describing his late queen as one who had "brought up even under her wing a nation that was almost begotten and born under her, that never shouted any other *ave* but for her name, never saw the face of any prince but herself."[25] Such verbal images are visually literalized in the Ditchley portrait. It represents the Queen as standing upon her land and sheltering it under her skirts, suggesting thereby a mystical identification of the inviolate female body of the monarch with the unbreached body of her land. At the same time, it affirms her distinctive role as the maternal protectress of her people. She is both "a Virgin Mother and a Maiden Queene"—both the Pelican and the Phoenix.[26]

This painting also compellingly asserts another aspect of Elizabeth's personal symbolism that derives from her body politic—namely, her princely rule; it affirms her power over her land and over its inhabitants. The Ditchley portrait is perhaps the most spectacular Elizabethan conjunction of cartographic and royal images. Indeed, if (in J. B. Harley's words) early modern maps were "spatial emblems of power in society," which "still retained some of the crucial communicative properties of pictures," then the Ditchley portrait is in some ways both picture and map.[27] In the painting, the Queen stands upon a cartographic image of Britain, closely imitating Christopher Saxton's 1583 printed map of England and Wales.[28] The map within the picture divides England into counties, each separately colored, and marks principal towns and rivers. Here it is important to emphasize the iconographic significance of placing the Elizabeth figure not on an image of the island of Britain but rather on a *map* of England and Wales. She is not positioned on a visual representation of a physical place; rather, she stands on a graphic representation of the political space that has already been imposed upon that place. The map inscribes territoriality upon the land, transforming part of an island into a state; and by the division of the state into the counties that constituted its core administrative units, its inhabitants are more precisely and securely marked as the monarch's subjects.

Roy Strong comments that "in the 'Ditchley' portrait Queen, crown, and island become one. Elizabeth is England, woman and kingdom are interchangeable."[29] This seems to me to be only partially true, for it elides the theme of sovereign power and rule that is emphasized both in the icon and in its accompanying verses. In melding the nurturant mother with the absolute ruler, the representational resources of the Ditchley portrait are concentrated not only upon Elizabeth's *identification with* England but also and primarily upon Elizabeth's *possession of* England. One of the most remarkable aspects of the Ditchley portrait is the deftness with which it employs both iconic and textual resources to synthesize cartographic, Petrarchan, and Marian tropes in the service of royal autocracy. In terms of its sheer scale—both its physical size and its imaginative scope, its realization of the divine source of royal power in the superhuman proportions of the royal body—the Ditchley portrait strikes me as perhaps the most brilliant Elizabethan equivalent of Holbein's icon of Henrician kingship (figs. 3, 4). Although it produces its effects by means radically different from Holbein's phallic symbolization of kingly *virtù*, the Ditchley portrait of Queen Elizabeth seems designed to elicit from its beholders feelings of awe and devotion, love and fear, and an unquestioning assent to their own subjection.

Policy in Pictures

In later sixteenth-century Europe, policy makers paid attention to pictorial representations of geopolitical conflict and negotiation. Such, at least, is the conclusion that could be drawn from a dispatch sent from London by the Spanish ambassador on 2 March 1583:

> The picture they sent from Flanders represents a cow, signifying the States, with his Majesty mounted thereon and spurring it till the blood flows. Orange is depicted milking the animal, whilst a lady, to represent the queen of England, is giving it a little hay with one hand, and holding out a porringer to Orange with the other, and Alençon is holding on by the tail.[1]

The allegorical panel painting to which Mendoza was presumably referring (fig. 36) epitomizes in both word and image the complexity of the political situation of the seventeen provinces that constituted the Low Countries: in addition to being collectively a site of convergence of Spanish, English, and French strategic interests, they were also divided among themselves in terms of their particular traditions, leadership, loyalties, and aspirations, and were individually riven by sectarian strife.[2]

This picture provides compelling evidence that it was not only appropriations of the royal image by its domestic and foreign enemies that were beyond the effective control of the Elizabethan regime but also those made by its clients and allies in the Low Countries, who employed the Elizabethan image in their efforts to promote an aggressive Anglo-Dutch opposition—religious, political, and military—to imperial Spain. Within the Queen's own Privy Council, such aims had long been championed by the Earl of Leicester and Sir Francis Walsingham, among others. However, the conservative Queen had long regarded full military and political engagement in the Low Countries

NOT LONGE TIME SINCE I SAWE A COWE.
DID FLAVNDERS REPRESENTE.
VPON WHOSE BACKE KINGE PHILIP RODE
AS BEING MALECONTNT.

THE QVEENE OF ENGLAND GIVING HAY
WHEARE ON THE COW DID FEEDE.
AS ONE THAT WAS HER GREATEST HELPE.
IN HER DISTRESSE AND NEEDE.

THE PRINCE OF ORANGE MILKT THE C[O]
AND MADE HIS PVRSE THE PAYLE.
THE COW DID SHYT IN MONSIEVRS HAN[D]
WHILE HE DID HOLD HER TAYLE.

FIGURE 36

Allegory of the Low Countries, with Philip II, Elizabeth I, William of Orange, and the duc d'Anjou. Artist unknown; ca. 1583. Oil on panel. Rijksmuseum, Amsterdam.

with deep suspicion, as a financially extravagant and strategically risky continental entanglement on behalf of those whose reformist religious beliefs and republican political tendencies she regarded with considerable suspicion. She was reluctant to commit herself to a direct alliance with those whom she uncomfortably perceived to be subjects in rebellion against their legitimate ruler—her fellow monarch, former benefactor, and archenemy King Philip of Spain.[3] In seeking to check Spanish power without recourse to open war, Elizabeth preferred to support the inept military and political adventures of a French Catholic prince—her sometime wooer, François, duc d'Anjou and formerly duc d'Alençon. In the absence of direct English intervention, Anjou had been invited into the Low Countries in order to counter Spanish hegemony, first as "Defender of the Liberties of the Low Countries" and then in 1581 as "Prince and Lord of the Netherlands." Although his election was facilitated by William of Orange, Anjou's regime was mistrusted by the more militant Dutch Protestants, who continued to hope for an explicit league with England. The latter finally materialized in 1585, leading to the Earl of Leicester's ostentatious but brief and ultimately disastrous episode as Governor-General of the Netherlands.[4]

The English inscription borne by the picture described by the Spanish ambassador represents the Queen of England as the savior of Flanders: "ONE THAT WAS HER GREATEST HELPE, / IN HER DISTRESSE AND NEEDE." This encomium comes at the expense, not only of the "MALECONTNT" [sic] King Philip, but also of the Protestant Prince of Orange (who "MILKT THE COW AND MADE HIS PVRSE THE PAYLE") and the French Catholic duc d'Anjou ("THE COW DID SHYT IN MONSIEVRS HAND / WHILE HE DID HOLD HER TAYLE"). Although it is a panel painted in oils, the style and tone of this work give it an affinity with the satirical print.[5] The inscription identifies the cow specifically with Flanders, and Mendoza's dispatch suggests that the picture's provenance was Flemish. Around this time, among strongly Reformist Flemings there was intense resentment toward their erstwhile protector, the duc d'Anjou, as well as mistrust of the Prince of Orange for what was perceived to be his collusion with the opportunistic and incompetent French occupiers.[6]

The intended viewers of the picture that so interested the Spanish ambassador were presumably the Queen and her advisers. If so, its intended purpose was to exhort Elizabeth to emulate the image by augmenting the financial and military resources already committed to the cause—and, perhaps, formally to assume an English protectorate of the Low Countries, as favored by some in the Dutch States General and in the English Privy Council. As expressed in a parliamentary speech prepared for delivery to the Queen in 1587, the hope was that the Low Countries "should of olde assured freindes become adopted chyldren to your Majesties, and felloe subjectes with our selves."[7] Whatever the details of the diplomatic and political maneuverings that gave rise to the picture, of primary concern here is way its images personify and gender the discourse of geopolitics. As the bountiful maternal body of the Flemish cow is subjected to various abuses and degradations by the three princes, six Flemish gentlemen steady her head and look for succor to the imposingly large and magnificently costumed figure of the English Queen. Her hands filled with rustic offerings of food and drink, Elizabeth appears in the left foreground as at once a goddess of the harvest and a regal personification of Charity.

In a roughly contemporaneous although more skillfully executed picture, King Philip again rides and spurs the theriomorphic Netherlands; but here the cow is being milked by the Duke of Alva, the Spanish military commander in the Low Countries, rather than by the Dutch Protestant William, Prince of Orange (fig. 37).[8] In benign contrast to the Spaniards' acts of brutal oppression and exploitation, Orange steadies the cow's horns while Queen Elizabeth feeds hay to the docile beast. An oddly sympathetic resonance between the English Queen and the Low Countries is created in each picture by virtue of the fact that both are represented as nurturingly maternal figures, in pictorial

FIGURE 37
Allegory of the Low Countries, with Philip II, Elizabeth I, William of Orange, the duc d'Anjou, and the
Duke of Alva. Artist unknown; ca. 1584–86. Oil on panel. Private collection. Photo courtesy of the
National Portrait Gallery, London.

fields otherwise occupied by men. In the second picture, as in the first, it
is Anjou who literally brings up the rear: As he pulls on the cow's tail, she
unceremoniously sprays his finery with her feces. Those responsible for this
painting were apparently looking to Queen Elizabeth to aid the Low Countries
against a resurgence of Spanish hegemony and to relieve them from their
reliance upon the opportunistic and incompetent Anjou; at the same time,
they were promoting the Prince of Orange as England's natural ally and agent
in this endeavor.[9]

These two variant pictures serve to suggest that, in certain instances, groups
or individuals within England's governing circle had a vested interest in, and
may even have encouraged or commissioned, the production and circulation
of foreign images that sought presumptuously to influence royal attitudes
and policies. As in the present examples, such images and their makers were
potentially objectionable to Elizabeth both in their policy implications and in
their indecorous tone toward their social betters. The latter included not only
the Queen herself but also foreign princes—and, in particular, Anjou, her
suitor and client, whose prestige had now become intertwined with her own.

These paired paintings exemplify the unstable and contentious nature of both policy making and picture making within the political culture of Elizabethan England.

As the preceding discussion has suggested, it is frequently misleading to speak impersonally of the Elizabethan *regime* or the Elizabethan *state*, if such terms are meant to imply a cohesive or homogeneous set of corporate policies, strategies, or interests. Roy Strong has noted that, unlike the Valois or Habsburg monarchs, Elizabeth "was never to have a court painter well paid by the crown and hence be able to sustain government control over her own image."[10] This is a crucial point, but its formulation is questionable to the degree that it implies that the Queen and her "government" were synonymous. Individuals and factions within the Privy Council and the political elite assiduously pursued their own interests and also habitually struggled over matters of policy, both among themselves and with their sovereign. These agendas and struggles frequently impressed themselves upon iconic, textual, and theatrical representations of Queen Elizabeth. Thus, not only were the monarch and her government unable to maintain effective control over the production and distribution of the royal image from unofficial and foreign sources, but the very notion of an "official" image is itself more vexed and less stable than it is usually considered to be. And, in any case, whatever the intent of "official" images, there was no guarantee that the perceptions of those who viewed them would conform to it.

Many entries in Elizabethan state papers demonstrate that ambassadors and other English agents abroad were always on the lookout for texts and images that defamed their Queen and so traduced the Elizabethan state. One office seeker, writing to Vice Chamberlain Sir Thomas Heneage in 1590, promoted himself on the basis of the loyal services he had performed in France in the prior decade, "as in adventuring my life in pulling down her Majesty's picture from a pair of gallows where it was hanged up."[11] In most cases, however, such loyal Elizabethans had little recourse other than to lodge formal protests, or to attempt the clandestine seizure and destruction of materials they found to be offensive. The dispatches addressed to Sir Francis Walsingham by Sir Edward Stafford, English ambassador in Paris during the 1580s, are especially revealing in this regard.[12] During this period, leading up to and immediately following the execution of Mary, Queen of Scots, in 1587, Paris was a hotbed for the production in both word and image of Marian apologetics and anti-Elizabethan invectives of Scottish, French, papal, and English expatriate Catholic provenance.

On 17 November 1583—which happened to be the anniversary of the Queen's accession, the high holiday of the Elizabeth cult—Stafford wrote in confidence to Walsingham regarding

> a fowle picture of the Q. majesties sett upp she beinge on horsback her left hande holdinge the brydell of the horse, with her right hande pullynge upp her clothes shewinge her hindparte Sir reverence. Uppon her hed written *la Reine d'Angleterre* verses under neethe signifiynge thatt yf anye Inglish man thatt passed by weere asked he kowlde tell whatt and whoose the picture was.
>   under ytt was a picture of *Monsieurs* verie well-drawen in his best apparell havynge uppon his fiste a hawke which continually bayted and kowlde never make her sytt styll.[13]

According to Stafford, copies were set up in three places around Paris, although they had disappeared by the time Stafford's agents went to find them. Stafford assumed that English Catholic exiles were among the perpetrators: "I am afrayde soome of our good Inglish men heere have a parte in ytt for I thinke theire are nott manye nawghtie people in the worlde as somme of them be." Having dallied for several years with the prospect of marrying Anjou ("Monsieur"), Elizabeth had finally rid herself of her ardent suitor in 1582. With Elizabeth's blessing and her clandestine financial support, Anjou departed for the Low Countries; by the time that these rude pictures appeared in Paris, however, his campaign had already ended in disaster and he had returned ignominiously to France.

In the "fowle picture of the Q. majesties" reported by Stafford, a mixture of religious, political, and national antipathies was being directed toward the supreme governor of the reformed English church and the head of the English state. What is relevant here is that these ideological antipathies were being given a compelling representational form in an *ad feminam* attack upon the person of Elizabeth Tudor—in a symbolic degradation of her regal and ecclesiastical authority by the exposure of her lower body and its base functions: "her right hande pullynge upp her clothes shewinge her hindparte Sir reverence." As the context suggests, and as other recorded instances verify, Stafford's interjection—"Sir reverence"—is an Elizabethan euphemism for defecation.[14] The use of scatological insult as a vehicle for political satire or dissent would seem to have had some currency in Elizabethan culture. In 1585, for example, one Peter Vanhill, "of St Mary's parish, Sandwich, labourer," was indicted for having said in public, "Shyte uppon your Queene; I woulde to god shee were dead that I might shytt on her face."[15] Stafford's report withholds specifics of the relationship between the Queen's picture and that of Anjou, which was positioned below it; still, Stafford does write that "in my opinion ytt towcheth

FIGURE 38
Queen Elizabeth and Pope Gregory XIII as Diana and Callisto, by Pieter van der Heyden; ca. 1584–85.
Engraving. © The Trustees of The British Museum.

more *Monsieurs* honor then the Q. yf everie bodye interprett ytt as I dooe."
Although the primary intent of the cartoon was presumably to vent anti-
Elizabethan sentiments and its purported agents were English Catholic exiles,
Stafford's comment suggests that the French prince was also being mocked and
degraded by the gross gesture imposed upon the image of the English Queen.
Such a scatological deflation may well be implied by the letter's emphasis on
how well Anjou's figure was drawn and how finely it was dressed. There would
seem to be a quite precise analogy, then, between this representation of Anjou
and those in the contemporaneous allegorical paintings discussed above (figs.
36, 37): in effect, the French prince—whom Elizabeth had nicknamed her
"frog"—gets the same treatment from the equestrian English queen as he
gets from the Dutch cow.[16] Although details are lacking, Stafford's comment
implies that while the Queen was being dishonored in the Parisian cartoon,
her representation was also a means of dishonoring Anjou, and that the latter
effect was grounded in the relative genders, poses, and spatial positions of
these two figures. In effect, this was an obscene twist upon the ubiquitous
satirical *topos* of the woman-on-top.[17]

To the image reported by Stafford, I wish to juxtapose another representation of the Queen, also made beyond the boundaries of the realm and at about the same time. This one is panegyrical rather than hostile; but, like the reported Parisian cartoon, it appropriates and works upon the gendered and sexualized royal body for its own polemical ends. By the mid 1580s—that is, within two years of the defamatory placard reported by Stafford—a Dutch Protestant engraving was in circulation that used Elizabeth to condemn the Pope and Catholic atrocities in the Low Countries (fig. 38).[18] The striking image engraved by Pieter van der Heyden is clearly a parody of Titian's mythological picture of Diana and Callisto; and the engraving's iconography and polemical thrust are fully intelligible only when they are read in relation to the image in Titian's painting (fig. 39).[19] Titian derives his subject from the second book of Ovid's *Metamorphosis* (2.451 ff.), in which the goddess of chastity discovers and punishes the pregnancy of one of her own nymphs. In Ovid's story, Callisto's predicament is the consequence of her rape by Jupiter, who had transformed

FIGURE 39

Diana and Callisto, by Titian; 1559. Oil on canvas. Duke of Sutherland Collection, on loan to the National Gallery of Scotland, Edinburgh.

himself into the likeness of Diana in order to approach Callisto unawares. Van der Heyden displaces onto the Pope the transsexuality of Ovid's pagan god, and simultaneously renders him a perverse parody of the pregnant Callisto. While its central focus is on antipapal satire, the engraving also constitutes a provocation to Philip II, the Low Countries' nominal sovereign. "Diana and Callisto" was one of a series of paintings on erotic Ovidian subjects executed by Titian for Philip of Spain—the scourge of the Dutch Protestants, Queen Elizabeth's sometime brother-in-law and suitor, and England's implacable foe.[20] By metamorphosing Titian's singular mythological painting into a replicable and easily disseminated vehicle of religio-political satire, Van der Heyden and his collaborators were engaged in a complex act of cultural appropriation. By exhorting the reluctant Queen of England to intervene in the Low Countries on behalf of the Protestants and against their Spanish and Catholic enemies, they were in effect using King Philip's magnificent artistic possession against him.

The right half of van der Heyden's print is occupied by a nude Elizabeth-Diana, crowned and enthroned, and attended by four of her nymphs. The latter are labeled in the print as allegories of the Dutch provinces of Holland, Guelderland, Zeeland, and Friesland. From her elevated position, Elizabeth-Diana gestures disdainfully toward the figure of Pope Gregory–Callisto, who occupies the lower left foreground. The Pope's shame is discovered by the Reformation allegories of Time and Truth, who have replaced the classical nymphs of Titian's painting. They reveal the Pope to be incubating a nest of allegorical eggs, from which his monstrous brood is hatching. These include such anti-Protestant atrocities as the assassination of William of Orange, the Inquisition, and the St. Bartholomew's Day Massacre. Inscribed in a cartouche in the lower right-hand corner of the print are verses in Dutch addressed to Elizabeth. While exalting her, they also caution her against "that crowned beast" which "causes many evil deeds"; she is enjoined to "remember the death of the Prince of Orange," who had recently been assassinated, and to succor the Low Countries against Spanish Catholic oppression.[21]

A favorite icon of the English Reformation displayed the King enthroned, with the Pope beneath his feet—a celebration of the Royal Supremacy as a reversal of the infamous submission of the Emperor Frederick Barbarossa to Pope Alexander III. A notable version of this icon is the woodcut of Henry VIII and Pope Clement VII, first printed in the 1570 edition of John Foxe's *Actes and Monumentes* (fig. 40). From about the same date, the anonymous painting of Edward VI as heir to the antipapal legacy of Henry VIII (fig. 21) incorporates a variant of this motif.[22] Van der Heyden's print translates the iconic topos of imperial triumph over papal tyranny into the language of erotic Ovidian

The Pope suppressed by K. Henry the eight.

Papa citò moritur, Cæsar regnabit vbiq, Et subito vani cessabunt gaudia cleri.

FIGURE 40

Henry VIII and Archbishop Cranmer holding the Bible in English, with Pope Clement VII under the King's feet. Artist unknown. Woodcut. Printed in John Foxe, *The Actes and Monuments*, 2nd ed. (London, 1570), 2.1201. By permission of the British Library (BL 4705.h.4).

myth, in which an enthroned goddess asserts her power and authority over her wayward handmaiden. It seems obvious that this was a conceit to which the artist's wit was prompted by the gender and sexual status of the Queen, and by her already established association with the iconography of Diana. In the print, the regal nudity of Elizabeth-Diana provides a striking contrast to the forced exposure of Gregory-Callisto. The masculine visage, papal tiara, female torso, and monstrous fertility of the latter seem to suggest a conflation of the effeminated Pope with his allegorical companion in sin, the Whore of Babylon.[23]

Religion, gender, sexuality, and social status interact in complex and curious ways when Elizabeth is associated with the militantly chaste virgin goddess of the hunt, at the same time that the Pope is associated with the unclean nymph who is Diana's disgraced attendant. The print hyperbolically reaffirms the maidenly virtue of the English Queen, who had been much defamed in Catholic propaganda, while personifying hypocritical false chastity in the Pope. In Titian's painting and its Ovidian source, the handmaiden had been a victim of the wrathful goddess; in the Van Heyden print, however, the Queen justly arraigns the Pope for his victimization of others. The print works its complex polemical ends by bringing to bear upon the grotesque body of the Pope pervasive cultural notions about gender hierarchy and about the rampant female sexuality that was held both to necessitate that hierarchy and to subvert it; and in the same paradoxical operation, the resources of misogyny serve to aggrandize the moral authority and political charisma of a female prince.

Although the Dutch print engraved by Van der Heyden and the Parisian cartoon reported by Stafford have antithetical polemical aims, they have in common the formulation of urgent religious and geopolitical agendas in terms of the shaming of a grotesque female body—a formulation articulated in a gesture of exposure, an act of discovery, which lifts the robes of propriety to reveal the obscenity beneath. Such misogynistically inflected body imagery is an essential element in the ideological armory of sixteenth-century conflict. For example, the same form of iconomachy is at work in the contemporaneous first book of *The Faerie Queene* (1590): Spenser's "Legende of Holinesse" initially confronts the Redcrosse Knight with the book-vomiting monster Errour and "her fruitfull cursed spawne of serpents small" (1.1.22); and ultimately it discovers the maidenly Duessa to be a hideously misshapen witch (1.8.46–49).[24] The description of Catherine de Medici and her sons in a 1587 House of Commons speech by Job Throckmorton provides a close textual analogue to Van der Heyden's pictorial image. Throckmorton declares that the dowager Queen of France

> hath not many (thankes bee to God) lefte of her loynes to pester the earth with. And those that she hath yet lyving ... she may have as much comforte of them as the adder hath of her broode.... Queen Mother may sure bragge ... that shee hath brought us into this world suche a litter ... whose principall delight (synce they came first out of the shell) hath bin in nothinge almost but in hypochrisye, filthynesse of life, and persecuting of the Church of God.[25]

In terms of agenda, imagery, and tone, this impassioned English speech devoted to the apocalyptic struggle for the soul of the Low Countries shows a remarkable affinity with the contemporaneous Dutch engraving.

Van der Heyden produces an ingeniously gender-bending variation upon such venerable antifeminist topoi, thus appropriating them to serve the purposes of antipapal rather than anti-Elizabethan satire. The engraving effects a reversal of gender types, in which a virtuous and heroic female prince sits in judgment upon a degradingly feminized pope. This paradox of gendered authority is compounded by the paradox that Elizabeth's desired leadership of the Protestant cause is symbolized in her identification with a *pagan* goddess. Through its iconic allusion to the subject of Titian's painting, the Dutch print achieves a visual similitude of Elizabeth-as-Diana. As we have seen in part two above, it was the usual practice of English artists or Netherlanders working in England to make the iconic connection between Elizabeth and Diana by means of a discreet crescent moon. In van der Heyden's engraving, the identification of the Queen with the goddess is mediated through pictorial quotation or parody; at the same time, however, the classical personification of the Queen is also being made both more precise and more central. Perhaps the most audacious aspect of this Dutch image is to break decisively with the decorum of English practice by presenting the Queen-as-Diana in the nude. It is likely that Elizabeth herself would have been deeply offended by her unauthorized representation in such a figure. It is also plausible that the godly would have considered this iconic strategy to have been tainted by pagan idolatry. Of course, if idolatrous associations had been activated in the minds of some who viewed the print, the consequence would have been to subvert the absolute contrast between the Queen and the Pope that the print was clearly intended to promote. To the extent that this presumably unintended effect was a latent possibility, Van der Heyden's manifestly celebratory image demonstrates that ideological contradiction was inherent in the iconography of Elizabeth.

Purity and Danger

The work of the geopolitical imaginary in later sixteenth-century Europe is exemplified in polemical images like van der Heyden's, which sharply personalize Elizabethan England's struggles with the Papacy and with Philippine Spain. The present chapter explores the personified confrontation of England and Spain by focusing upon the interplay of gender and nation in verbal and visual constructions of the Armada and in related representations of martial prowess. I would like to preface this exploration with a perspective from the periphery, by juxtaposing two English reports of how Irishmen in rebellion against England's queen expressed the Anglo-Spanish interaction and their own relationship to it.

My first example is contained in a letter written around 1586 and describes events in Connaught:

> The Commissioners were no sooner departed, than the rebels began to break down castles and burn towns. They made most odious speeches against her Majesty, saying, "What have we do with that *caliaghe*? How unwise are we, being so mighty a nation, to have been so long subject to a woman! The Pope and the King of Spain shall have the rule of us, and none other."[1]

The writer's invocation of the Gaelic word *caliaghe* or *cailleach*—signifying a hag—inflects this derogation of the Queen in terms of corrupt and malign female sexuality, sorcery, and bodily decay.[2] Irish subjection to England is thus cast explicitly in terms of a shameful inversion of gender hierarchy: By their fealty to the Pope and the King of Spain, true Irishmen overthrow tyrannous female regiment and reassert their heroic manhood. The declaration here attributed to the Irish rebels interlinks affiliations grounded in ethnicity, religion, and gender.

My second example, from an English field report on the Irish military campaign in 1600, includes the following remark: "All the way we burned all their houses in their fastnesses and woods. In one of them was found the Queen's picture behind the door, and the King of Spain's at the upper end of the table."[3] Here an image of Ireland's nominal sovereign, the English and Protestant Queen, has been displaced from the position of honor and reverence by an image of the Spanish and Catholic King—presumably, the recently deceased Philip II, who had repeatedly sought to exploit English vulnerabilities in Ireland. It appears that the relative disposition of these two royal portraits within a colonized domestic space was interpreted by the English as a confirmation of the inhabitants' treason.

Construed together, these two anecdotes encapsulate the topics dealt with in this chapter: the expression and manipulation of geopolitical dynamics within the symbolic space of textual and iconic representations; the gendered personification of the opposing strategic interests and national characters of England and Spain in contrasting images of Queen Elizabeth and King Philip; the tendency of Protestant propagandists to pose the opposition of the Queen of England to the King of Spain and the Pope in terms of an apocalyptic contest between the forces of good and evil—and of some Catholic propagandists to do likewise, but with the terms reversed.

The so-called "Armada" portraits of Queen Elizabeth contribute to the shaping of that complex and contingent event into an English national myth.[4] The paradoxical iconic strategy of these paintings is to embody a collective assertion of national strength and imperial ambition in the Queen's virginal self-containment. The version of the "Armada" portrait that I reproduce and discuss here is (like the 1579 "sieve" portrait, fig. 32) attributed to George Gower, who was appointed the Queen's Serjeant Painter in 1581 (fig. 41).[5] The Queen's stylized face, surrounded by a large lace ruff, appears like a sunburst between two distant maritime views, each of which is framed by columns. On the Queen's right, English fire ships advance toward the Spanish fleet; on her left, the remains of King Philip's *Armada Invencible* are tempest-tossed and wrecked upon the rocky coast of Ireland. As Roy Strong reads the image,

> The theme is that of imperial triumph for, whereas in both versions of the "Sieve" portrait a decade before, the terrestrial globe was relegated to the background with a motto prognosticating imperial expansion, it is here placed in the Queen's hand after the manner of the Roman emperors. This theme is emphasized in the crown which is deliberately placed above the globe.[6]

FIGURE 41
Elizabeth I (the "Armada" portrait), attributed to George Gower; 1588(?). Oil on panel. By kind
permission of His Grace the Duke of Bedford and the Trustees of the Bedford Estates.

To Strong's helpful explication of this conventional, if esoteric, imperial
iconography, I would add the suggestion of a more idiosyncratic, corporeal,
and gender-coded iconography. In effect, the latter imagines the Queen's body
politic in terms that derive from her female body natural. Both the "sieve"
and the "Armada" portrait groups make an iconic connection between the
English sovereign's virtuous chastity and the English nation's emerging power
and influence across the globe.

The corporeal iconography manifested in the "Armada" portraits developed as a visual equivalent for the proliferating literature on the Virgin Queen.
This, in turn, drew upon a rich tradition of panegyrical and descriptive discourses, both sacred and profane, deriving from the cult of Mary and from
scriptural sources, on the one hand, and from the iconography of Diana and
from Ovidian, Petrarchan, Neoplatonic, and pastoral literary conventions, on
the other.[7] In countless Renaissance erotic texts, poet-lovers catalogued their
ladies' parts in tropes comparing them to precious stones, metals, flowers, and
fruits. The "Armada" portraits work rather more obliquely than such blazons,
by displacing features of the Queen's numinous body onto the patterning and

decoration of the dress that covers it. The strategy is analogous to those involving the placement of the book and the attachment of the sieve in portraits that I have already discussed (figs. 8, 32); here, however, the mystico-political efficacy of the royal body is at its clearest. In all three of the extant "Armada" portraits, at the appropriate spot—the apex of the inverted triangle formed by the queen's stomacher—in the place of a codpiece, the beholder's attention is drawn to a lace ribbon that is tied in an unusually large and ostentatious bow. Resting upon this bow are a rich jewel in an elaborate setting and a large teardrop pearl pendant; both of them attached to a girdle that is also composed of precious stones and pearls. As in the Armada year portrait of Ralegh as the Queen's devotee (fig. 23), pearls are conspicuous here because they were Elizabeth's signature jewel and conventionally associated with chastity.[8]

In the case of the "Armada" portrait under discussion here, as in virtually every other instance of Elizabethan royal representation, issues of biography, sexuality, and gender were intertwined with issues of political and religious ideology. At once demure and provocative, the coy iconography of Queen Elizabeth's virgin-knot suggests a causal relationship between her sanctified chastity and the providential destruction of the Spanish Catholic invaders, the momentous event represented in the background of the painting. The security of the island realm, the strength and integrity of the English body politic, are thus made to seem mystically dependent upon the strength and integrity—the intact condition—of the Queen's body natural. The painting is an iconic essay on the theme of inviolable boundaries. A poetic analogue to this visual strategy may be found in George Chapman's *Hymnus in Cynthiam* (1594):

> Set thy Christall and Imperiall throne,
> (girt in the chast, and never-loosing zone)
> Gainst Europs Sunne directly opposit,
> And give him darknesse, that doth threat thy light.[9]

Chapman adapts the ubiquitous association of Elizabeth with the militantly virgin goddess Cynthia-Diana to a simultaneously cosmological and geopolitical conceit of gendered opposites, one in which the chaste English moon repulses the belligerent Spanish sun. It is apparent in both the picture and the poem that mystifications of the physiology of royal virginity are directly tied to the strategic calculations of state policy. As I have already suggested, the iconography of virginity that dominated royal representation in the decade prior to the Armada served the agenda of those who argued that its queen regnant had to remain impervious to foreign marital alliances if England was to remain strong and free, prosperous and Protestant. In effect, the visual argument of the Armada portrait is a vindication of the wisdom of that position—one that Elizabeth had now appropriated as her own.

Our source for the famous speech that the Queen is reported to have made to her hastily mustered forces at Tilbury at the time of the Armada has long been an undated letter by Dr. Leonel Sharp, who claimed to have been an eyewitness but was probably writing in 1623, some two decades after the Queen's death, and whose letter was not printed until the mid-seventeenth century.[10] Also extant is an undated manuscript draft of the speech, possibly in Sharp's hand, until recently ignored by Elizabethan scholars.[11] Although there is no definitive evidence that either of these slightly different texts constitutes an accurate record of the words spoken by the Queen at Tilbury camp on 9 August 1588, they do accord in their basic themes, metaphors, and rhetorical patterns with speeches that are attributable to Elizabeth, as do several other, more fragmentary, extant literary representations of the same event.[12] The existence of the manuscript of the Tilbury speech strengthens the credentials of Sharp's belated printed transcript. Even without it, however, I would still have chosen to quote and analyze Sharp's transcript of the speech here because it forms part of the cultural text that discursively constituted "the Queen," a cultural text from which Elizabeth drew and to which she herself was a major contributor. Although we cannot be sure of the precise relationship between this transcript and the words actually spoken by Elizabeth on that occasion, in style and substance it is wholly consistent with her public voice. Thus, in my analysis of the speech, the speaker whom I designate as Queen Elizabeth is to be identified with the royal persona collectively constructed by Elizabeth Tudor and her subjects. This compelling persona also presumably shaped Dr. Sharp's recollection and report of what he had originally heard and witnessed many years earlier.

Like the "Armada" portraits, Queen Elizabeth's address to her troops at the time of the Armada employs an identification of corporeal with geopolitical boundaries:

> My loving people, we have been perswaded by some, that are careful of our safety, to take heed how we commit our self to armed multitudes for fear of treachery: but I assure you, I do not desire to live to distrust my faithful, and loving people. Let Tyrants fear, I have alwayes so behaved my self, that under God I have placed my chiefest strength and safeguard in the loyal hearts and good will of my subjects. And therefore I am come amongst you . . . being resolved in the midst, and heat of the battaile to live, or die amongst you all, to

lay down for my God, and for my kingdom, and for my people, my Honour, and my blood even in the dust. I know I have the bodie, but of a weak and feeble woman, but I have the heart and Stomach of a King, and of a King of *England* too, and think foul scorn that *Parma* or *Spain*, or any Prince of Europe, should dare to invade the borders of my Realm, to which rather then any dishonour shall grow by me, I my self will take up arms, I my self will be your General, Judge, and Rewarder of everie one of your vertues in the field. . . . In the mean time my Lieutenant General shall be in my stead . . . not doubting but by your obedience to my General . . . and your valour in the field, we shall shortly have a famous victorie over those enemies of my God, of my Kingdomes, and of my People.[13]

Elizabeth's strategy of self-empowerment involves a delicate balance of contrary tactics. On the one hand, she invokes the feminine frailty of her body natural and the masculine strength of her body politic—a strength deriving from the love of her people, the virtue of her lineage, and the will of her God. In other words, she moderates the anomalous spectacle of martial feminine sovereignty by representing herself as the handmaiden of a greater, collective, and patriarchal will.[14] On the other hand, she subsumes this gesture of womanly self-deprecation within an assertion of the unique power that inheres in her by virtue of her office and nation. Her feminine honor, the chastity vested in a body natural that is vulnerable to invasion and pollution, is made secure by the kingly honor vested in her body politic.[15]

Elizabeth's speech presents the threat of invasion in the most intimate and violent of metaphors, as an attempted rape of the Queen by a foreign prince. Finding a metaphorical equivalent for the iconography of the "Armada" portrait, this speech gains rhetorical force from Elizabeth's identification of corporeal and geopolitical boundaries, from her subtle application of the land/body trope to herself. She identifies her virginal female body with the clearly bounded body of her island realm, threatened with violation by the Spanish sea and land forces masculinized and personified in King Philip and the Duke of Parma. Some of Elizabeth's subjects were less subtle in their use of this trope, particularly if they were appealing to the jingoism and xenophobia of a popular audience. For example, in one of the popular ballads he penned in response to the momentous events of 1588, Thomas Deloney focused upon the cargo of whips rumored to have been carried by the Armada, with which the invaders had supposedly planned to chastise the conquered English. Deloney activates the familiar Elizabethan sexual pun on "country" in writing that "Our noble Queene and Countrie first, / they did prepare to spoile." The rape of a gendered and sexualized England is literalized not only in the rape of the Queen but in the rape of her women subjects: "Our seelie women . . . their spoyle they ment to make," intending to take "their filthie lust / and pleasure," before whipping them. Thus would these "Romish Spanyards" have demonstrated their descent from the pagan Roman invaders who had raped and whipped an earlier British queen, "good Queene Voadicia."[16]

Shortly after the Queen's death, her appearance at Tilbury and the Armada victory were dramatized in the public theatre in part two of Thomas Heywood's *If You Know Not Me You Know Nobody*. As a prelude to Elizabeth's heroic entry with her army, Heywood brings on the admiral of the Armada, the Duke of Medina Sidonia, to make a hollow boast to his companions:

> I thinke we come too strong, what's our designe
> Against a petty Iland govern'd by a woman?
> I thinke instead of military men,
> Garnish'd with Armes and martiall Discipline,
> She with a feminine Traine
> Of her bright Ladyes beautifull'st and best,
> Will meete us in their smocks, willing to pay
> Their Maiden-heads for Ransome.[17]

In both Deloney's ballad and Heywood's play, as in the "Armada" portraits and the Queen's Tilbury speech, an alien threat that consolidates the collective interests of Englishmen also enables an identification of the English body politic with the female body of its monarch. An emphasis upon the virginity of that royal body transforms the monarch's problematic gender into the paradoxical source of her potency and the foundation of her subjects' collective welfare. However, the dynamics of the early modern gender-system ensured that the power ascribed to virginity was always fragile, not only because of a cultural assumption that it was a prelude to marriage and motherhood but also because it tended to arouse a masculine will to mastery: A virgin's purity was inherently dangerous to herself because it presented an invitation to pollution. Thus, in his *Discovery of Guiana*, Sir Walter Ralegh reminded his Elizabethan readers that King Philip's father, the Emperor Charles V, had "had the maidenhead of Peru"; and when he concluded his tract with the declaration that "Guiana is a countrey that hath yet her maidenhead," he was exhorting them to emulate the Spanish example in a collective act of cultural defloration that would manifest the imperial ambition of heroic Englishmen.[18]

The royal panegyrics that so extravagantly celebrated the magical power of virgin queenship during the later part of Elizabeth's reign were grounded in the fundamental socio-sexual realities of the age: In a world that was otherwise governed by lords, fathers, and husbands, the Queen's control over access to her own person was a vital source of her political power. Her authority over the realm was dependent upon her physical and symbolic control of her own body. The threatened Spanish violation of England's Virgin Queen would contaminate the blood of the lineage and dishonor not only the house of Tudor but the whole commonwealth. In Sharp's transcript of the Queen's Armada speech, the implied comparison is to Lucretia. Lucretia's rape by Tarquinius led to his exile and also to her suicide, which cleansed the social body and restored honor to Lucretia and to her husband and kinsmen. In contrast to the noble Roman matron, the royal English virgin determines to defend and preserve both herself and her state. Thus, latent in the imagery of the Armada speech and its oblique allusion to Lucretia is a contrast between the rape that constituted the foundational myth of Roman republicanism and the militant virginity that constituted the foundational myth of Elizabethan imperialism.[19]

In the Queen's declaration of her readiness "to lay down for my God, and for my Kingdom, and for my people, my Honour, and my blood, even in the dust," rhetorical power is generated from the strategic equivocation between masculine and feminine modalities of honor and of bloodletting, between military heroism and virgin sacrifice—or sacrificed virginity. We cannot be certain of how the Queen dressed or of what she said when she visited the camp at Tilbury; however, contemporary and subsequent reports concur in suggesting that her appearance and performance there had a charismatic effect upon her troops. The Earl of Leicester, her host at Tilbury, enthused at the time in a private letter to the Earl of Shrewsbury, that "our gratious Majestie hath byn here with me to see her camp & people, which so enflamyd the harts of her good subjects, as I think the wekest person amongst them ys able to mach the proudest Spaniard that dares land in England." According to this knowing and admiring observer, the hearts and stomachs of the weakest Englishmen there had been fortified by the *mascula vis* of their Prince.[20]

Not every Englishman was so roused by the Queen's Armada performance. It is worth pausing briefly over a dissenting account of her demeanor during the crisis, mentioned in passing in a report filled with news and gossip from one English Catholic expatriate to another. Writing from Antwerp to Father Persons in Madrid, Richard Verstegan is discussing the outcome of the treason trial of Sir John Perrot, formerly the Queen's Lord Deputy in Ireland:

> Sir John Parrat is not executed. The only thing that could be prooved against him was that he should say, when the Spanish Armada was on the seas, that the Queen was of a dastardly nature, and that he thoughte she did then bepisse

her smock (in thease tearmes the woordes were repeated at the barr), and that
he hoped to live the day that she should have nede of him.[21]

In his purported slur, Perrot expresses his contempt toward his sovereign
in terms that are both classed and gendered. The highly pejorative Elizabethan adjective "dastardly" connotes a cowardly and dull-witted nature that
is symptomatic of social baseness. Here Queen Elizabeth is said to have displayed her dastardliness by betraying her fear of the Spanish invasion in bodily
incontinence—in that involuntary leakage which in early modern culture was
widely regarded as symptomatic of womanly disability.[22] In this sense, the ma-
licious anecdote bears an inverse relationship to the celebrated speech on the
occasion of the Armada that is ascribed to Queen Elizabeth herself. Any pre-
tense that this queen regnant has the heart and stomach of a king of England
is unmasked when the body of a weak and feeble woman reasserts itself in its
incontinent fear. It is precisely because here the basis of the royal slander is
the Queen's cravenness rather than her insatiable lust that urinary semiotics
replace sexual ones. Whereas the speech at Tilbury grounds resistance to a
Spanish invasion in the Virgin Queen's mystical impermeability, the slur rehearsed in the courtroom presents the spectacle of a timorous woman who
leaks in fear at the prospect of a Spanish invasion. I am not claiming that
Perrot (or Verstegan) intended specifically to parody the Tilbury speech but
rather that these contrary texts preserve ways of thinking and speaking that
shared a common cultural matrix, however different their tone, occasion, and
intent. Their juxtaposition allows us to appreciate the rhetorical and strategic
mastery with which the ringing words ascribed to the Queen appropriated and
transmuted a conventional discourse of disparagement and contempt into an
idiosyncratic assertion of authority.

It has become customary to imagine and to represent Elizabeth's rhetorical
performance at Tilbury as a boldly innovative tactic, one designed to sur-
mount those liabilities of her gender that restricted her capacity to perform
in the theatre of war. Such Elizabethan tactics, however, appear to have had
immediate and direct precedents in those of her sister, England's prior queen
regnant. There is even a suggestive Marian precedent for Elizabeth's review of
her troops at Tilbury; and it is one with which Elizabeth herself would have
been very familiar. The momentous occasion was the mustering of forces in
East Anglia in July 1553 on behalf of Mary's claim to the throne, an occasion
which led to the collapse of the Northumberland regime and aborted the reign

of Queen Jane. A contemporary (1554) manuscript account of the coup and the first year of Mary's reign, written in Latin by a Catholic Marian sympathizer, describes how on the afternoon of 20 July 1553 the as yet unmarried Mary rode out of Framlingham castle in Suffolk on a white horse

> to muster and inspect this most splendid and loyal army.... Her majesty, now on foot, went round both divisions of the army speaking to them with exceptional kindness and with an approach so wonderfully relaxed as can scarcely be described, in consideration of their esteem for the sovereign, that she completely won over everyone's affections.[23]

According to this partisan narrative, Mary received the joyous news of her enemies' political collapse immediately thereafter.

This account concludes with a prayer that Philip of Spain "very soon will enter the beloved and long-sought embraces of our most honourable queen; and that some day, God willing, that pure and fertile womb will be made fruitful through the most noble seed of all Europe."[24] The Marian accession narrative ends in eager anticipation of Philip's arrival in England to consummate his marriage with Queen Mary, thus possessing England by possessing England's queen. Similar sentiments were expressed in a Latin epithalamium in honor of the marriage of Philip and Mary that was printed in London in 1554. Entitled *Philippeis*, the poem was characterized by its author, the Dutch humanist Hadrianus Junius, as a "Carmen heroicum," and it is replete with classical deities and epic machinery. Its hero is Philip; and the imperial destiny that Mercury enjoins him to fulfill is to sail to England, marry Mary, father a male heir, and restore the Golden Age to England and peace to all of Europe. The poem's subsidiary attention to Queen Mary is focused upon persuasions that she abjure virginity and submit to her destiny as the spouse and mother of kings. In an epilogue addressed to Philip, Junius writes of Britannia bestowing the scepter of rule upon him.[25] In the antithetical Elizabethan Armada narrative—as definitively articulated by Elizabeth herself at Tilbury—the English queen successfully defends her own virginity, the integrity of her state, and the welfare of her people by repelling the royal Spanish rapist.

As it happened, before Philip's arrival Mary faced and overcame a second violent threat to her throne within little more than six months of the first: this was Wyatt's Rebellion, which appears to have been catalyzed by the prospect of Mary's Spanish marriage, and to have had as its goal her deposition and replacement by Elizabeth. Writing at the end of the first decade of Elizabeth's reign—that is, two decades before the Armada—the chronicler

Richard Grafton described Mary's demeanor and speech during this second crisis in terms that resonate with accounts of Elizabeth at Tilbury:

> But more then marvaile it was to see that day the invincible heart and constancie of the Queene her selfe, who beyng by nature a woman, and therefore commonly more feareful then men be, shewed her selfe in that case more stoute then is credible. For she notwithstandyng all the fearefull newes that were brought to her that day, never abashed saiyng . . . farther, that she her selfe would enter the field to trye the truth of her quarell, and to die with them that would serve her, rather then to yelde one jote unto such a traytor as Wyat, and prepared her selfe accordingly. But by the apprehension of Wyat, that voyage tooke none effect.[26]

In the aftermath of the failed rebellion, Wyatt and a large number of co-conspirators were executed. Elizabeth herself was placed under arrest on suspicion of complicity, and was sent to the Tower. In order to survive and to succeed, she chose wisely which of her sister's lessons to repudiate and which to emulate.

I have been arguing that the "Armada" portraits and related texts involve an implicit troping of Queen Elizabeth in the similitude of land and body. Perhaps the fullest and most explicit iconic realization of such a trope is a curious Dutch engraving dated 1598, the year of King Philip's death. Whereas in the "Ditchley" portrait (fig. 35) the body of the Queen is superimposed upon a map of England, in this polemical print (fig. 42) the royal body itself is metamorphosed into a cartographic image, a map of Europe. This engraving appears to parody a cartographic image of Europa printed a decade earlier in Sebastian Münster's influential *Cosmographia* (fig. 43).[27] The polemical force of the parody is that in following the geo-corporeal alignment of the earlier personification, the crowned head of Elizabeth-Europa now occupies the Iberian peninsula. As discussed in part one, Philip II—the husband of Elizabeth's deceased half-sister, and briefly the King of England—was prepared to marry his sometime sister-in-law upon her accession, in order to re-secure the interests of the Catholic faith and the Habsburg dynasty. In a nice retort to the Spanish monarch's recurrent attempts to master and possess England, whether by marital or military means, the Dutch Protestant engraving shows Elizabeth literally occupying and possessing Spain—becoming its head. The engraving sharpens its anti-Spanish and anti-Catholic point by adding such choice details as the destruction of King Philip's *gran armada* and the discomfiture of the Pope, who appears to have abandoned Europe and is retreating

FIGURE 42
Elizabeth I as Europa. Artist unknown; 1598. Engraving. Ashmolean Museum, Oxford.

toward the Arctic region. The mighty, sword-bearing arm with which Elizabeth accomplishes these feats is formed from the island of Great Britain itself;
her other arm, which holds the orb of sovereignty, has absorbed the Italian
peninsula with its papal and Habsburg dominions.

This Dutch image of Elizabeth-Europa projects the prudent English queen
as a virago who champions the international Protestant cause and sweeps away
the Spanish tyrant and popish Antichrist. Such a representation may have been
welcome to militant Protestant reformers and to the hawkish faction within
Elizabeth's court and council, but the Queen herself is unlikely to have been
so appreciative. Münster's Europa is gowned; Elizabeth's body appears to be
nude, even though her face is framed by crown and ruff. The addition of
a remarkable anatomical detail further complicates the iconography of the
engraving: Elizabeth has one conspicuous bare breast. In another context,
we might associate this detail with verbal images of the Queen as a nursing
mother, or with the figure of Plenty who accompanies Elizabeth and Peace in
the circa 1572 painting of the Protestant succession (fig. 19). However, in the
strongly martial context of this print, the *absence* of a breast on the side of the

hernach angezeigt wird. Was aber Lands vber dem Mare Mediterraneum ligt gegen AFRICA
Mittag hinauß/ das wird alles zugeschriben Africe/vñ streckt sich gegen Orient hinauß begrentz.

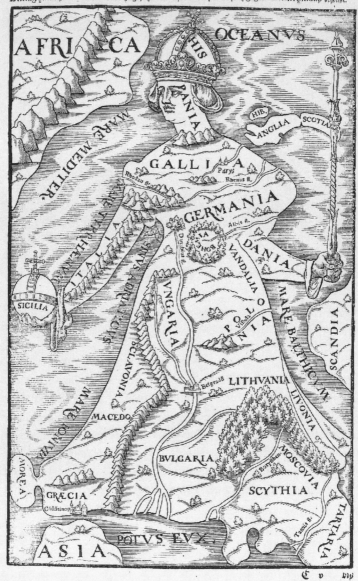

FIGURE 43
Europa. Artist unknown. Engraving. Printed in Sebastian Münster, *Cosmographia* (Basel, 1588), xli. By
permission of the Folger Shakespeare Library, Washington, DC.

queen's sword-bearing arm becomes equally conspicuous, and it suggests an Amazonian image of military prowess.[28]

An Amazonian representation of the Queen has a certain propriety in an engraving on the subject of European geopolitical and religious conflict. Nevertheless, in early modern culture, any allusion to the Amazons carried heavy ideological baggage. For example, in an unfinished dialogue, Francis Bacon imagined

> a land of Amazons, where the whole government public and private, yea the militia itself, was in the hands of women. I demand, is not such a preposterous government (against the first order of nature, for women to rule over men,) in itself void, and to be suppressed? I speak not of the reign of women, (for that is supplied by counsel and subordinate magistrates masculine,) but where the regiment of state, justice, families, is all managed by women.[29]

Bacon draws a sharp distinction between the matriarchal tyranny enforced in a hypothetical "land of Amazons" and a limited monarchy of the sort that Elizabethan subjects routinely praised. The latter preserved the patriarchal norm by prescribing masculine counselors and parliamentarians to constrain the prerogative of a queen regnant. The abhorrence evident in Bacon's speculation indicates why an explicit identification of Elizabeth as an Amazon seems to have been rare, particularly among the many encomia produced by her own subjects.[30] A conspicuous exception was made for the heroic Amazon queen Penthesilea, who may have been considered an acceptable and appropriate exemplar precisely because she sacrificed herself not for the Amazonian cause but for the cause of patriarchal Troy, the mythical place of origin of the Britons. Thus, in his execrable Armada poem *Elizabetha Triumphans* (1588), James Aske employed a simile of Penthesilea at Troy to describe Elizabeth at Tilbury: On this occasion, "our Queene (an Amazonian Queene)" displayed "courage wonderfull."[31] Penthesilea excepted, the Amazons' maintenance of a "monstrous regiment of women" and their unorthodox sexual and parental practices rendered them at best an equivocal instrument of royal compliment.

Merely by representing Queen Elizabeth as a female warrior, the various accounts of the visit to Tilbury that I have cited invite associations with an Amazon—but with the fundamental difference that the English queen leads an army of men. On the rare occasion when Elizabeth herself invoked such an association, she was too prudent to pursue it very far. In Sharp's transcript of her Tilbury speech, having resonantly declared, "I my self will take up arms, I my self will be your General, Judge, and Rewarder of every one of your vertues in the field," she concludes by delegating her authority to the Earl of Leicester: "In the mean time, my Lieutenant General shall be in my stead." Perhaps it was her reluctance to be passively subjected to masculine force—even a force intended to protect her against the aggression of others—that drove the Queen to make such an equivocal gesture at Tilbury, at once asserting and disavowing the role of a virago. Thomas Heywood captures Elizabeth's predicament when he has her say, at Tilbury, "Oh had God and Nature / Given us proportion man-like to our mind, / Wee'd not stand here fenc't in a wall of Armes, / But have beene present in these Sea alarmes."[32]

Throughout her reign, and increasingly in its later years, the most conspicuous and potentially the most dangerous arena in which the Queen's gender disabled her royal authority was in military affairs. In 1565, the Spanish ambassador de Silva reported that Elizabeth, upon being told of a Turkish victory over Christian forces, responded that she "was very sorry, and said she wished she was a man to be there in person"; two decades later, on the eve of the Armada, according to the Spanish ambassador Mendoza she declared that "although she was a woman and her profession was to try to preserve peace with neighboring princes, yet if they attacked her they would find that in war she could be better than a man."[33] In the former example, Elizabeth's expressed wish to participate personally in a war against the infidel resonates with the crusading exploits of her royal forebears and the heroes of chivalric romance; in the latter example, she seeks to impress upon her enemies that her gender in no way compromises her resolve to withstand an imminent foreign invasion. Underlying the Queen's distinct responses to these dissimilar occasions is the perception that the mere fact of her gender excluded her from a central arena of masculine emulation, honor, and fellowship, and that this exclusion put her at a distinct political disadvantage.[34] Such thoughts may have been in her mind during a 1597 interview recorded by André Hurault, Sieur de Maisse, the French Ambassador: "Speaking to her of the news from France, and that the King had caused his forces to march towards Brittany, she asked me if he would go in person. I said yes."[35]

Elizabeth's generals in the field—most notoriously, Leicester and Essex, who were also royal favorites—tended to be the most insubordinate and self-aggrandizing of her servants. But their conduct was at least in part a response to their own perceptions that the Queen was vacillating, parsimonious, and merely reactive in military affairs. This was a mindset that they ascribed primarily to her gender; and its perceived consequence was to frustrate the exercise of their own manly *virtù*, and thus the enhancement of their personal honor. In his memoir of his 1597 embassy to Elizabeth, de Maisse wrote that the Earl of Essex had confided to him that "they laboured under two things at this Court, delay and inconstancy, which proceeded chiefly from the sex of the

Queen."[36] Tellingly, in the 1595 correspondence between Essex and the Spanish exile Antonio Perez, Essex himself was figured as Aeneas, and Elizabeth as Juno, the capricious and vindictive queen of the gods who tried unsuccessfully to thwart the martial hero's imperial destiny.[37] Lest it be concluded that this issue was merely Essex's personal obsession, consider the retrospective judgment of his sometime rival, Sir Walter Ralegh, writing in the second decade of the seventeenth century: "If the late queen would have believed her men of war, as she did her scribes, we had in her time beaten that great empire in pieces, and made their kings kings of figs and oranges, as in old times. But her majesty did all by halves, and by petty invasions taught the Spaniard how to defend himself, and to see his own weakness."[38] Whether or not Ralegh was making a realistic assessment of Elizabethan England's potential military might, in his subjective perception that the Queen had frustrated that potential he was speaking on behalf of all "her men of war."

Elizabeth's own allusions to her *mascula vis* were usually displaced into her filial identification with Henry VIII; and her infrequent postures of militancy were almost always cast in terms of her providential status as a virginal instrument of the divine will. These themes are conspicuous in the speech with which she closed the Parliament of 1593. In discussing the war with Spain, the Queen told her parliamentarians that

> Many wiser Princes than my selfe you have had, but one only excepted (whom in the duty of a childe I must regard, and to whom I must acknowledge my selfe farre shallow) I may truely say, none whose love and care can be greater. . . .
>
> For mine owne part, I protest I never feared: and what fear was, my heart never knew. For I knew that my cause was ever just, and it standeth upon a sure foundation that I should not faile, God assisting the quarrell of the rightwise and such as are but to defende. Glad mought that King my greatest enemy be, to have the like advantage against me, if in truth for his owne actions he might truely so say.
>
> For in ambition of glorie I have never sought to enlarge the territories of my land, nor thereby to advance you. If I have used my forces to keepe the enemy farre from you, I have thereby thought your safetie the greater, and your danger the lesse. If you suppose I have done it in feare of the enemy, or in doubt of his revenge, I know his power is not to prevaile nor his force to feare me, having so mighty a protector on my side.[39]

In reflecting upon the long struggle against Spain and in making her own contribution to the construction of an Armada myth, Elizabeth emphasizes

not her place among the viragos of history and legend but rather her status
as both the pious daughter of her earthly father and the humble handmaiden
of her heavenly father. In her reiterated denials of personal fear, and in her
explanation for her repudiation of an expansionist foreign policy, she is engaged in a conspicuous effort to counter any perception that her gender has
negatively impacted the strength and security of the commonweal. Throughout the speech, in her repeated emphasis upon her "love towards" her subjects
and her "care over" them, any suggestion of maidenly frailty is supplanted by
an image of maternal strength. She insists that her triumph over Philip—"that
King my greatest enemy"—is grounded in the rightness of her cause.

In her speech to the Lords at the end of the 1601 Parliament, in what was
to be the final such public address of her reign, the sixty-nine-year-old queen
offered a summation of the problems and achievements of her foreign policy.
This she characterized as a history of resistance to, and triumph over, relentless
Spanish aggression and subversion; and at its heart she put her own role in
the defeat of the Armada:

> I have . . . bene content to be a taper of trewe virgin waxe to wast my self and
> spend my life that I might give light and comfort to those that lived under
> me. The strange devisis, practisis, and stratagemes never hard nor written of
> before that have bene attempted, not only against my owne person in which
> so many as acknowledge themselves beholding to my care and happie in my
> government have an interest, but by invasione of the state it self by those that
> did not only threaten to come, but came at the last in verie deed with their
> whole fleet, have ben in number many and by preparation dangerouse, though
> it hath pleased God to whose honor it is spoken without arrogation of anie
> praise or merit to my self, by many harde escapes and hasardes both of diverse
> and strange natures to make me an instrument of his holy will in deliveringe
> the state from danger and my self from dishonour.[40]

This royal rhetoric has similarities to that found in the Tilbury Armada
speech—notably in its identification of a threat to the body of the state with a
threat to the honor of the Queen and in its ascription of mystical potency to
the Queen's virginity. Elizabeth now presents the latter as emblematic of her
self-sacrifice for the common good rather than as the personal preference she
had so long and so tenaciously maintained against parliamentary pleas that
she marry. In a characteristic paradox, her attribution of all honor to God for
his special care—a demonstration of her humility and devotion—works to
enhance her own claim to honor and worship.

If, in her own retrospective allusions to the defeat of the Armada, Elizabeth
modestly eschewed the pose of a conquering hero, she could rely upon her

devoted subjects to supply the missing element of rant. Consider the following example, written during the 1590s by Henry Wotton:

> The Spaniard is in the opinion of all men, the terrour of Princes, the controller of Kings, the Monarch of the world. . . . It is he . . . that overlooketh with an eye of ambition, with a heart of covetousness, with a desire of superiority, with an unsatiable appetite of Sovereign Authority, the whole face, and the large precincts of Christendom. . . .
>
> Now if a woman hath presumed to encounter with this man; if a Queen of one Island hath undertaken to bridle a Prince of so many Nations, if her sole Forces have tamed his invincible power, her only counsel prevented his subtile practices; and his ambitious desires; if she alone hath hindred him to be . . . Commander of all the rest of the world, shall he not err that compareth *Hercules* with her? Or can any man deem him wise, that taketh her in any respect inferiour to *Julius Caesar*, mighty *Pompey*, or *Alexander the Great* ?[41]

Wotton's emphasis is upon the apparent incommensurability of these two antagonists—a contest between David and Goliath, but now enacted on a global scale: "a Queen of one Island" versus "the Monarch of the world." Thus, Wotton also emphasizes throughout his discussion the miraculous quality of the victory, a victory impossible without divine intervention. Wotton represents the Anglo-Spanish conflict in the graphically physical image of Elizabeth personally combating and bridling Philip. This is a daring invocation of one of the tropes of gender inversion that were a staple of the early modern discourse of female pride and unruliness. However, by his favorable comparison of Queen Elizabeth not to a familiar roster of viragos or female worthies but rather to the masculine heroes of antique myth and history, Wotton contains both the subversive potential and the misogynistic resonance in this allusion while simultaneously amplifying his royal encomium.

The paean that pours forth from Wotton is precisely what we would expect from one of Elizabeth's loyal subjects. What we might not expect is that the rhetoric of her enemies was sometimes remarkably similar. Of course, there are a few examples of Spaniards being as vituperative on the subject of Queen Elizabeth as Protestant Englishmen habitually were about King Philip and the Pope. Thus, in his 1588 sonnet "A la jornada de Inglaterra," Lope de Vega imagined the seaborne invasion in terms of a moralized *Odyssey*, in which the devout Philip II was a *cristiano Ulises* and the false Elizabeth *una sirena*. Here Philip's imagined voyage of conquest against Elizabethan England seems to parody his eroto-imperial voyage to Marian England, as imagined in the 1554 epithalamium by Hadrianus Junius. In the *canción* on the Armada that he wrote in 1588, Góngora portrayed a sexually rapacious and morally depraved Elizabeth—a figure familiar from the writings of English Catholic exiles like Sander and Allen: "Wife of many and of many the daughter-in-law, O infamous queen. No queen but a she-wolf, lustful and bestial!"[42]

Surely no Spaniard imagined the English queen's lupine nature more powerfully than did Lucretia de León, a young woman whose politically explosive dream visions were recorded and widely disseminated in Spain around the time of the Armada. On 14 December 1587, she dreamed of Queen Elizabeth seated with a dead and disemboweled lamb in her lap, thrusting her hands into the eviscerated cavity and bathing them in blood. In this dream, the Queen was accompanied by a woman dressed as a widow, who refused her invitation to drink the blood of the lamb; at this refusal, Elizabeth angrily unsheathed a sword and decapitated the woman. Richard Kagan plausibly suggests that this dream alludes to the execution of Mary, Queen of Scots, which had occurred a few months earlier.[43] It might be added that the image of the eviscerated lamb powerfully evokes the fate of Edmund Campion and other English missionary priests, whose martyrdom was vividly recounted in printed texts and images that circulated widely in Catholic Europe.[44] Four nights preceding this dream, and eight months before the defeat of the Armada, Lucretia dreamed of a naval battle in which Drake's forces destroyed the Armada.[45] These anti-Elizabethan visions were merely xenophobic episodes within a larger seditious dreamwork that had as its central thrust an indictment of King Philip's character and policies in all matters civic, foreign, and religious. In defaming the Queen of England, Lucretia de León and those who exploited her were challenging the authority and judgment of their own sovereign.[46]

Despite the poetic invectives and nightmare visions generated by a few of King Philip's Spanish subjects, Elizabeth's principal antagonists seem to have had a far more complex attitude toward her. For example, on the very eve of the Armada, the Venetian ambassador in Rome wrote to the Doge and the Senate:

> The Pope said he had news from Spain that the Armada was ready. But the English, too, are ready. "She certainly is a great Queen," he said, "and were she only a Catholic she would be our dearly beloved. Just look how well she governs; she is only a woman, only mistress of half an island, and yet she makes herself feared by Spain, by France, by the Empire, by all."[47]

Another reputed remark by Sixtus V—that "the distaff of the Queen of England was worth more than the sword of the King of Spain"—gives expression to the same ambivalent wonder at the spectacle of this "woman on top."[48] Sentiments similar to the Pope's were current at the Spanish court at the time of the Armada, according to the Venetian ambassador there: In mid-1587, he wrote (in cipher) that "the Spanish say that the King thinks and plans while the Queen of England acts, and that in earnest."[49] One of those Spaniards, Juan de Silva, Count of Portalegre, a nobleman and minister to King Philip, seems to have been as enthusiastic an admirer of Elizabeth as was any Englishman. He wrote to a friend in 1601 that the years "the queen of England has spent in the service of the world, will be the most outstanding known of in history."[50] The Irishmen invoked at the beginning of this chapter, who put "the Queen's picture behind the door, and the King of Spain's at the upper end of the table," were declaring their stand in a religious and political struggle of international scope; Juan de Silva was motivated instead by an aristocratic admiration of personal genius when, at about the same date, he proudly displayed in his home the portraits of King Philip's nemeses, Sir Francis Drake and the Queen of England.

PART FOUR

Resistances

In his *Admonition to the Nobility and People of England and Ireland* (1588), England's Cardinal-in-exile, William Allen, set out for his fellow countrymen the brief that would justify the Armada and its "godly purpose of restoringe the Catholike religion, and putting the realme in order." Toward the end of this incendiary pamphlet, Allen considered what sort of reception the foreign invaders/liberators and the returning exiles who would follow them might expect from Queen Elizabeth's subjects. Here is the gist of his analysis:

> Though never so great shewe be made, never so many raised against you, bicause moste of them be Catholikes or notoriously injured by heretikes, they be armed for us, they cannot strike, they will not fighte against their owne consciences.... Many others of them be indifferente, of neither, or no religion; whose witt and warynesse will be suche in this extremitie, and in so juste cause to desire a Change, that where by overthrow of the heretikes many shal be advaunsed, and by theire good successe no man bettered, in so great hassard of thinges, they will never adore the sun setting, nor follow the declininge fortune of so filthie, wicked, and illiberall a Creature.[1]

Allen's scenario was doubtless as excessively optimistic as that promoted by the self-styled liberators of latter-day Iraq. Nevertheless, his arguments remain of great historical interest. Indeed, from an ideological vantage point directly opposed to Allen's, Philip Sidney had acutely observed a similar political alignment a decade earlier, when he was seeking to counsel the Queen not to marry the duc d'Anjou:

> Your subjects ... are divided into two mighty factions, and factions bound upon the mighty knot of religion.

The one of them is to whom your happy government hath granted the free exercise of the eternal truth.... These ... are they your chief, if not your sole, strength.... The other faction ... is of the Papists; men whose spirits are full of anguish; some being forced to oaths they account damnable; some having their ambition stopped, because they are not in the way of advancement ... all burdened with the weight of their consciences.... With these, I would willingly join all discontented persons, such as want and disgrace keeps lower than they have set their hearts.... This double rank of people how their minds have stood, the Northern Rebellion and infinite other practices have well taught you.[2]

Although Allen was a tireless spokesman for "the other faction," his analysis has much in common with Sidney's earlier one; at the same time, it also anticipates those widespread conditions of religious dissention and political alienation, inflation and dearth, courtly factionalism and popular riot, that historians of the period have increasingly come to see as characterizing the 1590s and the final years of Elizabeth's reign.[3] Such ideological and material realities both necessitated and gave the lie to the ever more hyperbolic encomia of the aging and isolated queen.

Part four is concerned with cultural manifestations of the sectarian and popular dissention that was endemic in the Queen's domains, particularly during the last two decades of her reign. Chapter twelve considers how the international religious and geopolitical struggles manifested in the Armada were refigured in forms of resistance to royal authority that were enacted by Catholic and plebeian English subjects. Chapter thirteen analyzes some notable acts of symbolic violence against the royal image by disaffected Elizabethan subjects of varying religious persuasions, both in England and in Ireland. Chapter fourteen explores the religio-political struggle between the Elizabethan regime and its Roman Catholic opponents, as this was played out upon the Queen's two bodies and upon the bodies of those Catholic missionary priests whom the state executed for treason.

Vox Populi

King Philip of Spain doubtless hoped and prayed for total victory in his great enterprise against England, with a successful invasion precipitating a rising by English Catholics and full-scale rebellion in Ireland. Nevertheless, he was sufficiently prudent to plan for a more equivocal outcome, one that would leave his forces in a position strong enough to occupy parts of Kent or the Isle of Wight, and thus to extract valuable religious, territorial, and economic concessions from a hard-pressed Elizabethan regime. His final instructions to his commanders make this strategy clear:

> If (which God forbid) the result be not so prosperous that our arms shall be able to settle matters, nor, on the other hand, so contrary that the enemy shall be relieved of anxiety on our account (which God, surely, would not permit) and affairs be so counterbalanced that peace may not be altogether undesirable... there are three principal points upon which you must fix your attention. The first is, that in England the free use and exercise of our holy Catholic faith shall be permitted to all Catholics, native and foreign, and that those who are in exile shall be permitted to return. The second is, that all the places in my Netherlands which the English hold shall be restored to me; and the third is that they (the English) shall recompense me for the injury they have done to me, my dominions, and my subjects; which will amount to an exceedingly great sum.[1]

In June 1588, a few weeks after the King drafted these instructions, and with the Armada now an imminent threat, Sir Francis Walsingham wrote to Lord Burghley to express his alarm at the lack of English preparation: "I would to God the enemye were no more carefull to assayle than we to defend."[2] King Philip had good reason to believe that his contingency planning was for a worst-case scenario. The stunning failure of the Armada and the mythical status that this (non)event has subsequently assumed in the popular historical imagination have obscured the very real danger that a well-executed invasion of England would have posed to the Elizabethan regime.

When Elizabeth delivered her famous speech to some seventeen thousand hastily mustered troops at Tilbury on 18 August 1588, the danger of invasion had in fact already passed. It was then a week and a half after the last hostile contact between English and Spanish vessels in the English Channel; and what remained of the Spanish fleet under the Duke of Medina Sidonia had already been sighted rounding the Orkney Islands, heading toward the west coast of Ireland in an attempt to get back to Spain. At the time, however, the English seem to have thought that the return of a repaired and regrouped Armada was still a distinct possibility; and in Flanders the Duke of Parma had continued to embark thousands of seasoned troops in preparation for the cross-Channel invasion that the Armada had been intended to facilitate. Sir Walter Ralegh, an active participant in the events of Armada year, later reflected in his *History of the World* (1614) that

> when the choice of all our trained bands, and the choice of our Commanders and Captaines, shall be drawn together (as they were at *Tillburie* in the yeare 1588) to attend the person of the Prince, and for the defence of the Citie of *London*: they that remained to guard the coast, can be of no such force, as to encounter an Armie like unto that, wherewith it was intended that the Prince of *Parma* should have landed in *England*.[3]

If the planned rendezvous of the Armada with the army of Flanders had been accomplished, and if the invasion forces had successfully landed at their designated location on England's southern coast, at a place where the defenders were not expecting them, then it is far from clear that the military and political outcome would have favored Queen Elizabeth and her Protestant adherents.[4]

Given the inadequate and ill-prepared military resources of the Elizabethan regime, in the event of an invasion the Queen's fate would have been in the hands of her common subjects: the scope and intensity of their support for the Elizabethan status quo and their resistance to the Philippine innovation would have been decisive. The invaders hoped, and the defenders feared, that the Queen's Catholic subjects would rise in support of an invasion made in the cause of their faith. In the final event, their loyalties were not put to the test. Nevertheless, the Armada threat heightened the antipapist hysteria that characterized the Elizabethan regime and the English Protestant elite, and many English Catholics suffered in varying degrees as a consequence. At the end of August 1588, Robert Southwell wrote to Claudio Acquaviva, Father

General of the Jesuit Order, that "our rulers . . . after the peril of the Armada
had passed, and the army which they had enrolled on land had been disbanded,
turned their arms from foreign foes against their own sons, and with inhuman
ferocity vented the hatred they had conceived against the Spaniards on their
own fellow citizens and subjects."[5] Southwell's impassioned claim is doubtless
exaggerated; still, statistical evidence shows that executions of Catholics in
England peaked during the years 1586–91.[6]

It was the characteristic position of devout and beleaguered Elizabethan
Catholics to invoke conscience in their refusal of the royal supremacy in
matters spiritual. However, the Elizabethan Catholic community was hardly
monolithic in its position vis-à-vis the Elizabethan regime. Many in the
Catholic gentry and nobility adamantly professed their loyalty to the Queen
and her government in matters temporal, opposed the exile community's collaboration with Spain on patriotic grounds, and openly contested the politically subversive activities of those militant co-religionists who, like William
Allen, were living safely beyond the seas.[7] Their position was laid out in a
"Supplication . . . To the Queenes most excellent Majestie," probably written
in 1585. Like the reformed citizens of Norwich in 1578, these professedly loyal
Catholics declared a wish that their truth might be anatomized: "Would God
our hartes mighte be layd open to the perfect viewe of your Majestie and all
the world, no doubt our thoughtes shall appear correspondent to the expectation of so mercyfull a Queene in all lovinge, true, and faythfull subjection,
and would gieve due desert of mercye for reward."[8] The probable author was
Sir Thomas Tresham, a leading recusant gentleman, who also wrote a "humble protestation of my allegiance to her majesty," in which he vowed himself
religiously committed to "defending her royal person from violence, and pre-
serving this realm and all other her majesty's dominions from invasion, against
all persons without exception; be it prince, pope, or potentate whosoever."[9]
Tresham wrote that petition during one of his frequent stints of imprison-
ment; like other prominent recusants, he also suffered crushing fines for his
nonattendance at church. Those of Tresham's persuasion prudently espoused
loyalty to their queen and their native country in the hope of an eventual
amelioration of their conditions, and perhaps eventual toleration for their
faith. However, nothing that they might profess dispelled the suspicions of
the regime; and, for better or worse, no invasion put those professions to a
definitive test.

As Philip Sidney pointed out to the Queen in the passage quoted at the
beginning of part four, it was not only anguished Catholics whom the regime
had to be concerned about but also "all discontented persons, such as want
and disgrace keeps lower than they have set their hearts." In book one of

De republica anglorum, Sir Thomas Smith ends his top-down anatomy of the Elizabethan social order with "the fourth sort or classe amongst us"—adult males without real property, including day laborers, husbandmen, shopkeepers, and artisans: "These have no voice in our common wealth, and no account is made of them but onelie to be ruled, not to rule other."[10] Smith's judgment was no doubt widely shared within the Elizabethan political nation. Nevertheless, despite being denied any voice by their betters, those of the fourth sort continued to speak. And some of those speakers—not only men but also women, whom Smith found unworthy of mention—insisted upon making their voices heard, even though the authorities only acknowledged them in order to impose discipline and punishment.

Here I propose to consider a few of these comments, attributed to common Elizabethan subjects and dating from the later years of the reign. My examples are drawn from the published records of the Elizabethan assizes for five home counties—those areas of the realm most immediate to London and the court, and thus intimately tied both economically and ideologically to the dominant institutions of Elizabethan England. The sample of indictments is even more restricted in that some records are lost and some individual entries are lost, damaged, incomplete, or indecipherable. This, then, is merely a fragmentary record of those scandalous or seditious statements uttered aloud in the presence, or coming to the attention, of those willing to report them. In these counties as well as in others throughout England and Wales, many other Elizabethan subjects may have had seditious thoughts that were unuttered or unheard, or were uttered only to those to whom they were congenial or who, for some other reason, failed to report them to authorities. Thus, the relatively small number of indictments for scandalous words, sedition, or seditious words appearing in these records should not be taken necessarily to indicate that such thoughts and utterances were extremely unusual. Those that have fortuitously found their way into the historical record preserve traces of the *vox populi* speaking its resistance to the dominant order.[11]

This fragmentary archive suggests that the Elizabethan popular discourse of sedition had its material basis in physical privation, economic exploitation, and social injustice, but that such practical experiences were readily perceived and articulated in ideological terms. Sometimes the content of this reported seditious speech is explicitly religious, and sometimes it is explicitly socio-economic; in other instances, the languages of spiritual and material grievance are mixed. The *vox populi* characteristically grounded its complaints in the judgment that fundamental principles of Christian charity and long-established community customs were being violated by those who put their material self-interest above the common good, and that it was the sacred duty of those in authority to correct such abuses. In a rigidly authoritarian culture that occluded legitimate channels for dissent, the essential conservatism of this plebeian *mentalité* was likely to be manifested as religio-political heterodoxy. Sometimes evident in such heterodoxy was a skeptical attitude toward the authorizing fictions of worldly power. Such plebeian skepticism was frequently inflected by the venerable tradition of misogyny; and in this form it was deployed against the person of Queen Elizabeth, who incarnated that worldly power. Here I examine a few instances of reported popular sedition that give some credibility to Allen's wishful scenario of conjoined invasion and rebellion, and that do so by putting the Spaniards and their king to work in the collective articulation of a plebeian geopolitical imaginary.

The Spaniards' planned invasion route from the coast to the court lay through the county of Kent; and there exists evidence from both before and after the Armada that some in Kent might have welcomed them. The yeoman Samuel Alkyngton of Westgate, Canterbury, was indicted in 1584 for saying "he hoped to see the daye that the pope of Rome should have as great auctorytye and beare as great swaye in Inglande as ever he dyd in Rome; and that he hoped to se a change of religion in Ingland within these three years." And in the same year, Ralph Watson of Dover, a laborer, was indicted for saying, "This is a very evill land to lyve in except yt be for a man that hath a very good occupacion. I would yt were warre. I knowe a great many richemen in the land; I wold have some of ther money yf yt were so come to passe. I knowe a thowsand, yea and a thowsand that wold yt were come to passe so the Queene were dead."[12] Alkyngton appears to have been motivated primarily by religious sectarianism; Watson, by resentment of economic privation. Cardinal Allen reckoned that the "great hassard of thinges" precipitated by a Spanish invasion would embolden all manner of disaffected English subjects to repudiate their subjection to the existing order. He trusted that English Catholics (like Alkyngton) and others offended by the official religion would either rise up in support of the invasion or at least refuse actively to oppose it; and that those irreligious malcontents (like Watson) who had little to lose would seize upon the opportunity for personal gain that was proffered by a world turned upside down: "Many ... be indifferente ... whose witt and warynesse will be suche in this extremitie ... to desire a Change, that ... by overthrow of the heretikes many shal be advaunsed, and by theire good successe no man bettered." In his social history of early modern Kent, Peter Clark has observed that "by the mid-1590s there were quite a few non-Catholic members of the lower orders willing to declare their support for Philip of Spain."[13]

The records of the Hertfordshire assizes include the indictment of Stephen Slater, a weaver from Smithfield, London, who stood accused of having publicly said in 1585 "that kinge Phillipp was a father to Ingland and did better love an Inglyshe man then the Quenes Majesties did, for that he woulde geve them meete, drynck and clothe. And that he thoughte that the Quene was not Quene and supreme hedd of Ingland." The indictment reports Slater as complaining that "he was pressed to serve as a souldyer in Flaunders by comyssion and had not those thinges which he was promysed, and that yf her majestie were Quene, she had vylleynes under her."[14] His mistreatment by his own countrymen apparently led this embittered war veteran to embrace his former enemy. Slater was certainly not the only Englishman in the later years of Elizabeth's reign to voice his loyalty to the King of Spain. In some instances, Philip was paired with the Pope. Such was the accusation against a tailor from Finchingfield, Essex, named George Bynckes, who in 1592 was indicted for publicly saying

> that the poope is supreme hedd over all Christendome, and that Kinge Phillipp ys right kinge of Ingland. And that if he, the said George Bynckes, sholde be comanded to doe any service in the Queenes behalfe, the same wold goe ageynste his conscience. And that Capteyne Drake and his soldiers when they have gonne forth in the princes service doe robbe and spoyle the kinge of Spayne of his goods, which is the righte kinge of Ingland.[15]

Here "papist" sympathies are combined with adherence to King Philip and denunciation of Sir Francis Drake, England's national hero in the war with Spain; and this combination represents a wholesale rejection of the concerted efforts of the Elizabethan regime and the political nation to make Protestantism synonymous with Englishness.

Sentiments that "kinge Phillipp was a father to Ingland" and that "Kinge Phillipp ys right kinge of Ingland" may also speak to the sometimes overlooked fact that, before becoming King of Spain, Philip had indeed already been King of England. According to Cardinal Allen, one of the chief reasons Pope Sixtus V entreated Philip to undertake the Armada was "his singular love towards that nation wherof by mariage to *Holie Queene Marie* of blessed memorie he was once kinge."[16] Slater and Bynckes may well be remembering this, and looking to Philip as England's once and future king. As Allen implies, Philip had only reigned briefly by virtue of being the husband of Queen Mary, and his kingship of England was terminated upon her death. The failure of Slater or Bynckes to mention Queen Mary may suggest that dissident Catholic commoners shared a gender bias widespread among the English Protestant political elite: a conviction that gynecocracy was an unfortunate anomaly, and an urgent desire for a masculine succession.[17]

One of the most interesting recorded examples of antigynecratic popular seditious speech is that attributed in 1591 to a laborer from Great Wenden, Essex, named John Feltwell. According to the indictment against him, Feltwell had publicly said, "let us praye for a father for we have a mother already." When queried, he explained, "let us pray for a kinge"; and when it was responded that "[we] have a gracious queene already, wherfore wold you praye for a kinge?" he elaborated as follows:

> the Queene was but a woman and ruled by noblemen and the noblemen and gentlemen were all one and the gentellmen and fermers wold hold togeyther one with another so that poore men cold gett nothinge amonge them, and therfore we shall never have a mery world while the queene lyveth but yf we had but one that would ryse, I would be the next, or els I wold the Spaniards wold come in that we maye have some sport and then we wold have corne amonge them.[18]

As reported, the syntax of Feltwell's declaration may not be entirely coherent, but the structural principle of his thinking comes through clearly enough: Feltwell's seditious words constitute a kind of counterdiscourse to the familiar Elizabethan homily exhorting "Good Order and Obedience to Rulers and Magistrates," in that they are built upon an analogical series of paired and opposed identities and interests—between father and mother, king and queen, man and woman, gentle and base, landed and landless, English and Spanish.[19]

Elizabeth's 1588 Armada speech argued that she had the heart and stomach—the greatness of spirit, the courage and fortitude—of a king; and this was an argument authorized upon the political fiction of the Queen's Two Bodies. Such ideological subtleties were clearly of no consequence to Feltwell. His remark that "the Queene was but a woman" registers the collapse of the Elizabethan *arcana imperii* upon contact with the intransigent empiricism of the English husbandman. Although Feltwell's wish for a king/father might at first be taken for a simple prejudice against gynecocracy, it actually develops into a denunciation of Elizabeth's failure to exercise her royal prerogative and fulfill her pastoral responsibility: This queen/mother warrants deposition because, although the nominal ruler, she has allowed herself to be ruled by men. The men in question constitute a particular socio-economic group that interposes itself between the prince and her poor subjects, abusing both and undermining the very principle of commonwealth. Thus, Feltwell's manifest misogyny quickly modulates into what could be called an intimation of class consciousness: First he indicts the nobility, then the gentry in league with the nobility, and finally the yeomanry in league with the gentry; in short, he locates the common interest of distinct social status groups in their ownership of land, an economic interest that links them in a conspiracy against tenant farmers and the landless poor. As is characteristic of dissent among the disadvantaged during this period, Feltwell imagines structural change as a heady mixture of holiday and riot. But what is striking about his vision of social apocalypse is that it concludes by creating an opening for the alien: "I would the Spaniards would come in that we may have some sport." Here the English commons' best opportunity to effect a change in the material conditions of their existence is seen to lie in the Spanish violation of the Elizabethan social body.

Feltwell's invocation of Spain in the context of English popular rebellion was not his innovation; on the contrary, it appears to have been an established trope of plebeian seditious rhetoric in later Elizabethan England. For example, in 1596, John Feere, a brickburner, was indicted for saying, "I wold that all the Spanyerds of Spayne ware landed here in Ingland to pull out the boores and churles by the eares, and that twenty thowsand of them ware aboute Mr. Capells house (meaning Arthur Capell of Little Hadham, esq.) for then he wold turne unto them and should be much set by." And in 1598, Henry Danyell, a laborer, was indicted for saying "that he hoped to see such warre in this Realme to afflicte the rich men of this countrye to requite their hardnes of hart towards the poore. And that the Spanyards ware better then the people of this land and therefore he had rather that they were here than the rich men of this countrie."[20] These instances are typical of the way in which the language of popular resistance employed elements of global geopolitics in the service of local grievances. Another, of considerably greater complexity, is the abortive Oxfordshire Rising of 1596. This was precipitated by a combination of resentment against depopulation caused by enclosure for sheep farming, successive failed harvests and dearth, and the contraction of economic opportunity for young artisans and servants. Its leader was Bartholomew Steer, a carpenter, whose plan was to kill some of the county's leading gentleman sheep farmers and to plunder their estates. After turning Oxfordshire upside down, Steer planned to go on toward London, where he anticipated that the apprentices would rise up and join his revolution. In seeking to enlist his fellow carpenter Roger Symonds to the cause, Steer invoked the precedent of Spain: "The poore did once rise in Spaine and Cutt down the gent[lemen] and sithens that tyme they have lyved merily there."[21]

Sir Henry Lee was named among the leading Oxfordshire gentleman sheep farmers whose properties Bartholomew Steer intended to despoil. One of Queen Elizabeth's favorites and her longtime jousting champion, Lee

masterminded much of the pageantry we associate with the cult of Elizabeth. The ways in which the Queen showed her favor toward the rapaciously
acquisitive Lee included not only grants of lands, offices, and honors but
also commissions to compel bondmen on royal lands to buy their freedom
from him. Entrepreneurial English gentlemen found the power of compulsory
manumission over prosperous farmers who were still technically serfs to be
potentially lucrative.[22] This was a scheme that Lee had assiduously pursued
over the course of three decades, beginning in the 1570s; although it was not
one of the grievances enumerated by the rebels of Oxfordshire, it does convey
a sense of this lordly shepherd's attitude toward the humbler members of the
commonwealth.

Upon his deathbed, in an unprecedented moment of intimacy with his
son and heir, Shakespeare's King Henry IV counsels the future Henry V "to
busy giddy minds / With foreign quarrels"; and we hear at the very end of the
play that plans are already afoot for an invasion of France.[23] This is one secret
of state that remains as congenial to today's rulers as to those of Lancastrian
or Tudor England. The heterodox comments of Feere, Danyell, Feltwell, and
Steer work against this statecraft by refusing the mystifying abstraction of a
collective national interest that is forged in opposition to a foreign enemy.
These lowly Elizabethan subjects are led into such acts of practical demystification by their tangible experience of exploitation, injustice, and dearth
within the commonwealth and within the parish. Among the potential spoils
that awaited Steer and his fellows at Lee's Ditchley estate in 1596 would have
been the "Ditchley" portrait of the Queen, which had been commissioned in
celebration of her visit to Lee there during the royal progress of 1592 (fig. 35).
That prospective pillaging—and the angry desperation of "the fourth sort or
classe amongst us" that had precipitated it—casts a peculiarly ironic light back
upon the painting's refulgent image of the Queen, her feet securely planted
in Oxfordshire and her skirts benevolently covering her realm. Just as the imagery of the "Ditchley" portrait mobilizes loyalty to the Elizabethan regime
in terms of an identification with a natural mother, so the imagery of the "Armada" portrait (fig. 41) mobilizes loyalty in terms of opposition to the threat
of an alien invasion. In its repudiation of England's queen/mother and its
welcoming of the Spanish invaders, Feltwell's seditious discourse turns each
of those powerful icons upside down.

Defacing the Queen

Nicholas Sander's iconoclastic challenge to his Anglican opponents—"Breake if you dare the Image of the Queenes Majestie, or Armes of the Realme"—mockingly ascribed to them an idolatrous attitude toward the icons of the royal supremacy.[1] However, there is evidence that at least a few Elizabethan subjects did indeed dare to break or to disfigure the Queen's image or the royal arms, and that their motivations for doing so were various. In 1591, for example, the Privy Council was alarmed by reports of a "great riot" in Sussex during which the Queen's arms were "torne and pulled downe."[2] The precipitating cause of the riot is not reported, but it is likely to have been the dearth that was widespread at this date and had sparked numerous disturbances, both rural and urban. Although, in this instance, the origins of anti-Elizabethan iconoclasm may have been socio-economic rather than sectarian, most recorded cases appear to manifest a mixture of religious and political dissidence. The ways in which royal portraits were treated not only by the adherents but also by the enemies of the regime confirm that they were regarded not merely as representations of the body natural of the monarch but as charismatic symbols of the mystical body of kingship that inhered in the person of the Queen.

As is testified by the following dispatch from the Spanish ambassador in London to King Philip's Secretary, imitative magic was practiced upon images of the Queen in order to do her harm:

> A countryman has found, buried in a stable, three wax figures.... [T]he centre figure had the word Elizabeth written on the forehead and the side figures were dressed like her councillors ... the left side of the images being transfixed with a large quantity of pig's bristles as if it were some sort of witchcraft. When it reached the Queen's ears she was disturbed, as it was looked upon as an augury.[3]

Although the Queen and many of her subjects were apparently appalled by this discovery, Reginald Scot invoked these "three images of late yeeres found in a doonghill, to the terror & astonishment of manie thousands" in order to debunk the whole mentality of witch belief: "Such mischeefous pretenses . . . though they never can or doo take effect, the practisers be punished with all extremitie: bicause therein is manifested a traiterous heart to the Queene, and a presumption against God."[4] While denying supernatural efficacy to such image magic, Scot nevertheless affirmed the heinous nature of the practitioners' intent—at once high treason and a mortal sin.

Anxious concern for the welfare of the monarch, upon whom depended the stability of the entire socio-political order, led Elizabethan parliamentarians to criminalize a wide range of gestures, comments, and images that could be interpreted as expressing ill will toward Queen Elizabeth. And agents of the regime were vigilant in prosecuting any suspicious uses of the royal image that came to their attention. In 1571, for example, the Privy Council ordered the interrogation of several people in connection with "a boke painted wherein the Queen's Majesties image is with an arrowe in her mowthe."[5] This was a society in which "to compass, imagine, invent, devise, or intend" the bodily harm of the sovereign was to be guilty of high treason; a society in which it was felonious, and thus a capital offense, to so much as speculate about how long the Queen might live, "by setting or erecting of any figure or figures, or by casting of nativities, or by calculation, or by any prophesying, witchcraft, conjurations."[6] Here it must be emphasized that the state's conceptualization of the work of treason did not clearly separate the domain of the imagination from that of social action, the thought from the deed.

The scope of the surveillance and discipline that the Elizabethan regime sought to impose upon its subjects was totalitarian in its ambitions, although far beyond its capacity to implement effectively. Despite the regime's ambitiously conceived but haphazardly enforced controls, both dissident Elizabethan subjects and hostile aliens manifested their antipathy by mounting symbolic attacks upon the person of the prince—by ridiculing, destroying, or otherwise appropriating the royal image. And there is extant evidence not only of attacks upon authorized royal icons but also of unauthorized representations being made to order for defacement. In chapter ten, I touched upon some instances in which the Elizabethan image was appropriated and subjected to ridicule abroad. In the present chapter, I suggest the variety of forms that iconoclasm could take when Elizabethan subjects in England and Ireland directed their resistance toward the royal image. Here I shall juxtapose three instances of symbolic violence: the first ascribed to a radical religious nonconformist; the second, to a recusant English Catholic; the third, to a Catholic

Irish rebel. To a large degree, each of these examples owes its preservation in the historical record to the concerted disciplinary and documentary activity of the Elizabethan state, and to the work of the regime's agents in giving an exemplary narrative shape to the perceived depravity of its enemies.

William Hacket, an illiterate maltmaker and charismatic lay preacher, caused a commotion in the streets of London in 1591 when, declaring the Day of Judgment to be at hand, he and his two erstwhile apostles publicly denied the Queen's sovereignty and urged her deposition. Hacket, who styled himself "King of Europe" and claimed to be the Messiah, may have had connections with a small group of radical reformers within the Puritan movement. Whether or not Thomas Cartwright and other leading Presbyterians actually used Hacket to further their own agenda, the government certainly used the incident in a concerted effort to discredit them.[7] Hacket's indictment for high treason was based not only upon his seditious words but also upon his actions: he "did trayterouslie debruze and deface her Majestie's armes in one Kaye's house . . . inveighinge then and there bytterlie againste her Majestie." Furthermore, upon seeing the Queen's picture—presumably a popular print—on display in his lodgings, Hackett "did, with an iron instrument, villainouslie and trayterouslie deface the pycture, and especiallie that part of the picture which represented her Majestie's harte, raylinge most traiterously againste her Majestie's personne."[8] According to an officially sanctioned pamphlet written by Richard Cosin and printed after Hacket's execution, Hacket had confessed regarding his defacement of the Queen's arms, "that hee was mooved thereunto inwardly by the spirit, to take away her whole power of her authoritie. . . . Hee confessed also, that he was likewise moved to put out the Lyons and the Dragons eyes in the armes."[9] In seeking to put out the heraldic eyes in the royal arms, Hacket was making a violent if futile gesture of resistance to surveillance by the state.

Contemporary judgments of these iconophobic acts would have been colored by the varying ways in which Hacket's agency was perceived, and such perceptions would not have been disinterested. The Queen herself had already spoken in Parliament in 1585 to the effect that Catholics ("Romanists") and Puritans ("new-fanglenesse") were equally perilous to her realm, "and of the latar I must pronounce them daungerows to a kyngely rule, to have every man according to his owne sensure to make a doome of the validitie and privitie of his princes governement, with a comon vaile and cover of God's worde." This is precisely what Hacket had presumed to do, as he implied in his alleged confession: "Hee was mooved thereunto inwardly by the spirit, to take away her whole power of her authoritie." In a 1587 parliamentary speech, the Speaker of the House of Commons had gone so far as to accuse "these new-fangled refiners" called "Puritans" of enabling the anticipated Armada: "Abasing the sacred authority and Majesty of their prince, they do both joyne and concur with the Jesuits inn opening the dore and preparing the way to the Spanish invasion that is threatned against the realme."[10] Harassed religious reformers like Cartwright, who were anxious to disassociate themselves from Hacket, argued that he was merely a madman; contrariwise, those who disseminated the establishment line, like Cosin, argued that Hacket and his cohorts were the agents of a diabolically inspired conspiracy.[11] At Hacket's trial, the Attorney General dismissed arguments regarding the defendant's "franticke humours," emphasizing instead his leadership position within a carefully planned plot to overthrow the state. There followed a discourse by the Queen's Solicitor General, who averred that

> no treason was so dangerous to the estate as that proceeding from so base puddelles shaddowed with the glosse of a pretended holliness, forasmuch as yf a nobleman rebell, his meaninge ys onelie to usurpe the Crowne, not im-payringe the governmente; but ther can be no means to these peasants to accomplishe ther purpose, excepte by the absolute extirpation of all govern-mente, magistracy, nobility and gentrye, with the utter subversione and ruine of all lawes that should suppresse these ther trayterous actions.

The Solicitor General elaborated his telling distinction between an elite coup d'état and a popular revolution by inserting Hacket into a native tradition of insurrection stretching back two centuries through the Ket and Cade re-bellions to the Peasant's Revolt; to clinch the case, he identified as "the verye paterne of this conspiracy," the millenarian regime of the Anabaptist John of Leyden in Münster.[12] Within the interpretive framework constructed by the prosecution, Hacket's defacement of the Queen's picture and the royal arms was far more than a gesture of hostility toward the established church or the person of the monarch: It epitomized an assault upon the entire existing socio-political fabric and its metaphysical basis in the divinely created cosmic order. In other words, Hacket's purported actions made manifest the threat to the very principle of hierarchy that the newly established Elizabethan regime had sought to restrain in its 1560 proclamation against "the breaking or defacing of . . . any image of Kings, princes, or noble estates of this realm."[13]

A curious case from 1601 indicates that some among the Queen's English Catholic subjects, like a few on the radical fringe of the Puritan movement, manifested their resistance to the royal supremacy over the church by abusing the symbols of state. As if in answer to Nicholas Sander's call, some beleaguered recusants were apparently prepared to become iconoclasts. Government officials surmised that such malevolent motives were at work when they intercepted a chest bound for France that contained a small box, wherein was found "her Majesty's picture in metal, and a kind of mercury sublimate which had eaten in the metal." Having examined the contents of the box, William Waad, the Secretary to the Privy Council, declared to Sir Robert Cecil: "I cannot conceive he can have a good meaning that will place the picture of her Majesty's sacred person with such poison as hath endangered the apothecary's man that did but put it to his tongue."[14] The owner of the chest, one Thomas Harrison, was quickly interrogated:

> Being further asked what picture that is which he had . . . he answereth that it is a picture of a woman, but of whom he doth not know. . . . He put the picture in the box with the other mixture but a little before he went over [to France], for no other cause but because they were both of one substance. Being asked if it be not the picture of the Queen that which was in metal, he saith that he thinketh that Hillyard did make it amongst the models that he made for the seal of the Queen's picture.[15]

Under interrogation—which likely involved torture—Harrison began reluctantly to concede that the image immersed in chemicals might have been that of the Queen. However, he continued to insist that he had had no interest in the image itself; indeed, he tried to suggest that he had barely noticed it: His avowed interest was in alchemy—not, he implied, in witchcraft. Thus, his focus was not upon the image but rather upon the substance from which it was made; and he had placed the picture together with the solution for the eminently logical reason that they both contained mercury.

Harrison's deposition contains the striking detail that the incriminating image was "amongst the models" that Nicholas Hilliard had "made for the seal of the Queen's picture." Presumably, this was the second Great Seal of the reign (fig. 44), in use from 1586 until the Queen's death.[16] The Great Seal, the impression of which authenticated official documents of the highest import, was the symbolic instrument of royal authority, the Queen's fiat. The second Great Seal of Elizabeth bears the Queen's image on both obverse and reverse, the former a frontal and standing image and the latter a rare equestrian image of martial demeanor. On both sides, the Queen is shown in full majesty, crowned and holding orb and scepter, with heavenly rays shining down upon her head; on the obverse, her mantle is supported by hands extended from the clouds. As Roy Strong notes, this iconography projects a

FIGURE 44

The Second Great Seal of Elizabeth I, by Nicholas Hilliard and Anthony Dericke; 1584–86. Obverse and reverse. © The Trustees of The British Museum.

"sanctification of the monarchy."[17] The deposition implies that Harrison had had in his possession and had subjected to abuse an unusually potent royal image, thus compounding his apparent treason with sacrilege. Harrison, who during interrogation revealed that he had close ties to Catholic clerics in Paris, attempted to extricate himself from his dire circumstances by insisting upon a rigorously materialist explanation of the evidence against him. On the other hand, Secretary Waad—a zealous foe of papistry, who frequently interrogated missionary priests by torture—seems to have regarded what he called "the picture of her Majesty's sacred person" as a talisman, due the kind of reverence that he himself might have identified as idolatry had he observed it in the conduct of a Catholic toward a votive image of the Virgin Mary.[18] Indeed, when Elizabeth's agents first discovered the little box secreted within Harrison's chest, they may well have been expecting to find there a papistical idol or relic rather than a corroding image of Queen Elizabeth's "sacred person."

In strife-torn Ireland, Queen Elizabeth's other kingdom, Catholic resistance was intensified by the profound differences in language, culture, and socio-political organization among the indigenous Irish majority, the now largely assimilated old English elites, and the dominant minority of new English planters and administrators who were bent on securing their hegemony. In these complex circumstances, portraits of Queen Elizabeth were bestowed upon Gaelic chieftains and their wives in an effort to arouse their admiration and to secure their loyalty to the English crown.[19] It seems, however, that if the

Queen's unruly Irish subjects embraced the royal image, they sometimes did so only in order to deface it. The most notorious instance of image appropriation as a practice of Irish resistance concerns the rebel Sir Brian-na-Murtha O'Rourke, active in Connaught in the later 1580s. The incident is reported in a number of sources—all of them English but differing in details. One report claimed that O'Rourke had "made a wooden image for the Queen, and caused the same to be trailed at a horse's tail, and kernes and horseboys to hurl stones at it, every day"—implying that he was engaged in a kind of imitative magic like that attributed by some to the infamous wax dolls stuck with hog bristles or to Hacket's knife attack on the Queen's portrait.[20]

The most lurid and detailed account of O'Rourke's action is contained in a dispatch from the Elizabethan Lord Deputy in Ireland to Lord Burghley:

> O'Rourke about two or three years since having found in a church or in some other place an image of a tall woman wrote upon the breast thereof QUEEN ELIZABETH, which done he presently fell with such spiteful and traitorous speeches to rail at it, and otherwise so filthily to use it, as I protest unto your Lordship I abhor to remember, and can by no means frame my pen to write. During which time his barbarous gallowglasses . . . with their . . . axes striking the image one while on the head, another while on the face, and sometimes stabbing it in the body, never ceased until with hacking, and mangling they had utterly defaced it. And being nevertheless not contented herewith they, the more to manifest the malice of their traitorous hearts, fastened a halter about the neck of the image, and tying it to a horse tail dragged it along upon the ground, and so beating it with their axes, and railing most despitefully at it, they finished their traitorous pageant.[21]

What the Queen's servant imagines as a "traiterous pageant" is an extended scene of symbolic violence that parodies elements of a royal progress, of the iconoclastic outbursts accompanying the Protestant Reformation in England, and of those horrific public punishments prescribed for traitors by the Elizabethan state. Of particular interest is the suggestion that O'Rourke appropriated to his own wicked uses a church sculpture—perhaps an allegorical figure or the representation of a saint or biblical personage, or the funeral effigy of a woman of high rank. In this curious detail, a parody of Protestant iconoclasm against traditional religious images is fused with an act of Catholic iconoclasm against the Elizabethan image of state: Who, now, is the idolator, and who the iconoclast?

In the official articles indicting O'Rourke for high treason, the charge was made that

> Sir Bryan, contrary to the lawes of the Churche of Englande and Irland, did selebrate and keepe the feaste of the Natyvitie of our Lord God according to

the Romishe and Popishe computation; and most trayterously and wickedly
caused a woman's pycture to be drawne and draged after a horsse tayle through
his owne towne, where then he kept his Christmas, in the very pudle and myre
and like most fythy places, and did publishe and declare to the voulgare people
that the same was her highnes pycture, and that he caused the same to be
soe used in despighte and contempt of her Majesty, tearmynge her highnes the
mother and nurse of all herisies and heretiques.[22]

This narrative represents O'Rourke's violence against the head of the Elizabethan state and the supreme governor of its church as a logical consequence of his fealty to the Pope and the old religion. However, in the very
process of establishing the Elizabethan regime's charge of high treason against
O'Rourke, the official document attributes to him a countercharge of heresy
against the English Protestant establishment. "Tearmynge her highnes the
mother and nurse of all herisies and heretiques," the indictment ventrilo-
quizes a mocking Catholic perspective upon the Elizabethan regime, which
had appropriated the maternal Marian cult for the benefit of the Protestant
Virgin Queen. The English indictment against O'Rourke preserves within it a
fragmentary and distorted echo of that dissident voice which it seeks to silence.
This echo hints that O'Rourke's Christmastide rite of violence was directed
against what he himself may have experienced as the Anglicans' blasphemous
parody of the Nativity and the Virgin Mary. In describing the destruction
of a Marian votive image by order of the Queen at Edward Rookwood's estate in 1578, Richard Topcliffe wrote against those "who had sucked of the
idoll's poysoned mylke."[23] By "tearmynge her highnes the mother and nurse
of all herisies and heretiques," O'Rourke in effect reverses the polemical vec-
tor of Topcliffe's figure: In this reappropriation of the trope of nurture by the
Catholic imaginary, the "poysoned mylke" of false doctrine is being sucked
from the Elizabethan idol by benighted Protestants; and it is precisely by
his act of anti-Elizabethan iconoclasm that O'Rourke demonstrates his piety
and his obedience to the scriptural injunction to destroy idolatrous graven
images.

In the face of English military advances in Ireland, O'Rourke fled in 1591
to Scotland, where he apparently was seeking to recruit Scots mercenaries. In
an unusual legal move, the English crown formally requested his extradition
to England, and King James VI complied. On dubious jurisdictional grounds,
O'Rourke was indicted for high treason by an English grand jury. Among the
charges was the crime of lèse-majesté, made in reference to what was called
"the treason of the picture."[24] In punishment for his alleged abuse of the
Elizabethan royal image, English justice reenacted that abuse upon the Irish
chieftain's flesh. As recorded by the annalist John Stow,

> Upon Wednesdaie the 3 of November [1591], Bren O'Royrke was drawne to
> Tyborne, and there hanged, his members and bowels burned in the fire, his
> heart taken out, and holden up by the hangman, naming it to be the archtraytors
> heart, and then did he cast the same into the fire, then was his head stricken
> off, and his body quartered.[25]

It was reported that, upon the scaffold, O'Rourke refused to make obeisance
to the Queen; and, when taunted that he had bowed to idols, he retorted that
there was "a great difference between your queen and images of the saints."[26]
It may be impossible to determine how accurately these and similarly hostile
accounts represent the historical actions of Sir Brian-na-Murtha O'Rourke;
indeed, it has been suggested that the case against O'Rourke was merely a step
in an elaborate conspiracy within court circles to bring down Sir John Perrot,
English Privy Councilor and sometime Lord Deputy in Ireland.[27] At the least,
such accounts do offer compelling evidence that abuse of the royal image was
a powerful motivator, both for the agents of the Elizabethan regime and for
their enemies.

It is not always easy to ascertain precisely how either the iconoclasts or the
authorities construed the explicitly hostile acts that were committed against
the royal image. Were they to be understood merely as impulsive outbursts,
or as premeditated acts of imitative magic intended to cause the Queen material harm? In many instances, such precise distinctions were probably not
operative in the minds of either the perpetrators or the authorities. In other
instances, interpretation appears to have been tactical, and calculated for purposes of incrimination or disavowal that varied with the circumstances and
agendas of the interpreters. Official concern or ire was aroused not only by
overtly violent or seditious appropriations of the royal image but sometimes
also by actions that appear to us to indicate little more than a subject's casually
irreverent attitude toward symbols of authority. In yet other instances, suspect
attitudes toward the royal image served as collateral evidence that might reinforce a prejudgment of treason. Such was the case of Robert Dalby, a Catholic
missionary priest who was apprehended at the moment of his landing in
England, and who was executed in 1589:

> The judges openly declared that they found him guilty, because he professed
> himself to be a priest. Among other things objected against him was this, that
> a sixpence was found in his purse, on which the Queen's likeness was nearly
> rubbed off, and they said he would do the same to the Queen herself if he
> could.[28]

An ideologically embattled and politically insecure regime such as that of Elizabeth Tudor was likely to construe any less-than-idealized representation of the monarch or any less-than-reverential demeanor toward the royal image as a serious breach of decorum, if not as an outright indication of treasonous intent. Whatever the sympathies and intentions of those who created, sponsored, displayed, or possessed representations of the monarch merely as a consequence of their contact with the charismatic royal icon, they became participants in a potentially dangerous negotiation of symbolic power.

Secrets of the Heart

Cultures mold, mark, and sort the individual human bodies that compose the social body's members, and they do so in diverse ways. Elizabethan bodies were complexly coded, not only by means of the prescribed dress and comportment that constructed their social identities in terms of gender, age, occupation, and estate, but also through the explicit rules and implicit understandings that regulated both the distinctions and the interactions among social orders. The political fiction of the King's Two Bodies was a singular and privileged instance of such coding; and the combination of historical contingency and political agency that produced the Elizabethan discourse of the Queen's Two Bodies was an idiosyncratic variation upon that already special case.

One manifestation of the authority vested in the body of the Queen was her power over the bodies of her subjects. As summarized by Thomas Wilson in 1600, it was within the royal prerogative to

> pardon and give lyfe to the condemned or to take away the life or member
> of any subject at her pleasure, and none other in all ye Kingdom hath power
> of life and member but onely the Prince, noe not so much as to imprison or
> otherwise to punish any other, unless it be his servant, without the expresse
> comission from the Queen.[1]

Within legal limits, and as exercised in part through those who were delegated to act in her name, this female prince held the power of life and limb over every Englishman. In Elizabethan England, as elsewhere in early modern Europe, such power to judge and to punish was the practical manifestation of a dominant ideology of divinely sanctioned hierarchy. And it was a power most starkly materialized in the contrast between the anointed body of the monarch and the butchered body of the traitor, whose treason was explicitly construed by the statutes as threatening the life of the monarch.[2]

In anatomizing "the spectacle of the scaffold" under the ancien régime, Michel Foucault remarks that "the public execution is to be understood not only as a judicial, but also as a political ritual. It belongs, even in minor cases, to the ceremonies by which power is manifested." And in writing of the punishment of Edmund Campion and other Catholic missionary priests under the Elizabethan treason statutes, John Bossy remarks that such "examples of the execution of justice in England, attended as they were by a ritual cuisine requiring dissection of the victim, boiling of entrails and placing of heads in public situations, might well be considered sacrificial rites in the temple of monarchy."[3] By trying and executing Roman Catholics on political rather than on religious grounds, the Elizabethan regime sought not only to manifest its power (as Foucault and Bossy both compellingly argue) but also to legitimate that power in the face of the fundamental ideological challenge posed by its papist opponents. The Catholic missionary priests and their abettors made up a special category of deviant Elizabethan subjects, for while the state deemed them to be traitors and prosecuted them as such, they proclaimed themselves to be prisoners of conscience, loyal subjects who were being persecuted for their faith alone. A momentous ideological conflict was played out upon the living bodies and the dismembered remains of these Catholic traitors/martyrs.[4]

By means of their very first legislation—the 1559 acts of Supremacy and Uniformity—the Elizabethan regime and the Protestant political nation had effectively put Catholic subjects into the position of having to renounce their religious convictions and practices in order to demonstrate their loyalty to the state. As one such subject put it, "truth is made treason, religion rebellion."[5] William Allen pointedly argued the Catholic position that this policy was "to make traitors and not punish treasons."[6] And, as discussed at the opening of part four, even so staunch a Protestant as Philip Sidney was capable of appreciating, and reminding the Queen, that her Roman Catholic subjects were "men whose spirits are full of anguish; some being forced to oaths they account damnable; some having their ambition stopped, because they are not in the way of advancement . . . all burdened with the weight of their consciences."[7] The Catholic position in this ideological struggle will perhaps appear retrospectively to have been an enlightened plea for freedom of religion; nevertheless, it was the circumstantial product of the dire situation in which Elizabethan Catholics found themselves. After all, on the continent, torture had long been used by the Catholic Church in the prosecution of heresy; and it is clear that Cardinal Allen and his brethren had no intention of promoting ecumenism and religious toleration, should they ever succeed in restoring their apostate country to the Catholic fold.[8]

In 1559, newly Elizabethan Protestant reformers may have hoped or expected that the old faith would fade away within a generation; if so, they were to be disappointed. Although they were not the first missionary priests to return to England, the arrival of Edmund Campion and Robert Persons in 1581 heralded an enterprise that would continue throughout the second half of the Elizabethan reign. Thenceforth, the Protestant state and its dissident Catholic subjects were engaged in an unremitting public struggle to define the relationship between the temporal and spiritual domains, between politics and religion, treason and conscience, the royal prerogative and the liberties of the subject. The vociferous and sharply delineated ideological combat between the Protestant state and its resistant Catholic subjects opened up issues for consideration and debate that were beyond the power of either party to contain or control.

This combat—which touched the very foundations of the regime's legitimacy—was conducted through a range of cultural forms and performances. These included printed tracts, proclamations, poems, martyrologies, broadsheets and engraved prints, as well as public trials and executions. To cite the formative instance invoked by Bossy: the powerful personal challenge to the Queen's spiritual authority made by Campion both in speech and writing, the energies expended by the Protestant state to discredit him and to justify its own actions against him, and the profound and enduring impact of his martyrdom upon the English Catholic community all demonstrate that the Elizabethan regime struggled mightily but with only limited success to suppress this volatile discourse of treason and conscience. As Laurence Humphrey vividly put it in an address to the Earl of Leicester, "Campion dead bites with his friends' teeth . . . for . . . as a harvest of new men rose from the seed of the dragon's teeth, so one labour of ours only begets another and still another."[9] The present chapter examines the incarnation of this ideological struggle in the body of the Queen and in the bodies of her subjects.

Francis Bacon famously declared that the Queen did not wish "to make windows into men's hearts and secret thoughts, except the abundance of them did overflow into overt express acts and affirmations . . . impugning and impeaching advisedly and ambitiously her majesty's supreme power."[10] Of course, the limits of royal toleration depended upon where the distinction between private conscience and public agency was to be drawn—upon how those "overt express acts and affirmations" against the royal supremacy were to be defined, and by whom. Bacon, who was an active participant in and defender of interrogatory torture, defended royal surveillance as a defensive measure, only to be deployed against the imminent threat of treasonous acts.[11] The metaphor so subtlely employed by Bacon was crudely but vividly reimagined by John Baxter as the means by which the state could gain unbridled access to the innermost thoughts of its subjects. As mentioned above in part two, Baxter wishfully proposed that "if a window were framed in the brests of these discontented catholikes . . . her Majestie and the state-guiding counsell and all true friends to the kingdom might know their secret intentions."[12] Like Bacon, Baxter was here participating in the work of an antipapist imaginary that was rooted in tropes of Catholic secrecy, stealth, and dissembling.[13] Of course, to the degree that such Catholic practices were a reality, they were largely the unacknowledged consequences of the state's own repressive policies. Sir John Harington candidly observed that, as laws against Catholics became more and more harsh, "their practices grewe fowler and fowler; onely the question is (which in my conscience I cannot certainly decide) . . . whether their sinister practices drewe on these rigorous lawes, or whether the rigour of these lawes moved them to these unnaturall practices."[14]

Interrogation by torture, followed by public trial and execution—this was the sequential means by which such "secret intentions" could be probed, unmasked, published, and punished.[15] The corporal regime followed a methodical process. The accused were interrogated with the use of bodily torture in order to discover useful information; after trial and conviction, the condemned were hanged, cut down, and disemboweled; their hearts and entrails were displayed and burned; their heads were cut off; and their eviscerated bodies were quartered. The heads and quarters of the deceased were subsequently boiled and prominently displayed at strategic locations—if in London, then the quarters upon the four city gates and the heads upon London Bridge. In one of his illustrated martyrologies, Richard Verstegan includes several later stages of this passion play within the frame of a single engraving, with each vignette keyed by letter to a verbal description (fig. 45). The early modern state's practices of torture and execution are symptomatic of that "culture of dissection" that Jonathan Sawday sees epitomized in the Renaissance anatomy theatre.[16] Such practical procedures for processing the bodies of traitors were grisly materializations of the Elizabethan regime's intent to "know their secret intentions," an unmetaphoring of the will to anatomize their inward parts in order to reveal the malign truths secreted there. As Edgar bluntly puts it—in a Shakespearean play notably concerned with tyranny, torture, and conscience—"To know our enemies' minds we rip their hearts."[17]

FIGURE 45

"Crudelitas in Catholicis Mactandis" by Richard Verstegan. Engraving.
Printed in Richard Verstegan, *Descriptiones quaedam illius inhumanae et
multiplicis persecutionis, quam in Anglia propter fidem Catholicè Christiani*
(n.p., n.d. [1583–84?]). By permission of the President of St. Edmund's College
and the Archbishop of Westminster.

Under the direction of Lord Burghley and Secretary Walsingham, the use of
torture in the interrogation of captured missionary priests and various others
deemed to be traitors became a policy vigorously pursued by the Elizabethan
government.[18] By the early 1580s, Richard Topcliffe had become active in this
campaign; by the early 1590s, he was established as the most assiduous—and
most notorious—agent of the regime's concerted campaign against papistry.
Topcliffe was tireless in the pursuit and apprehension of clandestine priests and
appallingly zealous in interrogating them, giving evidence against them at trial,
and supervising their public executions. The writer of a 1594 letter in which
the Earl of Essex was praised for his skillful interrogation of the accused traitor
Dr. Roderigo Lopez concluded that "contrary to our Topcliffian customs . . . he

hath won with words more than others could ever do with racks."[19] It is clear that by this time, and not only in the eyes of Catholics, Topcliffe had come to personify the most questionable of the regime's activities.

Topcliffe conducted frequent interrogations by torture in a special room of his own house at Westminster, and he did so with the full knowledge and authorization of Queen Elizabeth and her privy councillors. It was there, in 1592, that he tortured Robert Southwell, the Jesuit priest and poet, whom he had personally apprehended. In *An Humble Supplication to Her Majesty*, which Southwell had written shortly before his capture and had apparently intended for print, his rhetorical strategy was to disbelieve that the Queen could be personally complicit in the cruel practices of her own regime:

> We presume that your Majestie seldome or never heareth the truth of our persecutions, your lenity and tenderness being knowne to be soe professed an enemy to these Cruelties, that you would never permit their Continuance, if they were expressed to your Highnes as they are practised upon us. . . . Let us be not so farr exiled out of the limits of all Compassion, as besides all other evills, to have it confirmed under your Majesties hand, *that we suffer no punishments for Religion*, suffering in proofe all punishments for nothing ells.[20]

We know—and Southwell presumably knew—that the Queen was well informed about what he called "the truth of our persecutions." In a letter to the Queen concerning Southwell's interrogation, Topcliffe declared proudly, "It may please your majesty to consider, I never did take so weighty a man." In the same letter, Topcliffe reported having Southwell manacled, "here within my strong chamber in Westminster churchyard"; and he offered to make himself the instrument through which the Queen could pluck out the heart of Southwell's mystery: "If your highness' pleasure be to know any thing in his heart, to stand against the wall, his feet standing upon the ground, and his hands but as high as he can reach against the wall . . . will enforce him to tell all; and the truth proved by the sequel."[21] Despite his boasts to the Queen, Topcliffe was apparently unsuccessful in wringing anything incriminating from Southwell's heart. On the other hand, his torture of Southwell seems to have made Topcliffe something of a pariah, whom the Privy Council found it convenient to disavow.[22] It was normal practice that after the condemned was cut down from the gallows, his heart was cut out by the hangman, who declared it to be the heart of a traitor as he exhibited it to the crowd. When Father Henry Garnett wrote of Southwell that "being afterwards disemboweled, his holy heart leaped in the hangman's hands," he was vividly making the point that Southwell's heart, like his soul, was unspotted. In the light of both traditional Christian iconography and the devotional practices of the Jesuit

order, Southwell's "holy heart" was the physical locus of his love for God; and
its butchery by the state was thus converted by Garnett into a kind of divine
sacrifice.[23]

Topcliffe's method of torturing Southwell was by then standard practice in
the interrogation of suspected Catholic subversives, as is clear from a warrant
issued to him by the Privy Council in 1590

> to examyn . . . Christofer Baylles alias Evers a Seamenary Priest, John Baylles
> tayller, Henry Goorney, Antony Kaye, and Jhon Coxed from tyme to tyme,
> and . . . to commytte them . . . unto such torture upon the wawle as is usuall for
> the better understanding of the trewthe of matters agenst her Majestie and the
> Stayte.[24]

The rack, which had earlier been the instrument of choice in such interrogations, was by this date being replaced by a quieter, cleaner, and more effective
method—one that did not require the operation of diabolical machinery but
merely used the weight of the victim's body as the means of its own agony.
James Heath writes that Topcliffe "was reported to have said, at Southwell's
trial, that he had the Council's letter to prove that he had been authorized
to torture the prisoner, short of death or maim."[25] Such justifications have
an alarming immediacy in the light of twenty-first-century revelations about
the terrorizing of prisoners in the so-called war on terror. A 2002 Justice
Department opinion solicited by then presidential counsel Alberto Gonzales
concluded that "physical pain amounting to torture must be equivalent in intensity to the pain accompanying serious physical injury, such as organ failure,
impairment of bodily function, or even death."[26] According to this standard,
Topcliffe's admitted acts of torture might not have constituted torture at all.

The Elizabethan regime had been made sufficiently uneasy and defensive
about its use of the rack during the prosecution of Campion and others that
a justification of its methods was published in 1583. This quasi-official text,
possibly authored by Burghley, was subsequently reprinted and translated
into several other languages. Its conclusion makes a case for the Queen as
a reluctant and tenderhearted torturer: "Torture hath been and is lawfully
judged to be used . . . for inquisition of truth . . . yet even in that necessary
use of such proceeding, enforced by the offender's notorious obstinacy, is
nevertheless to be acknowledged the sweet temperature of Her Majesty's mild
and gracious clemency."[27] Every execution of a Catholic for treason provided
an occasion to give the lie to Burghley's claim, and such opportunities were
eagerly embraced by the opposition. For example, William Allen wrote of
the Jesuit John Nelson's martyrdom that "he was cut downe before he was
halfe dead, dismembered and ripped up, and as the hangman plucked out his

hart, he lifted himself up a little, and as some that stode nere report, spake these wordes, I forgive the Q. and all those that were causers of my death."[28] Mixing piety with sensationalistic propaganda, Allen's brief narrative seizes upon the act in which the state incarnated its claim to have done justice upon a traitor, and makes of it a golden legend in which martyred charity confounds tyrannous cruelty.

The primary focus of this chapter is not upon celebrity victims like Edmund Campion or Robert Southwell but rather upon the strange case of Thomas Pormort, another of the missionary priests who were executed for treason and, in the eyes of the Catholic faithful, martyred in later Elizabethan England. Richard Topcliffe interrogated Pormort by torture, accused him at trial, and supervised his execution by hanging, disemboweling, and quartering in February 1592.[29] Some time late in that year, the expatriate English Catholic polemicist, printer and engraver Richard Verstegan sent a letter from Flanders to the Jesuit Robert Persons, who was then resident in Madrid. He enclosed a document headed "A copy of certain notes written by Mr Pormort Priest and Martir, of certaine speeches used by Top[clif] unto him whyle he was prisoner in the house and custody of the said Topclif. The which notes were since delivered to Wade one of the clarcks of the counsel, and by him shewed to the co[unsel] in November last 1592." Seven of the ten items enumerated in the report concern Pormort's charge that, during his interrogation, Topcliffe made him privy to his own intimacy with the Queen:

> Item, Topcliff told (unto the said priest) that he was so [great and] familiar with Her Majestie that he many tymes putteth [his hands] betweene her brestes and pappes, and in her neck.
>
> That he hathe not only scene her legges and knees [but feeleth them] with his hands above her knees.
>
> That he hathe felt her belly, and said unto Her Majestie that she h[ad] the softest belly of any woman kynde.
>
> That she said unto him, "be not thease the armes, legges and bo[dy] of King Henry?" to which he answered, "yea."
>
> That she gave him for a favour a whyte linen hose wroughte with whyte silke, etc.
>
> That he is so familiar with her that, when he pleaseth to sp[eake] with her he may tak her away from any company; and that she [is] as pleasant with every one that she dothe love.
>
> That he did not care for the Counsell, for that he had his aucthor[ite] from Her Majestie.[30]

This singular relation—reputedly first spoken in the torture chamber, and later recounted in the Privy Council chamber and the open courtroom—brings the Queen's *arcana imperii* into a startling convergence with the subject's illicit secrets, and incongruously yokes the monarch's *corpus mysticum* to the traitor's tortured flesh.

In Verstegan's report of Pormort's account of Topcliffe's (putative) words, there is nothing explicitly impugning the conduct of the Queen. It is Topcliffe's lewd and irreverent discourse about the Queen that is the immediate subject of censure. On the other hand, the salacious remarks that Pormort apparently attributed to Topcliffe arose within the context of a discourse about the Queen's sexual proclivities and practices that dated from at least the beginning of her reign. Defamatory gossip about Queen Elizabeth could be heard in the village as well as at court, and it also circulated widely on the continent. While largely irrecoverable, the gossip of the Queen's humblest subjects is partially documented in the extant assize records and is hinted at in letters and reports. For example, in 1580 an Essex laborer named Thomas Playfere was convicted of rumoring that "the Quene had two children by my Lord Robert (meaning the earl of Leicester)"; and a year later, one Henry Hawkins bettered the report: "The earl hath five children by the queen, and she never goeth on progress but to be delivered."[31] Such rumors effectively mocked the official cult of mystical royal virginity by insisting upon the physicality of the royal body, the carnal inclinations of the Queen. Hawkins's remark is especially interesting for its cynical explanation of the function of royal progresses, which played so important a role in projecting the Queen's charismatic authority among the commons and in monitoring the loyalties of regional magnates. The scandalous words of Playfere and Hawkins—and many others of a similar tenor in the records of local Elizabethan courts and in domestic and foreign state papers of the period—suggest in what varied and casual ways the royal body, and the royal fiction, might be manipulated by the Queen's subjects; and how easily such discursive manipulations might be construed by the ever anxious authorities as symptoms of a popular disenchantment that threatened the established order.

In addition to its informal, popular, oral dimension, this defamatory discourse had a more systematically polemical dimension, one that was characterized by rhetorically exorbitant printed defamations composed by learned enemies of the English Protestant state. The latter were part of the concerted effort of international Catholic forces—and, prominent among them, English exiles—to undermine the Queen's temporal and ecclesiastical authority by sensationalizing and excoriating her personal conduct. Preeminent examples of the genre are Edward Rishton's expanded edition of Nicholas Sander's

De origine ac progressu schismatis Anglicani (1585), which I have discussed in part one, and William Allen's *Admonition to the Nobility and People of England and Ireland Concerninge the Present Warres* (1588). Allen was a founder of the seminaries for English missionary priests at Douai, Rome, and Rheims. In writing his tract to prepare the way for the Spanish Armada and the Queen's overthrow, he made denunciations of Elizabeth's sexual depravity central to his argument. He wrote, for example, that with the Earl of Leicester "and divers others she hathe abused her bodie, against Gods lawes, to the disgrace of princely majestie & the whole nations reproche, by unspeakable and incredible variety of luste." Furthermore, he claimed that the real reason she chose not to marry—thereby putting the succession at risk and jeopardizing the collective welfare of her subjects—was not her supposed personal preference for virginity but precisely her rank promiscuity.[32] In the gendered rhetoric of Catholic polemic, Elizabeth, like her mother, was denounced as a whore. Of course, Protestant partisans employed exactly the same terms in order to vilify Mary, Queen of Scots, while Mary's Catholic supporters busily extolled her prudence and piety.[33] When cautioned for having called Mary a Jezebel in a parliamentary speech, Peter Wentworth responded, "did I not publish her openly in the last parlment to be the most notorious whore in all the world? And wherefore should I then be afraid to call her soe nowe againe?" And in the aftermath of Mary's execution, an English agent in Edinburgh reported to Walsingham a libelous epigram that addressed Elizabeth as "Jesabell that English whore."[34] If one of these queens was Una, then the other was Duessa: which was which depended on whether they were viewed from the Catholic or the Protestant side of the confessional divide.

Cecil ordered Cardinal Allen's *Admonition* suppressed as treasonous. A royal proclamation was issued on 1 July 1588, subjecting to martial law the importation, transcription, distribution, and possession of

> false, slanderous, and traitorous libels, books, and pamphlets . . . in covert and secret manner dispersed through this realm, wherein they do not only go about with most false and abominable lies to slander and dishonor her majesty . . . but also by subtle and pestilent persuasions to withdraw her highness' subjects from their due obedience, and to excite and stir up the people to take arms against God and their sovereign and to join with the foreign enemies and so to betray and yield themselves, their parents, kindred, and children, and their religion, country, and commonweal to be subjects and slaves to aliens and strangers.[35]

Such defamations as Allen's, distributed surreptitiously throughout the kingdom in the medium of print, had the imprimatur of hostile religious and civil authorities and were intended as justifications for the overthrow of the

Elizabethan state. For these reasons, they were far more alarming to the regime than were the occasional royal slanders to be heard in the ephemeral gossip of the Queen's disgruntled common subjects.

Thomas Pormort returned to England from the English seminary in Rome late in 1590, and was apprehended in September 1591. It was just four years following the printing, distribution, and suppression of Allen's tract that his acolyte Pormort accused his Protestant torturer of lewd speeches concerning the Queen's personal conduct—speeches that, by implication, seemed to give credence to the Catholic exiles' own polemics against Elizabeth and her minions. How are we to take this sensational claim? According to Pormort's reported testimony, Topcliffe had boasted that the Queen had (in the words of Cardinal Allen) "abused her bodie," both with himself and with "divers others." Thus, the moral depravity attributed to the heretical Elizabeth and her degenerate court by Allen, Rishton, and other Catholic polemicists was here being evoked in speeches attributed to one of the Catholics' most virulent antagonists. Rather than being the source of such wickedly defamatory accusations, Pormort could claim to have preserved his own innocence and his loyalty to the crown precisely by having informed against Topcliffe, who had so grossly sullied the reputation of their sovereign lady.

According to the independent account of another Catholic priest, named James Younge, Pormort had made these charges openly at his trial, where he stated that "Topcliffe had said unto him that he had used very secret dealing with the Queen, and had seen her bare above the knee. This Topcliffe spoke to Mr. Pormort when he thought to have persuaded him to recant, in hope to come to preferment by Topcliffe's means, being as it might seem in great favour with her Majesty."[36] Younge's account implies that Topcliffe was actually inventing his lewd narrative with the specific intention of impressing Pormort with his own power and influence, seeking thereby to entrap his captive and to triumph over his will by seduction rather than by torture. Playing the pander, Topcliffe was attempting to persuade Pormort to recant his own truth in exchange for the Queen's favor, which was to be procured by means of Topcliffe's intermediary patronage.

Even if Topcliffe had really undertaken such an unorthodox method for the curing of souls, could he reasonably have expected that such a service to the state would enhance his own credit with his masters? The preface to the notes Verstegan sent to Persons states that they were seen by the Privy Council; Lord Burghley and his associates would surely have found the remarks attributed to Topcliffe to be profoundly offensive—particularly when publicly recounted at Pormort's trial, as Younge reports they were, and no matter what Topcliffe's motivation might have been in uttering them. It is hardly surprising, therefore, that both at Pormort's trial and at his execution, Topcliffe vehemently protested Pormort's allegation. According to Younge's reputedly eyewitness account, at his trial Pormort "requested that he might be banished, but Topcliffe, his sworn enemy, withstood it forcibly"; and when the Archbishop sought a stay of execution in order to have Pormort counseled by chaplains, Topcliffe "went to the Lord Treasurer [Burghley], and got a mandamus to the Sheriff to execute the priest that self-same day." Younge goes on to record that at his execution Pormort "was enforced to stand in his shirt almost two hours upon the ladder in Lent time upon a very cold day, when Topcliffe still urged him to deny the words, but he would not."[37] Pormort had already endured torture, and he now faced a horrific death. Although we cannot finally determine which of these two men spoke "the truth," we can observe that Pormort not only manifested the spiritual resolve for martyrdom that characterizes the protagonists of all such narratives, but also performed an act of resistance, both against his torturer and against the regime that Topcliffe personified.

The active cooperation of the condemned was required if the civic and ecclesiastical agents who supervised the execution were to succeed in transforming a spectacle of cruelty into a penitential theatre of God's judgments. Public performances of confession and contrition upon the gallows would validate the justice of the punishment, salve the soul of the condemned, and powerfully impress upon the crowd an admonition to civic obedience and religious conformity.[38] In the preface to his account of the martyrdom of Campion and other priests in 1581, William Allen posed a powerful rhetorical question concerning the truth that was publicly professed at the moment of execution: "Can any man thinke that these men would lye to their damnation, at the very going out of their breath into the judgement of God?"[39] Precisely because dying words were commonly ascribed a special testimonial status, the representatives of the state and its church struggled mightily to effect a gallows conversion of the Catholic condemned—and, on occasion, to hasten their demise when it appeared that an obstinate victim was gaining control of the performance.

Just as the state intended public executions to serve as compelling lessons to the spectators, so the victims understood and sought to exploit their subversive potential as an inspiration to the persecuted faithful. As the missionary priest Anthony Middleton was reported to have said to Topcliffe as he stood upon the gallows at Clerkenwell on 6 May 1590: "If I had ten thousand deathes to suffer, I would suffer them for the Catholic Roman faith, & I hope my death shall confirm many Catholics in their faith, which are here present."[40] Both the etymological and the experiential roots of martyrdom were manifested in the public act of bearing witness to the truth of one's beliefs. As the Protestant martyrologist John Foxe put it, the work of martyrs was "to glorify God by their death, to subscribe and bear witness unto the truth by their blood, and, by the contempt of this present life, to witness that they do seek after a better life; by their constancy and steadfastness, to confirm and establish the faith of the Church, and to subdue and vanquish their enemy."[41] For Pormort, as for every Tudor martyr, whether Catholic or Protestant, the moment of public execution was at once the culminating trial of his or her faith and the supreme opportunity to exemplify its truth. And, in a less exalted sense, in Pormort's case it was not only the refusal to recant his faith but also the refusal to recant the accusation against Topcliffe himself that represented for believers a triumph of the victim's will over the wills of his adversaries and persecutors, a spiritual vanquishing of evil worldly powers.

It appears that such acts of resistance as Pormort's were not uncommon; and their occurrence serves to underline the profoundly performative and agonistic quality of such public executions. Such performances were not confined to established gallows sites such a Tyburn but were movable spectacles that could be enacted in venues that seemed most apt to the circumstances of the crime. Perhaps the earliest example was that of the Catholic layman John Felton. Felton was the daring soul who posted upon the gate of the Bishop of London's palace in St. Paul's churchyard the infamous Papal Bull *Regnans in Excelsis*, in which Pius V excommunicated and deposed Queen Elizabeth. Felton was swiftly tried for high treason; and he was hanged, disemboweled, decapitated, and quartered in front of that same gate on 8 August 1570.[42] Pormort himself was also hanged and quartered in Paul's churchyard—a place that modern Elizabethan scholars are more likely to associate with book stalls than with the butchering block. In Portmort's case, the gibbet was set up in front of the door of a haberdasher named Barrows. Barrows had been reconciled to the old faith by Pormort,

> which was known to Topcliffe, whereof he caused Barrows to accuse the priest, or else he should also be hanged and lose all his goods, by which fear he did so, standing at the gibbet, and confessing that he had offended God and her Majesty by being reconciled by the priest. At last the ladder was turned, and the priest was quartered after their manner.[43]

In the face of Pormort's resistance, Topcliffe was no doubt able to take some small comfort in having terrorized Barrows into playing his part.

By choosing to perform the execution at the scene of the crime, the state was framing punishment as expiation, thus conferring upon it the status of a ritual occasion and not merely a theatrical one. In the light of these site-specific spectacles, it would be interesting to know why, in the Armada year, a missionary priest named William Gunter was "hanged by the Theator," and another named William Hartley was "carried near the Curtain and there hanged."[44] Although both the Curtain and the Theatre were located in the suburb of Shoreditch, these examples do not reference the locality itself but rather the proximity of the gallows to the playhouse. Whether or not the environs of the public playhouses provided a venue for such events on other occasions, the conjunction of papistry and playing is certainly a suggestive one: after all, some Protestant preachers spoke of unreformed churches and playhouses as if they were synonymous; and, on the other side of the confessional divide, Richard Verstegan titled and framed the most incendiary of his illustrated tracts against the persecution of Catholics as a *Theatrum crudelitatum haereticorum nostri temporis* (1587).[45] The social space of Elizabethan London constituted a vast and complex venue for political theatre; and the public execution of Catholics for treason was one of the most spectacular, ideologically unstable, and potentially subversive genres to be performed there.[46] In 1597, Richard Burbage, William Shakespeare, and their partners in the Lord Chamberlain's Men had the abandoned Theatre surreptitiously dismantled and its timbers transported across the Thames to be used in construction of the Globe. The physical and mental space within which Shakespearean drama was conceived and performed was, like the drama itself, a stage for the enactment of conflicts between conscience and obedience, one haunted by cultural traces of the old faith and vexed by the ideological strains of religious reformation.

Catholics condemned as traitors who refused to act their assigned parts upon the gallows sometimes appear to have been responding to direct provocation. For example, in December 1591, when the Catholic layman Swithin Wells sought the blessing of the missionary priest Edmund Gennings before both of them were to be executed, an angry Topcliffe cried out, "You follow the Pope and his Bulls; believe me, I think some bulls begot you all"; this provoked Wells to respond, "If we have bulls to our fathers, thou hast a cow to thy mother." If this was an allusion to Queen Elizabeth, it was a sign of profound disrespect that undercut the formulaic protestations of loyalty made by all such condemned Catholic subjects. Wells immediately regretted and sought to excuse his loss of composure and spiritual serenity. He first chastised Topcliffe for baiting him, and then forgave him, declaring that "by your malice I am thus to be executed, but you have done me the greatest benefit that ever I could have had."[47] Having recovered his equilibrium, Wells was able to turn his tormentor into the instrument of his own transcendence.

In the same letter to Persons in which he recounts the executions of Wells and Pormort, Younge also recounts a more explicit example of a Catholic layman's defying Topcliffe at the moment of execution:

> [Brian] Lacey, now having the rope about his neck, was willed by Topcliffe to confess his treason. "For, saith he, there are none but traitors who are of thy religion."
>
> "Then," said Lacey, "answer me. You yourself in Queen Mary's days was a Papist, at least in show. Tell me, were you also a traitor?" At which the people laughed aloud.
>
> "Well," quoth Topcliffe, "I came not here to answer thy arguments. Thou art to answer me."
>
> "I have said," quoth the other, with smiling and cheerful countenance, and voice as merry as though he had been far from death. Anon the cart was drawn away, and he suffered to hang until he was dead.[48]

Through his reference to the Marian reign, Lacey not only ridiculed Topcliffe with an accusation of Topcliffe's own apparent temporizing, but he pithily historicized the whole vexed question of the relations between treason and conscience. His quip thus implied a fundamental challenge to the moral legitimacy of those whose power was about to take his life—including not only Richard Topcliffe but also Elizabeth Tudor, who had likewise conformed during the reign of her sister. Younge's account clearly implies that the crowd appreciated Lacey's wit and applauded his performance, for they were sufficiently sympathetic to demand that he be allowed to hang until he was dead before he was disemboweled and quartered. Likewise, when the sheriff ordered Robert Southwell to be cut down, there was "a great confused cry in the companie that he praied for the Queene, 'And therefore let him hang, till he be dead,' sayd they. And so he was not cut downe till he was senst, as far as could be perceaved."[49] Among those Elizabethan Catholics whom the state deemed to be the Queen's enemies, not all were so fortunate.[50]

Even if Younge's version of Pormort's trial was substantially accurate and Pormort's claim was true—if Topcliffe really did say such things, and did so for the tactical reasons claimed—this would not begin to explain why the fantasies purveyed by Topcliffe should have taken the specific form that they did, nor why he would have expected Pormort to find them compelling. Whether or not a salacious exchange actually took place between Pormort and Topcliffe in the intimacy of the latter's torture chamber, the purported account of that exchange which was spoken in open court and the notes based upon that account which were read by both the Privy Council and Father Persons constituted part of the *public* discourse about the Queen. As Younge's report makes explicit, their central theme was the power and influence that might accrue to the subject by virtue of his physical proximity to, and intimacy with, the charismatic body of his sovereign. This might be thought of as an instance in which early modern culture was operating within the modality of magical thinking. From a historical rather than an anthropological perspective, it was also a signal instance of that "migration of the holy" which endowed the royal body with an aura of the sacred power that traditional Catholic culture had invested in hallowed places, the relics of saints, and the consecrated host itself.

A pragmatically political form of such contagious magic was the basis for what David Starkey has called "the doctrine of 'representation through intimacy,'" and which he has expounded in the context of the workings of the Privy Chamber under Henry VIII. Starkey discusses the rise in importance of the Privy Chamber, and the rise in power and influence of its gentlemen-servants, in terms of the difficulties and dangers entailed in effectively delegating royal authority. As he summarizes his argument,

> The Privy Chamber, uniquely, served both of the "two bodies" that contemporary lawyers and theorists distinguished as making up the entity of "king." As the royal domestics, they attended on the king's personal, physical body; but as men of high birth and distinction they were also servants of the king in his other, public capacity as the embodiment of the "body politic" or the state itself.

Thus, the gentlemen of the Henrician Privy Chamber could be effectively employed, both "as simple vehicles of the royal will" and "as agents of royal policy: in diplomacy, military affairs and local government."[51] While acknowledging the significance in political and legal theory of the distinction between the King's Two Bodies, Starkey emphasizes that "in practice, as contemporaries usually stressed, both bodies fused in the actual person of the king 'for the time being.'"[52] Those who came into physical proximity with the monarch were also in the presence of the mystical body of kingship. In effect, the monarch was different in substance from his—or her—subjects. As Starkey emphasizes, among the members of the court, "what was peculiar to the Privy Chamber, what was theirs alone, was physical intimacy with the king. Only they were his body servants."[53] In practice, this meant that those of the Privy Chamber were also the monarch's intimate companions—dressing and undressing him, waiting upon him at his table and at his toilet, sharing his recreations and his confidences, and sleeping in his bedchamber. The source of these courtiers' special power and influence was their physical intimacy with the royal body, and their control over others' access to the royal presence.

The organization and political significance of the Privy Chamber were profoundly transformed by the accession of a queen. As summarized by Pam Wright, "the Elizabethan Privy Chamber was a household department in the narrowest sense of the term. It was the queen's *familia*, largely staffed by her cousins, and wholly by her chosen and direct dependents. And it was essentially female."[54] This staff was hierarchically organized into Ladies of the Bedchamber, Gentlewomen of the Privy Chamber (informally including the Maids of Honor), and the more menial Chamberers. The ladies who constituted the first group were the Queen's most intimate companions, and also had the keeping of the personal jewelry and the close stools that came into direct contact with her body. However, although their responsibilities as body servants were analogous to those of the Groom of the Stool and others in Henry VIII's Privy Chamber, the power that might accrue to them as a consequence was limited and informal. A queen regnant required body servants who were women, but precisely because they were women their official duties were confined to the monarch's domestic domain. As intimate observers of the Queen's opinions and moods, and as intermediaries between the Queen and her court, these ladies could be very influential in the transmission of intelligence and in the advancement of personal suits.[55] Yet the powerful administrative functions that had devolved upon certain members of the all-male Henrician Privy Chamber now accrued to William Cecil—the Queen's Secretary and subsequently her Lord Treasurer—and to other men of the Privy Council.

The intimate encounter purportedly claimed by Topcliffe conflates the role of royal body servant—which, in the case of the Queen, was practically restricted to women—with that of royal lover. The latter role was widely ascribed to a number of Elizabeth's favorites during the course of the reign, most notably to Robert Dudley, Earl of Leicester, and to Sir Christopher Hatton and Sir Walter Ralegh. Salacious gossip about the sexual liaisons of Elizabeth and Leicester had been rife from the beginning of the reign; and, as examples cited earlier in this and other chapters demonstrate, it was rehearsed by courtiers, commoners, foreign ambassadors, and Catholic propagandists alike. The gossip continued to circulate even after Leicester's death in 1588. Perhaps the most outrageous of such allusions is contained in a wittily obscene manuscript written shortly after Leicester's demise, and purporting to be an account of his "futile attempt to enter heaven and his subsequent reception in hell."[56] Appropriating the Queen's nickname for her favorite of favorites, this anonymous tract imagines "his Robinship's entertainment" in hell to be his copulation with "a naked feind in the forme of a lady": "to geve a charge with his lance of lust against the [c]enter of her target of proffe, and run his ingredience up to the hard hiltes into the unserchable botome of her gaping g[u]llfe. And ... drowen the member of his virillitye in the bottomeless barrel of her virginnitye, through which runeth a felde of unquenchable fier" (157). By this means, "the member wherewith he had most offended" will become the instrument of his eternal punishment. At the same time that it excoriates Leicester, this pornographic phantasmagoria subjects to carnivalesque mockery those secrets of state that were vested in the iconography of royal virginity.[57] Additionally, one of the wicked details in this satire on courtly depravity is aimed directly at Topcliffe. In the entourage appointed to wait upon "his Robinship" in hell, "rome was left for Toplief against he shuld come at his owen request to be his grome of his sole [stool]" (155). It may be purely coincidental, but this barb nevertheless provides a culturally congruent and diabolically apt parody of Topcliffe's imagined erotic intimacy with the Queen in her Privy Chamber. At the same time, the charismatic power acquired by royal body servants under Henry VIII is here being reduced to a dirty joke— on a par with the excretory satires that had degraded Anjou and Elizabeth a few years earlier.

A German traveler recorded observing Queen Elizabeth's open display of intimacy with Walter Ralegh during the Christmas festivities at court in 1584. This was the year in which Ralegh was granted a royal patent to possess and exploit Virginia, which had been named for the Virgin Queen. Von Wedel wrote that "it was said that she loved this gentleman now in preference to all others; and that may be well believed, for two years ago he was scarcely able to keep a single servant, and now she has bestowed so much upon him, that he is able to keep five hundred servants." In surveying the leading courtiers attending upon the Queen at this event, von Wedel had already noted Leicester, "with whom, as they say, the queen for a long time has had illicit intercourse," and Hatton, "the captain of the guard, whom the queen is said to have loved after Lester."[58] Leicester was a member of the nobility who had been an intimate companion of Elizabeth from before her accession. By contrast, Hatton and Ralegh were both private gentlemen of modest means who owed their spectacular rise entirely to the favor of the Queen. In the course of their court careers, each enjoyed as a sign of that favor the office of Captain of the Guard, the court officer who, in both physical and symbolic terms, protected and controlled access to the body of the Queen.

Hostile observers interpreted the Queen's ways with her favorites as evidence of that inherent female intemperance which made her unfit to rule; others may have appreciated that her behavior was a politic strategy intended precisely to maintain her rule over a court filled with proud, ambitious, and emulous men, in which either the dominance of a single favorite or the escalation of factionalism could prove her undoing. At the time of Pormort's accusation against Topcliffe, both of these dangers were becoming more tangible with the emergence of the young Earl of Essex as the undisputed favorite of the aging Queen.[59] The gossip that von Wedel's native English informants seem to have offered eagerly for notation in his diary is one of many indications that, within the world of the court, the Queen's perpetual virginity was not necessarily regarded as a literal truth. Instead, many within this social elite may have construed the Virgin Queen as a convenient political fiction, one from which they themselves derived indirect benefit. It was a collectively sustained mystery of state, quite distinct from the empirical question of whether or not Elizabeth Tudor had an intact maidenhead.

In the tract on the succession that he wrote at the very end of the reign, Sir John Harington also declared the Queen's virginity to be a "secrett of State," yet one about which he had intimate knowledge, knowledge that he was eager to share with his readers. This notable denizen of the Elizabethan court regarded the Queen's secret from a perspective almost diametrically opposed to that of von Wedel's informants. He wrote of his royal godmother that

> to make the world thinke she should have children of hir owne, she entertained
> till she was fiftye yeares of age mentions of marriage; and though in mynde she
> hath ever had an aversion and (as many think) in body some indisposition to
> the act of marriage, yet hath she ever made shewe of affection, and still doth
> to some men which in Courte wee tearme favourites, to hyde that debility,
> enduring rather to run into some obloquie among straungers of a fault that
> she could not commit, then to be suspected to want anything that belongs
> to the perfection of a faire ladie, and that this is most probable the man lyves
> yet to whom Sir Christopher Hatton...did sweare voluntarily, deeply, and
> with vehement asseveration, that he never had anie carnall knowledge of hir
> bodye, and this was also my mother's opinions, who was till the xxth yeare
> of hir Majestie's reigne of hir privie chamber, and had bene sometime hir
> bedfellowe.[60]

For Harington, both the Queen's formal marriage negotiations and her courtly dalliances constituted an elaborate and extended charade, a performance of erotic desire and sexual fecundity by a woman who was neither temperamentally disposed to the one nor physically capable of the other. Thus, from Harington's cynically misogynistic viewpoint, the defamatory gossip to which Elizabeth exposed herself by such performances not only was unfounded but served more securely to mask her womanly deficiencies. The deceased Sir Christopher Hatton's testimonial to the royal chastity is reported secondhand from an anonymous source; and by protesting too much it seems to inflame rather than to allay the salacious gossip that had circulated so widely and for so long regarding the Queen's carnality. Harington's final anecdote permits his readers vicariously to cross the threshold of the Privy Chamber: For unimpeachable testimony concerning the Queen's intact condition, we are invited into the royal bedchamber and, indeed, into the royal bed. Through the mediation of his natural mother and the informal power deriving from her office as royal body servant, Harington penetrates the *arcana imperii* of his royal godmother and stimulates his readers' transgressive fantasies. In thus sharing his secret knowledge—"now I come to this secrett of State, and mark it well, my deere countrimen" (39)—he also advertises his own privileged proximity to the charismatic body of the Queen.[61]

The words attributed to Topcliffe by Pormort include the claim not only to have seen but to have physically handled the royal body, and to have done so in an explicitly erotic way. The first three items from Verstegan's letter that I have quoted above—those focused upon the Queen's breasts, thighs, and belly—are not only gender-specific but are powerfully sexualized; and the intimate favor that the Queen bestows in the fifth item—not the conventional glove or handkerchief but rather "a whyte linen hose"—foregrounds the sexual innuendo contained in the courtly gesture.[62] The penultimate item—"That he is so familiar with her that when he pleaseth to speake with her he may take her away from any company, and that she [is] as pleasant with every one that she doth love"—has some basis in the claims to special trust and favor that appear frequently in Topcliffe's own letters to and about Elizabeth. For example, in a 1601 letter to Sir Robert Cecil, Topcliffe was much exercised about "a base clown" who was defaming her: "At my last being at Court, I revealed to the Queen herself that clown's scandalous speeches: and her pleasure was that I should apprehend him discreetly. . . . Unspeakably has her Majesty bound me with her sacred conceit and defence of my credit in the desperate times I have lived in."[63] It is on the basis of his intimacy with the Queen that Topcliffe can confidently claim special power and influence, and can manifest such contempt for the authority of the Privy Council.[64]

At first reading, the only words that are attributed to Elizabeth herself during the course of her purported encounter with Topcliffe may seem startlingly incongruous: She responds to the sexually provocative compliment that she has "the softest belly of any woman kynde," by asking rhetorically, "Be not thease the armes, legges, and body of king Henry?" Topcliffe can only assent: "he answered: 'Yea.'" I would argue that the subject's fantasy of royal intimacy culminates in this apparent non sequitur, in which the Queen asserts her masculinized body politic. Topcliffe's statement and Elizabeth's negative interrogative response constitute a simultaneous juxtaposition and identification of the erotically feminine body of Queen Elizabeth with the virile body of her much feared father. The energy released by this queer verbal exchange is not so much homoerotic as it is *monarchoerotic*; and the experience of the gentlemen-servants of King Henry's own Privy Chamber provides a relevant, albeit partial, gloss. From the perspective of the issues discussed above in part one, the Queen's response to Topcliffe is an idiosyncratic take on the familiar assertion of her legitimacy, in both filial and constitutional senses: her identification with Henry VIII marks Elizabeth as both his offspring and his successor, the fruit of his body natural and true inheritrix of the body politic of Tudor kingship. Thus, in physically handling the natural, "woman kynde," body of Elizabeth, her masculine subject is also mystically handling the immortal body politic of kingship, which is implicitly gendered male. The Queen's response to Topcliffe implies that although she may have "the softest belly of any woman kynde," she also has the heart and stomach of a king, and of a king of England too.

Many modern readers may be inclined to dismiss Pormort's reputed accusation as a lurid historical oddity; I would argue that, however odd, it is also historically meaningful. This anecdote is comprehensible in terms of the Elizabethan cultural logic that cross-gendered the royal bodies natural and politic—a cultural logic that was itself consequent upon the anomalous historical circumstance of an unmarried female prince. It would, I think, be a failure of historical perspective to reduce the anecdote to the merely prurient, and to dismiss it as such. The natural body of the almost sixty-year-old Queen was not in any simple or singular sense the subject of Topcliffe's purported fantasy. Incarnated in Elizabeth's natural body was the immortal body politic of kingship, and it was this eroto-political mystery that gave to the imagined encounter its extraordinary cultural charge.

Topcliffe's alleged intimacies with the Queen would have taken place within the inward rooms of the Privy Chamber, the sanctum sanctorum of monarcholatry, where none but the Queen's body servants and special favorites might enter. The rhetorical question that Pormort attributes to Elizabeth—"Be not thease the armes, legges, and body of king Henry?"—would have had a special resonance if that trysting place was imagined to be in or beyond the Privy Chamber at Whitehall Palace, which was still dominated by Holbein's imperious image of the arms, legs, and body of King Henry (figs. 3 and 4).[65] This Henrician invocation is especially powerful in the context of Pormort's struggle with Topcliffe, precisely because it was Henry who had initiated the royal supremacy in matters spiritual; and, in the eyes of Elizabethan Catholic apologists, it was also Henry who had initiated the Tudor state's practice of martyring Catholics for their faith when he executed Thomas More and others on charges of high treason. Refusal of the royal supremacy in matters spiritual was the ideological foundation upon which Pormort and his fellow victims were prosecuted by the Elizabethan regime; and the verbally dismembered image of King Henry attributed to his daughter hauntingly parodies the corporal punishment prescribed and exacted for that refusal.

When Topcliffe wrote his letter about the discovery and burning of a Marian idol at Edward Rookwood's estate in 1578, he implicitly contrasted that papistical illusion with what he called the "reall presence" of Queen Elizabeth herself.[66] Likewise, the fantasy attributed to Topcliffe by Pormort could be seen as a monarcholatrous parody of the Eucharistic sacrament as it was understood and experienced within the Catholic confession, and of the priest's privileged intermediary status in the performance of that mystery. As the priest James Younge interpreted the report at the time, by claiming the power to handle the Queen's Two Bodies, Topcliffe "thought to have persuaded [Pormort] to recant, in hope to come to preferment by Topcliffe's means, being as it might seem in great favour with her Majesty." The missionary priests, who had been trained abroad to minister to and to fortify the Catholic laity at home, were the primary target of the regime's antipapist campaign; and priests made up the overwhelming majority of its victims. In his printed tract *The Execution of Justice in England* (1583), Burghley set the message, tone, and imagery for this campaign:

> These disguised persons (called scholars or priests)...came hither by stealth...by commandment of the capital enemy, the Pope...with their hallowed baggages from Rome to poison the senses of the subjects, pouring into their hearts malicious and pestilent opinions against Her Majesty and the laws of the realm.[67]

At the same time, the priests themselves, and the extensive cultural apparatus that grew up to defend the mission and to sanctify its martyrs, appropriated the persecutions so as to inculcate what Anne Dillon characterizes as "a profound reverence among the laity for the priesthood."[68] Consider this account of Robert Sutton, a missionary priest hanged and quartered in 1588:

> When 3 of his quarters were taken downe after they had hanged a twelvemoneth in the ayer, all beinge consumed to the bones, the Index and the thome consecrated for the touche of Christ his bodie, were found whole and are so conserved.[69]

Accounts such as this vividly impressed upon the faithful both the miraculous nature of the host's transubstantiation and the charismatic aura of its celebrant.

This and other martyrdom accounts already quoted clearly demonstrate the persistence of late medieval modes of religious devotion and imagination among Elizabethan lay Catholics. Recent scholarship has emphasized that because Catholicism survived in Elizabethan England only as a clandestine religion, lack of ecclesiastical organization and control allowed a popular culture of miracles, visions, and exorcisms to flourish; and, furthermore, that "the seminary priests and Jesuits sent across the Channel after 1574 deliberately and skillfully harnessed supernatural power in their attempts to combat heresy, reinforce contested tenets, reclaim backsliders, and win converts to their cause."[70] Central to this process was an informal and unsanctioned popular beatification of martyred priests and the spontaneous generation of a cult focused upon their relics. William Allen described "the godly greedy appetite" among believers in England and on the continent "for any peece of their reliques, either of their bodies, haire, bones or garments, yea or any thing that hath any spot or staine of their innocent and sacred bloud."[71] Lucy Ridley certainly seems to have manifested a greedy appetite for the remains of Edmund Jennings, a priest executed in 1591:

> Mrs Lucy Ridley after much desire finding no means to get a relic, took one of his thumbs (happened to light on the ground just by the virgin one of the quarters showed to the people by the hangman at the door of Newgate where the quarters were to be boiled) as if she would touch it only reverently, and behold, the whole thumb remained in her hand: and she soon after became a nun of St Benet's order in Louvain, and liveth anno 1600.[72]

Whether the martyr's thumb fell or was pulled, it possessed Mistress Ridley as surely as she possessed it, and its charismatic power was such as to precipitate her spiritual transformation.

Those who were not so fortunate as to light upon a relic could nevertheless make the martyrs' remains the focus of their meditations and prayers: "Divers devoute people of our nation that can get no part of their sacred reliques, yet come as it were on pilgrimage to the places where their quarters or heades be set up, under pretence of gasing... there to do their devotion & praiers unto them."[73] A poem on Campion's martyrdom proclaims that

> His quarterd lims shall joyne with joy agayne,
> and rise a body brighter then the sunne,
> your blinded malice torturde him in vayne...
> We can not feare a mortal torment, wee,

> this Martirs blood hath moystned all our harts,
> whose partid quartirs when we chaunce to see,
> we learne to play the constant christians parts,
> his head doth speake, & heavenly precepts give.[74]

Thus, the public spectacles of corporal punishment intended to assert the authority of the state and to admonish its subjects could just as easily become the instruments of a fundamental challenge to the state's own spiritual legitimacy. The religious beliefs and practices that were focused upon the bodily remains of martyred Catholic priests in Elizabethan England must be seen not only in terms of a continuity with late medieval piety but also as a politicized rearticulation of that traditional piety, shaped in dialogue and struggle with the Elizabethan regime and Protestant political culture. Those late medieval beliefs and practices, anathematized and suppressed by Protestant reformers, were subtly appropriated by adherents of the Elizabethan regime in order to legitimate reformed monarchy and to enhance the charismatic power of the Queen's Two Bodies. Catholic supernaturalism did not merely persist in Elizabethan England but rather took on a new character under the relentless pressure of such hostile policies and attitudes. This politically potent counter-discourse of Catholic spirituality was made manifest when the traitor's vivisected body was transfigured into the saint's miraculous relics, and the gallows became a shrine.

Elizabethan monarcholatry conjoined unremitting antipapistry with a promotion of the monarch's sanctity through the appropriation of formerly Catholic religious concepts, practices, and images. This conjunction formed the ideological substructure not only for Topcliffe's outrage that Rookwood—a recusant who had harbored a clandestine idol of the Virgin Mary—should dare to approach Queen Elizabeth's "reall presence," but also for the notion that Topcliffe might persuade Pormort to exchange his spiritual calling for the Queen's service. The confrontation between Pormort and Topcliffe embodied and made manifest the intertwined struggles between opposing collective ideologies, antipathetic subjective beliefs, and inimical individual wills. Any retrospective attempt that we might make to adjudicate that confrontation—to locate and to fix "the Truth"—is forced up against the destabilizing question, "Whose truth?" It has not been my intention to discover which of these Elizabethans was telling the truth about their encounter and which was not. Instead, by sifting the available records that constitute their shared history, I have sought to explore the nexus of contradictory and alternative cultural truths that was incarnated when Pormort, Topcliffe, and the Queen converged.

PART FIVE

Time's Subject

In preparing policy papers for the Queen and the Privy Council, Lord Burghley was frequently led by his humanist training to set forth reasons pro and contra, arguing both sides of an issue in the process of advancing one of them. This was his favored method when evaluating the Queen's prospective marriage with the duc d'Anjou. One such paper, written in 1579 and endorsed by Burghley as a "Memoryall for the Queen's Majestie tochyng the matters of her marriage," lists among the "benyfytes like to growe by the marriage," that Elizabeth "shall have a husband to defend her, a chyld to revenge her & therby avoyde contempte in her latter yeres." Conversely, "contempte in her latter yeres" is listed as one of the "perrells that maye growe yf her Majestie do not marrye."[1] Burghley's argument makes clear the particularity of this perceived danger: The prospect that Queen Elizabeth might end her reign as an old, unmarried, and childless woman—and one who continued to resist declaring the succession—threatened to erode the charismatic power of her royal office and thus to destabilize the late Elizabethan polity. The Queen and her counselors clearly shared a concern that "contempte in her latter yeres" not prove a major problem if she persisted in the kind of life she had elected at the very beginning of her reign. It was then that she told her first parliament, in response to the first of their many petitions that she marry, "in the end, this shalbe for me sufficient, that a marble stone shall declare that a Queene, having raigned such a tyme, lived and dyed a virgine."[2]

At about the time that Burghley constructed his memorandum in measured support of the French marriage, Philip Sidney wrote a letter to the Queen in which he argued forcefully against it. In this letter, which circulated widely in manuscript, Sidney identified—and sought to dismiss by a mixture of counsel and flattery—the two arguments in favor of marriage which he attributed to Elizabeth herself: "fear of standing alone in respect of foreign dealings, and in home respects, doubt of contempt." In regard to the latter, Sidney wrote to the Queen that,

> as I take it, you imagine two natural causes thereof, and two effects you think you find thereof. The natural causes be length of government and uncertainty of succession; the effects be looking, as you term it, to the rising sun, and some abominable speeches certain hellish minded people have uttered.[3]

The position argued by Sidney and others in the party of Leicester and Walsingham did ultimately prevail. However, the possible consequences of that decision which were feared by Burghley and dismissed by Sidney also came to pass: rampant speculation and secret negotiation regarding the succession; the emergence of a counter-cult to the Queen's, focused upon the charismatic, youthful and heroic Earl of Essex, who was in many ways Sidney's ideological heir; and the proliferation of slanderous gossip, ribald jokes, and veiled satires about the aging Queen's sexuality, vanity, and parsimony.

In the tract on the succession to the crown that he wrote but prudently withheld from publication at the very end of Elizabeth's reign, Sir John Harington mentioned as "worth the observing" that "the two universities at the commencementes in the year 98 did both light on one question that bewraied a kynde of weerines of this tyme, *mundus senescit*, that the world waxed old; which question I know not how well it was ment, but I knowe how ill it was taken."[4] That both Oxford and Cambridge should choose this commencement theme at century's end is not in itself remarkable. Harington's point, however, is that Queen Elizabeth and perhaps many others inevitably interpreted it as an oblique allusion to the approaching end of the Elizabethan era and the demise of the Tudor dynasty: The Queen waxed old, and the state of the nation was characterized by a kind of collective malaise. Bacon later wrote that

> although she had the use of many both virtues and demonstrations that mought draw and knit unto her the heart of her people, yet nevertheless carrying a hand restrained in gift and strained in points of prerogative, could not answer the votes either of servants or subjects to a full contentment; especially in her latter days, when the continuance of her reign ... mought discover in people their natural desire and inclination towards change.[5]

And Bishop Godfrey Goodman recalled that "the court was very much neglected, and in effect the people were very generally weary of an old woman's government."[6] "Length of government and uncertainty of succession" had indeed caused restless and anxious subjects to look "to the rising sun."

Of course, there was no shortage of factors contributing to the profound and pervasive discontent that seems to have characterized the last Elizabethan decade. Among them were inflation, successive bad harvests, and the resulting poverty and underemployment; the cost in life and treasure of protracted conflicts in continental Europe, Ireland, and the New World; the increasingly repressive measures taken by the regime against religious nonconformity and social unrest; sharply increased factionalism and instability in court politics; and—as both Bacon and Goodman imply—a perceived contraction and abuse of the patronage system that stifled opportunity, frustrated ambition, and bred resentment and disaffection among a wide range of courtiers and clients, especially in the younger generation. Such issues, many of which were direct consequences of royal policies and practices, combined with a generalized apprehension at the end of the century and the reign to make the 1590s in England not a post-Armada golden age—as literary historians have sometimes represented it—but rather a time of widespread alienation and discontent.

As the comments of Harington and Goodman suggest, these effects were exacerbated not merely by the inevitable natural aging of the monarch but by cultural perceptions regarding the impact of time and age upon a monarch who was an unmarried woman. In part five, I explore that "contempte in her latter yeres" which was a politically consequential manifestation of those cultural perceptions, and also some of the strategies that Elizabeth and her regime mobilized in order to neutralize such contempt and to preserve the Queen's honor and her authority.[7] The discourse of contempt and the discourse of adulation were equally symptomatic of the Queen's last decade; and, as I shall suggest in what follows, the apparently antithetical tendencies toward excessive praise and demeaning ridicule were frequently intertwined. In chapter fifteen, I analyze the stylistic and political issues involved in the project of royal portraiture late in the reign, and the regime's attempts at control of the Queen's iconic image. In chapter sixteen, through the dispatches of foreign and English ambassadors, I explore some strategies of the Queen's sartorial display and self-presentation in her late years, and some ways in which gender politics colored the intelligence that she received. In chapter seventeen, I study anecdotal usages of the trope of the Queen's looking glass, which were employed to criticize or satirize Elizabeth around the time of her death. In an epilogue, I briefly consider King James's succession to the English throne and his attempts to appropriate the subject of Elizabeth.

A Queen of Shadows

Precisely at the turn of the century, there appeared in London, for public sale, prints from engraved equestrian portraits of several English noblemen who were also military heroes. These included Charles Howard, Earl of Nottingham and Lord Admiral (fig. 46), George Clifford, Earl of Cumberland (fig. 47), and Robert Devereux, Earl of Essex (fig. 48). In addition to these images, which were engraved by Thomas Cockson, another equestrian portrait of the Earl of Essex was printed in 1600 from an engraving by Robert Boissard.[1] All of these prints listed the titles and honors of their noble subjects and celebrated their heroic exploits. As significant as the publications themselves was the regime's response to them, which came in the form of a directive from the Privy Council to the Archbishop of Canterbury:

> There is of late a use brought up to engrave in brasse the pictures of noblemen and other persons and then to sell them printed in paper sett forth oftentimes with verses and other circumstances not fytte to be used. Because this custome doth growe common and indeed is not meete such publique setting forth of anie pictures but of her most excellent Majesty should be permytted yf the same be well done, we have for divers good respects thought good to praie your Grace that you will give direccion that hereafter no personage of any noblemann or other person shalbe ingraven and printed to be putt to sale publiquely, and those prints that are already made to be called in.[2]

It was the wide public distribution of such cheaply reproduced images that so concerned the Council; and the draconian solution proposed for dealing with them suggests that they were construed as being incipiently seditious. What is most telling about this order is that it demonstrates an official perception that the public sale of such prints put them in direct competition with those of

FIGURE 46

Charles Howard of Effingham, Earl of Nottingham and Lord Admiral, attributed to Thomas Cockson; 1599(?). Engraving. © The Trustees of The British Museum.

the Queen; and, thus, that they represented a palpable threat to the monopoly held by the royal image in the hearts and minds of the Elizabethan populace. The Council found objectionable not only the iconic images of these mighty Elizabethan subjects but also the accompanying texts; presumably this was because the rehearsal of their titles, honors, and military glories reinforced with evidence of noble blood and chivalric honor the already powerful visual symbolism of their manly prowess and bravery. As Francis Bacon had written in 1596, in cautioning the Earl of Essex against too aggressive a pursuit of military honors, he was a "man of a nature not to be ruled . . . of an estate not grounded to his greatness; of a popular reputation; of a military dependence: I demand whether there can be a more dangerous image than this represented

FIGURE 47

George Clifford, Earl of Cumberland, by Thomas Cockson; 1598–99. Engraving. © The Trustees of The British Museum.

to any monarch living, much more to a lady, and of her Majesty's apprehension?"[3] An aging female monarch who was apprehensive of "contempte in her latter yeres," and who feared her subjects' "looking . . . to the rising sun," had every reason to regard these images as dangerous indeed. The only images of authority deemed fit for the eyes of Elizabethan subjects were those of their Queen—and of her, only those that were "well done."

The portraiture of Queen Elizabeth presented an idiosyncratic convergence of otherwise separate and distinct representational traditions and visual canons, a convergence that was relevant neither to portraits of kings nor to those of queens who were royal consorts. This was precisely because, in the Elizabethan case, royal authority was embodied in a queen regnant, an unmarried woman whose personal symbolism and rhetoric fused the gendered stereotypes of kingly power and strength with those of feminine virtue and beauty. In the process of being regendered, the trope of the King's Two Bodies was fundamentally reshaped. When transferred to the two bodies of Queen Elizabeth, the emphasis of the trope was no longer solely upon the distinction between the mystical office of kingship and its transitory creaturely occupant but also upon the contrasting character of a woman monarch's public and private virtues. As Spenser expressed it in the Letter he appended to the 1590 edition of *The Faerie Queene*, Queen Elizabeth bore "two persons, the one of a most royall Queen or Empress, the other of a most vertuous and beautifull Lady."[4] As the embodiment of divinely sanctioned political authority, the former person was implicitly masculine, whereas the latter, private person was explicitly feminine.

To a poet as resourceful as Spenser, this complication posed not merely problems but also opportunities. Thus, in his Letter, Spenser identified the former, public person of the Queen with Gloriana, the Faerie Queene in whose service her knights were fashioned; and the latter, private person of the Queen, he identified primarily with the beautiful virgin huntress, Belphoebe. Gloriana does not appear as a character in the narrative of *The Faerie Queene*, whereas Belphoebe is a conspicuous presence in three of its six books. This contrast suggests a strategic choice by the poet, a choice undoubtedly due at least in part to the fact that the latter figure was so well accommodated to the allusive and oblique resources of literary representation—in particular, to the ubiquitous tropes of Ovidian and Petrarchan discourses. These resources were perfectly suited to the rhetorical manipulation of a virtuous and beautiful lady, but they were less well equipped to subject an empress. In other words, such polysemous erotic conventions structured Elizabethan relations of power in ways that could be advantageous to the skillful writing subject. The issue was trickier for painters, however, who—as many Renaissance poets, including Spenser himself, liked to remind them—were more bound than were poets to the representation of their subjects' extrinsic features, to the evidence of things seen.[5] In the special case of Queen Elizabeth's portraiture, feminine beauty was not only an artistic but also a political issue, and one that grew more sensitive as its subject grew older.

From the earliest years of the reign, the Elizabethan regime had been concerned to regulate the production and dissemination of the royal image. As early as 1563, it sought to suppress patriotic portraits made for popular consumption in the form of prints from woodcuts and engravings, ostensibly when these were deemed insufficiently skillful to do justice to the royal visage. In that year, a proclamation was drafted in an attempt to curtail the grievous and offensive "errors and deformities" in widely available representations of the Queen. The intent was to regulate the production and distribution of the royal image in all media, according to a single model approved by Elizabeth herself:

> Forasmuch as through the natural desires that all sorts of subjects and peo-
> ple, both noble and mean, hope to procure the portrait and picture of the
> Queen's majesty's most noble and loving person and royal majesty, all manner
> of painters have already and do daily attempt to make in short manner por-
> traiture of her majesty in painting, graving, and printing, wherein is evidently
> seen that hitherto none hath sufficiently expressed the natural representation
> of her majesty's person, favor, or grace, but that most have so far erred therein
> as thereof daily are heard complaints amongst her loving subjects; insomuch
> that for redress thereof her majesty hath lately been so instantly and importu-
> nately sued unto by the body of her council and others of her nobility not only
> to be content that some special commission painter might be permitted, by
> access to her majesty, to take the natural representation of her majesty, whereof
> she hath always been of her own disposition very unwilling, but also to pro-
> hibit all manner of other persons to draw, paint, grave or portray her majesty's
> personage or visage for a time until, by some perfect patron and example, the
> same may be by others followed.[6]

In the person of William Cecil, whose hand corrected the draft manuscript of the proclamation, the state proposed verisimilitude ("natural representa-tion") as the goal of royal portraiture. But it went further in seeking to treat the production and dissemination of the royal image as an ideological state appa-ratus: It required strict regulation, uniformity, and idealization in productions of the royal image; and it comprehended that the availability and wide dis-semination of such a "perfect patron and example" contributed indirectly to the maintenance of "loving subjects." To further the ends of this statecraft, it was deemed necessary that the Queen overcome her own apparent reluctance to sit for her picture.

However, as was the case in other attempts at cultural control undertaken by the Elizabethan government—the most notorious of which included those regulating dress and the public theatre—there was a conspicuous gap between the proclamation of intent to regulate and the process of effective enforcement.

The 1563 proclamation remained in draft. And in 1596, the regime was once again ordering the collection and destruction of such unofficial likenesses as might be objectionable to their royal subject. The *Acts of the Privy Council* record the following minute:

> A warrant for her Majesty's Serjeant Painter and to all publicke officers to yelde him their assistance touching the abuse committed by divers unskillfull artizans in unseemly and improperly paintinge, gravinge and printing of her Majesty's person and vysage, to her Majesty's great offence and disgrace of that beutyfull and magnanimous Majesty wherwith God hathe blessed her, requiring them to cause all suche to be defaced and none to be allowed but suche as her Majesty's Serjant Paynter shall first have sight of.[7]

More than thirty years on, the tone is stronger and more urgent than in 1563. Those without sufficient skill to present a true likeness of the Queen are not merely errant but abusive, and their work is unseemly. It is no longer the Queen's subjects but the Queen herself who takes offense; and the proposed remedy now includes the confiscation and destruction of extant offensive works and the subjection of future production to a process of review by a court official, analogous to the licensing of plays by the Master of the Revels. As we have already seen, in its 1600 order banning the public sale of noblemen's portraits, the Privy Council would find it necessary to reiterate that it was "not meete such publique setting forth of anie pictures but of her most excellent Majesty should be permytted *yf the same be well done*" (emphasis added).

Thus, to produce a "portraict" of the Queen was—at least, in theory—to come under the closest scrutiny of the Elizabethan government, and to risk the displeasure of every Elizabethan subject's "dearest dred."[8] Furthermore, the focus now was not merely upon "the natural representation of her majesty's person, favor, or grace," but upon defining the skillful artisan as one who, in representing "her Majesty's person and vysage," fully conveyed "that beuty-full and magnanimous Majesty wherwith God hathe blessed her." In other words, between 1563 and 1596, there was a subtle shift of emphasis in the reg-ulatory language from a verisimilar representation of the young queen's body natural—the "natural representation" of her "person, favor, or grace"—to an idealized representation of the aged queen's body politic—"that beutyfull and magnanimous Majesty wherwith God hathe blessed her." I suggest that the differences in emphasis and tone between the regulations on royal portraits drafted near the beginning and near the end of the reign are due at least in part to the growing gap between the Queen's Two Bodies. In other words, there was an increasing disjunction between the political ideal of the Queen's beauty, which was abstract and timeless, and an artistic project of "natural

representation" which by more sharply observing the realm of the senses indirectly contributed to the erosion of the royal charisma, to "contempte in her
latter yeres."

⋙

By the early 1590s, production of the royal image was dominated by the officially sanctioned pattern for "her Majesty's person and vysage" that Roy
Strong has called "the mask of youth." This aesthetic ideal correlated well
with one of Queen Elizabeth's most often invoked personal mottoes, *semper
eadem*, which suggested that she fused the moral virtue of constancy with a
personal exemption from time's depredations. As Sir John Davies put it in his
1599 *Hymnes of Astraea*, "In her shall last our *states* faire spring, / Now and for
ever flourishing."[9] On May Day 1600, the Earl of Cumberland presented an
ode to the Queen in which he addressed her as Cynthia:

> Only Time which all doth mowe,
>   Her alone doth cherish.
> Times yong howres attend her still,
> And her Eyes and Cheekes do fill,
>   With fresh youth and beautie:
> All her lovers olde do grow,
> But their hartes, they do not so.[10]

This passage and the setting in which it was originally performed epitomize
the late Elizabethan courtly imaginary at full tilt. The conceit of the Queen
as Cynthia renders her ever changing and ever the same, at once powerfully
attractive and utterly unattainable; her timelessly youthful beauty is adored by
her courtly lovers, who are constant in their love despite the mutability of their
own mortal bodies; the song is presented as part of the erotic rites of May Day,
thereby fusing courtly political theatre with popular festivity; the presenter is
the nobleman who was the Queen's official champion, and whose office it was
to defend the peerless beauty of his sovereign mistress against all challengers
during the annual Accession Day tilts. Nicholas Hilliard limned a splendid
miniature of Cumberland in this role straight out of chivalric romance, in
which he wears the Queen's jeweled glove in his hat as a favor and stands with
his lance at the ready (fig. 49).[11] Unlike the engraved print that promoted
him publicly as a military hero (fig. 47), this courtly miniature was unlikely
to arouse the Queen's apprehensions.

Hilliard was Elizabethan England's preeminent practitioner of the art of
limning—the painting of portrait miniatures in watercolor. Highly prized
and highly developed at the Elizabethan court, this art had perhaps stronger

FIGURE 49

George Clifford, Earl of Cumberland, by Nicholas Hilliard; ca. 1590. Watercolor miniature on vellum, mounted on panel. © National Maritime Museum, London.

affinities with manuscript illumination, jewelry making, and heraldry than it did with oil painting. An art of lustrous surfaces and clear colors, limning devoted equal attention to the physiognomy of the sitter and to the clothing, ornaments, jewelry, and armor that were held to be emanations the sitter's rank and virtue. In his *Treatise concerning the Arte of Limning*, Hilliard asserts that

> it is sweet and cleanly to use, and it is a thing apart from all other painting or drawing, and tendeth not to common men's use ... being fittest for the decking of princes' books, or to put in jewels of gold, and for the imitation of the purest flowers and most beautiful creatures in the finest and purest colours ... and is for the service of noble persons very meet, in small volumes, in private manner, for them to have the portraits and pictures of themselves, their peers, or any other foreign persons which are of interest to them.[12]

Hilliard suggests that its subject matter, refinement, and cost make limning an exclusively aristocratic art. Furthermore, he argues that only those who are gentlemen—whether by birth or manners—are fit to pursue this art.[13] Jewel-like in their brilliant coloring and fine detail, these miniatures were frequently covered by crystals and set in jewels or richly worked cases. In this format, the rare and exquisite portrait miniature distilled the essence of the sitter's rank-encoded nobility and grace.

It is to Hilliard's *Treatise concerning the Arte of Limning* that we owe our only textual evidence of the Queen's artistic opinions and preferences. There, à propos of the Queen's picture, Hilliard exhorts his readers not to forget that

> the principal part of painting or drawing after the life consisteth in the truth of the line ... for the line without shadow showeth all to a good judgment, but the shadow without line showeth nothing. ... This makes me to remember the words also and reasoning of Her Majesty when first I came in her Highness's presence to draw; who, after showing me how she noted great difference of shadowing in the works, and the diversity of drawers of sundry nations ... required of me the reason of it, seeing that best to show one's self needeth no shadow of place, but rather the open light. The which I granted. ...
>
> For beauty and good favour is like clear truth, which is not shamed with the light, nor need to be obscured. (85, 87)

Hilliard reports that, as a consequence of their conversation, the Queen "chose her place to sit in for that purpose in the open alley of a goodly garden, where no tree was near, nor any shadow at all" (87).

The Queen's preferences in portraiture are perhaps most strikingly presented in the late "Rainbow" portrait (fig. 25), in which the relatively flat, evenly lit "mask of youth" emphasizes line and effaces shadow. Nevertheless, it was not primarily in panel paintings but in the late Elizabethan portrait miniatures of Hilliard that the Queen's notion of the skillful artisan was most consistently realized. In the words of the 1596 Privy Council memorandum, it was Hilliard who could best represent her "beutyfull and magnanimous Majesty," and it was to his studio that royal patronage flowed. Characteristic is a miniature limned by Hilliard around 1600, set in a jeweled locket with a star-burst design on the case (fig. 50).[14] Like the contemporaneous "Rainbow" portrait—but without recourse to any arcane symbolism—this intimate picture evokes Elizabeth's mystical virginity by representing her as a young and radiant maiden, her bosom uncovered, and her unbound hair flowing onto her shoulders. Not only in its youthful and idealized rendering of the Queen's physiognomy but also more generally in its linear, decorative, and brilliantly colored style, the work of Hilliard and his followers exemplifies an aesthetic at variance with that evident in the work of his younger contemporary, Isaac Oliver.[15] The miniatures and drawings of Oliver, like the oil paintings of his brother-in-law Marcus Gheeraerts the Younger, reveal a pursuit of the norms of high Renaissance painting, including linear perspective, chiaroscuro, and plasticity of forms; and both artists began to gain important noble patronage during the 1590s.[16] In the "Ditchley" portrait (fig. 35), Gheeraerts used chiaroscuro to present a verisimilar image of the facial features of Queen Elizabeth at threescore years of age. Consequentially, the representation of her physiognomy is in strong stylistic tension with the highly decorative patterning of her clothed body and the exorbitant and idealizing conceit governing the whole work. A comparison with the stylistic seamlessness of the slightly later "Rainbow" portrait emphasizes the stylistic incongruity inhering in the "Ditchley" portrait. At about the same time that Gheeraerts painted the "Ditchley" portrait, Oliver limned a strikingly naturalistic miniature of the Queen (fig. 51). The apparent verisimilitude of this unfinished portrait was an experiment that was not repeated: this seems to have been Oliver's first and only commission from the Queen, who subsequently returned her favor to the studio of Hilliard, and to the "mask of youth."[17]

Hilliard shared the aversion to shadowing in pictures that he attributed to Queen Elizabeth. Whether the product of the artist's poor skill or judgment or the subject's physical or moral deficiency, "great shadow is a good sign in a picture after the life, of an ill cause" (*Treatise*, 87). Hilliard suggests that shadowing figures dissimulation; thus, he commends its application in a picture on the subject of Christ's betrayal by Judas Iscariot, "for there the matter consisteth chiefly in the traitorous act done by night" (89). There is an instructive *paragone* to be made between Hilliard's attitude toward the painterly shadowing of Queen Elizabeth and Spenser's attitude toward shadowing her in the

FIGURE 50
Elizabeth I, by Nicholas Hilliard; ca. 1600. Watercolor miniature, set in a jeweled locket, with a star-burst
design on the case. Victoria & Albert Museum, London; V&A Images.

metaphorical language of poetry. Spenser characterized *The Faerie Queene*
as a "continued Allegory, or darke conceit"; and, while acknowledging that
such writing was often "doubtfully . . . construed" and was subject to "geal-
ous opinions and misconstructions," he nevertheless sought to "shadow" "the
most excellent and glorious person of our soveraine the Queene" in Belphoebe
and a variety of other allegorical personages.[18] Unlike the literal shadowings

of the painter's royal portrait image, the figurative shadowings of the poet's allegorical discourse allowed both for dangerous constructions and for deniability.

In his treatise, Hilliard responds to the Queen's observations on shadowing with the flattering comment that "beauty and good favor is like cleare truth, which is not shamed with the light, nor neede to bee obscured." To this can be juxtaposed an almost contemporaneous remark in John Clapham's memoir of Elizabeth's reign. Having censured his recently deceased queen for her susceptibility to flattery, Clapham goes on to emphasize that the exemplary

FIGURE 51
Elizabeth I, by Isaac Oliver; ca. 1590–92. Watercolor miniature on vellum, mounted on card.
Victoria & Albert Museum, London; V&A Images.

value of history obliges those who write histories to be candid in discussing the vices of princes; and he concludes that "by flattery in describing their actions, like a painted face without a shadow to give it life, the credit of such things as are truly reported would be much doubted and diminished."[19] For Clapham, then, shadowing figures not deception or treachery but rather historical verisimilitude, and its absence puts the truth of the historical record into question. It is unlikely that Clapham's royal subject would have appreciated his historiographical meditations. On the contrary, it is evident from the pattern of royal patronage and the regulatory attempts of the Elizabethan government that, as she grew older, shadowing became too revealing of the work of time and mutability for a Queen whose motto was *Semper eadem*. Paradoxically, it was in shadows that Elizabeth's *arcana imperii* were revealed.

Mysteries of State

Maxims of State, a tract sometimes attributed to Sir Walter Ralegh, defined "mysteries, or sophisms of state" as "certain secret practices, either for the avoiding of danger, or averting such effects as tend not to the preservation of the present state, as it is set or founded."[1] As expounded by Machiavelli, this principle of statecraft tempered adherence to the norms of morality and justice with the prudential calculation of political interests.[2] In 1612, John Hayward presented to Henry, Prince of Wales, a history of the first four years of his late queen's reign that was particularly attentive to Elizabeth's skill in the practice of such mysteries. In his Jacobean account of Elizabeth's passage through London on the day before her coronation, Hayward notes Elizabeth's care regarding the royal furnishing of both herself and her train. Lifting a passage from Sidney's *Arcadia*, he commends the fledgling queen for

> knowing right well that in pompous ceremonies a secret of government doth much consist, for that the people are naturally both taken and held with exteriour shewes. . . . The rich attire, the ornaments, the beauty of Ladyes, did add particular graces to the solemnity, and held the eyes and hearts of men dazeled betweene contentment and admiratione.[3]

Henry Savile, who was the Queen's Greek tutor, included a note on the Tacitean phrase *arcana imperii* in his 1591 annotated translation of Tacitus's *History*. Here Savile is discussing "the secrete truethes of apparences in affaires of estate, for the masse of the people is guided and governed more by ceremonies and shewes then matter in substance."[4] Like Savile, Hayward had been a client of the Earl of Essex, and the Elizabethan government had deemed his prose history of Bolingbroke's usurpation of Richard II to be a seditious brief for the Queen's usurpation by Essex and his faction. Following the printing of his *First Part of the Reign of Henry IIII* (1599), Hayward was imprisoned for the duration of the Queen's reign. In echoing Savile's politic history and plagiarising Sidney's pastoral romance, Hayward applied to his Jacobean history of Elizabeth's reign the same Tacitean perspective upon the mysteries of state, or *arcana imperii*, that had characterized his notorious Elizabethan history of Henry IV's reign.[5]

"Dazeled betweene contentment and admiratione" captures nicely the amalgam of solace and awe that could hold "the eyes and hearts of men" in willing subjection to the charismatic power of the prince. In Haywood's narrative of Queen's Elizabeth's coronation entry, this was an effect produced by the combination of costume, ceremony, and feminine beauty. Hayward provides a shrewd retrospective account of Elizabeth's entry into her reign. Writing in the months following the Queen's death, John Clapham provides a useful counter-perspective to Hayward's when he discusses the altered circumstances in which she deployed this "secret of government" at the end of her reign: "In her latter time, when she showed herself in public, she was always magnificent in apparel, supposing haply thereby, that the eyes of her people, being dazzled with the glittering aspect of those accidental ornaments would not so easily discern the marks of age and decay of natural beauty."[6] This strategy seems to have worked well upon Thomas Platter, a Swiss traveler who saw the Queen at Nonesuch Palace in 1599. In his diary, Platter carefully recorded a detailed description of her gown, headpiece, jewelry, and gloves, concluding with the observation that "she was most gorgeously apparelled, and although she was already seventy four [*sic*], was very youthful still in appearance, seeming no more than twenty years of age."[7] However, three years later, when the Duke of Stettin-Pomerania and his entourage saw the Queen at Oatlands, his diarist observed more sharply: "To judge from portraits showing her Majesty in her thirtieth year, there cannot have lived many finer women at the time; even in her old age she did not look ugly, *when seen from a distance*."[8] The royal pageantry and iconography of late Elizabethan culture display an exorbitancy in verbal, visual, and sartorial rhetoric that seems intended to produce a symbolic compensation for the Queen's natural decline. Such "exteriour shewes" may have continued to be relatively effective in dazzling a majority of "the people"; however, in the eyes of at least some beholders, such hyperbolic strategies worked to the contrary effect, magnifying rather than mystifying the discrepancy between the Queen's natural and politic bodies, and thereby abetting that "contempte in her latter yeres" which she sought so assiduously to prevent.

The "exteriour shewes" in which Hayward perceived a secret of Elizabethan government have left historical traces not only in royal portraits and verbal descriptions of such pictures but also in texts that record the visual spectacle of the Queen's self-presentation. When she was in state—enrobed, bejeweled, bewigged, and painted—Elizabeth herself was a living icon, or, as either John Knox or William Allen might have put it, an idol. As the most immediately conspicuous and the most versatile manifestation of royal magnificence, costume was at the center of attention in royal portraiture and courtly ceremony. In their dispatches and diaries, foreign visitors to the English court almost invariably described in detail the Queen's features, carriage, wardrobe, and accessories; and in their reports to the Queen, English ambassadors frequently described the appearance, demeanor, and dress of foreign queens and court ladies—usually doing so precisely in order to draw an unfavorable comparison with their own unmatched mistress.

The Venetian Secretary Scaramelli had his first official audience with Queen Elizabeth just a few weeks before her death. He began his report to the Doge and Senate with the following description:

> The Queen was clad in taffety of silver and white, trimmed with gold; her dress was somewhat open in front and showed her throat encircled with pearls and rubies down to her breast. Her skirts were much fuller and began lower than is the fashion in France. Her hair was of a light colour never made by nature, and she wore great pearls like pears round the forehead; she had a coif arched round her head and an Imperial crown, and displayed a vast quantity of gems and pearls upon her person.[9]

It is clear from her reported remarks that the occasion was an important one for the aged Queen, and one very long in coming:

> Her countenance, which had hitherto been placid and almost smiling, assumed a graver aspect, and she said, "I cannot help feeling that the Republic of Venice, during the forty-four years of my reign, has never made herself heard by me except to ask for something; nor for the rest, prosperous or adverse as my affairs may have been, never has she given a sign of holding me or my kingdom in that esteem which other princes and other potentates have not refused. Nor am I aware that my sex has brought me this demerit, for my sex cannot diminish my prestige nor offend those who treat me as other Princes are treated, to whom the Signory of Venice sends its Ambassadors." (533)

It is the color, fabric, and style of the Queen's dress, and the size, shape, and abundance of her jewels that make the most immediate visual impact upon the Venetian Secretary. The intended effect was obviously to create an aura of imperial magnificence, one that put both the Queen and her Kingdom on an equal footing with *la Serenissima*. Elizabeth's blunt comment to Scaramelli reflected a forty-four year struggle: One of the challenges faced by the Elizabethan regime had always been to ensure that the Queen's sex did not diminish her prestige and thereby weaken England's stature in European affairs. The Venetian dispatch is a valedictory reminder that, in the case of Elizabeth Tudor, personal vanity was a manifestation of political necessity, of the imperative to preserve her *arcana imperii* against the increasing prospect of "contempte in her latter yeres."

The most detailed eyewitness accounts of the Queen's appearance are from late in the reign; and the richest single source is the private journal of André Hurault, Sieur de Maisse, the French ambassador who visited England in 1597. De Maisse recorded that at his first audience the Queen commenced by apologizing for being seen "in her night-gown [sa robe de nuit]"; it seems that she was more informally dressed than would normally have been the case for state occasions such as the reception of ambassadors. De Maisse continues:

> She was strangely attired in a dress of silver cloth, white and crimson.... She kept the front of her dress [robe] open, and one could see the whole of her bosom, and passing low [*tout sa gorge et assez bas*], and often she would open the front of this robe [*manteau*] with her hands as if she was too hot. The collar of the robe was very high.... She also had a chain of pearls and rubies about her neck. On her head she wore a garland of the same material and beneath it a great reddish-coloured wig, with a great number of spangles of gold and silver, and hanging down over her forehead some pearls.... On either side of her ears hung two great curls of hair, almost down to her shoulders.... Her bosom [*la gorge*] is somewhat wrinkled as well as [one can see for] the collar that she wears round her neck, but lower down her flesh is exceeding white and delicate, so far as one could see.
>
> As for her face, it is and appears to be very aged. It is long and thin, and her teeth are very yellow and unequal.... Many of them are missing so that one cannot understand her easily when she speaks quickly. Her figure is fair and tall and graceful in whatever she does; so far as may be she keeps her dignity, yet humbly and graciously withal.[10]

I have quoted at length from this description, in part because it seems to me to refract in words the visual image in the late "Rainbow" portrait (fig. 25): The maidenly coiffure, uncovered bosom, and adornments are very similar; the *manteau* may have been a mantle, or some other long outer garment, partially covering her upper body. On the other hand, the signs of physical aging— the wrinkled skin of her face and throat (*sa gorge*), her yellowed and missing teeth—are in stark contrast to the glowingly youthful beauty of the portrait image. Although the verbal portrait drawn by de Maisse frankly registers the ravages of age, it eschews the opportunity for maliciously misogynistic commentary that his private medium allowed him. On the contrary, he seems genuinely to admire Elizabeth's will to avoid "contempte in her latter yeres," and to resist the inexorable triumph of time: "So far as may be she keeps her dignity."[11]

The ambassador's second audience was deferred because, at the appointed time, "the Queen was ill and indisposed": "She was on the point of giving me audience, having already sent her coaches to fetch me, but taking a look into her mirror said that she appeared too ill and that she was unwilling for anyone to see her in that state; and so countermanded me" (*Journal*, 36). De Maisse had his audience on the following day. On this occasion, the Queen

> was clad in a dress [robbe] of black taffeta, bound with gold lace.... She had a petticoat [une robbe desoulz] of white damask, girdled, and open in front, as was also her chemise, in such a manner that she often opened this dress and one could see all her belly [l'estomach], and even to her navel [nombril].... When she raises her head, she has a trick of putting both hands on her gown and opening it insomuch that all her belly [l'estomach] can be seen. (36–37)

Janet Arnold suggests that this seemingly bizarre scene is likely due to the Frenchman's awkwardness in describing women's fashions at the English court.[12] Be that as it may, whatever the Queen was actually wearing, and in whatever manner she actually wore it, the ambassador's description represents her dress and demeanor as erotically provocative, and as intentionally so. De Maisse opens a window onto the performative culture of the late Elizabethan court, one that may help us better to understand how Pormort/Topcliffe might have fantasized telling the Queen that she had "the softest belly of any woman kynde."

The context that de Maisse provides for his second audience suggests that the Queen was at pains to compensate for the circumstance that had precipitated its postponement—her indisposition after "taking a look into her mirror." However, his perceptions of the vanity and melancholy of this personage in no way negate his numerous observations of her grace, vitality, and political cunning. In another description of her clothing, jewels, and bearing, de Maisse observes that she "walked in a manner marvellous haughty ... and I believe she did so expressly that I might see her while she pretended not to see me" (83). Indeed, in the very process of describing the Queen's preoccupation with the impact of her appearance upon her beholders, the ambassador demonstrates its impact upon himself.

Almost immediately following his description of the Queen's attire at his second audience, de Maisse relates the substance of the conversation that ensued, in which the Queen turned the talk to the subject of the French king's mistress: "Speaking of Brittany, she said that the King would no longer go there, and that it was made a present to a lady whom she knew not how to name. Afterwards she corrected herself; she said several times: 'Gabrielle, that is the name of an angel; but there has never been a female'" (37). Gabrielle d'Estrées had been created marquise de Monceaux and Duchess of Beaufort by Henri IV. Elizabeth appears to have gone out of her way to raise the matter in order to insinuate to the King's ambassador that "she knew not how to name" the King's mistress because her own modesty forbade her to name what that other lady was: she would only suggest that she was no angel. The subtext of Elizabeth's comment was presumably that she herself was utterly unlike Gabrielle d'Estrées, not only in her uncompromised chastity but also in her autonomous power: In Elizabethan England, a queen regnant bestowed estates and titles upon her masculine favorites. Elizabeth was making a similar point about gender and power (although one without an explicitly sexual dimension) when she revealed to de Maisse during a subsequent audience that "she had intercepted a letter that the Infanta Margerita sent to the late Duchess of Savoy. . . . She caused this letter to be sent to the Duchess of Savoy, telling her that she had no wish to know the affairs of the ladies" (56). Here Elizabeth demonstrates the efficiency of her intelligence network, while also making the point to her masculine interlocutor that she is a Prince who concerns herself not with "affairs of the ladies" but rather with matters of state.

In another comment reported by de Maisse, Queen Elizabeth performed an even more complex rhetorical operation upon the paradox of her two bodies:

> She spoke to me of the languages that she had learned, for she makes digressions very often, telling me that when she came to the Crown she knew six languages better than her own; and because I told her that is was great virtue in a princess, she said that it was no marvel to teach a woman to talk; it were far harder to teach her to hold her tongue. (110)

There is a sly wit at work in this off-handed gesture of apparent self-deprecation: After all, the speaker was a female prince, one who not only took great pride in her mastery of languages but also embraced the politic virtue of taciturnity in her personal motto *Video et taceo*—"I see and am silent."[13] Peter Burke has pointed to "two particularly important principles underlying the system of silence in early modern Europe," namely, that of respect or deference and that of prudence. A prominent example of the former is the silence of women, especially in public or in the presence of their husbands; a prominent example of the latter is "the dissimulation of princes and the discretion of the

wise." Burke remarks that Philip II, among other Spanish kings, was known
for his

> public taciturnity. Silence may have been their strategy to appear dignified, or it
> may have been a means of dissimulating their intentions. . . . Dissimulation and
> "prudent silence" (*prudentemente tacere*) was a central concern of the writers on
> "reason of state" and the art of discretion in the early modern period. . . . Their
> discussions drew heavily on the writings of Cornelius Tacitus.[14]

From the perspective of the tradition illuminated by Burke, it might be said that
Elizabeth's motto *Video et taceo* paradoxically incorporated both deferential
and prudential silence, and thus wittily incorporated the Queen's Two Bodies.
Returning to de Maisse's anecdote, we might say that, in ventriloquizing a
common misogynistic caricature of female garrulity, in making a joke at the
expense of women and sharing it with the ambassador, the Queen implied
to her male interlocutor that she herself was and was not a woman. At the
same time, however, in the process of inscribing the Queen's paradoxical
comment into his journal, de Maisse also reinscribed her within the very
gender stereotype that she had sought to appropriate: "She makes digressions
very often."

When the English queen introduced the topic of the French king's mistress
into her conversation with de Maisse, she may have been remembering a piece
of intelligence that she had received from her own ambassador in France,
Sir Henry Unton, less than two years prior. In a letter to Elizabeth sent from
France, in which he recounted his audiences with Henri IV, Unton digressed
as follows:

> [The King] sent for Madam *de Monceaux* [i.e., Gabrielle d'Estrées], telling me,
> that he would no more estrange himself now from me, then in former Tymes;
> and used many affectionate Wordes in her Commendation, among others, that
> she never intermeddled with his Affayres, and had a tractable Spyrite, whearin
> he spake not amiss; for she is heald to be incapable of Affaires, and verie simple.
> At her cominge he drew near to her, with great Reverence, houlding his Hatt at
> the first in his Hande; then he declared unto her, that I was so well known unto
> them both, as he doubted not but she would welcombe me; which she did,
> unmaskinge her self, and gracinge me with her best Favors; whearin I toke no
> great Pleasure, nor heald it any Grace at all. She was attyred in a playne Sattayne
> Gowne, with a Velvet Hood all over her Head . . . which became her verie ill;
> and, in my Opinion, she is altered verie much for the worse in her Complection
> and Favor, yeat verie grosselye painted. I am loath to mingle Toyes with serious
> Matters, yeat are such Circumstances sometymes not impertinent; and for
> myne I humbly crave Pardon, being willing rather to offend in Surplusage
> then Defect.[15]

As constructed in the exchange between the King and the ambassador, Madame de Monceaux's tractability and naïveté manifest the patriarchal principle of womanly frailty, which was widely asserted as an inherent disability that justified the subjection of women and their exclusion from the public sphere. When Queen Elizabeth told de Maisse that "she had no wish to know the affairs of the ladies," she implied both that she shared this understanding of female incapacity and that it did not apply to her.

Not only was Madame de Monceaux held to be "incapable of Affaires, and verie simple," but even in those very attributes of beauty, grace, and charm for which ladies were to be esteemed, the King's mistress was woefully lacking. In her fashion, visage, and bearing, as well as in her wit, her shortcomings reflected negatively upon the judgment and taste of Henri IV himself. Although he contemptuously dismissed it as a mere toy, Unton was clearly very willing to mingle gossip about Gabrielle d'Estrées with the serious matters of his intelligence: It was "not impertinent" because it subtly epitomized the inferiority of Frenchness to Englishness. More particularly, by implicitly judging both the mistress and her master in the light of the peerless Virgin Queen, Unton dutifully played to the vanity of his own master-mistress.

As the narrative in Unton's letter to the Queen continued to unfold, it disclosed with consummate rhetorical skill the strategy that underlay his anatomy of Madame de Monceaux:

> The King, after these Ceremonies passed . . . withdrew himself, requiring me to follow him into his Chamber, wher in a privat Place, between his Bed and the Wall, he asked me how I liked his Mistress, and whether I found her anye thinge changed. I answered sparingly in her Praise, and tould him, that if, without Offence I might speake it, that I had the Picture of a farr more excellent Mistress, and yet did her Picture come farr short of her Perfection of Beauty. As you love me (sayd he) shew it me, if you have it about you. I made some Difficulties; yett, uppon his Importunity, offred it unto his Viewe verie seacretly, houlding it still in my Hande: he beheald it with Passion and Admiration, saying, that I had Reason, *Je me rends*, protesting, that he never had seen the like; so, with great Reverence, he kissed it twice or thrice, I detay[n]ing it still in my Hand. In the Ende, with some kind of Contention, he toke it from me, vowing, that I might take my Leave of it, for he would not forgoe it for any Treasure; and that, to possesse the Favor of the lively Picture, he would forsake the World, and hould himself most happie, with many other most passionate Wordes. Then he did blame me (by whom, he sayd, he had written many passionate Letters . . . in not retourninge him any reciproke Favor from your Majesty, and did complayne of your Highness Neglect, and Disdayne of him, which was not the least Cause of his Discomfort. Whearuppon I replyed as fitt an Answer as I could, and as I found his Humour more or less apt of Apprehension. But I

found that the dombe Picture did drawe on more Speache and Affection from
him then all my best Argumentes and Eloquence. (718–19)

Recalling de Maisse's not unsympathetic verbal portrait of the aged and
declining Elizabeth, struggling to keep her dignity, we may construe Unton's
disdainful verbal portrait of Madame de Monceaux—"altered verie much for
the worse in her Complection and Favor, yeat verie grosselye painted"—as a
foil contrived to set off his royal reader. Unton's Elizabeth is *semper eadem*,
the ever-youthful Queen of Hearts represented in the miniatures produced
during the 1590s by Nicholas Hilliard—"yet did her picture come farr short
of her Perfection of Beauty."

Their diminutive size, fragility, and expense encouraged the treatment of
miniatures as private treasures, either locked away or carried upon the body.
Because, as Hilliard put it, such "small pictures" were to be "viewed of necessity
in hand near unto the eye" (*Treatise*, 87), the occasion of their viewing was
characteristically marked by physical intimacy and heightened passions. Such
were the conditions under which Sir Henry Unton and the king of France
together beheld and adored the picture of Queen Elizabeth. In the second
quotation from Unton's dispatch to the Queen, the scene has shifted from the
royal park into the King's bedchamber. In that "privat Place, between his Bed
and the Wall," the French king shared with the English ambassador highly
eroticized intelligence regarding the secrets of state. In his narrative, Unton
provides a paradigmatic setting for the viewing of the Queen's portrait in
miniature, one that inextricably combines intimate and extravagant sentiment
with high politics. Playing to the King's assumed role as the importunate
lover, Unton undertakes to double in the parts of go-between and rival; he
thereby presents himself to his own sovereign as an adept in those strategies
of erotic courtship through which she had long pursued a central aspect of
her statecraft. Unton's account of his coy way with the French king might well
be compared to Ralegh's description of his interaction with the natives of the
New World, written in the same year: "I shewed them her Majesties picture
which they so admired and honoured, as it had bene easie to have brought
them idolatrous thereof." As it happened, Elizabeth's picture was not the first
that Henri had worshiped: In a 1594 letter to Gabrielle d'Estrées, Henri told
her that he was writing to her seated at the foot of her picture, which he
adored only because she was its subject, not because it truly resembled her;
she was painted with all perfection only "dans mon ame, dans mon coeur,
dans mes yeux." The King's tone was more decorously courtly when he wrote
directly to his elderly ally and patroness, Queen Elizabeth, begging her to
forgive him for intercepting and keeping the portrait she had meant for his

sister: The representation of so great a beauty had been too strong a temptation for one who so loved and reverenced its subject.[16] Both the French king and the English ambassador knew well how to play their parts in the maintenance of the old queen's dignity.

The panegyrical motive in Unton's address to Elizabeth could hardly be clearer: "The dombe Picture did drawe on more Speache and Affection from him then all my best Argumentes and Eloquence." In this *paragone* of the visual and verbal arts, the idol of feminine beauty trumps the humanist's rhetorical powers—such, at least, is the assertion of Unton's courtly eloquence. Nevertheless, the apologetic justification that Unton also included—"I am loath to mingle Toyes with serious Matters, yeat are such Circumstances sometymes not impertinent"—suggests that he felt his manly self-esteem to have been compromised by this requisite descent into effeminating trifles. Perhaps he remembered Erasmus's caution that men should avoid the inclusion of "minor topics that are trivial and old-womanish" in their letters of counsel.[17] A comparison of Unton's letter to the Queen with the one that he wrote to Lord Burghley on the very same day suggests that the ambassador mingled those "Toyes with serious Matters" because he was confident that they would appeal to the woman in his prince. In his substantially longer dispatch to Burghley, Unton includes nothing of what I have quoted from his letter to the Queen; Madame de Monceaux is never mentioned, nor is the secret sharing of the Queen's picture in the King's bedchamber. Such toys would indeed have been construed as "impertinent" by Queen Elizabeth's sober old counselor. Instead, Unton gives Burghley a far more circumstantial account of his interviews with the King, and a series of intelligences about a wide range of political and diplomatic affairs in France and Spain.[18]

Whatever the actual dynamics of Elizabethan counsel, late Elizabethan royal panegyric represented the Queen as exercising absolute and unerring command over the process of sifting intelligence and determining policy. This theme was featured among the entertainments with which Elizabeth was greeted by Sir Robert Cecil—Burghley's son and political heir, and the Queen's principal secretary and chief intelligencer—when she visited him in 1602. For this occasion, John Davies had devised a conference between a gentleman usher and a courier. The courier had "inteligence" to bring to the Queen—namely, letters "from the Emperor of China." This provided an opportunity for lavish praise of the Queen's linguistic abilities, although Davies did not go so far as to claim that she spoke Chinese. During the course of the exchange, the courier asked, "what use dooth she make of her servants?" The usher replied, "She makes the same use of them as the mynde makes of the sences.

Many things she sees and heares through them; but the judgment and election are her owne."[19] Cecil's client was complimenting his master's mistress on her powers of discernment and on the autonomy of her will, on her mastery of the mysteries of state.

We might contrast to Davies's royal entertainment of 1602 the private memoir of the Queen's reign written in the months immediately following her death by John Clapham. Clapham, who had been a client and protégé of Robert Cecil's father, described the Queen during her later years

> as a prince who heareth and seeth for the most part with other men's ears and eyes, seldom discerning the truth of things, but looking in counterfeit glasses and receiving reports as they are delivered by parasites and tale-carriers, who first serve their own turns for advantage, and then either for favor commend their friends beyond desert, or for malice deprave without just cause such as they dislike. Such are the effects of flattery, a vice many times unpleasing even to them that practise it, and not to be tolerated by a prince without imputation of his weakness in judgment.[20]

In assessing his late queen, Clapham may concur with Davies that "many things she sees and heares through" the eyes and ears of her servants, but he dissents from the flattering claim that "the judgment and election are her owne." In fact, the relationship observed by Clapham inverts the conventional model of royal statecraft: Rather than a wise and feared master, the vain prince is the pliant instrument of her dissimulating and self-serving subjects.[21]

It is impossible to determine the precise relationship between the account in Unton's letter to Queen Elizabeth and the interview that actually took place between himself and King Henri IV. Of course, there is a possibility that he took the liberty to enliven his account with details of his own invention. But even if Unton's letter to the Queen were a relatively accurate relating of the events as he perceived them, the companion letter to Burghley would still act as a foil. The latter allows us to apprehend the degree to which assumptions about gender determined both the specific content and the rhetorical strategies of the intelligence that the Queen's loyal servants deemed appropriate for her eyes and ears. Near the beginning of the reign, then Secretary William Cecil reportedly had reprimanded the bearer of ambassadorial intelligence for discussing it with the Queen: "I have declared unto Mr. Secretary, what your Lordship thinketh of the General Council, who wished I had not told the Queen's Majesty a matter of such weight, being too much he said for a woman's knowledge."[22] We may wonder how much Burghley's attitudes had changed almost four decades later, and how sharp a distinction he would then have drawn between the capacities of Queen Elizabeth and those of Gabrielle d'Estrées. In writing his intelligence report to the Queen, Unton addressed her as one distinct from and superior to other women. At the same time, however, both by what he chose to say and by what he chose not to say, not only to her but also to Burghley, Unton reinscribed the Queen within the cultural norms of gender difference to which all of them were habituated.

Through the Looking Glass

In February 1603, shortly before the Queen's death, John Manningham recorded in his diary the following anecdote: "Sir Christopher Hatton and another knight made challenge whoe should present the truest picture of hir Majestie to the Q[ueene]. One caused a flattering picture to be drawne; the other presented a glas, wherein the Q[ueene] saw hir selfe, the truest picture that might be."[1] The scenario is one of typical courtly rivalry for the attentions and approval of the prince; however, because this prince is a woman, the scenario is also atypical in being predicated upon traditional gendered assumptions regarding the vice of vanity and its specular iconography. The conventional moral of the story is that truth is to be preferred before flattery, but this moral is enforced ironically: The politic courtier praises the Queen's moral virtue, flattering her with the implication that she disdains flattery. Hatton had been dead since 1591; and, in any case, the story is likely to have been apocryphal. Nevertheless, it is of historical interest not only because Manningham himself had found it sufficiently memorable to have taken the time to record it but also because it forms part of a larger corpus of such stories. The subject of the Queen and the Looking Glass appears in a number of anecdotes recorded around the time of Elizabeth's demise. These anecdotes inscribe in the medium of gossip the late Elizabethan theme of *mundus senescit* and all that it implied about the disenchantment of the old Queen's subjects.

Soon after Manningham made his diary entry, the Queen was dead; and shortly thereafter, Henry Chettle published *England's Mourning Garment* (1603), a memorial in the form of a fictionalized pastoral dialogue:

So farre was she from all nicenes, that I have heard it credibly reported, and know it by many instances to be true, that she never could abide to gaze in a mirror or looking glasse: no not to behold one, while her head was tyred and adornd, but simply trusted to her attendant Ladies for the comeliness of her attyre: and that this is true . . . I am the rather perswaded, for that when I was yong, almost thirtie yeeres agoe, courting it now and than: I have seene the Ladies make great shift to hide away their looking glasses if her Majestie had past by their lodgings.[2]

Chettle's pastoral speaker represents Elizabeth as abhorring mirrors. However, "that she never could abide to gaze in a mirror or looking glasse" is interpreted by this literary shepherd as evidence of her indifference to her own image. With an irony that is characteristic of Elizabethan pastorals, Chettle renders the Queen's often observed vanity as the occasion for an encomium to her lack of pride.

Other anecdotal evidence gives little reason to think that Manningham's queen preferred the truthful mirror to the flattering picture. In 1596, for example, Bishop Anthony Rudd preached a sermon at court on the delicate theme of infirmity in old age. He was recklessly forthright in holding a rhetorical mirror up to his royal auditor, observing that time had "furrowed her face and besprinkled her hair with meal"; in response, the Queen made it immediately known that his text displeased her.[3] In the memoir that he wrote in the months immediately following the Queen's death, John Clapham offered another version of the looking glass anecdote that treated the subject of royal flattery sententiously:

It is credibly reported that, not long before her death, [the Queen] had a great apprehension of her own age and declination by seeing her face, then lean and full of wrinkles, truly represented to her in a glass; which she a good while very earnestly beheld, perceiving thereby how often she had been abused by flatterers whom she held in too great estimation, that had informed her to the contrary.[4]

In Clapham's exemplary anecdote, Elizabeth's memento mori moment does not turn her thoughts toward heavenly verities but rather concentrates her mind upon hard political truths. Clapham might have made the misogynistic choice to focus upon the personal vanities of the female monarch; instead, he reflects upon the collective ethical dilemmas of courtly society and monarchical government: endemic corruption and sycophancy, and the constant danger that the subject's duty to proffer wise counsel will be perverted by narrow and ruthless self-interest.

Another perspective upon the royal mirror derives from a body of reported court gossip that is of considerably less moral probity than the observations of Clapham or Rudd, and that is casually but pervasively misogynistic. In the aftermath of her death, anecdotes of the Queen and the Looking Glass seem to have multiplied; and, unlike Chettle's, most of this gossip focused specifically on Queen Elizabeth's declining years. Ben Jonson seems to have been a good source of gossip, royal or otherwise; and Drummond records a couple of particularly wicked Jonsonian remarks about the late Queen's chastity and beauty. Of the former, he asserted "that she had a Membrana on her which made her uncapable of man, though for her delight she tryed many"—in effect, that she was rampantly unchaste, and remained a virgin only on a technicality. And of the latter, he maintained that "Queen Elizabeth never saw her self after she became old in a true Glass. they painted her & sometymes would vermilion her nose."[5] Here Jonson pithily confounds Manningham's simple opposition between the "flattering picture" painted to represent the Queen and the true picture revealed by her reflection in the mirror: For Jonson, the putatively "false" glass merely gives a truthful reflection of the "flattering picture" that has been falsely painted with cosmetics directly upon the old Queen's face. Jonson's conceit was apposite because Elizabethan miniatures and Elizabethan mirrors were similar in size, shape, ornamentation, and function.[6] He implies that Elizabeth's ladies-in-waiting had now become her limners, although perhaps they lacked Hilliard's skill in fashioning the mask of youth. A Jesuit in London named Anthony Rivers reported in a letter to Robert Persons that at the court's Christmas festivities in 1600 "it was commonly observed that . . . her Majesty . . . was continually painted, not only all over her face, but her very neck and breast also, and that the same was in some places near half an inch thick."[7] Jonson himself was a sometime Catholic; and just as his comment on his late queen's false chastity recycled earlier defamations by Sander and Allen, so his iconoclastic quip that "they painted her & sometymes would vermilion her nose" rendered the royal image not merely a false idol but a ridiculous one. Not only Jesuits but even Protestant ecclesiasts participated in this derisive discourse: in his memoir of the Jacobean court, Bishop Godfrey Goodman recalled that in the later years of Elizabeth's reign "there was . . . a report that the ladies had gotten false looking-glasses, that the queen might not see her own wrinkles."[8]

Mirrors made of several different materials and having quite different re-flective properties were available in late sixteenth-century England. Crystal glass mirrors were the newest and best of these—light, portable, easily main-tained, and reflecting clear and relatively undistorted images. Perhaps these were of the sort that the Queen's ladies had to hide from her sight. In any case, the anecdotal history of the Queen and the Looking Glass registers the shifting technology of mirrors and the impact of such changes upon the per-vasive cultural tropings of the mirror: as an exemplary image of personal conduct or public policy, to be either emulated or avoided; as an epitome of knowledge; as an emblem of human vanity and the mutability of earthy things; as a metaphor for the workings of conscience and moral self-scrutiny.[9] Clapham's version concerns itself with an issue that was central to Elizabethan political culture: How might subjects safely and effectively counsel or admonish their sovereign and remedy corruption in high places? And even the more trivial of the anecdotes examined here can make a claim to historical significance because they too point toward the vexed relationship between flattery and counsel. They are also indicative of the degree to which Elizabeth was indeed subject to "contempte in her latter yeres"—a contempt inflected by the same gender bias that figured *Vanitas* as a woman gazing at herself in a mirror.

The gossip being retailed concerning the late Queen was part of a venerable misogynistic discourse about female vanity, envy, and spite, a discourse in which old women were assigned an especially ignominious place. And this discourse was but the underside of that which venerated youthful female beauty and grace. In the Elizabethan case, at issue was the predicament of a ruler who—perhaps out of personal inclination, and undoubtedly out of political necessity—had exploited the charismatic potential of certain culturally constituted feminine ideals, ideals with which the accidents of nature and the ravages of time were becoming increasingly incompatible. As we have seen, when Isaac Oliver limned his unfinished miniature of the aging monarch in the early 1590s, he provided her with a looking glass in which she might see her wrinkles. He received no further patronage from the Queen, who preferred the flattering pictures offered by Hilliard. During the final decade of the reign, as if in compensation for Oliver's image, Hilliard's workshop produced numerous variations upon an idealized, youthful and beautiful royal visage. We may choose to comprehend such images in Neoplatonic terms, as visual allegories of the Queen's virtue and authority, as metaphorical portraits of her chaste mind, her beautiful soul. Yet there is considerable evidence that the whole enterprise of later Elizabethan royal panegyric was pervaded by a distinctly cynical air. The gossip that represented the Queen as a vain, foolish, and wrinkled old woman—an object of pathos or derision—sought thereby to divest her of the body politic of kingship, and to confine her within a body natural that was culturally defined by the perceived deficiencies of her gender, age, and marital status. It is in this sense that the quip attributed to the Earl of Essex, that "the Queen was cankered, and that her mind had become as crooked as her carcass," was not merely spiteful but seditious.[10] The lengthening tenure of Elizabeth's rule may have served to enhance her political experience and acumen, but it was also eroding the efficacy of precisely those symbolic forms through which her regime sought to secure the devotion of her subjects.

The looking glass anecdote plays a part in the manuscript narrative of the Queen's death that was written by Elizabeth Southwell four years after the event. Southwell was a granddaughter of the Lord Admiral, Charles Howard of Effingham, and a blood relative of Queen Elizabeth; as one of the royal maids of honor, she was in attendance on Queen Elizabeth at the time of the Queen's death and was also in attendance on her corpse during the royal obsequies. In 1605, Southwell and Robert Dudley, illegitimate son of the late Earl of Leicester, played out a romantic scenario of Shakespearean resonance: with Southwell disguised and cross-dressed as Dudley's page, the lovers eloped to the continent, where they converted to Catholicism and were married.[11]

In Southwell's account, presumably written early in her Italian exile, the episode of the mirror occurs after the onset of the Queen's final illness:

> She saw one night in her bed her bodie exceeding leane and fearefull in a light of fire, for the which the next daie she desired to see a true loking glass which in 20 yeares befor she had not sene but onlie such a one which of purpos was made to deceive her sight which glas being brought her she fell presently exclaiming at all those which had so much commended her and toke yt so offensivelie, that all thos which had befor flattered her durst not come in her sight. (20–27)

Like Clapham, Southwell describes a complicity between the courtier's flattery and the prince's vanity, and she focuses upon the belated moment of royal self-revelation. However, Southwell's account is quite distinctive in that it embeds this moralizing anecdote within a larger discourse: a contest for control of the Queen's Two Bodies waged between the dying Elizabeth and her chief counselor and Secretary of State, Sir Robert Cecil. Southwell consistently demonizes Cecil, to whom she indirectly attributes the onset of the Queen's fatal illness by means of sorcery. She represents him as seeking to manipulate his dying mistress and as contravening her deathbed wishes in order to deliver the crown to King James so to secure his own preeminent position under the new dispensation. The Machiavellian role played by Cecil intensifies the narrative's emphasis upon the Queen's weakness and disability, her increasing loss of control over her bodies natural and politic.

One detail in Southwell's account conveys with particular power the dissolution of Elizabeth's charisma and her divorce from the body politic of kingship. When the Queen died—without having named a successor—the assembled privy councillors departed for London to proclaim James as king, "leaving her bodie with charge not to be opened such being her desire, but Cecill having given a secret warrant to the surgeons they opened her" (79–81). Disemboweling was standard procedure in the sixteenth century, not only in the treatment of living traitors but also in the treatment of dead monarchs; and it had been customarily applied to the corpses of Elizabeth's Tudor predecessors. What made this case special was both the official status of the Queen as a virgin and the claim that men had handled, opened, and inspected her body against her wishes.[12] To have opened the Queen's corpse thus would have been to violate her *arcana imperii* in the most visceral of ways.[13]

Southwell dwells in sometimes lurid and wholly unsympathetic detail upon the physical infirmity and emotional distress of Queen Elizabeth in the last days of her life; and also upon the spectacular corruption of her corpse after death:

> My selfe that night there watching as one of them being all about the bodie which was fast nailed up in a bord coffin ... her bodie and head break with such a crack that spleated the wood lead and cer cloth. whereupon the next daie she was faine to be new trimmed up; whereupon they gave their verdics that yf she had not ben opened the breath of her bodie would a ben much worse. (84–91)[14]

By focusing so insistently upon the debility, corruption, and violation of the Queen's physical body, Southwell's account undermines any sense that the mystical body of English kingship had inhered in it. Among extant accounts, this one is uniquely insistent upon the late queen's bodily corruption—a difference made salient by the fact that Southwell was a Catholic convert and exile, whose manuscript was possessed and also redacted by the tireless Jesuit polemicist Robert Persons. This insistence was an effective means to demolish the late queen's sacral aura. As such, it complemented those earlier representations of Elizabeth's sexual depravity that were deployed by Catholic polemicists to undermine her temporal and spiritual authority and to counter the antipapist imaginary of Elizabethan Protestants.

Southwell may also have had in her mind an implied contrast between the polluted flesh of this persecutor of Catholics and the miraculously uncorrupted corpses sometimes ascribed to the Catholic martyrs themselves. An apposite example is that of Margaret Clitherow, a Catholic laywoman convicted of recusancy and of harboring a priest, who was pressed to death at York in 1586. It was reported that

> Mrs. Clitherow's body was buried beside a dunghill ... where it lay full six weeks without putrefaction, at which time it was secretly taken up by Catholics and carried on horseback a long journey, to a place where it rested six days

unbowelled, before necessary preservatives could be gotten, all which time it remained without corruption or evil savour.[15]

In this light, we might consider the possibility that Southwell's unsympathetic account of Queen Elizabeth's demise was shaped as a counter-narrative to the martyrologies of those Catholics who had been killed in her name.

The eminent historian and biographer of Elizabeth, J. E. Neale, long ago sought to protect both Elizabeth's reputation and the canons of historical criticism by discrediting not only Southwell's account but also some of the other anecdotes related here, including those of Clapham and Jonson.[16] Regarding Southwell's story, Neale dwelt upon both its sensationalism and what he regarded as the personal impropriety and suspect motives of its author—"a young woman of surpassing beauty, romantic in temperament and career...who had turned Catholic."[17] Neale's concern was to separate historical truth from falsehood, and thus he repudiated Southwell's account because "neither its author nor the circumstances under which it was written encourage trust in the narrative."[18] I, on the other hand, embrace not only Southwell's story but all of those other slanderous, flattering, or merely curious anecdotes and accounts addressed and analyzed in this book. And I do so not out of sheer perversity but because I am in pursuit of a historical truth different in kind from Neale's. Here and throughout this book, my primary concern has been to interpret the textual and iconic archive of subjective perceptions and ideological appropriations of the Queen. Whatever relationship it bears to empirical truth, and whether or not it provides trustworthy and accurate biographical information about Elizabeth Tudor, Elizabeth Southwell's manuscript account is nevertheless a valuable historical document. This is so because it records the subjective perceptions of one who had an intimate knowledge of the events related, and of the cultural ambiance in which they unfolded; and thus it allows us access to the workings of the collective Elizabethan imaginary through which those individual perceptions and feelings took on articulate form.

Epilogue: The Jacobean Phoenix

Despite almost half a century of relatively successful rule by a woman, and despite the propagation of a vast cultural discourse to justify and to celebrate that rule, much of the English political nation seems to have remained as fundamentally biased against gynecocracy at the end of Elizabeth's reign as it had been at the beginning. In the journal of his 1597 visit to England, de Maisse observed that the Queen's government "is fairly pleasing to the people, who show that they love her, but it is little pleasing to the great men and the nobles; and if by chance she should die, it is certain that the English would never again submit to the rule of a woman."[1] Sir John Harington, who wrote with an intimate knowledge of the Queen and her court, offers some confirmation of the ambassador's observation. He declares in his 1602 tract on the succession that

> Whensoever God shall call hir, I perceive wee ar not like to be governed by a ladye shutt up in a chamber from all her subjects and most of her servantes, and seen seeld but on holie-daies; nor by a childe that must say as his uncle bydes him ... but by a man of spirit and learning, of able bodye, of understanding mynde, that in the preceptes he doth give to his sonn shewes what we must look for, what we must trust to.[2]

In the person of King James VI of Scotland, Harington looks forward to an intellectually and physically virile succession, deferred since the demise of Henry VIII by the historical aberration of successive rule by a boy and two women, each without issue.

We shall probably never know whether James's accession was the consequence of Elizabeth's dying wish or a brief assumption of interregnal authority by the Elizabethan Privy Council. The latter scenario was, in fact, an eventuality for which Robert Cecil's father had planned as early as the 1560s.[3] Whether

Queen Elizabeth actually nominated King James as her successor or kept her own counsel to the last, when her death did finally arrive, the much anticipated and much feared breach was negotiated with relative ease—thanks in no small measure to the careful preparations of Robert Cecil. After a reign of almost half a century, throughout which the question of succession remained a continuous preoccupation of the political nation, a queen regnant without heirs of her body was peacefully succeeded by a foreign king. Nevertheless, royal family romance tainted James's legitimacy as it had Elizabeth's own. James derived his claims to both the Scottish and English thrones not from his father but from his mother—a queen regnant who was implicated in the murder of her consort, Lord Darnley, and who had been deposed by her own son's supporters in Scotland. Furthermore, Mary Stuart's rumored promiscuity had raised questions about James's own paternity and legitimacy. It is not entirely amiss to claim that James had two mothers and no father: His enormously complex and deeply ambivalent relationships to both Mary Stuart and Elizabeth Tudor were central to his political life and his royal identity, particularly during the years in which he was king of Scotland and an active candidate for the English throne. During much of this period, of course, Elizabeth was keeping James's natural mother under house arrest in England; and, eventually, she was reluctantly complicit in her own counselors' management of Mary's execution. In his letters to his English cousin and fellow monarch, James sometimes styled himself "Your most loving and devoted brother and son"; in her own letters to James, Elizabeth pointedly refused to acknowledge the filial claim, preferring to style herself his sister.[4]

At the time of Queen Elizabeth's demise and the proclamation of King James's accession, the Venetian ambassador in London reported home that "Elizabeth's portrait is being hidden everywhere, and Mary Stuart's shown instead with declaration that she suffered for no other cause than for her religion."[5] Whether this was accurate reporting or wishful thinking on Scaramelli's part, King James did subsequently undertake a postmortem rehabilitation of his mother, in tandem with a subtle but obviously calculated program to diminish the aura of his immediate predecessor on the English throne. There is no more striking example of this complex process at work than James's arrangement of the final resting places in Westminster Abbey for his two mothers and himself. As Julia Walker has shown, James had Elizabeth's remains removed from their original place in the central tomb that her grandfather Henry VII had built for himself and his consort, Elizabeth of York. James commissioned a new tomb for Elizabeth Tudor in a more obscure part of the Henry VII Chapel, where her coffin was place together with that of her half-sister, Mary Tudor. At the same time, the King commissioned a new tomb in the chapel for Mary Stuart, one larger and grander than Elizabeth's, and had Mary's remains reburied there. The space originally occupied by Elizabeth's remains, James now reserved for himself.[6]

Just as the pageantry of Elizabeth's coronation entry into London had emphasized her direct descent from Henry VII and Elizabeth of York, founders of the Tudor dynasty, so the pageanty accompanying James's English accession celebrated his Tudor lineage: In the pageant for the King's entry into London, he received a scepter from the figure of Henry VII.[7] Moreover, the new king underlined this identification in his opening address to his first English parliament. Reworking the genealogical imagery presented to Elizabeth at her entry into London on the day before her coronation, James enumerated for his new subjects the "great blessing[s] that GOD hath with my Person sent unto you":

> By my descent lineally out of the loynes of *Henry* the seventh, is reunited and confirmed in mee the Union of the two Princely Roses of the two Houses of LANCASTER and YORKE, whereof that King of happy memorie was the first Uniter.... But the Union of these two princely Houses, is nothing comparable to the Union of two ancient and famous Kingdomes, which is the other inward Peace annexed to my Person.[8]

Here James was not only effectively sidelining Elizabeth Tudor but also emulating her father, Henry VIII, whose own claim to have augmented the accomplishments of his father was recorded in the cartouche of Holbein's celebrated Whitehall wall painting (fig. 4). The reentombment of Elizabeth with Mary Tudor was less a sentimental affirmation of Tudor sisterhood than a symbolic relegation of both barren queens to the same genealogical dead end. Bacon tellingly remarked of James's accession that "seldom has a son succeeded to a father with such silence and so little change and perturbation."[9] James himself seems to have been intent on literalizing Bacon's similitude, by so emphatically representing himself not merely as Elizabeth's successor but also and preeminently as her grandfather's heir.

English attitudes toward their new Stuart king may well have begun to sour even before he reached London to be invested; and the subsequent disillusionment with James helped to foster a nostalgic mythologizing of the late queen and the Elizabethan age. Having written, in the memoir quoted above at the beginning of part five, that "the people were very generally weary of an old woman's government," Bishop Goodman continued as follows: "But after a few years, when we had experience of the Scottish government, then in disparagement of the Scots, and in hate and detestation of them, the Queen did seem to revive; then was her memory much magnified ... and in effect more solemnity and joy in memory of her coronation than was for the coming of

King James."[10] Goodman's emphasis is emphatically xenophobic; he represents the consequence of James's accession as a kind of foreign invasion that
usurped the privileges of native Englishmen. This presents a striking contrast
to the image of England and Scotland united in the person of the King, as
James himself had so forcefully represented it at the opening of his first English parliament: "What God hath conjoyned then, let no man separate. I am
the Husband, and all the whole Isle is my lawfull Wife; I am the Head, and
it is my Body."[11] By the time his first parliament had ended, the King was
already chastising the Commons for presuming upon his royal prerogative.
He told them in no uncertain terms that the return of a king meant an end to
the practices of mixed monarchy and parliamentary initiative that had taken
root during the interval of gynecocracy: "Precedents in the times of minors, of
tyrants, or women or simple kings [are] not to be credited."[12] The Elizabethan
political nation was about to learn what it meant to be ruled by a king.

In the immediate wake of the change, however, the novelty of a masculine
ruler seems to have generated some enthusiasm for James—"This Treasure
of a Kingdome (a Man Ruler) hid so many yeares from us . . . now brought
to light, and at hand," as Thomas Dekker enthused in the entertainment that
he wrote for performance at the King's London entry.[13] A sermon preached
before the new English king shortly after his accession described how, at the
death of Elizabeth, God

> did in the change of state so order all things, as that it might seeme no change at
> all. For when the rare Phoenix of the world, the queene of birds, which had for
> many yeeres gathered together, and safely covered Jerusalems children under
> her wings, was now through age to be turned into dust and ashes, though she
> appeared unto men to die, yet she died not, but was revived in one of her owne
> blood; her age renewed in his younger yeeres; her aged infirmities repaired in
> the perfection of his strength; her vertues of Christianitie and princely qualitie
> rested on him, who stood up a man as it were out of the ashes of a woman.[14]

Subsuming the maternal Pelican into the singular Phoenix, the preacher seeks
to appropriate the legacy of the Elizabethan political imaginary for a new
Jacobean mythopoeia: the half-century-long quest to provide for a masculine
succession to an unmarried queen is resolved when King James arises from
Queen Elizabeth's ashes. The mystical transfer of the body politic of kingship
is here realized in a transgendered political fantasy, one that sorted well with
James's initiative to absorb the late queen's charisma while circumscribing
her place in the cultural memory. That initiative was singularly unsuccessful,
however; and the measure of its failure is our enduring attraction to the subject
of Elizabeth.[15]

Abbreviations Used in the Notes and Bibliography

APC: *Acts of the Privy Council of England*

BL: British Library

CAR, Essex: *Calendar of Assize Records: Essex Indictments, Elizabeth I*

CAR, Kent: *Calendar of Assize Records: Kent Indictments, Elizabeth I*

CAR, Hertfordshire: *Calendar of Assize Records: Hertfordshire Indictments, Elizabeth I*

CAR, Surrey: *Calendar of Assize Records: Surrey Indictments, Elizabeth I*

CAR, Sussex: *Calendar of Assize Records: Sussex Indictments, Elizabeth I*

CSP, Domestic: *Calendar of State Papers, Domestic Series, of the Reigns of Edward VI, Mary, Elizabeth*

CSP, Foreign: *Calendar of State Papers, Foreign Series, of the Reign of Elizabeth*

CSP, Scottish: *Calendar of State Papers Relating to Scotland and Mary, Queen of Scots, 1547–1603*

CSP, Spanish: *Calendar of Letters and State Papers relating to English affairs, Preserved in, or originally Belonging to, the Archives of Simancas*

CSP, Venetian: *Calendar of State Papers and manuscripts relating to English affairs, existing in the archives and collections of Venice*

HMC: Historical Manuscripts Commission

HMC, *Salisbury*: *Calendar of the Manuscripts of the . . . Marquis of Salisbury . . . preserved at Hatfield House*

HMSO: His/Her Majesty's Stationery Office

PPE: *Proceedings in the Parliaments of Elizabeth I*

PRO: Public Records Office (London)

STC: *A short-title catalogue of books printed in England, Scotland, & Ireland and of English books printed abroad, 1475–1640*

TRP: *Tudor Royal Proclamations*

Notes

Introduction

1. More broadly, the field of early modern studies has been much enriched by work on vitally important but hitherto neglected topics such as gender and sexuality, and also by fresh and challenging perspectives on subjects of enduring significance that had for some time been out of academic fashion, such as religious belief and practice. I have benefited from such scholarship by many colleagues in early modern studies, working in and across several disciplines; and I have endeavored to acknowledge my engagement with their work in my notes and bibliography. A few of special importance should also be mentioned here at the beginning: Frances Yates and Roy Strong, whose pioneering work on the Elizabethan image fired my interest in the subject while I was a still a student; Susan Frye, Helen Hackett, and Carole Levin, who in their important studies of Elizabeth have engaged constructively with my own previously published work; Patrick Collinson, Susan Doran, John Guy, Anne McLaren, and Judith Richards, whose work on Elizabethan political culture has enlightened my understanding of my subject.

2. In a pioneering feminist essay on Queen Elizabeth, Allison Heisch polemically characterized her as exemplifying "the exceptional woman" as "honorary male." Heisch described "the co-optive and cooperative process by which Elizabeth was absorbed into the existing patriarchal system, de-sexed, elevated and hence transformed into a figure both above and distinct from other women"; and she lamented that as Queen, Elizabeth "did little to inspire other women to regard themselves with pride or to persuade men to regard them differently" ("Queen Elizabeth I and the Persistence of Patriarchy," 54). Most other recent scholars, myself included, have tended to agree that, as Susan Frye puts it, "Elizabeth herself was no feminist—in the sense that she did not concern herself with the situation of other women" (*Elizabeth I*, 21). But there is also general recognition that female Elizabethan subjects as well as subsequent generations of Englishwomen may nevertheless have found inspiration in Elizabeth's example—may, in short, have appropriated "the Queen" to their own gender-specific ends, as did men. For a suggestive study of such appropriations by seventeenth-century Englishwomen, see Mihoko Suzuki, "Elizabeth, Gender, and the Political Imaginary of Seventeenth-Century England." For an avowedly feminist study of Elizabeth that positions itself in opposition to Heisch's argument, see Philippa Berry, *Of Chastity and Power*, esp. 65. Berry does not mention Heisch; instead, she attributes the

position most forcefully argued by Heisch to Frances Yates and others, myself included. Women figure among the common Elizabethan subjects who were indicted for slanderous and seditious comments about the Queen. Most such hostile comments condemn her failure to conform to the behavioral norms imposed upon Elizabethan women and clearly internalized by many of them. A number of these are quoted by Carole Levin in *"The Heart and Stomach of a King,"* 66–90, and "'We shall never have a merry world while the Queene lyveth,'" although she does not emphasize the gender-specific significance of this refusal of the Queen's exceptionalism by other Elizabethan women. A significant corpus of writing by women subjects of Elizabeth has been recovered and published in recent years, and the body of enlightening scholarship about Elizabethan women as writing subjects continues to grow. This is material of the greatest interest and importance for a comprehensive understanding of Elizabethan culture, but is beyond the focus of this book.

3. These brief remarks are given some theoretical grounding in my "New Historicisms." A revised and condensed version was published as the prologue to my book *The Purpose of Playing*, 1–16. As I write there, "My invocation of the term 'Subject' is meant to suggest an equivocal process of *subjectification*: on the one hand, it shapes individuals as loci of consciousness and initiators of action, endowing them with *subjectivity* and with the capacity for agency; and, on the other hand, it positions, motivates, and constrains them within—it *subjects them to*—social networks and cultural codes that ultimately exceed their comprehension or control" (16).

4. In particular, see my essay "Spenser and the Elizabethan Political Imaginary." This and related published work will be incorporated in revised form in a book now in progress, "Form and Pressure: The Work of the Elizabethan Political Imaginary." The term "political culture" has come into favor among historians of Tudor-Stuart politics in order to mark a reorientation of their field of study, from a narrowly construed history of political institutions and events to one more broadly informed by social, cultural, and intellectual perspectives. In the words of John Guy, the study of political culture focuses on "the interrelationships of, and interactions between, people, institutions, and ideas," contextualizes and interprets "actions, structures, and concepts in mutually informing ways," and acknowledges "the classical, rhetorical, and iconographical traditions that underpinned the practices of politics" ("Introduction," in *The Tudor Monarchy*, ed. Guy, 7–8). As Dale Hoak summarizes it, "the difference between politics and political culture is essentially the difference between political action and the codes of conduct, formal and informal, governing those actions" ("Introduction," in *Tudor Political Culture*, ed. Hoak, 1). For a concise critical survey of "the intellectual and cultural turn" in the writing of Tudor political history, see Stephen Alford, "Politics and Political History in the Tudor Century." Also see the review essay by Natalie Mears, "Courts, Courtiers, and Culture in Tudor England," which characterizes the "New Tudor political history" as shifting emphasis from political institutions to "social connections and cultural influences," from the Privy Council to the court: "Tudor politics are increasingly defined as based on social networks rather than institutional bodies, making issues of access to, and intimacy with, the monarch central" (703).

5. For the term "monarcholatry," see John Bossy, *Christianity in the West 1400–1700*, 159.

6. In addition to "Spenser and the Elizabethan Political Imaginary," see the following works of mine: "Celebration and Insinuation," "'The perfecte paterne of a Poete,'" "'Eliza, Queene of Shepheardes' and the Pastoral of Power," "Gifts and Reasons," "'Shaping Fantasies,'" "The Elizabethan Subject and the Spenserian Text," "Spenser's Domestic Domain," and *The Purpose of Playing*, esp. 151–78.

7. See Roy Strong, *Gloriana*, 12. Although, in the course of this study, I take issue with Strong on a number of points, I am throughout much indebted to his seminal work on Elizabethan portraiture and pageantry.

8. To the degree that I infer "intention" in what I identify as the cultural work performed by particular pictures, it is a version of the "posited purposefulness" delineated by Michael Baxandall: "The account of intention is not a narrative of what went on in the painter's mind but an analytical construct about his ends and means, as we infer them from the relation of the object to identifiable circumstances. It stands in an ostensive relation to the picture itself" (*Patterns of Intention*, 109).

9. I adopt the term *ideologeme* from Fredric Jameson, who defines it as "the smallest intelligible unit of the essentially antagonistic collective discourses of social classes" (*The Political Unconscious*, 76). However, I construe neither ideology nor the ideologeme in so restrictively Marxian a way. My usage here encompasses the meanings I have described elsewhere: "Traditionally, 'ideology' has referred to the articulated principles serving as an agenda for concerted action by a particular sociopolitical movement or group, or, more generally, to the congeries of ideas, values, and beliefs common to any social group. In recent years, this vexed but indispensable term has in its broadest sense come to be associated with the processes by which subjects are formed, re-formed, and enabled to perform as conscious agents in an apparently meaningful world. Representations of the world in written discourse participate in the construction of the world: They are engaged in shaping the modalities of social reality and accommodating their writers, performers, readers, and audiences to multiple and shifting positions within the world that they themselves both constitute and inhabit" (*The Purpose of Playing*, 2–3).

Chapter One

1. Letter from John Coke to Thomas Cromwell, 22 May 1533; printed in *Original Letters, Illustrative of English History*, ed. Henry Ellis, 2nd series, 2.42–45; quotation from 44.

2. The former remark is quoted in G. R. Elton, *Policy and Police*, 278; the latter is printed in *Letters and Papers, Foreign and Domestic, of the Reign of Henry VIII*, 8.278.

3. Juan Luis Vives, *The Instruction of a Christen Woman*, facsimile ed., sig. T3r.

4. See, respectively, *CSP, Spanish*, 4.1062; and *CSP, Venetian*, 4.701.

5. As Bernard Capp has put it, "their action . . . was reproducing the common response of a wronged wife and her friends—to confront the other woman rather than the adulterous husband" ("Separate Domains?" 138–39).

6. On charivari, or rough music, see the following: "The Rites of Misrule," in Natalie Zemon Davis, *Society and Culture in Early Modern France*, 97–123; Martin Ingram, "Ridings, Rough Music, and the 'Reform of Popular Culture' in Early Modern England"; and "Rough Music," in E. P. Thompson, *Customs in Common*, 467–538. As concisely defined by Thompson, rough music denotes "a rude cacophony, with or without more elaborate ritual, which usually directed mockery or hostility against individuals who offended against certain community norms" (*Customs in Common*, 467); one of the offenses so mocked was remarriage.

7. See Simon Thurley, "Henry VIII: The Tudor Dynasty and the Church," in Christopher Lloyd and Simon Thurley, *Henry VIII: Images of a Tudor King*, 25.

8. Nicholas Sander's *De origine ac progressu schismatis anglicani* was first printed in Latin at Cologne in 1585, with a continuation on the Elizabethan church by Edward Rishton. I have used the modern English translation, *The Rise and Growth of the Anglican Schism*, trans. David Lewis; quotations from cxlvii and 100. The purpose of this notorious and influential work was

to recount in detail and to discredit thoroughly the progress of the Protestant Reformation in England from its beginnings in Henry's divorce up to the Elizabethan persecutions of recusants and missionary priests. This project was pursued largely by relentlessly cataloguing the moral depravity of individual historical agents from Henry and Anne to Elizabeth and Cecil. See, esp., book I, chs. 2, 5, 6, 14, 15, 17; book III, ch. 2; book IV, ch. 6. Some of the same charges against Elizabeth were retailed, during the 1570s and 1580s, in the tracts of William Cardinal Allen and other English Catholic exiles and in Franco-Scottish defenses of Mary, Queen of Scots. On the latter, see James Emerson Phillips, *Images of a Queen*, esp. 85–116, 143–70.

9. For the first quotation, see *The Works of Francis Bacon*, ed. Spedding et al. (1862 ed.), 11.405; unless otherwise indicated, all subsequent quotations from Bacon's work will be to this 15-vol. edition. For the second quotation, see Bacon, "A letter to the Lord Chancellor, Touching the History of Britain" (2 April 1605), in the 14-vol. edition of *The Works of Francis Bacon*, ed. Spedding et al. (1857–74; rpt., 1968), 10.250.

10. *In Felicem memoriam Elizabethae* (ca. 1608), in *The Works of Francis Bacon*, ed. Spedding et al., 11.425–42 (Latin text), 443–61 (English trans.); quotation from 450.

11. *The First Blast of the Trumpet against the Monstruous Regiment of Women* (1558), rpt. in *The Works of John Knox*, ed. Laing, 4.363–420; quotation from 373. All future parenthetical citations of *The First Blast* will be to vol. 4 of this edition.

12. "The Appellation from the Sentence Pronounced by the Bishops and Clergy: Addressed to the Nobility and Estates of Scotland, 1558," in Knox, *Works*, ed. Laing, 4.507. In his *History of the Reformation in Scotland* (1587), Knox wrote that "Princes ar nocht onlie bound to keip lawis and promeisses to thair subjectis, but also, that in case thai faill, thay justlie may be deposeit; for the band betwix the Prince and the Peopill is reciproce" (*Works*, ed. Laing, 2.457–58). For the context of Knox's writings in Calvinist political theory, see "The duty to resist," in Quentin Skinner, *The Foundations of Modern Political Thought*, 2.189–238. Also see Jane Dawson, "Revolutionary Conclusions: The Case of the Marian Exiles"; and Robert M. Kingdon, "Calvinism and resistance theory, 1550–1580."

13. Mention should be made here of the nine-day reign of Queen Jane in 1553. The dying Edward VI had been persuaded to exclude his bastardized and unmarried sisters from the succession, preferring instead the strongly Protestant Lady Jane Grey, wife of Lord Guildford Dudley and daughter-in-law of the de facto regent of England, the Duke of Northumberland. Thus, Jane was technically England's first queen regnant, and she was immediately followed by her two cousins. This brief dynastic interlude—what Bacon refers to in the earlier quoted passage as "the offer of an usurpation"—was in fact of considerable consequence for Elizabethan dynastic politics: Jane's sister, Lady Catherine Grey, married to Edward Seymour, son of the Edwardian Lord Protector Somerset, and herself the mother of two young sons, was perceived as a serious successor (or even a substitute) for the unmarried and childless Elizabeth during the early years of her reign. It was a threat that Elizabeth regarded with the utmost seriousness, judging by the ruthless way in which she dealt with Catherine, her husband, and their children. For important discussion of the Grey-Hertford claim in early Elizabethan dynastic politics, see Mortimer Levine, *The Early Elizabethan Succession Question 1558–1568*, 5–29; and Anne McLaren, "The Quest for a King," 277–81.

14. For evidence of Elizabeth's hostility to Knox due to the content and implications of his ill-timed book, see his letters to her and to Sir William Cecil, printed in Knox, *Works*, ed. Laing, 6.31–32 (to Cecil, 28 June 1559), 6.45–47 (to Cecil, 19 July 1559), 6.47–51 (to Elizabeth, 20 July 1559), 6.126–27 (to Elizabeth, 6 August 1561). In his 1559 letter to the Queen, Knox instructed her "to

ground the justness of your Authoritie . . . upoun the eternall providence of Him, who, contrarie to nature, and without your deserving, hath thus exalted your head. If thus in God's presence yee humble your self . . . a weake instrument, so will I with toung and pen justifie your Authoritie and Regiment, as the Holie Ghost hath justified the same in Deborah" (6.50). In reaction, Elizabeth annotated Knox's letter with the comment that his views on female regiment were "false, lewd, dangerous, and the mischiefs thereof infinite"; she concluded that "your purgation is worse than your book" (quoted in Anne McLaren, *Political Culture in the Reign of Elizabeth I*, 57).

15. John Aylmer, *An Harborowe for Faithfull and Trewe Subjectes, agaynst the late blowne Blaste, concerninge the Government of Wemen* (1559), facsimile ed., H4r–v. Future citations will be included within the text.

16. "Report of the Bishop of Aquila to the Emperor Ferdinand," London, 3 October 1559, trans. and printed in *Queen Elizabeth and Some Foreigners*, ed. von Klarwill, 127–37; quotation from 133.

17. Compare Dale Hoak, who characterizes Aylmer's book as "a paean to Parliament and the distinctive nature of the English constitution" ("A Tudor Deborah?" 76).

18. The sixteenth-century controversy regarding female rule has generated a considerable body of scholarship in recent years. In particular, I have benefited from the following studies: Constance Jordan, "Woman's Rule in Sixteenth-Century British Political Thought"; Judith M. Richards, "'To Promote a Woman to Beare Rule'"; and McLaren, *Political Culture in the Reign of Elizabeth I*, esp. 46–74. Important earlier studies include James Emerson Phillips, "The Background to Spenser's Attitude toward Women Rulers," and Paula Louise Scalingi, "The Sceptre or the Distaff." Also see Amanda Shephard, *Gender and Authority in Sixteenth-Century England*.

Chapter Two

1. For example, Leah Marcus writes that "as a young woman, Elizabeth had liked to place herself directly in front of the giant Holbein portrait of Henry VIII at Whitehall, challenging those present to measure her own bearing and authority" against those of her father (*Puzzling Shakespeare*, 55). She cites the biography by Paul Johnson, *Elizabeth I*, 79. A very similar assertion is made in Christopher Haigh, *Elizabeth I*, 21. None of these writers cites any Elizabethan source.

2. The Queen's address to a delegation from both houses of Parliament, delivered on 5 November 1566; printed in *PPE*, 1.145–49; quotation from 148. (Also see Elizabeth I, *Collected Works*, 93–98.) Compare her comments to the Parliament of 1593, two versions of which are printed in *PPE*, 3.28 and 3.173. (Also see Elizabeth I, *Collected Works*, 328–32.)

3. In 1515, the Venetian ambassadors described the English king in the following terms: "This most serene king is not only very expert in arms, and of great valour, and most excellent in his personal endowments, but is likewise so gifted and adorned with mental accomplishments of every sort that we believe him to have few equals in the world" (*CSP, Venetian*, 1.76; quoted in Sydney Anglo, *Spectacle, Pageantry, and Early Tudor Policy*, 116–17). On representations of Henry's learning and piety—the other essential components of his royal image—see John N. King, "Henry VIII as David."

4. The subject of this monumental work is Henry's first military campaign against France in 1513. For discussion of the painting and the events represented, see Lloyd and Thurley, *Henry VIII*, 44–45, 48–49. Regarding this and three related works, these authors argue that "internal evidence for dating . . . all points to their having been executed at the very end of Henry's reign" (45).

5. See Sydney Anglo, *The Great Tournament Roll of Westminster*. Vol. 1 is a detailed account of Henry's fashioning of his image as a magnificent warrior-prince, of the tournaments held during the first two decades of his reign, and of the contents of the *Great Tournament Roll*; vol. 2 is a complete facsimile of the *Roll*. The costumes of the king and his three fellow allegorical knights were each covered with hundreds of gold pieces; Sir Thomas Knyvet, who was disguised as *Ceure loyall*'s fellow knight, *Vailliaunt desyre*, bore in gold upon his codpiece the single word "desyer" (see Anglo, *Great Tournament Roll of Westminster*, 1.56 and n. 3).

6. A detailed analysis and contextualization of the painting, extensively illustrated, is to be found in Roy Strong, *Holbein and Henry VIII* (1967), reprinted with a new preface in Strong, *The Tudor and Stuart Monarchy*, 1.1–54; see esp. 31–49. I am indebted to Strong's discussion, and have also benefited from Lloyd and Thurley, *Henry VIII*, esp. 28–29. The present discussion revises and considerably expands one that I initially presented in "The Elizabethan Subject and the Spenserian Text" (1986).

7. The inscription, which was reproduced in the Restoration copy by Remigius van Leemput, was transcribed from the now-lost original by the Moravian Baron Waldstein when he visited London in 1600. See *The Diary of Baron Waldstein*, 57. Waldstein's editor provides the following translation (56):

> If you find pleasure in seeing fair pictures of heroes
>   Look at these! None greater was ever portrayed.
> Fierce is the struggle and hot the disputing; the question:
>   Does father, does son—or do both—the pre-eminence win?
> One ever withstood his foes and his country's destruction,
>   Finally giving his people the blessing of peace;
> But, born to do things greater, the son drove out of his councils
>   His ministers worthless, and ever supported the just.
> And in truth, to this steadfastness Papal arrogance yielded
>   When the sceptre of power was wielded by Henry the Eighth,
> Under whose reign the true faith was restored to the nation
>   And the doctrines of God began to be reverenced with awe.

The inscription makes clear that Holbein's painting (which, in van Leemput's copy, is dated 1537) participates in the articulation of an imperial ideology of English kingship. This articulation followed upon the Act in Restraint of Appeals (1533: 24 Henry VIII, c. 12), which declared in part that "This realm of England is an empire, and so hath been accepted in the world, governed by one supreme head and king having the dignity and royal estate of the imperial crown of the same, unto whom a body politic, compact of all sorts and degrees of people divided in terms and by names of spirituality and temporality, be bounden and owe to bear next to God a natural and humble obedience" (rpt. in *The Tudor Constitution*, ed. G. R. Elton, 344–49; quotation from 344).

8. Quoted in Strong, "Holbein and Henry VIII," 35; and also in Lloyd and Thurley, *Henry VIII*, 29. Strong (ibid., n. 20), points out that it is not absolutely certain that van Mander is referring to the Whitehall wall painting, and that he probably gained his knowledge of Holbein's portraits of Henry VIII at second hand from his master, Lucas de Heere, who was active in England during the second decade of Elizabeth's reign.

9. John Clapham, *Elizabeth of England: certain observations concerning the life and reign of Queen Elizabeth*, ed. Evelyn Plummer Read and Conyers Read, 49. In future references, this work

will be cited as Clapham, *Certain Observations*. Clapham was a gentleman-scholar and author of several works of history. His *Observations* were apparently written in the months immediately following the Queen's death. The two extant drafts remained in manuscript until the publication of the Reads' edition.

10. Stephen Gardiner, *De Vera Obedientia* (1535), quoted in Lloyd and Thurley, *Henry VIII*, 32.

11. See Strong, "Holbein and Henry VIII," 46–49. Jane Seymour, represented as Henry's consort in Holbein's painting, died twelve days following the birth of her son, on 24 October 1537. In terms of our calendar, the year 1537 would have run from 25 March 1537 to 24 March 1538. There is no certain evidence regarding the chronological relationship between the completion of the painting and either the birth of Prince Edward or the death of Queen Jane. In a variant Restoration copy of Holbein's Whitehall wall painting, also by Remigius van Leemput and perhaps commissioned by the late queen's relatives, the Seymour coat of arms appears upon the central altar in place of the inscription; in front of the altar, in the center foreground of the painting, stands the young Edward VI, in a pose that imitates his father's. See Strong, "Holbein and Henry VIII," 31, and plate 25 (the captions for plates 25 and 26 are reversed).

12. For discussion, see Oliver Millar, *Tudor, Stuart and Early Georgian Pictures in the Collection of Her Majesty the Queen*, 1.63–64; Strong, *Gloriana*, 49; Lloyd and Thurley, *Henry VIII*, 36–37. Millar dates the painting as ca. 1545; Strong, as ca. 1543–47; Lloyd and Thurley, as ca. 1545.

13. Strong, *Gloriana*, 49.

14. *The Winter's Tale*, 5.1.123–25. All quotations from Shakespeare's plays follow the texts and lineation of the Oxford edition, as reproduced in *The Norton Shakespeare*.

15. Excerpts from the second (28 Henry VIII, c. 7) and third (35 Henry VIII, c. 1) succession acts are printed in J. R. Tanner, *Tudor Constitutional Documents*, 389–95 and 397–400, respectively.

16. Painted ca. 1538/39, the portrait is inscribed with original Latin verses, signed by Richard Morison (a humanist scholar and client of Thomas Cromwell); I have used the translation printed in *Dynasties*, ed. Karen Hearn, 41.

17. On this pairing, dating, and attribution, see Roy Strong, *The English Icon*, 74. The paintings are catalogued and described in Millar, *Tudor, Stuart and Early Georgian Pictures*, 1.64–65; and in *Dynasties*, ed. Hearn, 49–50 (Edward) and 78–79 (Elizabeth). Both paintings have always been in the royal collection. Strong surveys the representations of Edward VI in *Tudor and Jacobean Portraits*, 1.87–94; he notes that "the placing of the legs firmly astride betrays . . . the definitive influence of the Whitehall wall painting of Henry VIII in projecting the official image of Edward VI. As a type it continued to be produced throughout the century" (93). The painting of Elizabeth is briefly discussed in Strong, *Gloriana*, 52; and in Janet Arnold, *Queen Elizabeth's Wardrobe Unlock'd*, 4, 18. Henry VIII died in January 1547; Edward's portrait, and possibly Elizabeth's, may have been executed shortly before Edward's accession. Millar, Strong, and Arnold all point out that, in the inscription on the painting, the term describing Elizabeth's relationship to the king is unclear: "Elizabetha / [Filia?/Soror?] Rex / Angliae."

18. Cranmer's portrait is signed by Gerlach Flicke and can be dated to 1545/46; it is catalogued and described in *Dynasties*, ed. Hearn, 48–49. On "the speaking portrait of the man of the book" in Tudor and Stuart painting, and for reproductions of numerous examples, see Margaret Aston, "Gods, Saints, and Reformers." On the figure of the holy book in Tudor Protestant iconography, see John N. King, *Tudor Royal Iconography*, 54–115; and, on Elizabeth's personal bible and prayer books, ibid., 104–15. A notable early Tudor precedent for the visual representation of the learned lady occurs in Hans Holbein's drawing of Thomas More's family, in which three of More's

daughters hold books, two of them open. The drawing was probably a study for a painting (ca. 1527) that is now lost.

19. The letter, dated from St. John's College, Cambridge, April 4, 1550, is printed in the original Latin in *The Whole Works of Roger Ascham*, ed. J. A. Giles, vol. 1, pt. 1, 181–93; I quote from the partial English translation, vol. 1, pt. 1, lxii–lxiv.

20. The letter is dated 15 May without year but ascribed to 1549 and printed in Elizabeth I, *Collected Works*, 35–36; quotation from 35. Arnold, *Queen Elizabeth's Wardrobe Unlock'd*, 18, connects the portrait attributed to Scrots with the one referred to in this letter, ascribing both to 1547. Lorne Campbell, *The Early Flemish Pictures in the Collection of Her Majesty the Queen*, xxvii–xxviii and n. 106, connects the letter to a portrait of Princess Elizabeth that King Edward commissioned from the miniaturist Levina Teerlinc in 1551. My discussion does not rely upon a direct connection between the letter and the picture attributed to Scrots. The portrait and the letter are also the subject of an essay by Susan Frye, published in German as "Elizabeth als Prinzessin"; my thanks to the author for a copy of a revised draft of the English-language original. Frye and I have independently arrived at some of the same conclusions in our studies of the portrait and the letter; her emphasis, however, is upon the youthful Elizabeth's strategic use of gift giving to negotiate her place in the dangerous world of Henrician and Edwardian court politics.

21. Roger Ascham to John Sturm, London, 11 April 1562; printed in *Original letters relative to the English reformation*, ed. Hastings Robinson, 2.64–72; quotation from 67–68. The original Latin text in printed in a separately paginated appendix, 39–44.

22. For example, Petruccio Ubaldini, an Italian *emigré* scholar living in Elizabethan London who had close connections to the court, wrote of the Queen as follows: "She is very clever at persuading and making insinuations. Furthermore, since she has a wide knowledge of the customs and histories of peoples, knows Latin, Greek and speaks Italian and French fluently, she is remarkably adept in dealing with foreigners. Through them, she thereby hopes to acquire outside her realm a reputation for wisdom and eloquence" (quoted and trans. in Francesca Bugliani, "Petruccio Ubaldini's Accounts of England," 181–82).

23. "The Qwene's Majestie's oration, made in the Parliament Howse, at the breakyng up there of, the xxix day of Marche, in *anno Domini* 1585"; printed in *PPE*, 2.31–32; quotation from 32. (Also see Elizabeth I, *Collected Works*, 181–83.) In an oration of welcome to the Queen when she visited Coventry in 1565, the town recorder lauded "the singular and manifold gifts of nature and grace ingrafted in your Royal person from your tender years, of your profound learning and policy, seldom to be found in any man comparable, much less in any woman" (printed in John Nichols, *The Progresses and Public Processions of Queen Elizabeth*, 1.193).

24. Translated from the Latin in Elizabeth I, *Collected Works*, 9–10; quotation from 10.

25. Marc Shell, *Elizabeth's Glass*, contains an annotated edition of her 1544 translation of Marguerite's text and of the "Epistle Dedicatory" and "Conclusion" written by John Bale for his 1548 printed edition, a facsimile of Elizabeth's handwritten presentation copy, and an introductory essay by the editor. All quotations are from this edition, and in future will be cited within the text; present quotation from 111. For the pious learning of Princess Elizabeth in the context of the writing and patronage activities of Queen Catherine Parr and other Protestant noblewomen, see John N. King, "Patronage and Piety." In *Tudor Royal Iconography*, King speculates that the Lady Elizabeth's portrait with a book "may have been influenced by the princess's stepmother, Catherine Parr, the Protestant sympathizer who controlled the education of both Elizabeth and Edward and who had a reputation for both bookishness and piety" (211). We might also remember that among some devoted reformers, Elizabeth's natural mother was admired not only for her

piety but also for her patronage of evangelical reformers and educational institutions, and for using her influence to promote the printing and dissemination of the Bible in English: See Maria Dowling, "Anne Boleyn and Reform."

26. Anne Lake Prescott, "The Pearl of Valois and Elizabeth I," 68. I am indebted to Prescott's cogent analysis of Elizabeth's manuscript text and its relationship both to Marguerite's original and to Bale's printed edition; and also to Patrick Collinson's characteristically learned and provocative essay "Windows in a Woman's Soul: Questions about the Religion of Queen Elizabeth I," in his *Elizabethan Essays*, esp. 93–104. In "Guilty Sisters," Susan Snyder suggests that the author and translator shared a resonant parallel of sibling rivalry and resentment: Elizabeth, like Marguerite, was an intellectually astute elder sister "subordinate, apparently forever, to a brother who was her inferior in age and natural powers" (454).

27. For discussion of some of these representations, see Leah S. Marcus, "Erasing the Stigma of Daughterhood"; Lena Cowen Orlin, "The Fictional Families of Elizabeth I"; Christine Coch, "'Mother of my Countreye'"; and "Gender and the Construction of Royal Authority in the Speeches of Elizabeth I," in Mary Beth Rose, *Gender and Heroism in Early Modern English Literature*, 26–54.

28. Compare Marc Shell's comment that "in the ideology of the sixteenth century, it was not merely that Elizabeth became a kind of Virgin Mary transformed to Protestant ends.... It was mainly that Elizabeth adjusted a specific ideological commonplace—that the Virgin Mary is at once the parent and spouse of God—to the general political requirements of her monarchal maturity" (*Elizabeth's Glass*, 67). On cultural resonances of the political problems raised by Tudor royal incest appearing in Elizabethan literature and drama, see Bruce Thomas Boehrer, *Monarchy and Incest in Renaissance England*, 42–85.

29. See Collinson, "Windows in a Woman's Soul," 98. This paragraph is indebted to his analysis. Collinson suggests (104–8) that similarly complex motives may have been operative in Thomas Bentley's *The Monument of Matrones: contening seven severall lampes of virginitie, or distinct treatises* (1582), a massive collection of prayers, meditations, and exempla for Elizabethan women in which the writings and the example of Queen Elizabeth herself are central. Not only does Bentley's encyclopedic work put a great many words into the mouths of God and the Queen, but it also includes a full reprint of Princess Elizabeth's translation of Marguerite. Maureen Quilligan, "Incest and Agency," studies the various sixteenth-century editions of Elizabeth's translations in order to suggest "how fantasized incestuous genealogies could provide profoundly enabling terms for female authority in the Renaissance" (209).

30. *CSP, Domestic*, 7.77, no. 37 (26 March 1556).

31. Report of England made by Giovanni Michiel, late Ambassador to Queen Mary and King Philip, to the Venetian Senate, 13 May 1557; trans. and printed in *CSP, Venetian*, vol. 6, pt. 2, 1057–58.

32. Henry Clifford, *The Life of Jane Dormer, Duchess of Feria*, 80. Dormer was a Lady of Queen Mary's Privy Chamber, slept in her bedchamber, and attended her at her death. At the accession of Elizabeth, Lady Dormer married the Count of Feria, King Philip's sometime representative in England, and moved permanently to Spain, where she subsequently became a benefactress of the English Catholic exiles. Clifford was a member of her household, possibly from before the end of the sixteenth century, until her death. The biography was written in 1643, but Clifford suggests he had begun it much earlier.

33. Printed in Georges Ascoli, *La Grande-Bretagne devant l'opinion française au XVIIe siècle*, 1.296–97; this book prints all of the French poems from the collection. For a detailed discussion of

the vilification of Queen Elizabeth in the *De Jezabelis* poems and other Franco-Scottish defenses of Mary, Queen of Scots, see Phillips, *Images of a Queen*, 85–116, 143–70.

34. William Allen, *An Admonition to the Nobility and People of England and Ireland concerning the present warres made for the execution of his Holines Sentence, by the highe and mightie King Catholicke of Spaine* (1588), facsimile ed., v, xi, xlvi, respectively. All future references will be to this edition, cited as Allen, *Admonition*.

35. Report of England made by Giovanni Michiel, late Ambassador to Queen Mary and King Philip, to the Venetian Senate, 13 May 1557; trans. and printed in *CSP, Venetian*, vol. 6, pt. 2, p. 1059.

36. *The Count of Feria's Dispatch to Philip II of 14 November 1558*, 331.

37. Count de Feria to the King, 25 November 1558, trans. and printed in *CSP, Spanish*, 1.7.

38. Letter to Robert Markham, 1606, printed in *The Letters and Epigrams of Sir John Harington*, 122.

39. *The Quenes Maiesties Passage through the Citie of London to Westminster the Day before her Coronation*, facsimile ed., 31–32. The authorship of the pamphlet is generally ascribed to Richard Mulcaster, although the planning and scripting of the pageants were the work of a committee. The pamphlet's text was followed closely by subsequent annalists and historians of the reign, such as Grafton and Hayward, and was reprinted in Holinshed; thus it remained available to readers throughout the reign.

40. Quoted from the English translation in the bilingual modern edition, *Thomas Chaloner's "In Laudem Henrici Octavi,"* 99. The work was written in Latin verse and printed in 1560 as *In laudem Henrici Octavi regis Angliae praestantissimi carmen panegyricum*; it was reprinted as part of a larger collection of Chaloner's Latin poetry in 1579, entitled *De Rep. Anglorum instaurada libri decem*.

Chapter Three

1. *The Quenes Maiesties Passage*, facsimile ed., 54.

2. *A Speciall Grace Appointed to Have Been Said after a Banket at Yorke, upon the Good Nues and Proclamacion Thear, of the Entraunce in to Reign over Us, of Our Sovereign Lady ELIZABETH... in November 1558*, sig. Aiii–Aiiii; as quoted in Judith M. Richards, "Love and a Female Monarch," 149.

3. See, for example, the following remarks made by Keith Thomas in his classic study, *Religion and the Decline of Magic*: "Although complete statistics will never be attainable, it can be confidently said that not all Tudor or Stuart Englishmen went to some kind of church, that many of those who did went with considerable reluctance, and that a certain proportion remained throughout their lives utterly ignorant of the elementary tenets of Christian dogma" (159); "it is certain that a substantial proportion of the population regarded organized religion with an attitude which varied from cold indifference to frank hostility" (172).

4. *The Quenes Maiesties Passage*, facsimile ed., 61.

5. See George Puttenham, *The Arte of English Poesie*, 260.

6. George Cavendish, *Metrical Visions*, ed. A. S. G. Edwards, 135–41; quotations (including the slashes) are from this edition, cited by line numbers. Cavendish had been a member of Wolsey's household during the Henrician period and later wrote *The Life and Death of Cardinal Wolsey*. He wrote his *Metrical Visions* during the Marian reign, concluding the collection—which remained unpublished during the Elizabethan period—with this epitaph.

7. An outstanding exception—one to which I am indebted in the following discussion—is the work of Judith M. Richards: see, especially, "Mary Tudor as 'Sole Quene'?"; and also the revisionist essay, "Mary Tudor, Renaissance Queen of England."

8. See *The chronicle of Queen Jane, and of two years of Queen Mary*, 14.

9. The event occured on 1 February 1554. The speech is recorded in John Foxe, *Acts and Monuments*, 6.414–15; Foxe claims to recount "the contents (at least the effect) . . . as near as out of her own mouth could be penned." Three weeks earlier, the imperial ambassadors reported to the Emperor that Queen Mary had told them that "she had already espoused her kingdom" and showed them her ring (trans. and printed in *CSP, Spanish*, 12.11; cited in Richards, "Mary Tudor as 'Sole Quene'?" 912, n. 92).

10. 1 Mary, st. 3, c. 1. For the possible context, see J. D. Alsop, "The Act for the Queen's Regnal Power, 1554"; also see McLaren, *Political Culture in the Reign of Elizabeth I*, 90–104.

11. *The Mirror for Magistrates*, ed. Lily B. Campbell, 419–20. The quoted passage was printed in the first edition of the *Mirror* in 1559; on its Marian provenance, see Campbell's Introduction, 13.

12. 1 Mary, st. 3, c. 2; quoted in Richards, "Mary Tudor as 'Sole Quene'?" 908–9.

13. The proclamation concerning the marriage treaty was issued on 14 January 1554, and is printed in *TRP*, 2.21–26; quotation from 21.

14. Susan Doran and Judith M. Richards have independently suggested that Queen Mary herself may have been more careful of her authority vis-à-vis her husband than either her contemporaries or most subsequent historians have perceived. On Mary not allowing "power and authority to slip from her hands into those of her husband," see Susan Doran, *Monarchy and Matrimony*, 8–9, and the works cited therein; on Mary's marriage as "much less a willful act, much more a carefully calculated (and, as it transpired) successful political act" for the preservation of her own and England's autonomy, see Richards, "Mary Tudor, Renaissance Queen of England" (quotation from 36). For a contrary perspective, see Glyn Redworth, "'Matters Impertinent to Women.'" Redworth concludes that, even when absent from England, "King Philip could wield a decisive influence quite at variance with the spirit of the marriage treaty" (605); and that although "Philip was content to exercise a temporary political dominance through being the husband of the Queen," (607) "whenever he so wished, Philip was politically the dominant partner" (611).

15. Philip II to Queen Elizabeth, 24 December 1559; calendared and paraphrased in HMC, *Salisbury*, 1.158.

16. Philip wrote to the Count de Feria at the beginning of 1559 that, despite some possible negative strategic consequences, "I nevertheless cannot lose sight of the enormous importance of such a match to Christianity and the preservation of religion which has been restored in England by the help of God. Seeing also the importance that the country should not fall back into its former errors which would cause to our own neighboring dominions serious dangers and difficulties, I have to place on one side all other considerations which might be urged against it and am resolved to render this service to God, and offer to marry the queen of England" (The King to the Count of Feria, 10 January 1559; trans. and printed in *CSP, Spanish*, 1.22). De Feria reported back to Philip that the wily Elizabeth "said after a time that she could not marry your Majesty as she was a heretic" (1.37); the King acquiesced graciously, instructing de Feria to "assure her that I will preserve the good friendship and brotherhood that I have hitherto maintained" (1.40).

17. For the proclamations announcing the terms of the marriage treaty between Mary and Philip and their regnal style, see *TRP*, 2.21–26 and 2.45–46, respectively. For the actions of the Privy Council, see *APC*, 5.53.

18. "Lord Keeper's opening speech, 25 January [1559]," printed in *PPE*, 1.33–39; quotation from 36.

19. On Mary's portraits, see Campbell, *The Early Flemish Pictures in the Collection of Her Majesty the Queen*, xxvi–xxvii; Joanna Woodall, "An Exemplary Consort," 198 and n. 14; Roy Strong, *Tudor and Jacobean Portraits*, 1.207–13, and for reproductions of Marian portraits by Mor, Eworth, and others, *Tudor and Jacobean Portraits*, vol. 2, plates 412–24.

20. Three autograph versions of Mor's portrait are extant. My discussion is much indebted to Woodall, "An Exemplary Consort." Mor's portrait is also briefly discussed in Hearn, *Dynasties*, 54–55; and in David Howarth, *Images of Rule*, 100–102. Recapitulating the venerable Protestant tradition of anti-Marian polemic, Howarth writes of Mary looking "furiously at us," of her "alarming physical presence," of the "powerful impression of fanaticism" in the image, of her "stare more reminiscent of a gargoyle than of a woman"; he concludes that "the picture is positively frightening because it is a likeness without mercy" (100–101).

21. Adam Zwetkovich to the Emperor Maximilian, London, 4 June 1565; trans. and printed in *Queen Elizabeth and Some Foreigners*, ed. von Klarwill, 218.

22. See Woodall, "An Exemplary Consort," 214–16.

23. See Hearn, *Dynasties*, 54–55, who continues that, "in contrast to the contemporary full-length image by Hans Eworth ... which works within English pictorial conventions, the type of seated format and aspects of the costume link [Mor's painting] with a visual 'genealogy' of Habsburg brides."

24. Philip's favorite, Ruy Gómez de Silva, writing from England shortly after the King's arrival there, concluded a letter to the Emperor's Spanish Secretary as follows: "The King fully realises that the marriage was concluded for no fleshly consideration, but in order to remedy the disorders of this Kingdom and preserve the Low Countries" (Ruy Gómez de Silva to Francisco de Eraso, from Winchester, 29 July 1554; trans. and printed in *Calendar of Letters, Despatches and State Papers Relating to the Negotiations between England and Spain*, 13.6). On Philip's attitude toward his English marriage and his role in governing Marian England, see D. M. Loades, *The Reign of Mary Tudor*, 109–47, 211–51; D. M. Loades, "Philip II and the Government of England"; and Redworth, "'Matters Impertinent to Women.'" Loades summarizes that "the whole pattern of Philip's involvement with England, and particularly after the failure of his dynastic hopes, indicates that he saw it primarily as a base and a source of supply for his perpetual struggle against France" ("Philip II and the Government of England," 191).

25. A number of such portraits are reproduced in Strong, *Gloriana*, 58–61. Strong writes that "the extremely depressing quality of Elizabeth's early portraits, which never rise above the mediocre, must be the consequence of the relinquishment of Eworth. ... The portraiture of the first ten years of her reign is therefore as tentative as her government. The politico-religious pressure demanding the projection of an image did not as yet exist and the notion of royal portraiture as loyalist propaganda had yet to be conceived" (*Gloriana*, 59, 61). A radically different explanation for the absence of an Elizabethan court portraitist is proposed in Nanette Solomon, "Positioning Women in Visual Convention": Solomon makes the interesting but undocumented suggestion that the absence of Eworth or "any dominant male artist in Elizabeth's court ... may best be understood in terms of Elizabeth's own determined avoidance of a powerful 'master' to shape her image artistically" (65).

26. The paintings are catalogued as P.23 and P.24, respectively, in Roy Strong, *Portraits of Queen Elizabeth I*, and discussed in Strong, *Gloriana*, 79–83.

27. Among the "Juelles geven to her Majestie at Newyer's-tide" in 1572–73 was "one juell of golde, wherein is a pellycane garnished with smale rubyes and diamonds," given by Lady Mary Sidney (Nichols, *Progresses and Public Processions of Queen Elizabeth*, 1.324); on New Year's Day, 1585, Lord Howard of Effingham gave "a juell of Golde being an Armlett containing xi. letters Being *Semper Eadem* garnished with Sparks of Rubyes . . . and in the midest Affenix [a phoenix] of golde garnished with Opalls" (quoted in Strong, *Gloriana*, 83); Strong cites several other examples on 82–83, and on 171, nn. 6, 11, 13. The Elizabethan antiquary and chronicler William Camden reports as one of Elizabeth's two most commonly used mottos, "SEMPER EADEM, whiche she as truely and constantly performed" (*Remains concerning Britain*, 182).

28. The Queen's answer to the Commons' petition, 28 January 1563; printed in *PPE*, 1.95. (Also see Elizabeth I, *Collected Works*, 70–72.)

29. Mary's address at the London Guildhall, following suppression of the Wyatt Rebellion, as recorded in Foxe, *Acts and Monuments*, 6.414–15.

30. For the first quotation, see D. M. Loades, *Mary Tudor: A Life*, 335; Loades cites no sources. For the second quotation, see Knox, *Works*, 3.296. Knox added, "that ever a woman, that suffred her selfe to be called the moste blessed Virgine, caused so muche bloud to be spilt for establishing of an usurped authoritie, I thinke is rare to be founde in Scripture or Historie" (294).

Chapter Four

1. Raphael Holinshed, *Chronicles of England, Scotland, and Ireland*, ed. Ellis, 4.140. On Elizabeth's accession, see 4.155–56.

2. The so-called "Allegory of the Tudor Succession" is catalogued in Strong, *Portraits of Queen Elizabeth I*, as P.82; P.89 is an anonymous copy from the 1590s, which updates the Queen's costume; and E.28 is an engraving by William Rogers from the 1590s, which is also based upon the early 1570s succession picture. All three are discussed in Strong, *Gloriana*, 70–77; on de Heere's original, also see Jan van Dorsten, *The Radical Arts*, 58–59, and Margaret Aston, *The King's Bedpost*, 128–30.

3. On a visit to "the Royal palatium, Witehal" in 1602, a diarist accompanying the Duke of Stettin-Pomerania recorded seeing "a portrait of King Henricus octavus, with his son Eduardus, the last of the family, on his arm. On either side there stand his two daughters" (Gottfried von Bülow, "Diary of the Journey of Philip Julius, Duke of Stettin-Pomerania, through England in the year 1602," 23).

4. For the text and a translation of the Bull, and the text of the answering "Act against the bringing in and putting in execution of bulls and other instruments from the see of Rome" (1571: 13 Eliz. I, c. 2), see *The Tudor Constitution*, ed. Elton, 414–21.

5. See *The Quenes Maiesties Passage*, facsimile ed., 46–47.

6. Anne Hooper to Henry Bullinger, Frankfort, 11 April 1555; printed in *Original letters relative to the English Reformation*, ed. Robinson, 1.114–15. In a postscript, Hooper writes, "Your [god-daughter] Rachel sends you an English coin, on which are the effigies of Ahab and Jezebel" (115).

7. All scriptural quotations are from the 1560 ed. of the Geneva Bible.

8. As noted in Michael Leslie, "The Dialogue between Bodies and Souls," 18, 21. Leslie cites such stylistic distinctions so as to make the point that at least some painters working in England were obviously acquainted with and had mastered contemporary continental styles, and thus that the dominant English style was more a matter of cultural—and ideological—choice than one of mere provinciality or cultural isolation.

9. In Rogers' engraving after de Heere's painting, produced in the 1590s, the second stanza of the accompanying text reads as follows:

> Now Prudent Edward dyinge in tender youth,
> Queen Mary then the Royall Scepter swayd:
> With foraine blood she matcht and put down truth,
> Which England's glory suddainly decayd:
> Who brought in warr & discord by that deed.
> Which did in common wealth great sorow breed.

10. As Aston puts it, "*Edward VI and the Pope* is . . . a historical painting of a different kind, which allegorizes a particular scene or moment, instead of setting the generations together with a deliberate disregard for chronological time. Is Elizabeth, in whose reign this group was likewise painted, perhaps present by implication, as the contemporary holder of that supreme responsibility of ensuring the enduring life of the Word?" (*The King's Bedpost*, 131).

11. *An Harborowe for faithfull and trewe subjectes*, B4v and L3r, respectively.

12. *CSP, Foreign*, 1.524–34, no. 1303 (1 September 1559); quotations from 525, 527.

13. *William Latymer's Chronickelle of Anne Bulleyne*, ed. Maria Dowling, 46. The editor notes that "the manuscript would seem to be a working copy rather than one prepared for presentation to the queen" (27). No other manuscript copies are extant, and the text was not printed during the reign.

14. An intriguing anomaly is a jeweled locket ring belonging to Elizabeth that opens to reveal portrait miniatures of Anne Boleyn and Elizabeth as Queen. It hints that her private sentiments regarding her parents may have been very different from her public representations. The ring is reproduced and catalogued in *Elizabeth*, ed. Susan Doran, 12–13, where it is dated ca. 1575.

15. Catalogued as P.98 in Strong, *Portraits of Queen Elizabeth I*.

16. According to Roy Strong, "vast numbers of copies of varying size and period survive" that are based upon the frontal image of King Henry VIII in Holbein's Whitehall wall painting; notable among them are three versions of a full-length portrait of the king painted during the reign of Elizabeth and either signed by or attributed to Hans Eworth (*Tudor and Jacobean Portraits*, 1.159).

17. See Levin, "*The Heart and Stomach of a King*," 91–104.

18. Francis Bacon, "The Beginning of the History of Great Britain," in *Works*, ed. Spedding et al., 11.408.

Part Two

1. Originally printed in *The second tome of homelyes* (1563), and reprinted in *The Two Books of Homilies Appointed to be Read in Churches*, 1859 ed., 167–272; quotation from 250. All references to the Elizabethan homilies will be to this edition. This three-part sermon constitutes a *summa* of official reformed attitudes on the subject. The homilies were prescribed texts for sermons in state churches, where (at least, in principle) regular attendance by all subjects was compulsory. Thus, they were a primary medium through which political, doctrinal, and moral orthodoxies were disseminated and Elizabethan subjects were interpellated.

2. On the rich religious culture of Catholic England on the eve of the Reformation, see the magisterial study by Eamon Duffy, *The Stripping of the Altars*. John Bossy, *Christianity in the West 1400–1700*, is a trenchant essay on traditional religion in the late medieval west and its transformation during the early modern period.

3. Quotations from Bossy, *Christianity in the West 1400–1700*, 155 and 159, respectively. Bossy's argument also marks a point of departure for Richard McCoy, *Alterations of State*, an insightful study of the shifting fortunes of sacred kingship in early modern English culture.

4. On the role of Queen Elizabeth as providential monarch, see Anne McLaren, "Prophecy and Providentialism in the Reign of Elizabeth I"; and Alexandra Walsham, "'A Very Deborah'?"

5. Nowell's remark is quoted in Patrick Collinson, *Elizabethan Essays*, 116.

6. See the studies collected in *The Reign of Elizabeth I*, ed. John Guy, and especially the editor's Introduction, "The 1590s: The second reign of Elizabeth I?" 1–19; also see McLaren, *Political Culture in the Reign of Elizabeth I*, 8–9, 159–60, 238–39. On the emergence of the cult of royal virginity as a strategy of resistance to the Queen's prospective French marriage, see Susan Doran, "Juno versus Diana."

Chapter Five

1. See *TRP*, 2.117–32; quotations from 117–18, 123. On religious polemics and state policies concerning the use of images and the practice of iconoclasm in Tudor England, see two important studies by Margaret Aston: *England's Iconoclasts*, vol. 1: *Laws against Images*, and *The King's Bedpost*.

2. Dated from Windsor, 19 September 1560; printed in *TRP*, 2.146–48; quotation from 146–47.

3. See, for example, the reference to the Catholics' "lewd distinction of Latria and Dulia: where it is evident that the Saints of God cannot abide that as much as any outward worshipping be done or exhibited to them," in "The Third Part of the Homily against Peril of Idolatry," *Two Books of Homilies*, 230. Sir John Harington, an unusually ecumenical Elizabethan, nevertheless scorned "the notable superstition used in worshipping of images, mainteined by the Roman church. In which, notwithstanding all their distinctions of Latria & Dulia . . . yet it is all too apparent that the vulgar sorte do worshippe very stockes and stones" (*A Tract on the Succession to the Crown* [1602], ed. Clements R. Markham, 116).

4. Sander, *The Rise and Growth of the Anglican Schism*, 172.

5. Allen, *Admonition*, xiii.

6. Thomas Bilson, *The True Difference between Christian Subjection and Unchristian Rebellion* (1585), 560; quoted in Sydney Anglo, *Images of Tudor Kingship*, 16.

7. Nicholas Sander, *A Treatise of the Images of Christ and his Saints* (1567), 109; quoted in Roy Strong, *Gloriana*, 38–39. On religious controversies regarding the status of royal images and ceremonies during the reign of Elizabeth, see the important discussions in the following works: Strong, *Gloriana*, 38–41; Anglo, *Images of Tudor Kingship*, 10–28; Helen Hackett, *Virgin Mother, Maiden Queen*, esp. 201–11; Aston, *The King's Bedpost*, 97–107.

8. Elizabethan Accession Day celebrations have been most fully studied by Roy Strong. See, in particular, *The Cult of Elizabeth*, 117–62; and also see his earlier study, "The Popular Celebration of the Accession Day of Queen Elizabeth I."

9. Allen, *Admonition*, xxv.

10. Maurice Kyffin, *The Blessednes of Bryttaine, or A Celebration of the Queenes Holyday* (1587), rpt. in *Fugitive Tracts*, ed. W. C. Hazlitt, vol. 2, unpaginated.

11. Excerpts from Sir William Segar, *Honor Military, and Civill* (1602), rpt. in Nichols, *The Progresses and Public Processions of Queen Elizabeth*, 3.41–50; quotation from 46–47.

12. See John Strype, *Annals of the reformation and establishment of religion, and other various occurrences in the Church of England during Queen Elizabeth's happy reign*, 3.1.177 (italics in

original); in future references, this work will be cited as Strype, *Annals of the reformation*, and all references will be cited by volume, part, and page.

13. *The First Blast of the Trumpet against the Monstrous Regiment of Women*, in Knox, *Works*, ed. Laing, 4.391.

14. John Whitgift, *A most godly and learned sermon preached at Pauls crosse the 17 of November, in the year of our Lorde 1583*, B7r.

15. Thomas Holland, *Paneguris D. Elizabethae, Dei gratiâ Angliae, Franciae, & Hiberniae Reginae*, H3v and H4v, respectively. The quotation is from the "Apologie or Defence of the Church and Common-wealth of England for their annuall celebration of Q. Elizabeths Coronation day the 17. of Novemb.," appended to this 1601 printing of Holland's 1599 Accession Day sermon. Also see Hackett, *Virgin Mother, Maiden Queen*, 207–11; and McCoy, *Alterations of State*, 65–67.

16. See John Howson, *A Sermon preached at St. Maries in Oxford, the 17. day of November, 1602*: "We swarme with Papistes . . . our chiefe divines whom some note under the name of *Formalists*, are ready to joine both heart and hand with them, to the incredible incourAGEMENT of all sortes of Romanistes, and to the dishonour of her Majesties government, the discredit of this Christian societie, the disparagement of their own judgements and discretion, who wound to the heart that religion they pretend to defend" (25).

17. Ibid., 26, 27.

18. Dated London, 11 February, 1603, and printed in *The Letters of John Chamberlain*, ed. Norman Egbert McClure, 1.185.

19. *The Diary of John Manningham of the Middle Temple, 1602–1603*, ed. Robert Parker Sorlien, 221. Also discussed in Hackett, *Virgin Mother, Maiden Queen*, 240.

20. Clapham, *Certain Observations*, 112, 113.

21. Of the Queen's demise, Dekker writes that "[s]he came in with the fall of the leaf and went away in the spring—her life, which was dedicated to virginity, both beginning and closing up a miraculous maiden circle, for she was born upon a Lady Eve and died upon a Lady Eve, her nativity and death being memorable by this wonder." See *The Wonderful Year* (1603), rpt. in Thomas Dekker, *Selected Prose Writings*, ed. E. D. Pendry, 37. For an important discussion of this and other elegies for Elizabeth in a similar vein, see Hackett, *Virgin Mother, Maiden Queen*, 213–21.

22. Clapham, *Certain Observations*, 30–31.

23. See Patrick Collinson, "The Elizabethan Exclusion Crisis and the Elizabethan Polity," 82. Also see the studies collected in *The Reign of Elizabeth I*, ed. Guy.

24. Clapham, *Certain Observations*, 90.

25. Edward Dyer to Christopher Hatton, 9 October 1572; printed in Harris Nicholas, *Memoirs of the Life and Times of Sir Christopher Hatton, K.G.*, 17–19; quotation from 18.

Chapter Six

1. Sander, *The Rise and Growth of the Anglican Schism*, 284–85.

2. See Frances Yates, *Astraea*, 29–120, 215–19; Strong, *The Cult of Elizabeth* and *Gloriana*. The more extreme implications of the work of Yates and Strong have been challenged in Anglo, *Images of Tudor Kingship*; John N. King, "Queen Elizabeth I"; and Hackett, *Virgin Mother, Maiden Queen*.

3. Yates, *Astraea*, 79. Compare her concluding reflections on "the romance of the Accession Day tilts": "The cessation of the observance of saints' days and other festivals of the church . . . must have been felt as a great lack. . . . The annual pageant of Protestant chivalry, in honour of the

holy day of the Queen's accession, skillfully used the traditions of chivalrous display to build up the Queen's legend as the Virgin of the Reformed Religion . . . and to present the spectacle of the worship of her by her knights in the ritual of chivalry as a new kind of regularly-recurring semi-religious festival" (*Astraea*, 109).

4. Richard Topclyffe to the Earl of Shrewsbury, 30 August 1578, printed in Edmund Lodge, *Illustrations of British History, Biography, and Manners*, 2.187–91; quotation from 188–89. Most contractions have been expanded, and future references will be incorporated into the text. My discussion of Topcliffe's letter has been informed by those in Marcus, *Puzzling Shakespeare*, 83–87; and Hackett, *Virgin Mother, Maiden Queen*, 1–6. The accounts of the 1578 Norwich entertainments written by Bernard Garter and Thomas Churchyard, both in print within days of the visit, are conveniently reprinted in an appendix to *Records of Early English Drama*, ed. David Galloway, 243–330. The two pamphlets will be quoted from this edition, and page references will be included within my text. For an illustrated narrative account of the whole progress, see Zillah Dovey, *An Elizabethan Progress*. Relying largely upon Dovey, F. W. Brownlow includes a discussion of the 1578 progress and Topcliffe's place within it in "Performance and Reality at the Court of Elizabeth I," 5–12. The narratives of Churchyard and Garter are also discussed in R. Malcolm Smuts, "Occasional Events, Literary Texts and Historical Interpretations," 188–92. Smuts rightly emphasizes the importance of evaluating these texts "in the context of print culture during late 1578 and 1579, when they appeared and began to circulate," and he reads them as "oppositionist tracts" in the controversy over the marriage negotiations with Anjou (191). I did not see the essays by Brownlow or Smuts until after the completion of my study.

5. See Margaret Aston, "Iconoclasm in England," 192. Although she does not mention the 1578 Suffolk case, Aston elucidates the iconoclastic tradition of which it is an idiosyncratic instance. She does briefly discuss the Rookwood incident in *England's Iconoclasts*, 1.318.

6. On this office under Elizabeth, see Pam Wright, "A Change in Direction," 154.

7. See *The Lives of Philip Howard, Earl of Arundel, and of Anne Dacres, His Wife*, 22–25.

8. See Julian Yates, "Parasitic Geographies."

9. John Baxter, *A Toile for Two-legged Foxes* (London, 1600), 109–10; as quoted in Yates, "Parasitic Geographies," 65.

10. "The Second Part of the Homily against Peril of Idolatry," in *The Two Books of Homilies*, 187.

11. For the religious and political agenda that was the setting for the 1578 progress to Norfolk and Suffolk, see Diarmaid MacCulloch, "Catholic and Puritan in Elizabethan Suffolk." I am indebted to this essay for my understanding of the local context of Topcliffe's letter. Also see the discussion of the 1578 progress in Mary Hill Cole, *The Portable Queen*, 141–44. Cole maintains that "by staying with recusant hosts and supporting local Puritans during the progress of 1578, Elizabeth sought the middle ground of religious inclusion" (144)—an interpretation of the agenda of the progress significantly different from my own.

12. PRO, SP 15/25/113; quoted in Diarmaid MacCulloch, *Suffolk and the Tudors*, 196–97. On Leicester's influence in East Anglia and his role in arranging the progress, see MacCulloch, ibid.; and also A. Hassell Smith, *County and Court*, 39–41, 79.

13. That the campaign was already under way is evident from the later part of Topcliffe's letter to Shrewsbury (189–90), in which he transmits instructions directly from the Queen and Cecil that Shrewsbury is to apprehend, examine, and incarcerate "a detestable Popish preest" (189) active in his vicinity.

14. For an analysis of the Campion affair that sets it in the context of a broad ideological struggle over the legitimacy of the Elizabethan state and the limits of its authority, see the

important essay by Peter Lake and Michael Questier, "Puritans, Papists, and the 'Public Sphere' in Early Modern England." Citing an unpublished paper by Thomas M. McCoog, Lake and Questier discuss "the connections between the Jesuit enterprise of 1580 and the Anjou Match" (612).

15. See Doran, "Juno versus Diana," 272; also, Dovey, *An Elizabethan Progress*, 127. On de Mauvissière's dealings with the Earl of Oxford and his cohort, see John Bossy, "English Catholics and the French Marriage 1577–81."

Chapter Seven

1. On Ralegh's portrait, also see Strong, *Tudor and Jacobean Portraits*, 1.256–57, and vol. 2, plate 505; also Strong, *The Cult of Elizabeth*, 74. The same motto had been incorporated into Ralegh's seal as Lord and Governor of Virginia (1584), which had been named for the Virgin Queen; for a reproduction, see *The Roanoke Voyages 1584–1590*, ed. David Beers Quinn, 1.147.

2. "The 11th: and last booke of the Ocean to Scinthia," lines 53–56, in *The Poems of Sir Walter Ralegh*, ed. Agnes Latham, 27. For the identification of Ralegh as "water," see the letter from Sir Thomas Heneage to Sir Christopher Hatton, 25 October 1582, printed in Nicholas, *Memoirs of the Life and Times of Sir Christopher Hatton*, 277–78, and the introductory note by the editor, 275–76.

3. Aston, "Gods, Saints, and Reformers," 205. The relevant scriptural passage—and the only scriptural reference to Artemis/Diana—is Acts 19:24–35.

4. The painting is catalogued and discussed in Erna Auerbach and C. Kingsley Adams, *Paintings and Sculpture at Hatfield House*, 92–93; unsigned and undated, it is currently attributed to the Flemish artist Frans Floris and dated ca. 1560. That the picture probably belonged to Lord Burghley or his son Robert Cecil is inferred from the fact that it has been listed—as a "picture of Diana"—in inventories at the Cecil properties of Hatfield House and Salisbury House since the early seventeenth century.

5. In "The Work of Gender in the Discourse of Discovery," I analyze the textual strategies and contradictions of Ralegh's *Discoverie* in the context of Elizabethan masculine subject-formation in "the New World."

6. Sir Walter Ralegh's *Discoverie of the large, rich, and beautifull Empire of Guiana* was first published separately in London in 1596 and went through three editions in that year; it was soon reprinted in the second edition of Richard Hakluyt's *The principal navigations, voyages traffiques & discoveries of the English nation*, 3 vols. (1598–1600). I quote Ralegh's *Discoverie* from the 1903 twelve-volume edition of Richard Hakluyt, *The Principal Navigations . . .*, 10.339–431; quotation from 415. Subsequent citations of Ralegh's *Discoverie* will be to vol. 10 of this edition.

7. For a detailed discussion of the imagery of the Drake Jewel and its imperial and occult contexts, see Karen C. C. Dalton, "Art for the Sake of Dynasty"; and for speculation on the relationship of the jewel to Drake's portrait, see Kim F. Hall, *Things of Darkness*, 222–26. Marcus Gheeraerts the Younger's 1591 portrait of Drake wearing the jeweled miniature of the Queen is reproduced in color in *Elizabeth*, ed. Doran, p. 136, fig. 132.

8. See Strong, *Gloriana*, 120–23, for discussion and reproductions of a number of these cameos and medals. Strong traces the origins of the fashion to the 1584 Bond of Association, an act of collective loyalty to the Queen by the English political nation, and a pledge to hunt down any and all who attempted her assassination. See the illustrated catalogue in Strong, *Portraits of Queen Elizabeth I*, for the Queen's image appearing on selected cameos (128–33), medals (134–40),

and coins (141–44). The Hatton portrait is catalogued in Strong, *Tudor and Jacobean Portraits*, 1.136, where the suggestion is made that it may be a seventeenth-century copy.

9. Queen Elizabeth is obliquely addressed and frequently invoked throughout the text of Ralegh's *Discoverie*; Ralegh's patrons—Charles Howard, the Lord Admiral of England, and Sir Robert Cecil, the Queen's Secretary of State—are addressed in an initial epistle and throughout the text; a general readership of English gentlemen, adventurers, and potential investors and colonists is directly addressed in a second epistle and at the close of the work.

10. "Of the Voyage for Guiana," Sloane MSS., 1133, fol. 45; printed in Walter Ralegh, *The Discovery of the Large, Rich, and Beautiful Empire of Guiana*, ed. Sir Robert W. Schomburgk, 135–53; quotation from 135. In his unsubstantiated attribution of this manuscript to Ralegh's authorship, Schomburgk effaces the striking differences in tone and emphasis between the two texts.

11. See "The first voyage made to the coastes of America, with two barkes, wherein were Captaines Master Philip Amadas, and Master Arthur Barlowe, who discovered part of the Countrey, now called Virginia, Anno 1584: Written by one of the said Captaines, and sent to sir Walter Raleigh, knight, at whose charge, and direction, the said voyage was set foorth," originally printed in Richard Hakluyt, *Principall Navigations, Voiages and Discoveries of the English nation* (1589); I quote from the edition in *The Roanoke Voyages 1584–1590*, ed. Quinn, 1.112, 113–14.

12. Thomas Harriot, *A Briefe and true report of the new found land of Virginia* (1590), facsimile edition; quotations from 48 and 26, respectively.

13. Baines's "note Containing the opinion of . . . Christopher Marly Concerning his damnable . . . Judgment of Religion, and scorn of Gods word" was presented to the Elizabethan Privy Council in 1593; I quote it from the reprint in C. F. Tucker Brooke, *The Life of Marlowe*, 98–100. A copy of the note was sent to the Queen. A decade earlier, Baines had been ordained a priest at the English seminary in Rheims under William Allen, and had himself confessed in writing to opinions very similar to those he subsequently ascribed to Marlowe: See Roy Kendall, "Richard Baines and Christopher Marlowe's Milieu." For a brilliant reading of Marlowe's heterodoxy as "the unintended consequence of an educational program designed to yoke literacy to belief, and eloquence to religion," see David Riggs, "Marlowe's Quarrel with God"; quotation from 20. Ralegh's relationship to Renaissance heterodoxy is studied in Ernest A. Strathmann, *Sir Walter Ralegh*; Strathmann draws a sharp distinction between Ralegh's manifest philosophical skepticism and his avowed religious orthodoxy. On Harriot's notoriety among his contemporaries—in part, an indirect campaign to discredit Ralegh—see Jean Jacquot, "Thomas Harriot's Reputation for Impiety." In his unpublished memoir of Elizabeth's reign, Clapham prudently commented that Ralegh "was commonly reputed an atheist, by reason of his profane speeches, perverting the words and senses of Holy Scripture. But whether they proceeded from a desire to maintain argument only and to make a show of his wit, or from a corrupt judgment in matter of religion I will not take upon me to censure" (*Certain Observations*, 93).

Chapter Eight

1. Formerly referred to as the "Blackfriars" picture, the painting is catalogued as P.101 in Strong, *Portraits of Queen Elizabeth I*. In *The English Icon*, 240, Strong attributes the painting to Robert Peake and dates it ca. 1600. His fullest discussion of the work and its context, with reproductions of numerous details, can be found in *The Cult of Elizabeth*, 17–55.

2. See, respectively, Yates, *Astraea*, 79; and Strong, *Gloriana*, 155.

3. Strong, *The Cult of Elizabeth*, 16.

4. Strong, *The Cult of Elizabeth*, 52. It should be noted that although the account of this painting in Strong's *Gloriana* (157–61) is basically an elaboration of that in *The Cult of Elizabeth*, it does temper some of the earlier book's claims for the "Rainbow" portrait as a "sacred icon." I have discussed the "Rainbow" portrait in greater detail in "Idols of the Queen," esp. 139–48.

5. Allen, *Admonition*, vi.

6. I quote from the text of *The Lady of May* in *Miscellaneous Prose of Sir Philip Sidney*, ed. Katherine Duncan-Jones and Jan van Dorsten, 31. This edition uses as its copy-text the first printed version, in the 1598 edition of Sidney's *Arcadia*; however, it incorporates readings from the Helmingham Hall manuscript, notably the final speech by Rombus for which that manuscript is the sole authority. The Helmingham Hall manuscript is printed in Robert Kimbrough and Philip Murphy, "The Helmingham Hall Manuscript of Sidney's *The Lady of May*." Although here I am concerned only with its epilogue, elsewhere I have discussed *The Lady of May* in detail: See my "Celebration and Insinuation."

7. On the relationship of Peele's play to Elizabethan court culture, see my essay "Gifts and Reasons."

8. Thomas Churchyard, *A Discourse of the Queenes Majesties entertainement in Suffolk and Norffolk* (1578), quoted in Nichols, *The Progresses and Public Processions of Queen Elizabeth*, 2.222–23.

9. *Records of Early English Drama*, ed. Galloway, 297. Future citations will be included within the text.

10. For an important discussion of this genre, see Wendy Wall, *The Imprint of Gender*, 111–67; and, for a nuanced discussion of the vexed relationship between event and text, see Sandra Logan, "Making History."

11. Thomas Churchyard, *A Handeful of Gladsome Verses, given to the Queenes Majesty at Woodstocke this Prograce, 1592* (1592; rpt. in *Fugitive Tracts Written in Verse*, ed. Hazlitt, vol. 1, unpaginated).

12. There is documentary evidence that the then aged Churchyard was granted a respectable royal pension in 1597: See Allan Griffith Chester, "Thomas Churchyard's Pension."

13. See Charles A. Rahter, *A Critical Edition of Churchyard's Challenge*, 183.

14. Anglo, *Images of Tudor Kingship*, 127–28.

15. Puttenham, *The Arte of English Poesie*, ed. Willcock and Walker, 299, 302, 186, respectively. For discussion of Puttenham's own courtly performance in the *Arte*, see my essay "Of Gentlemen and Shepherds," 433–52.

16. Kevin Sharpe argues for a similarly dialogical and agonistic perspective on "the politics of rhetoric and display" in his synoptic review essay, "Representations and Negotiations." In this essay, Sharpe reviews "recent interdisciplinary work on theatre and poetry, painting and pageant, vital to historians of politics," and he enjoins his fellow historians to attend to the "critical methods" developed by literary critics and art historians "to illuminate the performance and reception of texts in early modern culture" (853). Also see the review essay by Helen Hackett, "Dreams or Designs, Cults or Constructions?"; Hackett presents a methodological critique focused on studies of Queen Elizabeth, and she gives greater emphasis to gender issues than does Sharpe.

Part Three

1. The quoted words are those of Edmund Plowden, Elizabethan common lawyer, in his commentary on the 1563 Duchy of Lancaster case (*The commentaries, or Reports of Edmund Plowden*, 212a–213). On this Elizabethan secularization of "medieval political theology," see the

magisterial study of Ernst H. Kantorowicz, *The King's Two Bodies*, esp. 7–32. In *The Queen's Two Bodies*, Marie Axton studies the development of the concept by Tudor common lawyers and its articulation in drama and spectacle associated with the Elizabethan Inns of Court.

2. Mary Douglas, *Natural Symbols*, xix–xx, vii, respectively.

3. On the learned medical and anatomical discourse deriving from Galen that underpinned these notions, see Thomas Laqueur, *Making Sex*, esp. 63–148. As Laqueur explains, this discourse provided a "one-sex" model in which distinctions of male and female were matters of degree but in which manhood was nevertheless the measure of the model's fulfillment. Lyndal Roper adds the salutary proviso that "what Laqueur is actually describing is the discourse of medical theory. It is not apparent that it was by means of such theory that early modern people understood their bodies. Rather, their culture rested on a very deep apprehension of sexual difference as an organizing principle of culture" (*Oedipus and the Devil*, 16).

4. Among many recent studies of the construction of Woman in early modern English culture, both learned and popular, see the following important works: Ian Maclean, *The Renaissance Notion of Woman*; Linda Woodbridge, *Women and the English Renaissance*; Anthony Fletcher, *Gender, Sex and Subordination in England 1500–1800*; Audrey Eccles, *Obstetrics and Gynaecology in Tudor and Stuart England*; Gail Kern Paster, *The Body Embarrassed*. Also see Peter Stallybrass, "Patriarchal Territories." In the course of charting "the production of a normative 'Woman' within the discursive practices of the ruling elite" (127) in early modern England, Stallybrass makes a number of telling observations about the place of the Queen in this process; particularly relevant here is his remark that "as the nation-state was formed according to new canons of incorporation and exclusion, so was the female body refashioned. In this refashioning, Elizabeth functioned both as emblem of national 'integrity' and as embarrassing contradiction" (130).

5. Mary Douglas, *Purity and Danger*, 138, 145.

Chapter Nine

1. E. K. Chambers, *The Elizabethan Stage*, 1.19.

2. Nichols, *The Progresses and Public Processions of Queen Elizabeth*, 1.xxxviii. In his collection, Nichols prints full rolls for five years of the reign. I have discussed the political significance and cultural resonance of such prestations in "Gifts and Reasons."

3. Puttenham, *The Arte of English Poesie*, 302.

4. Guerau de Spes to Zayas, London, 9 January 1571; trans. and printed in *CSP, Spanish*, 2.298.

5. This secret negotiation can be followed through de Quadra's dispatches of 1561–62, printed in vol. 1 of *CSP, Spanish*; for a balanced interpretation, see Doran, *Monarchy and Matrimony*, 45ff.

6. According to the intelligence of de Quadra, the Spanish ambassador, Elizabeth had set this game going in an audience with Lethington, Secretary to Mary, Queen of Scots. In an enciphered dispatch to King Philip, de Quadra recounted the audience as purportedly told to him personally by Lethington. As an example of the precariously intimate terms in which diplomacy was conducted at the court of Elizabeth, this dispatch deserves to be quoted at length: "The Queen said that if his mistress would take her advice and wished to marry safely and happily she would give her a husband who would ensure both, and this was Lord Robert, in whom nature has implanted so many graces that if she [Elizabeth] wished to marry she would prefer him to all the princes in the world. . . . Lethington says that he replied that this was a great proof of the love she bore to his Queen, as she was willing to give her a thing so dearly prized by herself, and he thought the Queen his mistress, even if she loved Lord Robert as dearly as she (Elizabeth) did, would not marry him and so deprive her of all the joy and solace she

received from his companionship. . . . He says the Queen said to him she wished to God the earl of Warwick his brother had the grace and good looks of Lord Robert in which case each could have one. . . . Lethington was anxious to escape from this colloquy by bringing on the subject of the succession which he knew would shut her mouth directly, and therefore told her that the Queen his mistress was very young yet, and what this Queen might do for her was to marry Lord Robert herself first and have children by him, which was so important for the welfare of the country, and then when it should please God to call her to himself she could leave the queen of Scots heiress both to her kingdom and her husband. In this way it would be impossible for Lord Robert to fail to have children by one or other of them who would in time become Kings of these two countries, and so turning it to a joke he put an end to the conversation." (Bishop Quadra to the King, London, 28 March 1563; translated and printed in *CSP, Spanish*, 1.313.) Apparently, neither Leicester nor Mary had any enthusiasm for Elizabeth's proposition, and it is difficult to assess how seriously she herself took it. For narratives of the intertwined courtship strategies through which both Elizabeth and Mary pursued their political interests, see, for Mary, Jenny Wormald, *Mary Queen of Scots*, 129–66; and for Elizabeth, Doran, *Monarchy and Matrimony*, passim.

7. Guzman de Silva to the King, London, 17 August 1566; printed in *CSP, Spanish*, 1.518. Emphasis added.

8. For a detailed analysis of the stages of this courtship in the context of international politics, see Doran, *Monarchy and Matrimony*, 130–94. François, formerly duc d'Alençon, inherited this title when his brother Henri became King of France. Henri was the duc d'Anjou with whom Elizabeth had been negotiating marriage in 1571. Unless otherwise indicated, my references to Anjou are to François, who as heir apparent to the French throne was most frequently referred to in England during this period as *Monsieur*.

9. See John Stubbs, *John Stubbs's Gaping Gulf*, ed. Lloyd E. Berry, 3–4. Subsequent variations on this trope of invasion include the following: "Considering how Spain dotes upon that drunken harlot of Rome, I would be loath that either France or Spain should have such a porter here to let them in at a postern gate as Monsieur is" (38); "This match . . . lays the reins at random on the neck of this horse of hidden treason and sets a rider of choice upon him for the nonce, yea, and opens all the ports to foreign enemies" (77).

10. See *John Stubbs's Gaping Gulf*, ed. Berry, 68–69.

11. Issued 27 September 1579; reprinted in *TRP*, 2.445–49; quotation from 449.

12. See the paintings catalogued as P.43–46 in Strong, *Portraits of Queen Elizabeth I*; the painting I discuss is catalogued as P.43, the Plimpton "sieve" portrait. In Strong, *Gloriana*, the first two of these "sieve" portraits are dated 1579, and the second two ascribed to ca. 1580–83; see his important discussion of the whole group in *Gloriana*, 94–107. In a later portrait, ca. 1585–90, attributed to John Bettes the Younger, the Queen also holds a gold sieve (see Strong, *Portraits*, P.54; Strong, *Gloriana*, plate 119).

13. As J. B. Harley has pointed out, the "imperial" theme in Elizabethan culture was multidimensional: "The idea of Empire . . . was manifest in the nationalist drive to overseas expansion; it was rooted in the wider Renaissance conception of world-empire; and it was translated into an Elizabethan imperialism expressed in terms of royal supremacy over both church and state" ("Meaning and Ambiguity in Tudor Cartography," 33). For detailed analysis of the Siena "sieve" portrait, see Strong, *Gloriana*, 100–107. Strong attributes the work to Cornelius Ketel, but it has also been attributed to Quentin Massys the Younger.

14. Strong, *Gloriana*, 96. The origins of the legend are classical but it would probably have been familiar to a courtly Elizabethan audience through the Triumph of Chastity in Petrarch's

Trionfi. This poem was also a ready source for another striking symbol of royal chastity: the crowned ermine upon the Queen's sleeve in the "Ermine" portrait, attributed to William Segar and dated 1585. On the "Ermine" portrait, see Strong, *Gloriana*, 112–15. Paster makes the excellent point that "the trope comparing women and water appears in a subverted form in the famous iconographic depiction of female virginity as a sieve that does not leak.... The association of Elizabeth with Tuccia's sieve ... serves to separate her from womankind as a whole—and thus from the contradictions of a woman ruler" (*The Body Embarrassed*, 50).

15. Geffrey Whitney, *Whitney's "Choice of Emblemes,"* facsimile ed., 68.

16. For the device, see Camden, *Remains concerning Britain*, 182. One of the New Year's gifts to the Queen in 1590 was "A Juell roundelett of golde Lyke a Syve" (BL, Add. 5751A, f. 223; quoted in Arnold, *Queen Elizabeth's Wardrobe Unlock'd*, 38).

17. On the importance of this distinction for Elizabethan visual culture, see Leslie, "The Dialogue between Bodies and Souls." Leslie makes the point that "very few Elizabethan portraits are in any way emblematic. They may share some kinds of imagery with emblems; but in aim, process, and structure they are fundamentally different. Few portraits are intended to tell us of general moral concepts: rather they are designed to express the 'filosofia del cavaliere,' the 'segretto dell'animo' of the sitter. In short, they are *impresa*-like" (24).

18. As reported in a letter from Thomas Smith to Lord Burghley, from the French court at Blois, 22 March 1571; printed in Dudley Digges, *The Compleat Ambassador*, 193–98; quotation from 196. Catherine de' Medici was relating to Smith and Walsingham a conversation she had had with her son, Henri, duc d'Anjou. More than a decade earlier than the conversation reported by Smith, at the time of the marriage negotiations involving the Queen and the Archduke Charles of Austria, the Emperor Maximillian II instructed Adam Zwetkovich, his emissary to Elizabeth, that he should act with circumspection should he "learn, not from conjectures but from sure judgements and from the general opinion, that the integrity of the morals and life of Her Highness is not such as becomes a Princess." Zvetkovich subsequently reported of the Queen that "she would fain vindicate herself to Your Imperial Majesty against all the slander that had been cast at her, and she hoped that Your Imperial Majesty would find that she had all the time acted in all matters with due decorum and attention"; he added that "I have through several persons made diligent inquiries concerning the maiden honour and integrity of the Queen, and have found that she has truly and verily been praised and extolled for her virginal and royal honour, and that nothing can be said against her." These letters, dated 15 March 1565 and 4 June 1565, respectively, are translated and printed in *Queen Elizabeth and Some Foreigners*, ed. Victor von Klarwill, 205–9, 213–36; quotations from 207, 217, 231. At about this time (17 August 1566), Guzman de Silva, the Spanish ambassador in England, was reporting to King Philip that the French ambassador had sworn to him that the Queen had slept with Dudley on the prior New Year's night (see *CSP, Spanish*, 1.520). Defamatory gossip on the subject of the Queen's sexual conduct is usefully surveyed in Levin, *The Heart and Stomach of a King*, 66–90. Also see the essays collected in *Dissing Elizabeth*, ed. Julia M. Walker.

19. See, for example, the ribald anecdote recounted by Puttenham in *The Arte of English Poesie*, 272.

20. See Doris Adler, "The Riddle of the Sieve," which convincingly connects the "sieve" portraits to the Anjou courtship and to the iconography of the duc d'Anjou himself. Also building upon the foundational work of Strong and of Yates (*Astraea*, 114–20), other recent studies by literary scholars have focused upon the Siena "sieve" portrait: See Constance Jordan, "Representing Political Androgyny," which presents an ingenious interpretation of the painting

as wittily figuring an androgynous Queen; and Jonathan Goldberg, *Sodometries*, 43–47, which focuses upon what Goldberg sees as the permutations of desire evoked by the background figures.

21. See George Peele, *Polyhymnia Describing, The honourable Triumph at Tylt, before her Majestie, on the 17. of November last past. . . . With Sir Henrie Lea, his resignation of honour at Tylt* (1590); rpt. in *The Life and Works of George Peele*, 1.232.

22. See Strong, *Gloriana*, 134–41, for reproductions of details and analogues, a transcription and partial reconstruction of the sonnet inscribed on the canvas, and a commentary different from but complementary to my own. Also see the monograph by Karen Hearn, *Marcus Gheeraerts II*, which briefly discusses the Ditchley portrait (31–34) in the context of Gheeraerts's oeuvre and biography. Strong notes that Sir Henry Lee was a major patron of Marcus Gheeraerts the Younger; and he surmises that the portrait was executed in connection with Lee's retirement and the entertainments that alluded to it during the Queen's visit to Ditchley in 1592. Eighteenth-century visitors to Ditchley recorded seeing the painting there. On Lee's relationship to the Queen and her entertainments at Ditchley, see E. K. Chambers, *Sir Henry Lee*.

23. Sir John Harington, *Nugae antiquae*, ed. Henry Harington, 2.140–41. Sidney opened his imprudent "Letter . . . to Queen Elizabeth, Touching Her Marriage with Monsieur" (1579) with an address to his "Most feared and beloved, most sweet and gracious Sovereign" (*Miscellaneous Prose of Sir Philip Sidney*, ed. Duncan-Jones and van Dorsten, 46).

24. On the popularity of this cult in pre-Reformation England, see Duffy, *The Stripping of the Altars*, 264.

25. *The Wonderful Year* (1603), in Dekker, *Selected Prose Writings*, ed. Pendry, 33.

26. The phrase "A Virgin Mother and a Maiden Queene" occurs in the anonymous elegy "Singultientes Lusus," printed in *Sorrowes Joy; or, A Lamentation for our late deceased Soveraigne Elizabeth, with a triumph for the prosperous Succession of our gratious King James* (1603), rpt. in John Nichols, *The Progresses, Processions, and Magnificent Festivities of King James the First*, 1.15.

27. Harley, "Meaning and Ambiguity in Tudor Cartography," 22, 24.

28. See Victor Morgan, "The Cartographic Image of 'the Country' in Early Modern England," 151.

29. Strong, *Gloriana*, 136.

Chapter Ten

1. Bernardino de Mendoza to Juan de Idiaquez, King Philip's Secretary, London, 2 March 1583; trans. and printed in *CSP, Spanish*, 3.449. The anonymous painting is now in the Rijksmuseum, Amsterdam; see Pieter J. J. Van Thiel et al., *All the Paintings of the Rijksmuseum in Amsterdam*, p. 638, no. A 2684. Although there ascribed to the "English school ca 1585," the reference in Mendoza's dispatch implies a Flemish provenance for the painting and a date no later than 1583. In mid-1584, within weeks of each other, Anjou died and Orange was assassinated.

2. For guidance through this historical thicket, I have relied primarily upon Geoffrey Parker, *The Dutch Revolt*.

3. For an extended narrative of the unfolding of English policy in the Low Countries, see Wallace T. MacCaffrey, *Queen Elizabeth and the Making of Policy, 1572–1588*, 217–401; and the same author's *Elizabeth I*, 249–98. On the radical ideas of resistance to rulers and popular sovereignty developed in the course of the Dutch revolt, see Martin van Gelderen, *The Political Thought of the Dutch Revolt 1555–1590*.

4. On the pageantry and propaganda of Leicester's tenure in the Netherlands, see Roy Strong and J. A. Van Dorsten, *Leicester's Triumph*; on its religious ideology, see "A Puritan crusade? The

Composition of the Earl of Leicester's Expedition to the Netherlands, 1585–86," in Simon Adams, *Leicester and the Court*, 176–95.

5. A Dutch print is extant (reproduced in Strong and Van Dorsten, *Leicester's Triumph*, 74) that appropriates the allegorical conceit shared by this painting and another to be discussed below. However, unlike either of these paintings, the print employs the conceit in order to express disgust with the self-serving motives of the Earl of Leicester, the Low Countries' erstwhile English savior: in the print, it is Philip II who pulls the cow backward by the tail and Anjou who pulls her forward by a rope that breaks, while it is Leicester himself who milks the cow until the pail overflows and he draws blood. Considered together, these three pictures demonstrate a form of iconic conversation, debate, and parody as vigorous as any taking place within the textual domain.

6. See, for example, Pieter Geyl, *The Revolt of the Netherlands 1555–1609*, 189–90; and Parker, *The Dutch Revolt*, 199–207. Anjou journeyed from England to Antwerp early in 1582, in an entourage that included the Earl of Leicester and the Prince of Orange, there to be invested as Duke of Brabant. According to the contemporary narrative of his entry, he was honored by the city as its savior from the tyranny of King Philip, and was celebrated with civic pageantry as magnificent and extensive as any that Elizabeth received within her own kingdom; see "The Roiall Interteinement of the Right High and Mightie Prince, Francis, the French King's onelie Brother, by the Grace of God Duke of Brabant, Anjou, Alanson, Berrie. &c. into the Citie of Antwerpe," in Nichols, *Progresses and Public Processions of Queen Elizabeth*, 2.354–85.

7. "Proposed speech to the Queen on the Low Countries, February 1587," printed in *PPE*, 2.309.

8. This painting is catalogued as no. 9 among those in the addenda of Strong, *Portraits of Queen Elizabeth I*; it is undated and unattributed. Strong comments that "the allegory presumably related to the treaty between Elizabeth and the Provinces in August 1585 which led to the expedition of the Earl of Leicester" (159), although he offers no evidence for this specific occasion. He does not catalogue the Rijksmuseum painting. The political and diplomatic context in which these two pictures were generated is outlined in Strong and Van Dorsten, *Leicester's Triumph*, 1–19.

9. In *Dynasties*, ed. Hearn, 87, this painting is dated ca. 1586 on the basis of similarities to other images of Philip II and Queen Elizabeth from around that date. The fact that by 1586 both William of Orange and François, duc d'Anjou, had been dead for two years makes me skeptical of this late dating.

10. Strong, *Gloriana*, 12.

11. Michael Moodye to Sir Thomas Heneage, 18 December 1590; printed in HMC, *Salisbury*, 4.77. I owe this reference to Strong, *Gloriana*, 41.

12. For Stafford's efforts to suppress the verbal and visual propaganda of English Catholic exiles, see, for example, the following entries in *CSP, Foreign*: for the years 1583–84: nos. 305–6, 314–18, 341, 369, 376, 416, 491, 522; and for 1584–85: nos. 33, 68, 207. Most of these dispatches concern illustrated books produced by the English Catholic expatriate Richard Verstegan. For a narrative of Stafford's persistent but unsuccessful attempts to suppress Verstegan's work and to procure his punishment, see A. G. Petti, "Richard Verstegan and Catholic Martyrologies of the Later Elizabethan Period," 70–77.

13. PRO, London, SP 78/10, no. 79. I have modernized usage of "u" and "v" and have expanded some contractions. For advice and assistance in transcribing Stafford's difficult hand, I am most grateful to Laetitia Yeandle, curator of manuscripts at the Folger Shakespeare Library, Washington, DC, and to Mary Robertson, curator of manuscripts at the Huntington Library,

San Marino, California. Stafford begins the letter as follows: "Sir besyde this thatt I have writte to yow in this other letter, I thowght good to advertyse your honor of a thinge which I thowght nott fytte to putt in my other letter and for my parte think ytt nott good to be spredd abroade."

14. See *Oxford English Dictionary*, s.v. "Sir-reverence," sense 2, "Human excrement." The earliest printed occurrence cited in *OED* is from Robert Greene, *Ned Browne* (1592): "His face . . . and his Necke, were all besmeared with the soft sirreverence, so as he stunck." This phrase is elided by Strong in his partial transcription of Stafford's letter (*Gloriana*, 168, n. 82), and is censored in the transcription printed in *CSP, Foreign*, July 1583–July 1584, p. 218, no. 246.

15. See *CAR, Kent*, no. 1479, p. 246. Indicted for seditious words on 1 April 1585, Vanhill was found guilty and sentenced to hang, presumably as a consequence of his having treasonously wished for the Queen's death.

16. It was Elizabeth's practice to nickname her favorites and counselors, often as animals. Whatever her reason for calling Anjou her frog, he seems to have accepted it happily as a term of endearment, styling himself "vostre grenoille" in addresses to Elizabeth. See Doris Adler, "Imaginary Toads in Real Gardens," who argues that printed references to frogs and toads were unusually plentiful in England between 1579 and 1581, and that many of these encoded opposition to the proposed royal marriage.

17. For the classic study of this cultural trope, see Davis, *Society and Culture in Early Modern France*, 124–51.

18. Engraved by Pieter van der Heyden, possibly from someone else's design; and catalogued in Strong, *Portraits of Queen Elizabeth I*, as E.14. On the basis of its allusion to the assassination of the Prince of Orange and its indictment of Pope Gregory XIII, Strong maintains that the engraving was issued between July 1584 and April 1585, the dates of their respective deaths. I have benefited from the discussion of the print's iconography in Fritz Saxl, "Veritas filia temporis," esp. 209–10. David Howarth's summary judgment is that the print is "little more than a scatological cartoon . . . concocted by a rabble with whom Elizabeth was forced to come to terms in the interests of *realpolitik*" (*Images of Rule*, 115). The catalogue of Van der Heyden's works is dominated by biblical subjects and moral allegories, a number of them engravings after pictures by Pieter Brueghel the Elder: See F. W. H. Hollstein, *Dutch and Flemish Etchings, Engravings and Woodcuts, ca. 1450–1700*, 9.26–32.

19. Titian's painting had been completed by 1559; it is possible that Van der Heyden knew it indirectly, through an engraving made by Cornelis Cort in 1566. However, as Harold E. Wethey notes in his catalogue raisonné to *The Paintings of Titian* (3.143), in some of its details Cort's engraving more closely resembles Titian's second version of the subject (ca. 1566; and now in the Kunsthistorisches Museum, Vienna) than it does the version of ca. 1556–59. Cort's engraving is reproduced in *The Paintings of Titian*, vol. 3, plate 216.

20. Titian conceived of and executed "Diana and Callisto" in tandem with his "Diana and Actaeon," both of which included the erotic subject of Diana in her bath; according to his correspondence, they were completed at about the same time and sent together to Philip in 1559 (see Erwin Panofsky, *Problems in Titian*, 154 and n. 42). Other Ovidian paintings produced by Titian for Philip II, and possibly conceived as pairs, include his "Danaë" (second version) and "Venus and Adonis," and his "Rape of Europa" and "Liberation of Andromeda by Perseus." On this whole series of *poesie* (the term used by Titian in his letters to Philip II), see Panofsky, *Problems in Titian*, 149–68; David Rosand, "*Ut pictor poeta*"; and Jane C. Nash, *Veiled Images*.

21. I am grateful to Marguerite Oosterbaan Walk and to Cynthia Walk for a translation of the Dutch inscriptions.

22. The woodcut (fig. 40) shows Henry VIII enthroned, holding the Bible, with Archbishop Cranmer at his right hand and Pope Clement VII beneath his feet; it bears the title, "The Pope suppressed by K. Henry the eight." For analysis and other examples of the trope of the Pope's discomfiture, see Aston, *The King's Bedpost*, 135–55; and King, *Tudor Royal Iconography*, 116–81.

23. See Revelation 17:4: "And the woman was araied in purple & skarlat, & guilded with golde, & precious stones, and pearles, and had a cup of golde in her hand, ful of abominations, and filthines of her fornication." The *Geneva Bible* glosses this woman as "the Antichrist, that is, the Pope with ye whole bodie of his filthie creatures... whose beautie onely standeth in outwarde pompe & impudencie and craft like a strumpet"; it glosses the contents of her cup as "false doctrines & blasphemies." The inscriptions in Dutch included in Van der Heyden's print identify the Pope as both "the crowned brood hen" and "the Antichrist." The latter identification was also popular among Elizabethan Protestants: For example, in a fiery 1587 House of Commons speech on the subject of the Low Countries, Job Throckmorton asserted that "yt is an argument unawnswerable, to prove the Pope to bee that man described in the Apocalypse, I meane that man of sinne, that beast with the marke in his foreheadde, to prove him, I say, to be Antichrist" (*PPE*, 2.277–89; quotation from 279). See Peter Lake, "The Significance of the Elizabethan Identification of the Pope as Antichrist," for a nuanced analysis of how this identification functioned as part of "an activist ideology for the Protestant ruling class, both in its domestic administrative duties and in the direction of national policy in the theatre of European war and diplomacy" (177).

24. All citations from *The Faerie Queene* follow the edition of A. C. Hamilton; citation is by book, canto, and stanza.

25. *PPE*, 2.277–89; quotation from 280.

Chapter Eleven

1. Printed in *Calendar of the Carew Manuscripts*, 2.431.

2. See Christopher Highley, "The Royal Image in Elizabethan Ireland," 64.

3. "The Lord Deputy's Journey in the Queen's County," 26 August 1600; printed in *Calendar of the Carew Manuscripts*, 3.432.

4. For a trenchant analysis of the formation of this myth and its significance "in shaping Englishmen's perceptions of themselves and of the Spanish and Dutch," see F. Fernández-Armesto, "Armada Myths"; quotation from 38–39.

5. The three extant Armada portraits are catalogued in Strong, *Portraits of Queen Elizabeth I*, as P.64 (reproduced here), P.65, and P.68. For discussion, see Strong, *Gloriana*, 130–33; Janet Arnold, "The 'Armada' Portraits of Queen Elizabeth I," who focuses on costume and jewelry; and Andrew Belsey and Catherine Belsey, "Icons of Divinity," 11–15, who build upon my earlier published work on the subject.

6. Strong, *Gloriana*, 132. Peter Barber points out that the Queen's imperial gesture is aimed specifically against the Spanish Empire: "Elizabeth, while expressing imperial aspirations through the globe/orb, is placing her hand over *North America* and is pointing at the Spanish Main and South America, possible areas of English expansion" ("England II," 96, n. 180).

7. On the relationship of royal iconography to such profane discourses—including the Ovidian, Petrarchan, Neoplatonic, and pastoral—see Elkin Calhoun Wilson, *England's Eliza*; Leonard Forster, *The Icy Fire*, 122–47; Berry, *Of Chastity and Power*. And, on its relationship to sacred discourses, see King, *Tudor Royal Iconography*, 182–226; King, "Queen Elizabeth I"; Peter McClure and Robin Headlam Wells, "Elizabeth I as a Second Virgin Mary"; Hackett, *Virgin Mother, Maiden Queen*.

8. In a chapter titled "The Politics of Pleasure; or, Queering Queen Elizabeth," in her book *The Renaissance of Lesbianism in Early Modern England*, Valerie Traub takes my own earlier published reading of the Armada portrait as a point of departure in arguing that "it is the clitoral body of Elizabeth, not the imagined threat of the phallus, that reigns over the Armada portrait" (133). Appropriating the painting for the discourse of twenty-first century sexual politics, she writes that "the drop pearl in the Armada portrait emblematizes the erotic self-assertion of the most powerful woman in the realm, figuratively announcing Elizabeth's sovereign right to her own pleasures" (130). I am grateful to Professor Traub for sharing this chapter with me in advance of publication.

9. *Hymnus in Cynthiam*, lines 116–19, in *The Poems of George Chapman*, ed. Phyllis Brooks Bartlett. *Hymnus in Cynthiam* was originally printed in Chapman's *The Shadow of Night: Containing Two Poeticall Hymnes* (1594).

10. See "Dr. [Leonel] Sharp, to the Duke of Buckingham," in *Cabala, Mysteries of State*. In his letter, Sharp relates that he had been a preacher in the service of the Earl of Leicester in 1588 and had been present at Tilbury during the Queen's visit: "The Queen . . . rode through all the Squadrons of her Army, as Armed *Pallas* attended by Noble Footmen, *Leicester*, *Essex*, and *Norris*, then Lord Marshal, and divers other great Lords. Where she made an excellent Oration to her Army, which, the next day after her departure, I was commanded to re-deliver to all the Army together, to keep a Publick Fast." This explains his possession of a transcript of the Queen's speech, "and no man hath it but my self."

11. The manuscript version of this speech (BL Harleian MS 6798, art. 18) bears the subscription, "Gathered by on ye heard itt, and was commaunded to utter it to ye whole army ye next day, to send itt gathered to the Queen herself." The hand has been identified as Sharp's, and the undated draft may be contemporaneous with the event recounted. Sharp's printed letter and the manuscript version are printed together and compared in Janet M. Green, "'I My Self': Queen Elizabeth I's Oration at Tilbury Camp." (Also see Elizabeth I, *Collected Works*, 325–26, which uses the manuscript version as its copy text but notes significant variants from the *Cabala* text.)

12. For an informative analysis of various verbal and iconic accounts of the event, and of the process by which the event was elaborated into a national and Protestant myth, see Susan Frye, "The Myth of Elizabeth at Tilbury." Apparently unaware of the existence of the manuscript draft, Frye emphasizes the fact that Sharp is writing his letter at least three dozen years after the event and that he is concerned to show the nefarious parallels between Spanish policies in 1588 and 1623. Her point is well taken but it does not thereby discredit Sharp's account of the earlier events.

13. *Cabala, Mysteries of State*, 373.

14. Although very different in its details, another text claiming to represent the gist of the Queen's speech at Tilbury demonstrates basically the same gender-specific rhetorical strategies: "[F]or what are these proud Philistines, that they should revile the Hoast of the living God? I have been your Prince in peace, so will I be in warre[;] neither will I bid you goe and fight, but come and let us fight the battell of the Lord[.] [T]he enemie perhaps may challenge my sexe for that I am a woman, so may I likewise charge their mould for that they are but men, whose breath is in their nostrels" (William Leigh, *Queene Elizabeth, Paraleld in Her Princely Vertues, with David, Joshua, and Hezekia* [1612], The Second Sermon, 92; quoted in Frye, "The Myth of Elizabeth at Tilbury," 101–2). As Frye points out, this speech is repeated almost word for word as the inscription beneath a wall painting of Queen Elizabeth at Tilbury in the chancel of St. Faith's Church, Gaywood, Norfolk; the painting bears the date of 1588 but may be later. These texts may

not offer corroboration of the specifics of Sharp's version of the speech, but they do reinforce the impression that whatever the Queen did in fact say drew from the same relatively limited corpus of phrases, images, and tropes—a corpus that she had been building and refining since the very inception of her reign.

15. In her enlightening chronological survey of Elizabeth's gendered self-representations in her speeches, Janel Mueller argues that it is in the Tilbury speech "that Elizabeth must be said to first unambiguously claim possession of the virtue of courage.... At this point of supreme crisis Elizabeth conflates masculine and feminine gender in her woman's body with its king's heart and stomach. Then, as general, judge, and rewarder of virtues in the field, she puts her androgynized anatomy into action" ("Virtue and Virtuality," 235, 237).

16. "A new Ballet of the straunge and most cruell Whippes which the Spanyards had prepared to whippe and torment English men and women: which were found and taken at the overthrow of certaine of the Spanish Shippes, in July last past, 1588" (1588; rpt. in *The Works of Thomas Deloney*, ed. F. O. Mann, 479–82). In a companion ballad of "The Queenes visiting of the Campe at *Tilsburie* with her entertainment there," Deloney devotes a stanza to the speech made to the troops by "King *Henryes* royall daughter" that has a strong affinity with Sharp's transcription: "Never let your stomackes faile you. / For in the midst of all your troupe, / we our selves will be in place: / To be your joy, your guide and comfort, / even before the enemies face" (1588; rpt., Deloney, *Works*, 474–78). On the myth of Boadicia in early modern England and its relevance to the controversy over female authority, see Jodi Mikalachki, *The Legacy of Boadicea*. Apparently, rumors of intended Spanish atrocities were rife in post-Armada England. An Italian spy in the pay of the Spanish king wrote from London on 7 September 1588 that "it is publicly stated here that the Spanish prisoners confess they had orders, if they were victorious, to kill every Englishman over seven years old. They say they brought two kinds of whips...one for men and the other for women.... This is the reason these people are so enraged with the Spaniards. Their anger would certainly be justified if the above and other similar things were true" (trans. and printed in *CSP, Spanish*, 4.421).

17. Thomas Heywood, *If You Know Not Me You Know Nobody*, ed. Madeleine Doran, lines 2577–84. The second part of the play was originally printed in 1606, and reprinted in 1633 with additions to the Armada ending, including the scene among the Spaniards from which I quote here. On the representation of Elizabeth in the two parts of Heywood's play, and the significance of the changes in her representation as the play was revised and reprinted during the course of the early seventeenth century, see Teresa Grant, "Drama Queen." In numerous works printed and reprinted throughout the early seventeenth century, Heywood propounded a posthumous image of his late queen as a virtuous and heroic female champion of the English people and the Protestant cause; see Georgianna Zeigler, "England's Savior."

18. Ralegh, *The Discoverie of the Large, Rich and Beautiful Empire of Guiana*, 346, 428. See my essay "The Work of Gender in the Discourse of Discovery."

19. On his visit to the Queen's palace of Hampton Court in 1600, Baron Waldstein saw displayed in one of the galleries a painting "of Tarquin and Lucretia with the inscription 'Amissa pudicitia superstes esse nequeo'"—that is, "having lost my chastity I cannot go on living" (*Diary of Baron Waldstein*, 153). On the significance of the Rape of Lucretia for late Elizabethan political culture, see Annabel Patterson, *Reading between the Lines*, 297–310. The Siena "sieve" portrait (fig. 33) emphasizes the theme of imperial chastity by its inclusion of an imperial pillar with inset scenes of Aeneas abandoning Dido and subduing his desires in order to fulfill his Roman destiny: here Aeneas is to be read as an exemplar for Elizabeth.

20. The Earl of Leicester to the Earl of Shrewsbury, "from the Camp, this 15 of August [1588]," printed in Lodge, *Illustrations of British History, Biography, and Manners*, 2.376–77; I have expanded contractions. The phrase "*mascula vis*" or "manly character" is used in a Latin epigram on Elizabeth attributed to George Buchanan and printed in Camden's *Remains concerning Britain*, ed. Dunn, 306. Camden introduces it as having been made upon a picture of the "most potent, and prudent" Queen Elizabeth:

Cuius imago Deae, facie cui lucet in una,
    Temperie mixta, Juno, Minerva, Venus?
Est dea: quid dubitem? cui sic conspirat amice
    Mascula vis, hilaris gratia, celsus honos:
Aut Dea si non est, Diva est quae praesidet Anglis
    Ingenio, vultu, moribus aequa Deis.

Dunn provides the following translation: "Whose picture is it? A goddess in whose face shine in happy mixture June, Minerva, and Venus? She is a goddess; why should I doubt it? Her strength, her manly character, her blithe charm, and her noble reputation combine in harmony. Or if she is not a goddess, she is a deity who rules the English, the equal of the gods in wit, beauty, and character" (504–5). Interestingly, Camden pairs two epigrams on Elizabeth's portrait with two on the portrait of Mary, Queen of Scots. One of the latter includes praise of Mary's *mascula virtus* (307), a phrase very similar to the *mascula vis* of Elizabeth.

21. Endorsed and dated by Persons, 3 August 1592; printed in *The Letters and Despatches of Richard Verstegan*, ed. Anthony G. Petti, 59. The official account of Perrot's trial on the trumped-up charge of high treason does not mention this accusation, although it attributes to him a number of other contemptuously misogynistic comments about the Queen. Among these, two are particularly relevant to the one retailed by Verstegan: Perrot's expression of discontent at having "to serve a base bastard piss-kitchin woman," and his assertion that he was "the fittest man in England to have the keeping of her body." See "The Trial of Sir John Perrot, Lord Deputy of Ireland, at Westminster, for High Treason: 34 Eliz. April 27, A.D. 1592," in *A Complete Collection of State Trials*, ed. T. B. Howell, 1.1315–34; quotation from 1321.

22. On "the potential shamefulness of the association of women and water," see Paster, *The Body Embarrassed*, 23–63; quotation from 47.

23. See "The *Vita Mariae Angliae Reginae* of Robert Wingfield of Brantham," ed. and trans. Diarmaid MacCulloch; quotation from 265. In "Mary Tudor, Renaissance Queen of England," Judith M. Richards cites a narrative by a Spanish merchant resident in London to the same effect (32). Furthermore, she points out that Mary's performance had a precedent in the actions of her mother, Catherine of Aragon, when she acted as regent in the absence of King Henry VIII, and (as Peter Martyr pointed out to Erasmus at the time) that Catherine was imitating her own mother, Queen Isabella of Castile (30–35). This suggests an intriguing juxtaposition of Mary's Spanish and matrilineal dynastic heritage to Elizabeth's English and patrilineal one.

24. "*Vita Mariae Angliae Reginae*," ed. and trans. MacCulloch, 293.

25. Hadrianus Junius, *Philippeis, sev, in Nuptias Divi Philippi . . . et Heroinae Mariae* (London, 1554). My thanks to Adrienne Eastwood, who alerted me to this work and provided me with references and a photocopy of the edition in the British Library (BL 807 c 21). For more on Hadrianus Junius and his significance for Tudor religious polemic and iconography, see Aston, *The*

King's Bedpost, 176–99; on Junius's epithalamium as a bid for patronage, see Chris L. Heesakkers, "The Ambassador of the Republic of Letters at the Wedding of Prince Philip of Spain and Queen Mary of England."

26. *Grafton's Chronicle*, 2.542–43. Richard Grafton's *Chronicle*, which begins with the creation of the world and ends with the accession of Elizabeth, was first printed in 1569.

27. See Winfried Schleiner, "*Divina virago*," 164–67; my thanks to Professor Schleiner for so cheerfully enduring my queries. The Dutch engraving of Elizabeth is catalogued in Strong, *Portraits of Queen Elizabeth I*, as E.32.

28. Regarded by sixteenth-century Europeans as the paragon of civilization, Europa was represented in cartographical images as fully clothed, in contrast to the seminude personifications of savage Africa and America. The partial nudity and martial demeanor of the Elizabeth figure suggest a conflation of an Amazon with a personification of America. For the female personifications of the continents and their early modern iconography, see Claire le Corbeiller, "Miss America and Her Sisters."

29. "An Advertisement Touching an Holy War," in *The Works of Francis Bacon*, ed. Spedding et al., 13.214.

30. Queen Elizabeth is also celebrated as an Amazon by the Hungarian humanist Stephen Parmenius, in *De Navigatione* (1582), a Latin poem celebrating Sir Humphrey Gilbert's projected voyage to the New World. See *The New Found Land of Stephen Parmenius*, ed. and trans. David B. Quinn and Neil M. Cheshire, p. 88, line 93. The ubiquity of Amazonian representations in Elizabethan culture can be gleaned from the valuable survey by Celeste Turner Wright, "The Amazons in Elizabethan Literature." On Amazonian representations of Queen Elizabeth, see Schleiner, "*Divina virago*"; Montrose, "'Shaping Fantasies'"; Gabriele Bernhard Jackson, "Topical Ideology"; and Marcus, *Puzzling Shakespeare*, 51–105. For a recent queering of the topic, see Kathryn Schwartz, *Tough Love*.

31. James Aske, *Elizabetha Triumphans* (1588), facsimile ed., 23–24. Aske's representation of Elizabeth's speech to the troops is consistent in tone and theme, though not in detail, with those of Sharp and others to which I have already referred. Aske has the Queen declare that "we ... Wilbe our selfe their noted *Generall*. / Ne deare at all to us shalbe our life ... But in the midst and very heart of them, / *Bellona*-like we meane as then to march" (26). Aske also includes the topos of the Queen's resemblance to her father: "Although she be by Nature weake, / Because her sex, no otherwise can be: / Yet wants she not the courage of her Sire, / Whose valour wanne this Island great renowne" (2). Seventeenth-century panegyrists of Elizabeth elaborated the details of her self-presentation into a more fully Amazonian form. According to William Camden, "The Queene, with a Kingly courage, mounted on horsebacke, and holding in her hand the trunchion of an ordinary Captaine, made a review of her Army, & campe, which was at *Tilbury*, walkes up and downe, sometimes like a Woman, and anon, with the countenance and pace of a Souldier, and with her presence and words fortifieth the courages both of the Captaines and Souldiers beyond all beliefe" (*Annales*, 3.283). Thomas Heywood, in one of his several accounts of the Queen, described her as having been "habited like an *Amazonian* Queene, Buskind and plumed, having a golden Truncheon, Gantlet, and Gorget, Arms sufficient to expresse her high and magnanimous spirit" (*The Exemplary Lives and Memorable Acts of Nine the Most Worthy Women of the World*, 211). For more on posthumous representations of Queen Elizabeth as an Amazon, see Schleiner, "*Divina virago*."

32. Thomas Heywood, *If You Know Not Me You Know Nobody*, part 2, ed. Doran, lines 2545–48 (1606 version).

33. See, respectively, Guzman de Silva to the King, 13 August 1565, trans. and printed in *CSP, Spanish*, 1.467; and Sampson's Advices from England, 26 February 1587, trans. and printed in *CSP, Spanish*, 4.17–18. ("Sampson" was the code name of Antonio de Escobar, agent in France of Don Antonio, the Portuguese pretender, who himself was living in exile at the Elizabethan court; "Sampson," however, was also in the pay of King Philip, and was here giving secret intelligence to Spain.)

34. Elizabeth was not alone among female monarchs in wishing herself a soldier. In 1562, Thomas Randolphe wrote to William Cecil from Scotland, with the following intelligence about Mary, Queen of Scots: "In all these garbullies, I assure your honour I never sawe her merrier, never dismayde, nor never thought that stomache to be in her that I fynde! She repented nothynge but when the lardes and other at Ennernes came in the mornynges from the wache, that she was not a man to knowe what lyf yt was to lye all nyghte in the feeldes, or to walke upon the cawsaye with a jacke and knapschall, a Glascowe buckeler and a broode swerde" ([Thomas] Randolphe to [William] Cecill, 18 September 1562; printed in *CSP, Scottish*, 1.651).

35. André Hurault, *A Journal of All that was Accomplished by Monsieur de Maisse, Ambassador in England from King Henri IV to Queen Elizabeth Anno Domini 1597*, trans. and ed. G. B. Harrison and R. A. Jones, 109. In future references, this work will be cited as De Maisse, *Journal*.

36. De Maisse, *Journal*, 115.

37. See Paul E. J. Hammer, *The Polarisation of Elizabethan Politics*, 242, and the citations there to Gustav Ungerer, *A Spaniard in Elizabethan England*. On the shifting fortunes of the aristocratic honor code in Tudor political culture and its critical role in the Essex revolt, see the seminal essays collected in Mervyn James, *Society, Politics and Culture*, 308–465.

38. "A discourse touching a marriage between Prince Henry of England, and a daughter of Savoy," in *The Works of Sir Walter Ralegh*, 8.246.

39. "Elizabeth's speech at the close of Parliament," 10 April 1593; printed in *PPE*, 3.28–29. (Also see Elizabeth I, *Collected Works*, 328–32.)

40. "Queen Elizabeth's speech in Parlement," 19 December 1601; printed in *PPE*, 3.278–79. Taking the occasion of her first parliament following the death of Philip II in 1598, the Queen went on to vex the ghost of her sometime "brother": "Even that potent prince the king of Spain, whose sowle I trust be nowe in heaven, that hath so manie waies assayled both my realme and me as had manie provocationes of kindnesse by my juste proceedings as by hard measure he hath returned effectes of ingratitud. It is neither my manner nor my natur to speake ille of those that ar deade, but that in this case it is not possible without some touche to the author to taxe the injurie" (279). (Also see Elizabeth I, *Collected Works*, 346–54.)

41. Sir Henry Wotton, *The State of Christendom*, 84–85. Posthumously printed in the mid-seventeenth century, the work was written during the 1590s.

42. My translation; the original reads, "Mujer de muchos, y de muchos nuera! / ¡Oh reina infame; reina no, más loba / Libidinosa y fiera!" Lope de Vega's *Á la Jornada de Inglaterra* and Luis de Góngora's *Á la Armada que el Rey Felipe II Nuestro Señor Envió Contra Inglaterra* are quoted from the texts in Cesáreo Fernandez Duro, *La Armada Invencible*, 1.237–39. Spanish literary responses to the Armada are surveyed in P. Gallagher and D. W. Cruickshank, "The Armada of 1588 Reflected in Serious and Popular Literature of the Period"; and Ron Keightley, "An Armada Veteran Celebrates the Death of Drake." Although some attacks were directed specifically against Elizabeth and Drake, on the whole it appears that the kind of generalized prejudice that Englishmen directed toward Spaniards, the Spanish reserved for the Turks.

43. See Richard Kagan, *Lucretia's Dreams*, 70–71. I am indebted to Kagan's study for my knowledge of this fascinating episode and my understanding of its context.

44. See Anne Dillon, *The Construction of Martyrdom in the English Catholic Community, 1535–1603*.

45. See Kagan, *Lucretia's Dreams*, 75–76. This was only one of several Armada dreams reported by Lucretia.

46. There is evidence of a related phenomenon in Elizabethan England: Catholic priests promoted (and perhaps also instigated) a number of cases of young maidens who experienced visions in which the truths of Roman Catholicism were affirmed and the Queen and her regime condemned; see Alexandra Walsham, "Miracles and the Counter-Reformation Mission to England," 805–6.

47. Giovanni Gritti, Venetian Ambassador in Rome, to the Doge and Senate, 19 March 1588; trans. and printed in *CSP, Venetian*, 8.345.

48. See Ludwig Freiherr von Pastor, *The History of the Popes*, 22.32.

49. Hieronimo Lippomano, Venetian Ambassador in Spain, to the Doge and Senate, 21 May 1587; trans. and printed in *CSP, Venetian*, 8.277.

50. For this and the following reference, see Henry Kamen, *Philip of Spain*, 319–20.

Part Four

1. Allen, *Admonition*, li and llvi–lvii, respectively.

2. "Letter . . . to Queen Elizabeth, Touching her Marriage with Monsieur," in *Miscellaneous Prose of Sir Philip Sidney*, ed. Duncan-Jones and van Dorsten, 47–48.

3. This perspective has been forcefully articulated in *The Reign of Elizabeth I*, ed. Guy. Although most of the contributions to this volume deal with social elites and high politics, a relevant and valuable exception is Jim Sharpe, "Social Strain and Social Dislocation, 1585–1603." On popular dissent in the period, which manifested itself both in hostile words and violent acts, I have found the following valuable: Joel Samaha, "Gleanings from Local Criminal Court Records"; Peter Clark, "Popular Protest and Disturbance in Kent, 1558–1640"; John Walter, "A 'Rising of the People'?"; Roger B. Manning, *Village Revolts*; Nick Cox, "Rumours and Risings"; Carole Levin, "'We shall never have a merry world while the Queene lyveth'"; Adam Fox, "Rumour, News and Popular Political Opinion in Elizabethan and Early Stuart England."

Chapter Twelve

1. "Sealed document which the Duke of Medina Sidonia was to deliver to the Duke of Parma only in case the latter should land in England. In any other event, the document was to be returned to His Majesty" (April 1588), trans. and printed in *CSP, Spanish*, 4.250–52; quotation from 251.

2. Quoted in Judith Richards, "Before the 'Mountaynes Mouse,'" 32. Richards concludes that "the realm was not impressively united, and was not very responsive in the face of so great a danger" (ibid.).

3. Sir Walter Ralegh, *The History of the World*, ed. C. A. Patrides, 347.

4. See Colin Martin and Geoffrey Parker, *The Spanish Armada*, 265–77. They write that "England lacked all the vital resources to resist an invasion: if ever the Armada had landed, there were neither fortifications, troops nor money enough to stop the Spaniards" (269). For an evaluation of recent research on the strategic and logistical issues, see the review article by Simon

Adams, "The Gran Armada." Adams comments that "the real strength of the Army of Flanders lay in its core of tough, able and experienced officers and NCOs of all ranks; whether they would have carried the day in an unfamiliar operation is an open question" (248).

5. Printed in the original Latin and in English translation in *Unpublished Documents Relating to the English Martyrs*, vol. 1, *1584–1603*, ed. John Hungerford Pollen, 321–28; quotation from 325. All future citations of *Unpublished Documents Relating to the English Martyrs* will be to volume 1.

6. See Geoffrey F. Nuttall, "The English Martyrs 1535–1680."

7. For a detailed study of the vexed circumstances of loyal Elizabethan Catholics and their conflicts with their militant co-religionists, see Arnold Pritchard, *Catholic Loyalism in Elizabethan England*; also see Gillian E. Brennan, "Papists and Patriotism in Elizabethan England." On the range of positions concerning both religious and political resistance that evolved among Elizabethan Catholics over the course of the reign, see Peter Holmes, *Resistance and Compromise*.

8. "Petition of Loyal Catholic Subjects to the Queen," printed in HMC, *Report on Manuscripts in Various Collections*, 3.37–43; quotation from 38.

9. Printed in Strype, *Annals of the Reformation*, 3.2.81–82.

10. Sir Thomas Smith, *De republica anglorum*, 46. Although this work was first printed posthumously in 1583, Smith wrote it during the early 1560s, when he was the Queen's ambassador to France.

11. The assize records for the home circuit during the reigns of Elizabeth and James are calendared in ten volumes edited by J. S. Cockburn. In a separate volume, he discusses in detail the operation of the assizes and the processes of indictment, prosecution, and judgment; see Cockburn, *Calendar of Assize Records*. On the terminology regarding sedition and its legal history during the period, see Samaha, "Gleanings from Local Criminal Court Records"; and Roger B. Manning, "The Origins of the Doctrine of Sedition."

12. Quotations from *CAR, Kent*, nos. 1275 and 1322; pp. 214 and 221, respectively. For some post-Armada Kent indictments of a similar tenor, see nos. 1757 and 2391, pp. 290 and 393, respectively. Also see *CAR, Sussex*, no. 1760, p. 344; *CAR, Hertfordshire*, no. 751, p. 118; *CAR, Essex*, no. 1624, p. 277.

13. Peter Clark, *English Provincial Society from the Reformation to the Revolution*, 250.

14. *CAR, Hertfordshire*, no. 1592, p. 27.

15. *CAR, Essex*, no. 2356; p. 390.

16. Allen, *Admonition*, xlix.

17. On this preoccupation of the Elizabethan political nation, see McLaren, "The Quest for a King."

18. *CAR, Essex*, no. 2245; p. 273. Also see E. G. Emmison, *Elizabethan Life*, 57. In his survey of the assize records for Elizabethan Essex, Emmison cites a petition from some of Feltwell's neighbors that he was "a very troublesome and contentious person who prosecuteth divers frivolous suits against them to their great charge and vexation."

19. In particular, I am thinking of the following passage at the opening of the first part of "An Exhortation Concerning Good Order and Obedience to Rulers and Magistrates": "Every degree of people, in their vocation, calling, and office, hath appointed to them their duty and order. Some are in high degree, some in low; some kings and princes, some inferiors and subjects; priests and laymen, masters and servants, fathers and children, husbands and wives, rich and poor; and every one have need of other. . . . Where there is no right order, there reigneth all abuse, carnal liberty, enormity, sin, and Babylonical confusion. Take away kings, princes, rulers, magistrates, judges, and such estates of God's order . . . all things shall be common; and there must follow all

mischief and utter destruction both of souls, bodies, goods, and commonwealths" (*Two Books of Homilies Appointed to be Read in Churches*, 105–6).

20. For Feere, see *CAR, Hertfordshire*, no. 751, p. 218; for Danyell, see *CAR, Kent*, no. 2589, p. 425.

21. From the official transcript of Roger Symonds's examination, quoted in Walter, "A 'Rising of the People'?" 108. Walter's monograph is the definitive study of the rising.

22. See Alexander Savine, "Bondmen under the Tudors," esp. 270–75; Diarmaid MacCulloch, "Bondmen under the Tudors," esp. 100–101.

23. See Shakespeare, *2 Henry IV*, 4.3.34–43, and 5.5.99–102.

Chapter Thirteen

1. See above, chapter five.

2. *APC*, 21.4.

3. Bernardino de Mendoza to Gabriel Zayas, London, 8 September 1578; trans. and printed in *CSP, Spanish*, 2.611. Elizabeth's mage, John Dee, may have been referring to this notorious incident when he recorded that "My carefull and faithfull endeavours was with great speede required . . . to prevent the mischiefe, which divers of her Majesties Privy Councell suspected to be intended against her Majesties person, by means of a certaine image of wax, with a great pin stuck into it about the brest of it, found in Lincolnes Inn fields" (*The Compendious Rehearsal* [1592], in John Dee, *Autobiographical Tracts*, ed. James Crossley, 21; the entry is undated).

4. Reginald Scot, *The Discoverie of Witchcraft* (1584), bk. 16, ch. 3, p. 275.

5. *APC*, 8.31.

6. The first quotation is from the Second Treasons Act of Elizabeth (1571; 13 Eliz. c. 1), excerpts reprinted in *Tudor Constitutional Documents*, ed. Tanner, 413–17; quotation from 413. The second quotation is from the "Act against seditious words and rumours uttered against the Queen's most excellent Majesty" (1581; 23 Eliz. c. 2); excerpts reprinted in *Witchcraft in England, 1558–1618*, ed. Barbara Rosen, 56–57. The latter act also condemned those who "shall . . . maliciously by any words, writing, or printing, wish, will, or desire the death or deprivation of our sovereign lady the Queen's Majesty." On the complex history of Tudor treason legislation, see John Bellamy, *The Tudor Law of Treason*, 9–82.

7. On the context of the Hacket episode in the struggle between Presbyterianism and the state church, see Patrick Collinson, *The Elizabethan Puritan Movement*, 385–431; and Alexandra Walsham, "'Frantick Hacket.'"

8. "Memorandum of the arraignment, at Newgate, of William Hacket, of Northamptonshire, for high treason" (26 July 1591); printed in HMC, *Fourteenth Report, Appendix, Part IV. The Manuscripts of Lord Kenyon*, 607.

9. Richard Cosin, *Conspiracie for Pretended Reformation* (1592), 61; quoted in Curtis Charles Breight, "Duelling Ceremonies," 55. Analogous iconoclastic practices are familiar to us from contemporary history. Compare, for example, the following dispatch filed during the 2003 U.S. invasion of Iraq: "With trepidation still strong among the Iraqis, much of the celebrating today was done by American marines, who tore down every larger-than-life image of Mr. Hussein that decorated the town. They pried one loose by tying it to the bumper of a troop carrier, and another by cutting it up with a dagger. 'Feels good,' Oscar Guerrero, a marine from San Antonio, said as he ran his blade through the canvas likeness of the Iraqi leader. 'I wish he were here in person'" (Dexter Filkins, "Muted joy as troops capture an Iraqi town," *New York Times*, late edition, 22 March 2003, p. A1).

10. See "Queen's speech at Close of Parliament, 29 March 1585," and "Part of Speaker's speech, 2 March 1587 (?)," printed in *PPE*, 2.32 and 2.332, respectively. (For the former, also see Elizabeth I, *Collected Works*, 181–83.) At the 1593 arraignment of the Brownist Henry Barrowe for seditious writing, it was charged that not only "the Papistes" but also radical Protestants were "pioneers for the King of Spaine, the one beginning at the one end, and the other at the other end; and so at the last they woulde mete at the harte of the midle" (as reported in a letter from Richard Verstegan to Father Persons, 30 April 1593; printed in *The Letters and Despatches of Richard Verstegan*, ed. Petti, 144–47; quotation from 145).

11. See Walsham, "'Frantick Hacket,'" 38 ff.

12. "Memorandum," in *The Manuscripts of Lord Kenyon*, 609.

13. See above, chapter five.

14. William Waad to Sir Robert Cecil, 3 October 1601; printed in HMC, *Salisbury*, 11.404.

15. Examination of Thomas Harrison by Lancelot Brown and W. Ward [Waad/Wade?], 4 October 1601; printed in HMC, *Salisbury*, 11.406. I owe my awareness of this incident to Helen Hackett, who discusses it in *Virgin Mother, Maiden Queen*, 211–13.

16. Roy Strong notes that "in 1587 Hilliard was rewarded with the lease of certain lands 'in respect of his paynes lately employed in the engraving of the greate seale of Englande'" (*Portraits of Queen Elizabeth I*, 148).

17. Strong, *Gloriana*, 110.

18. For evidence of the role of William Waad (or Wade) in interrogations by torture during the late 1580s and 1590s, see James Heath, *Torture and English Law*, passim.

19. See Nicholas Canny, "Dominant Minorities," 59 and n. 41. For a broader discussion of the cultural and ideological complexities of early modern Ireland, see Nicholas Canny, "Identity Formation in Ireland."

20. See "Sheane McCongawney's Relation . . . delivered to the Lord Deputy and Council the 13th of August, anno '93"; excerpts printed in *Calendar of the Carew Manuscripts*, 3.76.

21. Lord Deputy Fytzwilliam to Lord Burghley, 9 April 1589; printed in *Calendar of State Papers Relating to Ireland*, 142–43. O'Rourke is also discussed in Highley, "The Royal Image in Elizabethan Ireland."

22. See "The Deposition of Sir Richard Bingham towchinge the 32 Articles against O'Rourk, latlie sent over into England"; printed in *The Egerton Papers*, ed. J. Payne Collier, 144–57; quotation from 147–48 (I have expanded contractions). Also see Sir Richard Bingham to Lord Burghley, 6 April 1589; redacted in *Calendar of State Papers Relating to Ireland*, 141.

23. See above, chapter six.

24. For a detailed discussion of the affair in its legal and political contexts, see Hiram Morgan, "Extradition and Treason-Trial of a Gaelic Lord."

25. John Stow, *The Annales of England* (London, 1605), 1267–9; quoted in Morgan, "Extradition and Treason-Trial of a Gaelic Lord," 285.

26. See the entry on Sir Brian-Na-Murtha O'Rourke in the *Dictionary of National Biography*, 14: 1158–60; quotation from 1159.

27. Hiram Morgan suggests this in "Extradition and Treason-Trial of a Gaelic Lord," and argues it more fully in "The fall of Sir John Perrot." The official record of Perrot's trial for high treason includes another version of O'Rourke's iconoclastic transgression. According to this account, he "took down a Picture, and did write Elizabeth thereupon; and using the same in most contemptuous and despiteful manner, tied the same to a horse-tail, and he with others dragged it in the dirt, and hacked it with gallow-glass axes, signifying how they would have

used her majesty if they had her in their power" ("The Trial of Sir John Perrot," in *A Complete Collection of State Trials*, ed. Howell, 1.1324).

28. See "Selections from the Stonyhurst Manuscripts," in John Hungerford Pollen, *Acts of English Martyrs Hitherto Unpublished*, 329–30.

Chapter Fourteen

1. Thomas Wilson, *The State of England Anno Dom. 1600*, 37–38.

2. For a comprehensive overview, see Bellamy, *The Tudor Law of Treason*.

3. See, respectively, Michel Foucault, *Discipline and Punish*, 47; Bossy, *Christianity in the West 1400–1700*, 158.

4. See two seminal essays by Peter Lake and Michael Questier: "Agency, Appropriation and Rhetoric under the Gallows," and "Puritans, Papists, and the 'Public Sphere' in Early Modern England." Much of this material is brought together in revised form in "Protestants, Puritans, and Papists," section 2 of Peter Lake with Michael Questier, *The Antichrist's Lewd Hat*; see esp. 187–280. My own perspective on the ideological struggle between the Elizabethan Protestant state and its dissident Catholic subjects is indebted to the work of Lake and Questier.

5. Thomas Alfield, *A True Reporte of the Death & Martyrdome of M. Campion, & M. Sherwin, and M. Bryan* (1582), facsimile ed., unpaginated. Some 189 Catholics were executed for treason during the reign of Elizabeth, of whom 112 were missionary priests trained in the continental seminaries. Of the 63 lay Catholics executed, three were women. For the demographics of the Elizabethan Catholic martyrs, see Dillon, *The Construction of Martyrdom in the English Catholic Community*, 3–4, n. 9. By comparison, approximately 290 Protestants were burned as heretics during the Marian reign. Of the relatively few who were clerics, several were prelates; the vast majority of victims, however, were laypeople and primarily from artisanal groups, with women and youths conspicuous among them. For the demographics of the Protestant martyrs, see A. G. Dickens, *The English Reformation*, 2nd ed., 293–301.

6. Allen's work was anonymously published as *A brief historie of the glorious martyrdom of XII. reverend priests . . .* (1582); quotation from C4v.

7. "Letter . . . to Queen Elizabeth, Touching her Marriage With Monsieur," in *Miscellaneous Prose of Sir Philip Sidney*, ed. Duncan-Jones and van Dorsten, 47–48.

8. As Allen obliquely put it, no "annoiaunce or alteration" was intended as a consequence of the invasion, "savinge so muche as the estates of the realme shall agree upon with his holiness, and Majestie, for the restitution and preservation of the Catholike religion, and necessary punishment of the pretended. . . . There shall be as greate care had of every Catholike & penitent person, as possibly can be" (*Admonition*, l).

9. Laurence Humphrey, dedicatory epistle to *Jesuitismi pars prima* (London, 1582), translated in Arthur F. Marotti, "Southwell's Remains," 49. For a detailed analysis of the ideological import and resonance of Campion's case, see Lake and Questier, "Puritans, Papists, and the 'Public Sphere' in Early Modern England."

10. "Certain Observations Made upon a Libel Published this Present Year, 1592," in Bacon, *Works*, ed. Spedding et al., 8.146–208; quotation from 178. The "libel" in question was Richard Verstegan's tract *A declaration of the true causes of the great troubles, presupposed to be intended against the realme of England* (1592). In his postmortem appraisal of Elizabeth, *In felicem memoriam Elizabethae*, Bacon embarks upon a lengthy digression in defense of the severity of Elizabethan policies toward Catholics.

11. Among those whom Bacon was personally authorized to torture were not only a number of missionary priests but also Bartholomew Steer and his co-conspirators in the Oxfordshire Rising of 1596: See Heath, *Torture and English Law*, 224–25 and passim. In "Subjected Bodies, Science, and the State," Page duBois makes a convincing case for the interconnections between Bacon's roles as torturer, royal counselor, and natural philosopher. In making a related point, Elizabeth Hanson notes that Bacon was "apparently the only English lawyer who actually asserted that torture was permissible in English juridical practice" (*Discovering the Subject in Renaissance England*, 25–26).

12. John Baxter, *A Toile for Two-legged Foxes* (London, 1600), 109–10; as quoted in Julian Yates, "Parasitic Geographies," 65.

13. The classic study of this antipapist imaginary is Carol Weiner, "The Beleaguered Isle." In her recent study of seventeenth-century English writings negatively linking Catholicism and disorderly women, Frances Dolan suggests that "perhaps because of their greater numbers but less visible presence in England, their resemblance to their antagonists, and their problematic status as 'natives,' Catholics provoked more prolific and intemperate visual and verbal representation and more elaborate and sustained legal regulation than any other group" (*Whores of Babylon*, 8). Interesting in the light of this observation is one of the "Questions propounded to don Pedro de Valdes," a Spanish captain captured and interrogated following the demise of the Armada: "How would they have known the catholic from the protestant?" he was asked (Strype, *Annals of the reformation*, 3.2.551).

14. Harington, *A Tract on the Succession to the Crown*, ed. Clements R. Markham, 104.

15. Elizabeth Hanson makes the point that "the structure of interrogatory torture posits a victim in possession of hidden information that the torturer must struggle to uncover, and therefore produces a narrative of discovery, a movement from unknowing, through labor, to an encounter with truth.... The truth at issue in torture is objective primarily because it is *thought of* as an object, something that can be covered and therefore dis-covered" (*Discovering the Subject in Renaissance England*, 25, 26).

16. See Jonathan Sawday, *The Body Emblazoned*.

17. Shakespeare, *The Tragedy of King Lear*, 4.5.252. In the Duke of Cornwall's staged blinding of Gloucester, in the rebellion of Cornwall's nameless servant against his master's monstrous cruelty, and in Gloucester's own defiance of his torturer, the early modern theatre presents perhaps its most excruciating and compelling affirmation of the moral imperative to resist tyranny and to bear witness against atrocities.

18. Heath, *Torture and English Law*, 93–147, provides a detailed account of torture as it was regulated and practiced by the Elizabethan state; an appendix (206–28) prints more than fifty extant torture warrants issued by the Elizabethan Privy Council between 1559 and 1601.

19. Sir Anthony Selden to Anthony Bacon, 2 March 1593/4; printed in Thomas Birch, *Memoirs of the reign of Queen Elizabeth*, 1.160.

20. Robert Southwell, *An Humble Supplication to Her Majestie*, ed. R. C. Bald, 44–45; italics in original. Although not printed until 1600, the text circulated earlier in manuscript. Topcliffe acquired a manuscript copy in 1594, which he loaned to Francis Bacon; according to Bald (xii), this probably occurred when Topcliffe and Bacon were working together on the interrogation of Henry Walpole, another Jesuit who had been imprisoned with Southwell.

21. The letter is subscribed "Here at Westminster with my charge and ghostly father, this Monday the 22nd of June, 1592," and signed "Your majesty's faithful servant, Ryc. Topclyff"; printed in Strype, *Annals of the reformation*, 4.185–86. (Also see Heath, *Torture and English Law*,

129–30.) According to a dispatch written by Richard Verstegan to Father Persons and dated 3 August 1592, "Because the often exercise of the rack in the Tower was so odious, and somuch spoken of of the people, Topclif hath aucthoritie to torment priestes in his owne house, in such sorte as he shall thinck good; whose inhuman cruelty is so great, as he will not spare to extend any torture whatsoever. Our Lord of His infynite mercy strengthen and comforte this good father and all such as shall fall into his mercilesse handes." This letter, which discusses Topcliffe's apprehension and torture of Robert Southwell, is printed in *The Letters and Despatches of Richard Verstegan*, ed. Petti, 57–60; quotation from 58.

22. In a letter to Roger Baynes at Rome, dated 13 May 1595, Richard Verstegan noted that "Topcliffe has been put in the Marshalsea prison by order of the Council for abusing his authority. It is possible that Topcliffe has been imprisoned in order to demonstrate the innocence of the Council, as if he had exercised such great cruelty on his own account without authority" (trans. from the Italian, in *The Letters and Despatches of Richard Verstegan*, ed. Petti, 232). In one of the letters that he wrote to the Queen from prison, Topcliffe boasted that "I have helped [something missing???] more trators then all noble menn and gentilmenn about your Coorte, your Cownsellers excepted.... And now at Easter, in steade of a Communyon, many an *Aleluya* wilbe sunge of preests and trators in presons and in ladyes' cloasettes for Topclyffe's fawle, and in farder kingdomes also" (Harleian MSS 9889, fol. 185; quoted in *Letters and Despatches of Richard Verstegan*, ed. Petti, 232, n. 1). In a subsequent letter to Baynes, dated 30 June 1595, Verstegan suggested that the regime, under criticism for the brutality of its methods, was using Topcliffe as a scapegoat: "Topclif is released oute of prison, but his comission is taken from him. They endeavour to perswade the world that thease hard courses were against the Queene's mynde. This course is thought to proceede from feare and cowardize—they may perhapps think to profitt more by this then by rigour" (242).

23. For the quotation, see "A brief discourse of the condemnation and execution of Mr. Robert Southwell," manuscript account by Henry Garnett, printed in *Records of the English Province of the Society of Jesus*, 1.375. For an introduction to the complex early modern symbolism of this organ, see Scott Manning Stevens, "Sacred Heart and Secular Brain.".

24. Printed in *Unpublished Documents Relating to the English Martyrs*, ed. Pollen, 1.179.

25. Heath, *Torture and English Law*, 130.

26. U.S. Department of Justice, Office of Legal Counsel, "Memorandum for Alberto R. Gonzalez, Counsel to the President, Re: Standards of Conduct for Interrogation under 18 U.S.C. §§2340–2340A," dated August 1, 2002 and signed by Jay S. Bybee, Assistant Attorney General; quotation from p. 1. Document accessed online through the Web site of the *Washington Post*, www.washingtonpost.com.

27. "A Declaration of the favorable dealing of Her Majesty's Commissioners appointed for the examination of certain traitors and of tortures unjustly reported to be done upon them for matters of religion," reprinted in Robert N. Kingdon's edition of William Cecil's *The execution of justice in England* and William Allen's *A true, sincere and modest defense of the English Catholics*, 45–50; quotation from 49. Kingdon attributes the tract to Cecil. Elizabeth Hanson notes that in *De republica anglorum* (1583), Sir Thomas Smith claims that torture is not used in England, while Sir Edward Coke, writing in the 1620s, asserts that it is without justification and should not be used in England. Hanson concludes that "although there is evidence that torture may have been used occasionally in England from the reign of Richard III, it was during Elizabeth's reign that interrogatory torture became increasingly a recognized, although unusual, part of the prosecution of important cases of felony.... Torture in England remained an *ad hoc* practice

remarkable for its discontinuity from the legal discourse to which it presumably should have belonged" (*Discovering the Subject in Renaissance England*, 28–29).

28. Allen, *Brief historie of the glorious martyrdom of XII. reverend priests*, D7v.

29. According to John Stow's *Annales*, "Thomas Pormort was convicted of two several high treasons, the one for being a Seminary priest, and the other for reconciling John Barwys, haberdasher" (quoted in Richard Challoner, *Memoirs of Missionary Priests*, ed. John Hungerford Pollen, 186). According to an anonymous manuscript catalogue of martyrs (ca. 1594), Pormort "through extremitie of torture got a rupture" (printed in *Unpublished Documents Relating to the English Martyrs*, ed. Pollen, 292).

30. The letter is undated but is endorsed 1592 by its recipient, Father Persons; it is printed in *Letters and Despatches of Richard Verstegan*, ed. Petti, 97–98. (It is also printed in *Unpublished Documents relating to the English Martyrs*, ed. Pollen, 210, with a phrase censored.) Petti prints the letter from Verstegan's holograph, which is now damaged and partially indecipherable; words in brackets are supplied by the editor from a seventeenth-century transcription. The clandestine priest used the alias Whitgift, and a marginal note in Verstegan's dispatch indicates that he was a godson of Archbishop Whitgift. John Whitgift, then Archbishop of Canterbury and the only churchman appointed to the Elizabethan Privy Council, was an unremitting opponent of Puritan reformers, as well as of Catholics. Two of the three remaining items recorded in Verstegan's dispatch attack Whitgift, including the claim that "Topclif offred (this priest) his liberty yf he would sa[y] that he was a bastard of the Archbishope's of Canterbury [and] that the Archbishop had maintained him beyonde the seas" (97).

31. For Playfere, see *CAR, Essex*, no. 1112, p. 195; for Hawkins, see the report from Thomas Scot to the Earl of Leicester, March 1581, in *CSP, Domestic*, 2.12.

32. See Allen, *Admonition*, xix–xxi. Rishton's expanded edition of Sander's book was translated into French, Spanish, Italian, and German, and went into fifteen editions, becoming "one of the most popular books in sixteenth century Europe" (Dillon, *The Construction of Martyrdom in the English Catholic Community*, 81).

33. For example, in *A Defence of the Honour of Marie Quene of Scotlande* (Rheims? 1569), John Leslie, Bishop of Ross, defended the virtue of his recently deposed queen against charges of adultery and complicity in the murder of her husband, praised her motherly care for her people, and argued that she be restored to the Scottish throne and recognized by Elizabeth as heir to the English throne; and in his *Theatrum crudelitatum haereticorum nostri temporis* (Antwerp, 1587), Richard Verstegan placed the recently executed Mary as the final and culminating figure in his Catholic martyrology. For Mary's divided reputation in the later sixteenth century, see the invaluable study by James Emerson Phillips, *Images of a Queen*; and, for an interesting survey of the intertwined and changing reputations of Mary and Elizabeth from their own time until the Victorian era, see Jayne Elizabeth Lewis, *Mary Queen of Scots*.

34. For the former, see "Peter Wentworth's examination by committee, 8 February [1576]," in *PPE*, 1.438; for the latter, see Robert Carvell to Sir Francis Walsingham, 6 March 1587, printed in *CSP, Scottish*, 9.330–31 (as quoted in Phillips, *Images of a Queen*, 129).

35. See *TRP*, 3.13–17; quotation from 15.

36. James Younge relates the capture, arraignment, and martyrdom of Pormort in the postscript to a letter, dated from Douai, 9 February 1595, to Father Persons in Spain. This is printed (with some passages censored) in Pollen, *Acts of English Martyrs Hitherto Unpublished*, 118–20; excerpts are also printed in *Unpublished Documents Relating to the English Martyrs*, ed. Pollen, 1.209, from which I quote here.

37. For this quotation and the previous one from Younge, see Pollen, *Acts of English Martyrs Hitherto Unpublished*, 120 and 119, respectively.

38. In "'Last Dying Speeches,'" J. A. Sharpe studies the topos of "making a good end" in seventeenth-century accounts of public executions for felony. In narrating the execution of the Thane of Cawdor, Shakespeare's Malcolm presents a paradigm case of this Foucauldian operation: "Very frankly he confessed his treasons, / Implored your highness' pardon, and set forth / A deep repentance. Nothing in his life / Became him like the leaving it" (*Macbeth*, 1.4.5–8). Shakespeare's dramatic strategy is homiletic, although ironically so: Macbeth has inherited the thane's taint with his title, but this regicidal usurper will not be so easily reassimilated into the body politic.

39. Allen, *Brief historie of the glorious martyrdom of XII. reverend priests*, B6r.

40. From an anonymous contemporary manuscript account, printed in *Unpublished Documents Relating to the English Martyrs*, ed. Pollen, 182–86; quotation from 186.

41. Foxe, *Acts and Monuments*, 5.611; I owe this reference to Dillon, *The Construction of Martyrdom in the English Catholic Community, 1535–1603*, 3.

42. For the official version of these events, see J. Partridge, *The End and Confession of John Felton* (1570), rpt. in *A Complete Collection of State Trials*, ed. T. B. Howell, 1.1085–88; and, for a dissenting perspective, see the narrative by Felton's daughter, Frances Salisbury, printed in Pollen, *Acts of English Martyrs Hitherto Unpublished*, 209–12. According to the latter account, on the gallows Felton bequeathed to the Queen the diamond ring that he wore.

43. See the account by James Younge, printed in Pollen, *Acts of English Martyrs Hitherto Unpublished*, 120. Pormort's quartering in Paul's Churchyard is also reported in the manuscript "Catalogue of Martyrs from 1588–1594," printed in *Unpublished Documents Relating to the English Martyrs*, ed. Pollen, 292.

44. For Gunter, see the manuscript "Catalogue of Martyrs from 1588–1594," printed in *Unpublished Documents Relating to the English Martyrs*, ed. Pollen, 289; for Hartley, see Peter Penkevel, "Relation of the sufferings in England from 1584–1591," printed in Pollen, *Acts of English Martyrs Hitherto Unpublished*, 288.

45. Anne Dillon, *The Construction of Martyrdom in the English Catholic Community, 1535–1603*, 243–76, provides a detailed analysis of the images and descriptions in Verstegan's *Theatrum crudelitatum* and a discussion of the work's importance in internationalizing the English Catholic cause and enlisting support for the Armada. Also see Chistopher Highley, "Richard Verstegan's Book of Martyrs." On the conjunction of antipapistry and antitheatricalism in Protestant polemic, see Lake with Questier, *The Antichrist's Lewd Hat*, 447–54.

46. Lake and Questier make the salutary point that these executions staged neither an unequivocal triumph of state hegemony nor a strictly binary ideological struggle but rather were "sites for a variety of ideological and emotional struggles, waged between a number of ideological fragments or factions, both catholic and protestant, clerical and lay"; the result, they conclude, "was an inherently unstable event, a species of dialogue, a partly scripted, partly extemporized series of exchanges between catholic victim, the secular and clerical representatives of protestant authority . . . and the crowd" (*The Antichrist's Lewd Hat*, 269, 280).

47. Manuscript account, endorsed by Persons as "Relation of Martyrs, by Mr. James Younge, Priest. Written from Douay, February, 1595"; printed in Pollen, *Acts of English Martyrs Hitherto Unpublished*, 98–117; quotation from 108. Younge claimed to be an eyewitness in close physical proximity to these events.

48. See Pollen, *Acts of English Martyrs Hitherto Unpublished*, 110; for additional accounts of martyrs defying Topcliffe at their deaths, see 317 and 322.

49. "Leake's Relation of the Martyrdom of Father Southwell," printed in *Unpublished Documents Relating to the English Martyrs*, ed. Pollen, 333–37; quotation from 336.

50. For example, the missionary priest Edmund Gennings, who was executed immediately following Swithin Wells, "being bade to confess his treason and so doubtless the Queen would pardon him, answered, 'I know not ever to have offended her etc. If to say mass be treason, I confess to have done it and glory in it etc.' At which Topcliffe enraged, giving him leave to say no more, and scarce to recite the Pater noster, made him be turned off the ladder, and the rope immediately cut. The martyr stood on his feet, then the hangman tripping up his heels, cut off his members and disbowelled him" (anonymous draft of the "Life and Death of Edmund Genings," 1603; printed in *Unpublished Documents Relating to the English Martyrs*, ed. Pollen, 207). Younge's purportedly eyewitness account substantially corroborates this later one (see Pollen, *Acts of English Martyrs Hitherto Unpublished*, 109).

51. See David Starkey, "Intimacy and Innovation," 83–84; also see Starkey's earlier, more detailed study, "Representation through Intimacy."

52. Starkey, "Representation through Intimacy," 188; the quoted phrase is from Plowden's *Reports*.

53. Starkey, "Representation through Intimacy," 207.

54. Wright, "A Change in Direction," 172. The information in this paragraph derives from Wright's study, to which I am indebted for my understanding of the special character and organization of the Privy Chamber under Queen Elizabeth.

55. For example, according to Paul E. J. Hammer, one factor in the undoing of the Earl of Essex was that "unlike Leicester and now Robert Cecil, Essex failed to create a network of effective support among the women of the privy chamber" ("'Absolute and Sovereign Mistress of her Grace'?" 49). In *Of Chastity and Power*, Philippa Berry claims with some justice that "the noblewoman or lady-in-waiting has characteristically been elided from contemporary critical views of the Elizabethan court" (79); her avowedly "feminist reading" (7) of Elizabethan court culture argues that "during the last years of the reign this hidden feminine dimension of Elizabethan courtliness received increasing attention in contemporary literature, with Elizabeth frequently represented as another Diana surrounded by her nymphs" (82).

56. This is the characterization of its scenario by D. C. Peck, who transcribes and edits the manuscript in "'News from Heaven and Hell': A Defamatory Narrative of the Earl of Leicester." The title is not original but is bestowed by Peck and intended to reflect the tract's parody of the newsletter genre. All quotations are from this edition; the present quotation from 142. Future citations will be included within the text. For a detailed study of the tradition of written defamations of Leicester, see the Introduction and editorial apparatus of *Leicester's Commonwealth*, ed. D. C. Peck. *Leicester's Commonwealth* (1584), the magnum opus of this genre, was the work of English Catholic expatriates. Satirical references to the Pope and purgatory suggest that "News from Heaven and Hell" was not of Catholic provenance, but it was certainly the work of one of Leicester's foes within the world of the Elizabethan court.

57. The passage reads like a grotesque variation on the charges of sexual depravity against Elizabeth and Leicester that were made in print earlier in the same year by Cardinal Allen (see *Admonition*, xviii–xxii). Furthermore, the two occurrences, in close proximity, of the phrase "gaping gulf"—the first referring to Leicester's greed (156), the second to his infernal companion's lust (157)—seem calculated to recall Stubbs's incendiary 1579 pamphlet against the Queen's French marriage, in which Stubbs clearly implies that Elizabeth's pursuit of her own desires imperils the

commonwealth and the gospel. The Stubbs allusion in "gaping gulf" is also noted in Brownlow, "Performance and Reality at the Court of Elizabeth I," 19, n. 36.

58. "Journey through England and Scotland made by Lupold von Wedel in the years 1584 and 1585," quotations from 265 and 263, respectively.

59. For an important analysis of the changing pattern of royal favor over the last half of the reign, see Hammer, "'Absolute and Sovereign Mistress of her Grace'?"

60. Harington, *A Tract on the Succession to the Crown*, ed. Markham, 39–41. The anonymous manuscript is dated December 1602; Harington's authorship is undisputed. It appears to have circulated in manuscript at the time of composition but remained unprinted until the nineteenth century.

61. For an acute analysis of Harington's use of writing as a means of self-promotion and pursuit of office, see two studies by Jason Scott-Warren: *Sir John Harington and the Book as Gift*, and "Harington's Gossip." As Scott-Warren demonstrates in detail, Harington's Elizabethan writings are characterized by the complex relationship between his assiduous courtship of royal patronage and his critical attitude toward the Queen's policies and her style of rule. In the context of the present chapter, it is also worthy of note that Harington's *Tract on the Succession to the Crown* contains a lengthy and sharply critical analysis of the Queen's increasingly harsh treatment of Catholics: See esp. 103–4.

62. This alleged favor is equivalent to the royal garter received by Anjou, which he swore never to part with as long as he lived: See "The Duke of Anjou to the Queen" (1581?), redacted in HMC, *Salisbury*, 2.478.

63. "Richard Topclyffe to Sir Robert Cecil," 14 December 1601; printed in HMC, *Salisbury*, 11.519–20. In his reply of 2 January 1601/02, Cecil writes "I have also delivered to her Majesty your letter, who hath commanded me to give you thanks for your great care and diligence . . . she is contented . . . that you shall have a warrant sent you for down for this fellow's apprehension" (HMC, *Salisbury*, 12.2–3).

64. As previously mentioned, Topcliffe was briefly imprisoned in 1595 and again in 1596 at the behest of the Privy Council, in the first instance for maligning some of the privy councillors. From prison, he wrote to the Queen to protest his treatment: "By this disgrace . . . the freshe deade boanes of Father Southwell at Tyburne . . . will daunce for joye" (BL, Harley MS 9889; as quoted by William Richardson in his article on Topcliffe in the *Oxford Dictionary of National Biography*). Topcliffe's friction with the Council is also discussed in the entry on him in *The History of Parliament*, 3.513–15.

65. For floor plans and a detailed discussion of "the inward chambers" of Tudor royal palaces, with particular attention to Whitehall during the reign of Henry VIII, see Simon Thurley, *The Royal Palaces of Tudor England*, 135–43. Thurley explains that "the inward chambers from the door of the privy chamber onwards, fell under the control of the King's Privy Chamber, the privy chamber being not only a room but the organization which populated and governed the inward rooms. The inward chambers were divided into an outer and an inner sanctum for the King" (135). The privy chamber itself, where Holbein's wall painting was located, was the most "public" of these privy spaces, beyond which lay the royal bedchamber, stool-room, and other "secret lodgings," including the king's closet, secret wardrobe, and secret jewel-house. Holbein's wall painting of Henry VIII is also invoked by Carole Levin in her brief discussion of Pormort's accusations against Topcliffe: See Levin, *The Heart and Stomach of a King*, 141–42.

66. See above, chapter six.

67. Cecil, *The execution of justice in England*, ed. Kingdon, 39.

68. Dillon, *The Construction of Martyrdom in the English Catholic Community*, 109.

69. "Catalogue of Martyrs from 1588–1594," printed in *Unpublished Documents Relating to the English Martyrs*, ed. Pollen, 291.

70. Walsham, "Miracles and the Counter Reformation Mission to England," 781. Also see Dillon, *The Construction of Martyrdom in the English Catholic Community*, esp. 72–113; and Marotti, "Southwell's Remains: Catholicism and Anti-Catholicism in Early Modern England."

71. Allen, *Brief historie of the glorious martyrdom of XII. reverend priests*, C7v.

72. "A brief relation of the life and death of Mr Edmund Jennnings priest, martyred 10 Dec. 1591 in London," printed in *Unpublished Documents Relating to the English Martyrs*, ed. Pollen, 207. This appears to have been an early draft of a pamphlet published on the continent in 1614.

73. Allen, *Brief historie of the glorious martyrdom of XII. reverend priests*, C7v.

74. Verses appended to Alfield, *A True Reporte of the Death & Martyrdome of M. Campion, & M. Sherwin, & M. Bryan*. These verses begin with the celebrated line, "Why do I use my paper inke, and penne," subsequently set to music by William Byrd.

Part Five

1. Printed in HMC, *Salisbury*, 2.239–45; quotation from 245. Burghley dated the memorandum "Marche 1578," which in new style would be 1579.

2. "Queen's reply to petition to marry, 10 February [1559]"; printed in *PPE*, 1.45. (Also see Elizabeth I, *Collected Works*, 56–60.)

3. "A Letter Written by Sir Philip Sidney to Queen Elizabeth, Touching Her Marriage with Monsieur," in *Miscellaneous Prose of Sir Philip Sidney*, ed. Duncan-Jones and Van Dorsten, 46–57; quotations from 51 and 53.

4. Harington, *A Tract on the Succession to the Crown*, ed. Markham, 104.

5. See "The Beginning of the History of Great Britain," in *The Works of Francis Bacon*, ed. Spedding et al., 11.409.

6. Godfrey Goodman, *The Court of King James the First*, ed. John S. Brewer, 1.97.

7. For a related study with very different emphases, see Frye, *Elizabeth I*, 97–147, which focuses on Spenser's poetry and Essex's rebellion.

Chapter Fifteen

1. Cockson also engraved an equestrian portrait of Charles Blount, Earl of Devonshire, which cannot be dated before 1603. All of these are catalogued in vol. 1 of Arthur M. Hind, *Engraving in England in the Sixteenth and Seventeenth Centuries*, 192, 243–46, 240–50, and reproduced as plates 109, 125–27.

2. 30 August 1600; printed in *APC*, 30.619–20.

3. Letter "To my Lord of Essex, from Mr. Bacon," 4 October 1596; printed in *The Works of Francis Bacon*, ed. Spedding et al., 9.40–45; quotation from 41. See Richard C. McCoy, *The Rites of Knighthood*, 79–102, where the equestrian prints of Essex are put into the context of his political career.

4. "A Letter of the Authors expounding his whole intention in the course of this work: which for that it giveth great light to the Reader, for the better understanding is hereunto annexed," dated 23 January 1589 and addressed to "the Right noble, and Valorous, Sir Walter Raleigh," in

The Faerie Queene, ed. A. C. Hamilton, 714–18; quotation from 716. All references are to this edition.

5. Spenser structures the proem to book III of *The Faerie Queene* as a *paragone* of poetry and painting, his argument being that the poet is superior to the painter in rendering a portrait of the Queen, although even he must fall short of her perfections. On Spenser's poetic resourcefulness in representing the Queen "in mirrours more then one" (3.Proem.5), see my essays, "The Elizabethan Subject and the Spenserian Text" and "Spenser and the Elizabethan Political Imaginary." On the "traditions of the *descriptio personarum* and the *paragone* of the literary and the painted" and their centrality to the representation of feminine beauty in Renaissance portraiture, see Elizabeth Cropper, "The Beauty of Woman"; quotation from 181.

6. The draft for the proclamation is printed in *TRP*, 2.240–41; quotation from 240.

7. An undated minute of 1596, printed in *APC*, 26.69.

8. The oxymoron is Spenser's, and is used three times in *The Faerie Queene*: once in direct address to the Queen (1.Proem.4); and twice in reference to allegorical personifications of the Queen—as Una (1.6.2), and as Belphoebe (4.8.17).

9. "Hymne III, To the Spring," in *The Poems of Sir John Davies*, ed. Robert Krueger, 72. Camden, *Remains concerning Britain*, ed. Dunn, remarks on *Semper eadem* as one of Queen Elizabeth's most commonly used "heroical devises" (182).

10. Originally printed in 1602 in the miscellany, *A Poetical Rhapsody*; it appears there as the final poem in the book, with a heading indicating that it was sung on May Day 1600 "before her sacred Majestie at a shew on horsebacke, wherewith the right Honorable the Earle of Cumberland presented her Highnesse." I quote it from Wilson, *England's Eliza*, 317–18.

11. The picture is catalogued in Roy Strong, with V. J. Murrell, *Artists of the Tudor Court*, 134–35. Strong dates the picture ca. 1590, and suggests that it may have been made to commemorate Cumberland's succession to the post of Champion at the 1590 Accession Day tilts, when Sir Henry Lee retired.

12. Nicholas Hilliard, *A Treatise concerning the Arte of Limning*, ed. R. K. R. Thornton and T. G. S. Cain, 63, 65; for the sake of clarity, I quote from the editors' modernized and reconstructed text, which is printed with their transcription of the manuscript on facing pages. The treatise is apparently unfinished, and appears to have been drafted ca. 1600. Future citations will be included within the text. On Tudor miniatures, the techniques of limning, and Elizabeth I and her limners, see Strong with Murrell, *Artists of the Tudor Court*, 9–27, 117–32; and, for a suggestive exploration of the resonances between Elizabethan miniatures and sonnets, see Patricia Fumerton, *Cultural Aesthetics*, 67–110.

13. At the opening of the extant manuscript, Hilliard writes as follows: "I wish it were so that none should meddle with limning but gentlemen alone, for that it is a kind of gentle painting, of less subjection than any other.... Here is a kind of true gentility, when God calleth: and doubtless though gentlemen be the meetest for this gentle calling or practice, yet not all; but natural aptness is to be chosen and preferred, for not every gentleman is so gentle spirited as some others are" (Hilliard, *A Treatise concerning the Arte of Limning*, 63, 65). One of the most remarkable features of Hilliard's work is its relatively lengthy opening disquisition on limning in relationship to issues of rank, status, and labor, which aligns this otherwise technical treatise with the genre of the courtesy book. From this perspective, Hilliard's *Arte of Limning* is analogous to Puttenham's *Arte of English Poesie*.

14. On the "mask of youth," see the following studies by Roy Strong: *Portraits of Queen Elizabeth I*, 94–97; *The Cult of Elizabeth*, 46–54; *Gloriana*, 146–51; and, with Murrell, *Artists of the*

Tudor Court, 126–32. The Hilliard miniature in the jeweled locket is catalogued as M.21 in Strong, *Portraits of Queen Elizabeth I*, and is fully described in Strong with Murrell, *Artists of the Tudor Court*, 128. Although primarily associated with miniatures, the "mask of youth" is also evident in such large-scale oil paintings as the "Procession" picture (fig. 31) and the "Hardwick" portrait, both dating from around the turn of the century, as well as in the "Rainbow" portrait (fig. 25). These paintings are catalogued as P.101, P.95, and P.100, respectively, in Strong, *Portraits of Queen Elizabeth I*.

15. The commonly invoked terms in which I have described Hilliard's style have been challenged in a stimulating essay by Gloria Kury, "'Glancing Surfaces.'" Kury makes the salutary point that "the terms of description—flat, decorative, line, colour—though they seem neutral and fair, actually serve to activate norms of picturing derived from an Italian Renaissance paradigm of representation. Generally speaking a Tudor picture is being judged against an Italian exemplar of the fifteenth or sixteenth century whenever it is described.... Flatness/depth: what allows difference to emerge and be judged, the singular norm implicit in the coupling, is a conception of picturing that denies significance to the physical means producing shape or likeness, while giving precedence to an illusion of three-dimensional space" (395). I take her point; however, I am not working within the normative disciplinary traditions of art history, and my usage is intended to be merely descriptive and not evaluative.

16. The "Rainbow" portrait has sometimes been attributed either to Gheeraerts or to Oliver. Should one of these attributions ever be substantiated, we would be forced to conclude that the painter was instructed to abandon his own style in order to conform to the alien style of Hilliard, and to the clear preferences of the Queen.

17. There is an illustrated, descriptive catalogue of miniatures and drawings by Oliver in Strong with Murrell, *Artists of the Tudor Court*, 97–116; and a profusely illustrated catalogue of portraits signed by or attributed to Gheeraerts the Younger in Strong, *The English Icon*, 269–304. On Oliver and the Queen, see Strong with Murrell, *Artists of the Tudor Court*, 124–26, and Strong, *Gloriana*, 142–45. For a detailed description of Oliver's miniature of the Queen, see Jill Finsten, *Isaac Oliver*, 2.27–30. Both Strong and Finsten suggest that the unfinished state of the miniature may indicate that it was intended for use as a pattern, and both surmise that it may also have remained unfinished due to the dissatisfaction of the Queen. In any event, only one finished miniature is known to be derived from it, and even there the features have been softened; the same is true of the popular 1592 engraving by Crispin de Passe, which also apparently derives from Oliver's image. The several paintings of the Queen that derive her image from the "Ditchley" portrait by Gheeraerts also soften her facial features. For reproductions of these paintings, see Strong, *Gloriana*, plates 142, 143, 152.

18. These phrases come from "A Letter of the Authors expounding his whole intention in the course of this work," in *The Faerie Queene*, 714–18.

19. Clapham, *Certain Observations*, 97.

Chapter Sixteen

1. *Maxims of State*, printed in *The Works of Sir Walter Ralegh*, 8.1–34; quotation from 8.

2. On the discourse of *ragione di stato* and the Machiavellian tradition, see Skinner, *The Foundations of Modern Political Thought*, 1.248–54; Richard Tuck, *Philosophy and Government 1572–1651*; Victoria Kahn, *Machiavellian Rhetoric*. On the commingling of reason of state, mysteries of state, and Tacitism in the late sixteenth and early seventeenth centuries, see Peter Burke, "Tacitism, scepticism, and reason of state"; and on the convergence of Machiavellian discourse

with that of the *arcana imperii* in Tudor England, see Peter S. Donaldson, *Machiavelli and Mystery of State*, 1–110. On "the new secular *arcana imperii* of absolutism" in early modern England as a "political theology" with medieval and ecclesiastical roots, see "Mysteries of State: An Absolutist Concept and Its Late Mediaeval Origins," in Ernst H. Kantorowicz, *Selected Studies*, 381–98; quotation from 382. Although Kantorowicz's emphasis is on King James's articulation of his royal prerogative, this issue was also central to Queen Elizabeth's interactions with her parliamentarians.

3. Sir John Hayward, *Annals of the First Four Years of the Reign of Queen Elizabeth*, ed. John Bruce, 15. Hayward's account of Elizabeth's coronation entry ultimately derives from Mulcaster's 1559 account, which was reprinted in 1604. In the quoted passage, Hayward is plagiarizing from Sidney's *Arcadia*: concerning arrangements for the trial of Pyrocles, Musidorus, and Gynecia, Sidney writes that "Euarchus did wisely consider the people to be naturally taken with exterior shows far more than with inward consideration of the material points; and therefore in this new entry into so entangled a matter he would leave nothing which might be either an armour or ornament unto him; and in these pompous ceremonies he well knew a secret of government much to consist" (Philip Sidney, *The Countess of Pembroke's Arcadia*, ed. Katherine Duncan-Jones, 324). On Hayward's liberal borrowings from Sidney's *Arcadia* in this work, see Lisa Richardson, "Elizabeth in Arcadia"; and, for an analysis of Sidney's "Old" *Arcadia* in relation to mid-Elizabethan political culture, see Blair Worden, *The Sound of Virtue*, esp. 209–94.

4. Henry Savile, trans., *The ende of Nero and beginning of Galba* (Oxford, 1591); the passage occurs in Savile's separately paginated Annotations, 6. On the place of Savile's Tacitus in late Elizabethan historiography and politics, see David Womersley, "Sir Henry Savile's Translation of Tacitus and the Political Interpretation of Elizabethan Texts."

5. For an annotated text of Hayward's history of Henry IV, with an account of its political context, printing, and suppression, see *The First and Second Parts of John Hayward's The Life and Raigne of King Henrie IIII*, ed. John J. Manning. Francis Bacon recounted that when the Queen asked him if he considered Hayward's history to be treasonous, he responded that he thought it not treasonous but rather felonious: "I told her, the author had committed very apparant theft: for he had taken most of the sentences of Cornelius Tacitus, and translated them into English, and put them into his text" (quoted in Manning's edition of Hayward, 2).

6. Clapham, *Certain Observations*, 86.

7. *Thomas Platter's Travels in England 1599*, trans. Clare Williams, 192.

8. "Diary of the Journey of Philip Julius, Duke of Stettin-Pomerania, through England in the Year 1602," ed. von Bülow, 53 (emphasis added).

9. Giovanni Carlo Scaramelli, Venetian Secretary in England, to the Doge and Senate, London, 19 February 1603; translated and printed in *CSP, Venetian*, 9.531.

10. De Maisse, *Journal*, 24, 25–26. Future citations will be included in the text. This translation is based upon a modern copy of a seventeenth-century transcript of the now lost original manuscript. Both de Maisse's French descriptions of the Queen and their modern English translations are somewhat vexed, especially regarding the terminology used to describe the Queen's wardrobe. Here I have found the discussion in Arnold, *Queen Elizabeth's Wardrobe Unlock'd*, 7–10, especially helpful; I have incorporated, in brackets, some of Arnold's quotations of the French terms that appear in the transcript. Also see Lisa Jardine, *Reading Shakespeare Historically*, 19–34, 162–70.

11. The discussion of de Maisse in the text and notes of Jardine, *Reading Shakespeare Historically*, 21–24, 163–65, is largely a critique of my own earlier discussion of de Maisse in "'Shaping

Fantasies.'" Jardine makes much of my use of the word "actual" in my discussion there of de Maisse's representation of the Queen, and I take her point about its dubious referential implications. But I must also take issue with her own reading of de Maisse, on both textual and historical grounds. Her stated reason for discussing de Maisse's text is that it "turns out to be particularly relevant to Desdemona's case in *Othello*" (21). This dubious claim is based upon the following assertion: "In the case of the Catholic Hurault de Maisse's two descriptions, glimpses of female flesh . . . cannot be accommodated to his version of female decorum. The detailed richness of the dress, furthermore, in conjunction with the suggestions of indecency, reinforces the anxiety about 'whoredom' (since finery and extravagant dress was customarily associated with prostitution)" (23). Jardine offers no textual evidence for de Maisse's sense of violated decorum or for his anxiety about whoredom, presumably because none exists. Instead, for evidence that finery was customarily associated with prostitution, she cites studies of urban, mercantile societies in sixteenth-century Germany and Italy that are not pertinent to the case at hand. Jardine also fails to clarify the immediate relevance of identifying de Maisse as a Catholic; surely the most relevant cultural code operative here is not religious but courtly and monarchical. An ambassador from the promiscuous court of Henri IV was hardly likely to be outraged by "suggestions of indecency" in Elizabeth's dress and demeanor; in any case, he would have expected a queen regnant to manifest royal magnificence in "finery and extravagant dress," for this was entirely in conformity with the "conventions of decorum" (24) that structured the elite society in which he customarily moved. It is also hard to square Jardine's unsupported assertion that de Maisse's description of Elizabeth is a version of "'woman spoken badly of'" (24) with the considerable textual evidence to the contrary: "Her figure is fair and tall and graceful in whatever she does; so far as may be she keeps her dignity, yet humbly and graciously withal" (De Maisse, *Journal*, 26); "It is a strange thing to see how lively she is in body and mind and nimble in everything she does" (De Maisse, *Journal*, 61); "Save for her face, which looks old, and her teeth, it is not possible to see a woman of so fine and vigorous disposition both in mind and body" (De Maisse, *Journal*, 82).

Also see the cogent critique of Jardine's analysis of de Maisse in Steven Mullaney, "Mourning and Misogyny," esp. 146–47, n. 28. Mullaney's essay advances the provocative thesis that "it is in late Elizabethan and early Jacobean revenge tragedy that the aging and posthumous body of Elizabeth is most fully engaged and problematized, in an apprehensive interplay of mourning and misogyny, revisionary desire and aggression, idealization and travesty" (144–45).

12. Arnold, *Queen Elizabeth's Wardrobe Unlock'd*, 9; also see Jardine, *Reading Shakespeare Historically*, 164, n. 14.

13. William Camden, the Elizabethan antiquary and chronicler of the Queen's reign, cites the motto as one of two "which she as truly and constantly performed" (*Remains concerning Britain*, ed. Dunn, 182).

14. See Peter Burke, *The Art of Conversation*; quotations from 135, 136, 134, respectively.

15. Sir H[enry] Unton to her Majesty, from Coucy, Feb. 3, 1595/6; printed in *A collection of state papers relating to affairs in the reign of Queen Elizabeth, from the year 1571 to 1596*, ed. William Murdin, 717–19, quotation from 718–19.

16. My quotation and paraphrased translation of the French originals, which are printed in *Recueil des lettres missives de Henri IV*, ed. M. Berger de Xivrey, 4.292–94. The editor places the undated letter to Queen Elizabeth immediately following the letter to Gabrielle d'Estrées, principally for thematic reasons.

17. "On the Writing of Letters" [*De conscribendis epistolis*], trans. Charles Fantazzi, in *Collected Works of Erasmus: Literary and Educational Writings 3*, ed. J. K. Sowards, 191.

18. Sir H. Unton to the Lord Treasurer, from Coucy, February 3, 1595/6; printed in *A collection of state papers relating to affairs in the reign of Queen Elizabeth, from the year 1571 to 1596*, ed. Murdin, 719–24. I have encountered other examples, suggesting that this may well have been standard practice among Elizabeth's ambassadors. Thus, when on 16 December 1576 Sir John Smith wrote separate letters to the Queen and Burghley from the French court at Saint-Dié, only in the letter to Elizabeth did he describe the French queen mother, princesses, and ladies of the court, concluding with the declaration that "there were besides other ladies, young and old, fair and foul, to the number of nine or ten, but this I do assure your Majesty by my faith that there is more beauty in your Majesty's little finger than there is in any one lady that there was, or in them all" (*CSP, Foreign*, 11.446–47). And when, on 11 June 1577, Dr. Thomas Wilson wrote separate letters to the Queen, Burghley, and Walsingham from Brussels concerning his interview with Don John of Austria, he related to the Queen alone that he "shewed hym Your Majesties picture, whiche I had borrowed of Mr Fowke Grevil," at which viewing Don John "desired earenstlie of me to have Your Majesties entier stature and makinge, and the sooner the better" (printed in *Relations politiques des Pays-Bas et de l'Angleterre, sous le règne de Philippe II*, 9.335–41; quotation from 336). I owe the latter reference to Strong, *Gloriana*, 167, n. 40.

19. "A Conference betweene a Gent. Huisher and a Post, before the QUEENE, at MR. SEC-RETARYE's House. By JOHN DAVIES," printed from manuscript in Nichols, *Progresses and Public Processions of Queen Elizabeth*, 3.76–77. Nichols places the event at the Cecils' Theobalds estate in 1591; Strong, *Gloriana*, dates it 1600. Mary C. Erler, "Sir John Davies and the Rainbow Portrait of Queen Elizabeth," demonstrates that it forms a part of the entertainments written by Davies for Cecil's entertainment of the Queen in 1602; these ended with the gift of a mantle, which Erler identifies with the mantle in the "Rainbow" portrait.

20. Clapham, *Certain Observations*, 96–97. Elsewhere in his memoir, Clapham averred that "as for flatterers, it is certain that she had many too near her, and was well contented to hear them. Howbeit, though it be a great fault in princes to endure such kind of persons about them, yet it is more tolerable in them to be flattered and praised sometimes for such virtues as they have not than to be hated and despised for known vices" (90).

21. Here it may be recalled that about the time he was flattering the Queen with these entertainments, Cecil was engaged in secret intelligence with King James VI of Scotland, smoothing the way for James's succession to the English throne and positioning himself to profit by it: See *Correspondence of King James VI. of Scotland with Sir Robert Cecil and Others in England, during the Reign of Queen Elizabeth*, ed. John Bruce, 1–32.

22. "Mr. [R. J.] Jones to Sir Nicholas Throkmorton," dated "The last of November, 1560"; printed in *Miscellaneous State Papers from 1501 to 1726*, ed. Hardwicke, 1.167. I own this reference to R. B. Wernham, *Before the Armada*, 237.

Chapter Seventeen

1. See *The Diary of John Manningham of the Middle Temple, 1602–1603*, ed. Robert Parker Sorlien, 188.

2. Henry Chettle, *Englandes Mourning Garment* (1603), facsimile ed., E2r.

3. See Arnold, *Queen Elizabeth's Wardrobe Unlock'd*, 5.

4. Clapham, *Certain Observations*, 96.

5. "Ben Jonson's Conversations with William Drummond of Hawthornden," in *Ben Jonson*, ed. C. H. Herford, Percy Simpson, and Evelyn Simpson, 1.141–42. The first assertion is a crude

variant on the disability alluded to by Harington in his *Tract on the Succession to the Crown*, discussed above in chapter fourteen.

6. See Debora Shuger, "The 'I' of the Beholder," 21.

7. In a letter dated London, 13 January 1601, printed in *Records of the English Province of the Society of Jesus*, ed. Foley, 1.8. Ironically, Rivers's observation of Elizabeth echoes Unton's report to Elizabeth herself of Gabrielle d'Estrées, "verie grosselye painted."

8. Goodman, *The Court of James I*, 1.164.

9. For a suggestive account of the changing technology of mirrors and its impact upon the mirror metaphor in early modern England, see Rayna Kalas, "The Technology of Reflection"; and, for a provocative discussion of the relationship between Renaissance mirror metaphors and theories of mind, see Shuger, "The 'I' of the Beholder."

10. See Walter Bourchier Devereux, *Lives and Letters of the Devereux, Earls of Essex*, 2.131.

11. For a transcription of Southwell's manuscript, with valuable annotation and commentary, see Catherine Loomis, "Elizabeth Southwell's Manuscript Account of the Death of Queen Elizabeth." I quote Southwell's text from this transcription, citing by the line numbers supplied there.

12. In her assertion that Cecil secretly ordered the Queen's body disemboweled, thus contravening Elizabeth's explicit wishes to the contrary, Southwell's account apparently departs from all others. On this topic, see Loomis, "Elizabeth Southwell's Manuscript Account," 493–96.

13. Writing in the mid-seventeenth century, with the understanding that the Queen had not been opened, Francis Osborne implied that the reason was to protect her sexual honor and to suppress questions regarding the succession. He made this suggestion during his discussion of Elizabeth's troubling of gender norms: "Her Sex did beare out many impertinencies in her words and actions . . . but especially in her *Treaties* relating to Marriage: Towards which some thought her uncapable by nature, others too propense." (As we have seen, according to William Drummond, Ben Jonson had maintained that she was both "uncapable" and "too propense.") Osborne then goes on to relate an anecdote about King Henri IV of France, who held that "*There were three things inscrutable to intelligence*," the third of them being "*Whether Queene Elizabeth was a maid or no*: which may render al reports dubious that come from meaner Men: yet it may be true that the Ladies of her bedchamber denied to her body the ceremony of *searching* and imbalming, due to dead Monarchs: But that she had a Son bred in the State of *Venise*, and a Daughter I not not where nor when . . . I neglect to insert, as fitter for a *Romance*, then to mingle with so much truth and integrity as I professe" (*Historical memoires on the reigns of Queen Elizabeth and King James*, 60–62). Despite his profession of integrity, Osborne's *occupatio* recycles the gossip about Elizabeth's promiscuity and illegitimate children that had been rife during her reign; and, by innuendo, this provides a strategic reason for the decision to go against tradition and to leave the body of the dead Queen unopened.

14. There is no corroboration elsewhere in the historical record for this ostensibly eyewitness account of what Loomis has dubbed "Elizabeth's exploding corpse" ("Elizabeth Southwell's Manuscript Account," 499). Southwell herself implies that it was hushed up: "No man durst speak yt publicklie for displeasing *Secretarie Cecill*" (91–92).

15. "A Yorkshire Recusant's Relation" (1586?), manuscript printed in *The Troubles of Our Catholic Forefathers Related by Themselves*, ed. John Morris, 3.99. Alexandra Walsham, "Miracles and the Counter Reformation," notes that "many manuscript accounts . . . told how the disemboweled bodies of the martyrs . . . defied physical corruption" (790); and that "like the corpses of medieval saints, the dismembered remains of early modern martyrs were often reputed to have discharged a fragrant perfume before being removed for embalming" (795).

16. See Neale's 1925 essay, "The Sayings of Queen Elizabeth," reprinted in J. E. Neale, *Essays in Elizabethan History*, 85–112; see esp. 107–12, where he discusses narratives of Elizabeth's death, giving special attention to Southwell's.

17. Neale, *Essays in Elizabethan History*, 110. Cecil, whom Southwell made the villain of her piece, managed the official version of the events in question, managed them successfully, and profited spectacularly from the consequences. If Southwell's motives are assumed to be suspect while Cecil's are not, part of the reason may lie in the perception that he was a statesman, while she was "a young woman of surpassing beauty, romantic in temperament and career . . . who had turned Catholic."

18. Neale, *Essays in Elizabethan History*, 111. Southwell was not alone in questioning the authorized version of the succession—that on her deathbed the Queen had explicitly designated the King of Scots as her heir. As Clapham guardedly put it at the time, "these reports, whether they were true indeed or given out of purpose by such as would have them so to be believed, it is hard to say. Sure I am they did no hurt" (Clapham, *Certain Observations*, 99). It is also the case that although he was dedicated to the memory of William Cecil, his late patron, Clapham demonstrated a prudently Tacitean circumspection regarding Robert Cecil, "of whom I will forbear at this time to make further mention, for that he now liveth in good prosperity, whereof I wish the happy continuance for the love and duty which I owe unto his house and particularly to himself. For howsoever a man may write of such as are living he may easily purchase blame or dislike" (104).

Epilogue

1. De Maisse, *Journal*, 11.

2. Harington, *Tract on the Succession to the Crown*, 51.

3. See two seminal essays by Patrick Collinson: "The Monarchical Republic of Queen Elizabeth I" (1986), reprinted in his *Elizabethan Essays*, 31–57; and "The Elizabethan Exclusion Crisis and the Elizabethan Polity."

4. See, for example, James's letters to Elizabeth of 27 June 1585 and 3 August [?] 1585, printed respectively in *Letters of Queen Elizabeth and King James VI. of Scotland*, ed. John Bruce, 14–15, and *Letters of King James VI and I*, ed. G. P. V. Akrigg, 64–65. In the former letter, James addresses Elizabeth as "Madame and dearest sister," and in the latter as "Madame and mother"; in both, he signs himself "Your most loving and devoted brother and son." For a suggestive argument that "James's interest in prosecuting witches may . . . have been related to his ambivalent relations with his two 'mothers,'" see Deborah Willis, *Malevolent Nurture*, 117–58; quotation from 125.

5. Giovanni Carlo Scaramelli, Venetian Secretary in England, to the Doge and Senate, 24 April 1603; trans. and printed in *CSP, Venetian*, 10.10.

6. See Julia M. Walker, "Reading the Tombs of Elizabeth I." Also see Jennifer Woodward, *The Theatre of Death*, 67–147, for much interesting information on the funerals, effigies, and tombs of Mary Stuart and Elizabeth Tudor. McCoy, *Alterations of State*, offers a brilliant reading of the shifting fortunes of sacred kingship in early modern England in terms of the successive reappropriations of the Henry VII Chapel at Westminster. McCoy points out that Henry VII had originally planned his chapel as a shrine for Henry VI, whom he intended to have canonized, with the hope that his own remains would benefit from their proximity to the sanctified corpse of his forebear (*Alterations of State*, 26–28).

7. Thomas Dekker, *The Magnificent Entertainment given to King James, and Queene Anne his Wife, and Henry Frederick the Prince, Upon the Day of his Majestie's Triumphant Passage (from*

the Tower) through his Honorable Citie (and Chamber) of London (1604); rpt. in Nichols, *The Progresses, Processions, and Magnificent Festivities, of King James the First*, 1.346.

8. The speech, delivered by the King on "The First Day of the first Parliament," 19 March 1604, is reprinted in King James VI and I, *Political Writings*, ed. Johann P. Somerville, 132–46; quotation from 134–35.

9. *In felicem memoriam Elizabethae*, in *The Works of Francis Bacon*, ed. Spedding et al., 11.452.

10. Goodman, *The Court of King James the First*, ed. Brewer, 1.97–98. The early seventeenth-century foundations of the historiographical and biographical afterlife of Queen Elizabeth, and the complex history of appropriation of Elizabeth and the Elizabethan age throughout the century, have been the subject of much interesting and important recent research. In this epilogue, I have benefited in particular from Curtis Perry, *The Making of Jacobean Culture*, and John Watkins, *Representing Elizabeth in Stuart England*.

11. King James VI and I, *Political Writings*, ed. Somerville, 136. In a speech to both houses of parliament on 21 March 1610, James further expounded the patriarchal analogy of Jacobean kingship: "A father may dispose of his Inheritance to his children, at his pleasure. . . . So may a King deale with his Subjects" (*Political Writings*, ed. Somerville, 182). As Judith M. Richards has observed, James was replacing "Elizabeth's preferred public language of reciprocity" with "an authoritative style, an irresistible obligation of obedience" ("The English Accession of James VI," 532).

12. Quoted in J. P. Kenyon, "Queen Elizabeth and the Historians," 52. I owe this reference to Anne McLaren, "The Quest for a King."

13. Dekker, *The Magnificent Entertainment given to King James*, 338. In the printed version of the entry entertainments, Dekker describes this as "A Device (projected downe, but till now not publisht) that should have served at his Majestie's first Accesse to the Citie."

14. Henry Hooke, *A Sermon Preached Before the King at White-Hall, the Eight of May. 1604 . . . Jerusalems Peace* (London, 1604), sigs. C2v–C3; quoted in Perry, *The Making of Jacobean Culture*, 156–57. John Watkins notes that "references to James as a phoenix rising from Elizabeth's ashes figure more frequently in accession commemorations than any other topos" (*Representing Elizabeth in Stuart England*, 17). Surely the most rhetorically opulent version is that put into the mouth of Archbishop Cranmer in Shakespeare and Fletcher's *Henry VIII* or *All is True*, which dates from about a decade after the Queen's death and the King's accession. Here it takes the form of a prophecy on the occasion of the infant Elizabeth's christening (5.4.17–54).

15. A number of recent studies address aspects of the myth of Elizabeth, from its origins in early seventeenth-century nostalgia and polemic to its most recent accretions and appropriations. Perhaps the most comprehensive works are Michael Dobson and Nicola J. Watson, *England's Elizabeth*; and Julia M. Walker, *The Elizabethan Icon: 1603–2003*. Among other recent studies of the modern and postmodern Elizabeth, see in particular "Romancing the Queen," in Barbara Hodgdon, *The Shakespeare Trade*, 110–70; Richard Burt, "Doing the Queen"; and Thomas Betteridge, "A Queen for All Seasons."

Bibliography

Acts of the Privy Council of England. Ed. John Roche Dasent. New Series. 43 vols. London: HMSO, 1890–1949.

Adams, Simon. "The Gran Armada: 1988 and After." *History* 76 (1991): 238–49.

————. *Leicester and the Court: Essays on Elizabethan Politics.* Manchester: Manchester Univ. Press, 2002.

Adler, Doris. "Imaginary Toads in Real Gardens." *English Literary Renaissance* 11 (1981): 235–60.

————. "The Riddle of the Sieve: The Siena Sieve Portrait of Queen Elizabeth." *Renaissance Papers* (1978): 1–10.

Alfield, Thomas. *A True Reporte of the Death & Martyrdome of M. Campion, & M. Sherwin, and M. Bryan.* Facsimile ed. English Recusant Literature 1558–1640, vol. 56. Menston, Yorkshire: Scolar Press, 1970.

Alford, Stephen. "Politics and Political History in the Tudor Century." *Historical Journal* 42 (1999): 535–48.

Allen, William. *An Admonition to the Nobility and People of England and Ireland Concerning the Present Warres made for the execution of his Holines Sentence, by the highe and mightie Kinge Catholike of Spaine.* 1588. Facsimile ed. English Recusant Literature 1558–1640, vol. 54. Menston: Scolar Press, 1971.

————. *A briefe historie of the glorious martyrdom of XII. reverend priests, executed within these twelvemonethes for confession and defence of the Catholike faith But under the false pretence of treason.* Rheims [?], 1582. STC 369.5.

Alsop, J. D. "The Act for the Queen's Regnal Power, 1554." *Parliamentary History* 13 (1994): 261–76.

Anglo, Sydney. *The Great Tournament Roll of Westminster: A Collotype Reproduction of the Manuscript.* 2 vols. Oxford: Clarendon Press, 1968.

————. *Images of Tudor Kingship.* London: Seaby, 1992.

————. *Spectacle, Pageantry, and Early Tudor Policy.* Oxford: Clarendon Press, 1969.

Arnold, Janet. "The 'Armada' Portraits of Queen Elizabeth I." *Apollo* 129, no. 326 (April 1989): 242–46.

————. *Queen Elizabeth's Wardrobe Unlock'd.* Leeds: W. S. Maney, 1988.

Ascham, Roger. *The Whole Works of Roger Ascham.* Ed. J. A. Giles. 2 vols. 1865; rpt., New York: AMS Press, 1965.

Ascoli, Georges. *La Grande-Bretagne devant l'opinion française au XVIIe siècle*. 2 vols. Paris: J. Gamber, 1930.

Aske, James. *Elizabetha Triumphans*. 1588. Facsimile ed. Amsterdam: Theatrum Orbis Terrarum, 1969.

Aston, Margaret. *England's Iconoclasts*. Vol. 1, *Laws against Images*. Oxford: Clarendon Press, 1988.

―――. "Gods, Saints, and Reformers: Portraiture and Protestant England." In *Albion's Classicism: The Visual Arts in Britain, 1550–1660*. Ed. Lucy Gent. New Haven: Yale Univ. Press, 1996. Pp. 181–220.

―――. "Iconoclasm in England: Rites of Destruction by Fire." In *Bilder und Bildersturm im Spätmittelalter und in der frühen Neuzeit*. Ed. Bob Scribner and Martin Warnke. Wolfenbütteler Forschungen, Bd. 46. Wiesbaden: In Kommission bei Otto Harrassowitz, 1990. Pp. 175–202.

―――. *The King's Bedpost: Reformation and Iconography in a Tudor Group Portrait*. Cambridge: Cambridge Univ. Press, 1993.

Auerbach, Erna, and C. Kingsley Adams. *Paintings and Sculpture at Hatfield House*. London: Constable, 1971.

Axton, Marie. *The Queen's Two Bodies: Drama and the Elizabethan Succession*. London: Royal Historical Society, 1977.

Aylmer, John. *An Harborowe for Faithfull and Trewe Subjectes, agaynst the late blowne Blaste, concerninge the Government of Wemen*. 1559. Facsimile ed. Amsterdam: Theatrum Orbis Terrarum, 1972.

Bacon, Francis. *The Works of Francis Bacon*. Ed. James Spedding, Robert Leslie Ellis, and Douglas Denon Heath. 15 vols. Boston: Brown & Taggard, 1862.

―――. *The Works of Francis Bacon*. Ed. James Spedding, Robert Leslie Ellis, and Douglas Denon Heath. 14 vols. 1857–74; rpt. New York: Garrett Press, 1968.

Barber, Peter. "England II: Monarchs, Ministers, and Maps, 1550–1625." In *Monarchs, Ministers, and Maps: The Emergence of Cartography as a Tool of Government in Early Modern Europe*. Ed. David Buisseret. Chicago: Univ. of Chicago Press, 1992.

Baxandall, Michael. *Patterns of Intention: On the Historical Explanation of Pictures*. New Haven: Yale Univ. Press, 1985.

Bellamy, John. *The Tudor Law of Treason*. London: Routledge & Kegan Paul, 1979.

Belsey, Andrew, and Catherine Belsey. "Icons of Divinity." In *Renaissance Bodies: The Human Figure in English Culture c. 1540–1660*. Ed. Lucy Gent and Nigel Llewellyn. London: Reaktion Books, 1990. Pp. 11–35.

Ben Jonson. Ed. C. H. Herford, Percy Simpson, and Evelyn Simpson. 11 vols. Oxford: Clarendon Press, 1925–51.

Berry, Philippa. *Of Chastity and Power: Elizabethan Literature and the Unmarried Queen*. London: Routledge, 1989.

Betteridge, Thomas. "A Queen for All Seasons: Queen Elizabeth I on Film." In *The Myth of Elizabeth*. Ed. Susan Doran and Thomas S. Freeman. New York: Palgrave Macmillan, 2003. Pp. 242–59.

Birch, Thomas. *Memoirs of the reign of Queen Elizabeth, from the year 1581 till her death*. 2 vols. London: Printed for A. Millar, 1754.

Boehrer, Bruce Thomas. *Monarchy and Incest in Renaissance England: Literature, Culture, Kinship, and Kingship*. Philadelphia: Univ. of Pennsylvania Press, 1992.

Bossy, John. *Christianity in the West 1400–1700.* Oxford: Oxford Univ. Press, 1985.

————. "English Catholics and the French Marriage 1577–81." *Recusant History* 5 (1959): 2–16.

Breight, Curtis Charles. "Duelling Ceremonies: The Strange Case of William Hacket, Elizabethan Messiah." *Journal of Medieval and Renaissance Studies* 19 (1989): 35–67.

Brennan, Gillian E. "Papists and Patriotism in Elizabethan England." *Recusant History* 19 (1988): 1–15.

Brooke, C. F. Tucker. *The Life of Marlowe.* London: Methuen, 1930.

Brownlow, F. W. "Performance and Reality at the Court of Elizabeth I." In *The Mysteries of Elizabeth I.* Ed. Kirby Farrell and Kathleen Swaim. Amherst: Univ. of Massachusetts Press, 2003. Pp. 3–20.

Bugliani, Francesca. "Petrucchio Ubaldini's Accounts of England." *Renaissance Studies* 8 (1994): 175–97.

Bülow, Gottfried von. "Diary of the Journey of Philip Julius, Duke of Stettin-Pomerania, through England in the Year 1602." *Transactions of the Royal Historical Society,* n.s. 6 (1892): 1–67.

Burke, Peter. *The Art of Conversation.* Ithaca: Cornell Univ. Press, 1993.

————. "Tacitism, Scepticism, and Reason of State." In *The Cambridge History of Political Thought 1450–1700.* Ed. J. H. Burns with the assistance of Mark Goldie. Cambridge: Cambridge Univ. Press, 1991. Pp. 479–90.

Burt, Richard. "Doing the Queen: Gender, Sexuality, and the Censorship of Elizabeth I's Royal Image in Twentieth-Century Mass Media." In *The Mysteries of Elizabeth I.* Ed. Kirby Farrell and Kathleen Swaim. Amherst: Univ. of Massachusetts Press, 2003. Pp. 267–77.

Cabala, Mysteries of State. In *Letters of the Great Ministers of K. James and K. Charles.* London, 1654.

Calendar of Assize Records: Essex Indictments, Elizabeth I. Ed. J. S. Cockburn. London: HMSO, 1978.

Calendar of Assize Records: Hertfordshire Indictments, Elizabeth I. Ed. J. S. Cockburn. London: HMSO, 1975.

Calendar of Assize Records: Kent Indictments, Elizabeth I. Ed. J. S. Cockburn. London: HMSO, 1979.

Calendar of Assize Records: Surrey Indictments, Elizabeth I. Ed. J. S. Cockburn. London: HMSO, 1980.

Calendar of Assize Records: Sussex Indictments, Elizabeth I. Ed. J. S. Cockburn. London: HMSO, 1975.

Calendar of Letters, Despatches and State Papers Relating to the Negotiations between England and Spain. Ed. Royall Tyler. 14 vols. London: HMSO, 1954.

Calendar of the Letters and State Papers Relating to English Affairs Preserved in, or originally Belonging to, the Archives of Simancas. Ed. Martin Hume. 4 vols. London: HMSO, 1892–99.

Calendar of State Papers and manuscripts relating to English affairs, existing in the archives and collections of Venice, and in other libraries of Northern Italy. Ed. Rawston Brown. 7 vols. London: HMSO, 1864.

Calendar of State Papers, Domestic Series, of the Reigns of Edward VI, Mary, Elizabeth, 1547–1625. Ed. Robert Lemon and M. A. E. Green. 12 vols. London: Longman, Brown, Green, Longmans, & Roberts, 1856–72.

Calendar of State Papers, Foreign Series, of the Reign of Elizabeth. Ed. Joseph Stevenson et al. 23 vols. London: Longman, Green, Longman, Roberts, & Green, 1863–1950.

Calendar of State Papers Relating to Ireland, of the Reign of Elizabeth, 1588, August–1592, September. Ed. Hans Claude Hamilton. 1885; rpt., Nendeln, Liechtenstein: Kraus Reprint, 1974.

Calendar of State Papers Relating to Scotland and Mary, Queen of Scots, 1547–1603. Ed. Joseph Bain, William K. Boyd, and J. D. Mackie. 13 vols. London: HM General Register House, 1898–1969.

Calendar of the Carew Manuscripts, Preserved in the Archiepiscopal Library at Lambeth, 1515–1624. Ed. J. S. Brewer and William Bullen. 6 vols. 1867–73; rpt., Nendeln, Liechtenstein: Kraus Reprint, 1974.

Camden, William. *Annales.* Trans. London, 1625. STC 4497.

———. *Remains concerning Britain.* Ed. R. D. Dunn. Toronto: Univ. of Toronto Press, 1984.

Campbell, Lorne. *The Early Flemish Pictures in the Collection of Her Majesty the Queen.* Cambridge: Cambridge Univ. Press, 1985.

Canny, Nicholas. "Dominant Minorities: English Settlers in Ireland and Virginia, 1550–1650." In *Minorities in History.* Ed. A. C. Hepburn. New York: St. Martin's Press, 1979. Pp. 51–69.

———. "Identity Formation in Ireland: The Emergence of the Anglo-Irish." In *Colonial Identity in the Atlantic World, 1500–1800.* Ed. Nicholas Canny and Anthony Pagden. Princeton: Princeton Univ. Press, 1989. Pp. 159–212.

Capp, Bernard. "Separate Domains? Women and Authority in Early Modern England." In *The Experience of Authority in Early Modern England.* Ed. Paul Griffiths, Adam Fox, and Steve Hindle. New York: St. Martin's Press, 1996. Pp. 117–45.

Cavendish, George. *Metrical Visions.* Ed. A. S. G. Edwards. Columbia, SC: Univ. of South Carolina Press, 1980.

Challoner, Richard. *Memoirs of Missionary Priests.* Ed. John Hungerford Pollen. London: Burns, Oates & Washbourne, 1924.

Chaloner, Thomas. *Thomas Chaloner's "In Laudem Henrici Octavi."* Ed. John B. Gabel and Carl C. Schlam. Lawrence, KS: Coronado Press, 1979.

Chamberlain, John. *The Letters of John Chamberlain.* Ed. Norman Egbert McClure. 2 vols. Philadelphia: American Philosophical Society, 1939.

Chambers, E. K. *The Elizabethan Stage,* 4 vols. Oxford: Clarendon Press, 1923.

———. *Sir Henry Lee: An Elizabethan Portrait.* Oxford: Clarendon Press, 1936.

Chapman, George. *The Poems of George Chapman.* Ed. Phyllis Brooks Bartlett. 1941; rpt. New York: Russell & Russell, 1962.

Chester, Allan Griffith. "Thomas Churchyard's Pension." *PMLA* 50 (1935): 902.

Chettle, Henry. *Englandes Mourning Garment.* 1603. Facsimile ed. Amsterdam: Theatrum Orbis Terrarum, 1973.

The chronicle of Queen Jane, and of two years of Queen Mary. Ed. John Gough Nichols. 1850; rpt., New York: AMS Press, 1968.

Clapham, John. *Elizabeth of England: certain observations concerning the life and reign of Queen Elizabeth.* Ed. Evelyn Plummer Read and Conyers Read. Philadelphia: Univ. of Pennsylvania Press, 1951.

Clark, Peter. *English Provincial Society from the Reformation to the Revolution: Religion, Politics and Society in Kent 1500–1640.* Hassocks, Sussex: Harvester Press, 1977.

———. "Popular Protest and Disturbance in Kent, 1558–1640." *Economic History Review,* 2nd ser. 29 (1976): 365–81.

Clifford, Henry. *The Life of Jane Dormer, Duchess of Feria.* Transcribed by E. E. Estcourt. Ed. Joseph Stevenson. London: Burns & Oates, 1887.

Coch, Christine. "'Mother of my Countreye': Elizabeth I and Tudor Constructions of Mother-hood." *English Literary Renaissance* 26 (1996): 423–50.

Cockburn, J. S. *Calendar of Assize Records: Home Circuit Indictments, Elizabeth I and James I, Introduction.* London: HMSO, 1985.

Cole, Mary Hill. *The Portable Queen: Elizabeth I and the Politics of Ceremony.* Amherst: Univ. of Massachusetts Press, 1999.

A collection of state papers relating to affairs in the reign of Queen Elizabeth, from the year 1571 to 1596. Ed. William Murdin. London, 1759.

Collinson, Patrick. *Elizabethan Essays.* London: Hambledon Press, 1994.

———. "The Elizabethan Exclusion Crisis and the Elizabethan Polity." *Proceedings of the British Academy* 84 (1994): 51–92.

———. *The Elizabethan Puritan Movement.* Berkeley: Univ. of California Press, 1967.

A Complete Collection of State Trials. Ed. T. B. Howell. 21 vols. London, 1816.

Correspondence of King James VI. of Scotland with Sir Robert Cecil and Others in England, during the Reign of Queen Elizabeth. Ed. John Bruce. 1861; rpt., New York: AMS, 1968.

The Count of Feria's Dispatch to Philip II of 14 November 1558. Ed. and trans. M. J. Rodriguez-Salgado and Simon Adams. Camden Miscellany 28. London: Royal Historical Society, 1984.

Cox, Nick. "Rumours and Risings: Plebeian Insurrection and the Circulation of Subversive Discourse around 1597." In *Subversion and Scurrility: Popular Discourse in Europe from 1500 to the Present.* Ed. Dermot Cavanagh and Tim Kirk. Aldershot, Hampshire: Ashgate, 43–57.

Cropper, Elizabeth. "The Beauty of Woman: Problems in the Rhetoric of Renaissance Portraiture." In *Rewriting the Renaissance: The Discourses of Sexual Difference in Early Modern Europe.* Ed. Margaret W. Ferguson, Maureen Quilligan, and Nancy J. Vickers. Chicago: Univ. of Chicago Press, 1986. Pp. 175–90, 355–59.

Dalton, Karen C. C. "Art for the Sake of Dynasty: The Black Emperor in the Drake Jewel and Elizabethan Imperial Imagery." In *Early Modern Visual Culture: Representation, Race, and Empire in Renaissance England.* Ed. Peter Erickson and Clark Hulse. Philadelphia: Univ. of Pennsylvania Press, 2000. Pp. 178–214.

Davies, John. *The Poems of Sir John Davies.* Ed. Robert Krueger. Oxford: Clarendon Press, 1975.

Davis, Natalie Zemon. *Society and Culture in Early Modern France.* Stanford: Stanford Univ. Press, 1975.

Dawson, Jane. "Revolutionary Conclusions: The Case of the Marian Exiles." *History of Political Thought* 11 (1990): 257–72.

Dee, John. *Autobiographical Tracts.* Ed. James Crossley. N.p.: Chetham Society, 1851.

Dekker, Thomas. *Selected Prose Writings.* Ed. E. D. Pendry. Cambridge, MA: Harvard Univ. Press, 1968.

Deloney, Thomas. *The Works of Thomas Deloney.* Ed. F. O. Mann. Oxford: Clarendon Press, 1912.

Devereux, Walter Bourchier. *Lives and Letters of the Devereux, Earls of Essex, in the Reigns of Elizabeth, James I, and Charles I, 1540–1646.* 2 vols. London: John Murray, 1853.

The Diary of Baron Waldstein, A Traveller in Elizabethan England. Trans. G. W. Groos. London: Thames & Hudson, 1981.

The Diary of John Manningham of the Middle Temple, 1602–1603. Ed. Robert Parker Sorlien. Hanover, New Hampshire: Univ. Press of New England, 1976.

"Diary of the Journey of Philip Julius, Duke of Stettin-Pomerania, Through England in the Year 1602." Ed. Gottfried von Bülow. *Transactions of the Royal Historical Society,* n.s. 6 (1892): 1–67.

Dickens, A. G. *The English Reformation.* 2nd ed. University Park, PA.: Pennsylvania State Univ. Press, 1991.

Dictionary of National Biography. Ed. Leslie Stephen and Sidney Lee. 34 vols. London: Oxford Univ. Press, 1921.

Digges, Dudley. *The Compleat Ambassador*. London, 1655.

Dillon, Anne. *The Construction of Martyrdom in the English Catholic Community, 1535–1603*. Aldershot, Hampshire: Ashgate, 2002.

Dobson, Michael, and Nicola J. Watson. *England's Elizabeth: An Afterlife in Fame and Fantasy*. Oxford: Oxford Univ. Press, 2002.

Dolan, Frances E. *Whores of Babylon: Catholicism, Gender and Seventeenth-Century Print Culture*. Ithaca: Cornell Univ. Press, 1999.

Donaldson, Peter S. *Machiavelli and Mystery of State*. Cambridge: Cambridge Univ. Press, 1988.

Doran, Susan. "Juno versus Diana: The Treatment of Elizabeth I's Marriage in Plays and Entertainments, 1561–1581." *Historical Journal* 38 (1995): 257–74.

————. *Monarchy and Matrimony: The Courtships of Elizabeth I*. London: Routledge, 1996.

Dorsten, Jan van. *The Radical Arts: First Decade of an Elizabethan Renaissance*. Leiden: Leiden Univ. Press, 1970.

Douglas, Mary. *Natural Symbols: Explorations in Cosmology*. 1970; rpt., with a new introduction by the author, New York: Pantheon, 1982.

————. *Purity and Danger: An Analysis of Concepts of Pollution and Taboo*. Harmondsworth, England: Penguin Books, 1966.

Dovey, Zillah. *An Elizabethan Progress: The Queen's Journey into East Anglia, 1578*. Phoenix Mill, England: Alan Sutton, 1996.

Dowling, Maria. "Anne Boleyn and Reform." *Journal of Ecclesiastical History* 35 (1984): 30–46.

duBois, Page. "Subjected Bodies, Science, and the State: Francis Bacon, Torturer." In *Body Politics: Disease, Desire, and the Family*. Ed. Michael Ryan and Avery Gordon. Boulder: Westview Press, 1994. Pp. 175–91.

Duffy, Eamon. *The Stripping of the Altars: Traditional Religion in England 1400–1580*. New Haven: Yale Univ. Press, 1992.

Eccles, Audrey. *Obstetrics and Gynaecology in Tudor and Stuart England*. Kent, Ohio: Kent State Univ. Press, 1982.

The Egerton Papers. Ed. J. Payne Collier. London: Camden Society, 1840.

Elizabeth: The Exhibition at the National Maritime Museum. Ed. Susan Doran; David Starkey, Guest Curator. London: Chatto & Windus in assoc. with The National Maritime Museum, 2003.

Elizabeth I. *Collected Works*. Ed. Leah Marcus, Janelle Mueller, and Mary Beth Rose. Chicago: Univ. of Chicago Press, 2000.

Elton, G. R. *Policy and Police: The Enforcement of the Reformation in the Age of Thomas Cromwell*. Cambridge: Cambridge Univ. Press, 1972.

————, ed. *The Tudor Constitution: Documents and Commentary*. Cambridge: Cambridge Univ. Press, 1960.

Emmison, F. G. *Elizabethan Life: Disorder*. Chelmsford, Essex: Essex County Council, 1970.

Erasmus, Desiderius. *Collected Works of Erasmus: Literary and Educational Writings 3*. Ed. J. K. Sowards. Toronto: Univ. of Toronto Press, 1985.

Erler, Mary C. "Sir John Davies and the Rainbow Portrait of Queen Elizabeth." *Modern Philology* 84 (1987): 359–71.

Fernández-Armesto, F. "Armada Myths: the Formative Phase." In *God's Obvious Design: Papers for the Spanish Armada Symposium, Sligo, 1988*. Ed. P. Gallagher and D. W. Cruickshank. London: Tamesis Books, 1990. Pp. 19–39.

Fernandez Duro, Cesáreo. *La Armada Invencible*. 2 vols. Madrid: Est. tipográfico "Sucesores de Rivadeneyra," 1884–85.

Finsten, Jill. *Isaac Oliver: Art at the Courts of Elizabeth I and James I*. 2 vols. New York: Garland, 1981.

Fletcher, Anthony. *Gender, Sex and Subordination in England 1500–1800*. New Haven: Yale Univ. Press, 1995.

Forster, Leonard. *The Icy Fire: Five Studies in European Petrarchism*. Cambridge: Cambridge Univ. Press, 1969.

Foucault, Michel. *Discipline and Punish: The Birth of the Prison*. Trans. Alan Sheridan. New York: Pantheon, 1978.

Fox, Adam. "Rumour, News and Popular Political Opinion in Elizabethan and Early Stuart England." *Historical Journal* 40 (1997): 597–620.

Foxe, John. *Acts and Monuments*. Ed. George Townsend. 8 vols. 1843–49; rpt. New York: AMS Press, 1965.

Frye, Susan. *Elizabeth I: The Competition for Representation*. New York: Oxford Univ. Press, 1993.

———. "Elizabeth als Prinzessin: Frühe Selbsdarstellung in Portrat und Brief." In *Der Körper der Königin: Geschlecht und Herrschaft in der höfischen Welt seit 1500*. Ed. Regina Schulte. Frankfurt: Campus Verlag, 2002. Pp. 49–66.

———. "The Myth of Elizabeth at Tilbury." *Sixteenth Century Journal* 23 (1992): 95–114.

Fugitive Tracts Written in Verse Which Illustrate the Conditions of Religious and Political Feeling in England and the State of Society There During Two Centuries. Ed. W. C. Hazlitt. 2 vols. N.p.: Privately printed, 1875.

Fumerton, Patricia. *Cultural Aesthetics: Renaissance Literature and the Practice of Social Ornament*. Chicago: Univ. of Chicago Press, 1991.

Gallagher, P., and D. W. Cruickshank. "The Armada of 1588 Reflected in Serious and Popular Literature of the Period." In *God's Obvious Design: Papers for the Spanish Armada Symposium, Sligo, 1988*. Ed. P. Gallagher and D. W. Cruickshank. London: Tamesis Books, 1990. Pp. 167–83.

The Geneva Bible: A facsimile of the 1560 edition. With an introduction by Lloyd E. Berry. Madison: Univ. of Wisconsin Press, 1969.

Geyl, Pieter. *The Revolt of the Netherlands 1555–1609*. 2nd ed. London: Ernest Benn, 1958.

Goldberg, Jonathan. *Sodometries: Renaissance Texts, Modern Sexualities*. Stanford: Stanford Univ. Press, 1992.

Goodman, Godfrey. *The Court of King James the First*. Ed. John S. Brewer. 2 vols. London: R. Bentley, 1839.

Grafton, Richard. *Grafton's Chronicle; or, History of England*. 2 vols. London, 1809.

Grant, Teresa. "Drama Queen: Staging Elizabeth in *If You Know Not Me You Know Nobody*." In *The Myth of Elizabeth*. Ed. Susan Doran and Thomas S. Freeman. New York: Palgrave Macmillan, 2003. Pp. 120–42.

Green, Janet M. "'I My Self': Queen Elizabeth I's Oration at Tilbury Camp." *Sixteenth Century Journal* 28 (1997): 421–45.

Guy, John, ed. *The Reign of Elizabeth I: Court and Culture in the Last Decade*. Cambridge: Cambridge Univ. Press, 1995.

———, ed. *The Tudor Monarchy*. London: Arnold, 1997.

Hackett, Helen. "Dreams or Designs, Cults or Constructions? The Study of Images of Monarchs." *Historical Journal* 44 (2001): 811–23.

———. *Virgin Mother, Maiden Queen: Elizabeth I and the Cult of the Virgin Mary*. New York: St. Martin's, 1995.

Haigh, Christopher. *Elizabeth I*. London: Longman, 1988.

Hakluyt, Richard. *The Principal Navigations Voyages Traffiques & Discoveries of the English Nation*. 12 vols. Glasgow: James MacLehose & Sons, 1903.

Hall, Kim F. *Things of Darkness: Economies of Race and Gender in Early Modern England*. Ithaca: Cornell Univ. Press, 1995.

Hammer, Paul E. J. "'Absolute and Sovereign Mistress of her Grace'? Queen Elizabeth I and Her Favourites, 1581–1592." In *The World of the Favourite*. Ed. J. H. Elliott and L. W. B. Brockliss. New Haven: Yale Univ. Press, 1999. Pp. 38–53.

———. *The Polarisation of Elizabethan Politics: The Political Career of Robert Devereux, 2nd Earl of Essex, 1585–1597*. Cambridge: Cambridge Univ. Press, 1999.

Hanson, Elizabeth. *Discovering the Subject in Renaissance England*. Cambridge: Cambridge Univ. Press, 1998.

Harington, John. *The Letters and Epigrams of Sir John Harington*. Ed. Norman Egbert McClure. Philadelphia: Univ. of Pennsylvania Press, 1930.

———. *Nugae antiquae*. Ed. Henry Harington. 3 vols. 1779; rpt. Hildesheim, Germany: Georg Olms, 1968.

———. *A Tract on the Succession to the Crown*. Ed. Clements R. Markham. 1880; rpt., New York: Burt Franklin, 1970.

Harley, J. B. "Meaning and Ambiguity in Tudor Cartography." In *English Map-Making 1500–1650*. Ed. Sarah Tyacke. London: British Library, 1983. Pp. 22–45.

Harriot, Thomas. *A briefe and true report of the new found land of Virginia: The Complete 1590 Theodor de Bry Edition*. Facsimile edition. New York: Dover, 1972.

Hayward, John. *Annals of the First Four Years of the Reign of Queen Elizabeth*. Ed. John Bruce. 1840; rpt., New York: AMS Press, 1968.

———. *The First and Second Parts of John Hayward's The Life and Raigne of King Henrie IIII*. Ed. John J. Manning. London: Royal Historical Society, 1992.

Hearn, Karen, ed. *Dynasties: Painting in Tudor and Jacobean England 1530–1630*. New York: Rizzoli, 1996.

———. *Marcus Gheeraerts II: Elizabethan Artist*, with a technical essay by Rica Jones. London: Tate Publishing, 2002.

Heath, James. *Torture and English Law: An Administrative and Legal History from the Plantagenets to the Stuarts*. Westport, CT: Greenwood Press, 1982.

Heesakkers, Chris L. "The Ambassador of the Republic of Letters at the Wedding of Prince Philip of Spain and Queen Mary of England: Hadrianus Junius and his Philippeis." In *Acta Conventus Neo-Latin Abulensis: Proceedings of the Tenth International Congress of Neo-Latin Studies*. Ed. Rhonda Schnur. Tempe, Arizona: Arizona Center for Medieval and Renaissance Studies, 2000. Pp. 325–32.

Heisch, Alison. "Queen Elizabeth I and the Persistence of Patriarchy." *Feminist Review* 4 (1980): 45–55.

Heywood, Thomas. *The Exemplary Lives and Memorable Acts of Nine the Most Worthy Women of the World*. London, 1640.

———. *If You Know Not Me You Know Nobody*, Part 2. Ed. Madeleine Doran. Oxford: Malone Society, 1935.

Highley, Christopher. "Richard Verstegan's Book of Martyrs." In *John Foxe and His World*. Ed. Christopher Highley and John N. King. Aldershot, Hampshire: Ashgate, 2002. Pp. 183–97.

———. "The Royal Image in Elizabethan Ireland." In *Dissing Elizabeth: Negative Representations of Gloriana*. Ed. Julia M. Walker. Durham, NC: Duke Univ. Press, 1998. Pp. 60–76.

Hilliard, Nicholas. *A Treatise concerning the Arte of Limning*. Ed. R. K. R. Thornton and T. G. S. Cain. Ashington, Northumberland: Mid Northumberland Arts Group, 1981.

Hind, Arthur M. *Engraving in England in the Sixteenth and Seventeenth Centuries*. 3 vols. Cambridge: Cambridge Univ. Press, 1952–64.

Historical Manuscripts Commission. *Calendar of the Manuscripts of the . . . Marquis of Salisbury . . . preserved at Hatfield House*. 24 vols. London: HMSO, 1883–1976.

————. *Fourteenth Report, Appendix, Part IV. The Manuscripts of Lord Kenyon*. London: HMSO, 1894.

————. *Report on Manuscripts in Various Collections*. 8 vols. London: HMSO, 1901–14.

The History of Parliament: The House of Commons 1558–1603. Ed. P. W. Hasler. 3 vols. London: HMSO, 1981.

Hoak, Dale. "A Tudor Deborah? The Coronation of Elizabeth I, Parliament, and the Problem of Female Rule." In *John Foxe and His World*. Ed. Christopher Highley and John N. King. Aldershot, Hampshire: Ashgate, 2002. Pp. 73–88.

————, ed. *Tudor Political Culture*. Cambridge: Cambridge Univ. Press, 1995.

Hodgdon, Barbara. *The Shakespeare Trade: Performances and Appropriations*. Philadelphia: Univ. of Pennsylvania Press, 1998.

Holinshed, Raphael. *Chronicles of England, Scotland, and Ireland*. Ed. Henry Ellis. 6 vols. 1807–8; rpt., New York: AMS Press, 1965.

Holland, Thomas. *Paneguris D. Elizabethae, Dei gratia Angliae, Franciae, & Hiberniae Reginae. A sermon preached at Pauls in London the 17. of November ann. Dom. 1599 . . . and augmented in those places wherein, for the shortnes of the time, it could not there be then delivered. Whereunto is adjoyned an apologeticall discourse, whereby all such sclanderous accusations are fully and faithfully confuted, wherewith the honour of this realme hath beene uncharitably traduced by some of our adversaries in forraine nations, and at home, for observing the 17. of November yeerely in the forme of an holy-day*. Oxford, 1601. STC 13597.

Hollstein, F. W. H. *Dutch and Flemish Etchings, Engravings and Woodcuts, ca. 1450–1700*. 43 vols. Amsterdam: Menno Hertzberger, 1949.

Holmes, Peter. *Resistance and Compromise: The Political Thought of the Elizabethan Catholics*. Cambridge: Cambridge Univ. Press, 1982.

Howarth, David. *Images of Rule: Art and Politics in the English Renaissance, 1485–1649*. Berkeley: Univ. of California Press, 1997.

Howson, John. *A sermon preached at St. Maries in Oxford, the 17. day of November, 1602. in defence of the festivities of the Church of England, and namely that of her Majesties coronation*. Oxford, 1602. STC 13884.

Hurault, André. *A Journal of All That Was Accomplished by Monsieur de Maisse, Ambassador in England from King Henri IV to Queen Elizabeth Anno Domini 1597*. Trans. and ed. G. B. Harrison and R. A. Jones. Bloomsbury: Nonesuch Press, 1931.

Ingram, Martin. "Ridings, Rough Music, and the 'Reform of Popular Culture' in Early Modern England." *Past & Present* 105 (1984): 79–113.

Jackson, Gabriele Bernhard. "Topical Ideology: Witches, Amazons, and Shakespeare's Joan of Arc." *English Literary Renaissance* 18 (1988): 40–65.

Jacquot, Jean. "Thomas Harriot's Reputation for Impiety." *Notes and Records of the Royal Society of London* 9 (1952): 164–87.

James, Mervyn. *Society, Politics and Culture: Studies in Early Modern England*. Cambridge: Cambridge Univ. Press, 1986.

Jameson, Fredric. *The Political Unconscious*. Ithaca: Cornell Univ. Press, 1981.

Jardine, Lisa. *Reading Shakespeare Historically*. London: Routledge, 1996.

Johnson, Paul. *Elizabeth I: A Study in Power and Intellect*. London: Weidenfeld & Nicholson, 1974.

Jordan, Constance. "Representing Political Androgyny: More on the Siena Portrait of Queen Elizabeth I." In *The Renaissance Englishwoman in Print: Counterbalancing the Canon*. Ed. Anne M. Haselkorn and Betty S. Travitsky. Amherst: Univ. of Massachusetts Press, 1990. Pp. 157–76.

———. "Woman's Rule in Sixteenth-Century British Political Thought." *Renaissance Quarterly* 40 (1984): 421–51.

Kagan, Richard. *Lucretia's Dreams: Politics and Prophecy in Sixteenth-Century Spain*. Berkeley: Univ. of California Press, 1990.

Kahn, Victoria. *Machiavellian Rhetoric: From the Counter-Reformation to Milton*. Princeton: Princeton Univ. Press, 1996.

Kalas, Rayna. "The Technology of Reflection: Renaissance Mirrors of Steel and Glass." *Journal of Medieval and Early Modern Studies* 32 (2002): 519–42.

Kamen, Henry. *Philip of Spain*. New Haven: Yale Univ. Press, 1997.

Kantorowicz, Ernst H. *The King's Two Bodies*. Princeton: Princeton Univ. Press, 1957.

———. *Selected Studies*. Locust Valley, NY: J. J. Augustin, 1965.

Keightley, Ron. "An Armada Veteran Celebrates the Death of Drake: Lope de Vega's *La Dragontea* (1598)." In *England and the Spanish Armada*. Ed. Jeff Doyle and Bruce Moore. Canberra: University of New South Wales and Australian Defence Force Academy, 1990. Pp. 79–111.

Kendall, Roy. "Richard Baines and Christopher Marlowe's Milieu." *English Literary Renaissance* 24 (1994): 507–52.

Kenyon, J. P. "Queen Elizabeth and the Historians." In *Queen Elizabeth I: Most Politick Princess*. Ed. Simon Adams. London: History Today, 1984. Pp. 52–55.

Kimbrough, Robert, and Philip Murphy. "The Helmingham Hall Manuscript of Sidney's *The Lady of May*: A Commentary and Transcription." *Renaissance Drama*, n.s. 1 (1968): 103–19.

King James VI and I. *Letters of King James VI and I*. Ed. G. P. V. Akrigg. Berkeley: Univ. of California Press, 1984.

———. *Political Writings*. Ed. Johann P. Somerville. Cambridge: Cambridge Univ. Press, 1994.

King, John N. "Henry VIII as David: The King's Image and Reformation Politics." In *Rethinking the Henrician Era: Essays on Early Tudor Texts and Contexts*. Ed. Peter C. Herman. Urbana: Univ. of Illinois Press, 1994. Pp. 78–92.

———. "Patronage and Piety: The Influence of Catherine Parr." In *Silent But for the Word: Tudor Women as Patrons, Translators, and Writers of Religious Works*. Ed. Margaret Patterson Hannay. Kent, OH: Kent State Univ. Press, 1985. Pp. 43–60.

———. "Queen Elizabeth I: Representations of the Virgin Queen." *Renaissance Quarterly* 43 (1990): 30–74.

———. *Tudor Royal Iconography*. Princeton: Princeton Univ. Press, 1989.

Kingdon, Robert M. "Calvinism and Resistance Theory, 1550–1580." In *The Cambridge History of Political Thought 1450–1700*. Ed. J. H. Burns with the assistance of Mark Goldie. Cambridge: Cambridge Univ. Press, 1991. Pp. 193–218.

———, ed. *The execution of justice in England, by William Cecil; and A true, sincere, and modest defense of English Catholics, by William Allen*. Ithaca: Cornell Univ. Press, 1965.

Knox, John. *The Works of John Knox*. Ed. David Laing. 6 vols. Edinburgh: James Thin, 1895.

Kury, Gloria. "'Glancing Surfaces': Hilliard, Armour, and the Italian Model." In *Albion's Classicism: The Visual Arts in Britain, 1550–1660*. Ed. Lucy Gent. New Haven: Yale Univ. Press, 1996. Pp. 395–425.

Lake, Peter. "The Significance of the Elizabethan Identification of the Pope as Antichrist." *Journal of Ecclesiastical History* 31 (1980): 161–78.

Lake, Peter, and Michael Questier. "Agency, Appropriation and Rhetoric under the Gallows: Puritans, Romanists and the State in Early Modern England." *Past & Present* 153 (November 1996): 64–107.

———. "Puritans, Papists, and the 'Public Sphere' in Early Modern England: The Edmund Campion Affair in Context." *Journal of Modern History* 72 (2000): 587–627.

Lake, Peter, with Michael Questier. *The Antichrist's Lewd Hat: Protestants, Papists and Players in Post-Reformation England.* New Haven: Yale Univ. Press, 2002.

Laqueur, Thomas. *Making Sex: Body and Gender from the Greeks to Freud.* Cambridge, MA: Harvard Univ. Press, 1990.

Latymer, William. *William Latymer's Chronickelle of Anne Bulleyne.* Ed. Maria Dowling. Camden Miscellany 30. London: Royal Historical Society, 1990. Pp. 23–55.

Le Corbeiller, Claire. "Miss America and Her Sisters: Personifications of the Four Parts of the World." *Metropolitan Museum of Art Bulletin,* 2nd ser. 19 (1961): 209–23.

Leslie, John. *A Defence of the Honour of Marie Quene of Scotlande.* 1569. Facsimile ed. English Recusant Literature 1558–1640, vol. 12. Menston: Scolar Press, 1970.

Leslie, Michael "The Dialogue between Bodies and Souls: Pictures and Poesy in the English Renaissance." *Word and Image* 1 (1985): 16–30.

Letters and Papers, Foreign and Domestic, of the Reign of Henry VIII, 1509–47. Ed. J. S. Brewer, J. Gairdner, and R. H. Brodie. 21 vols. London: HMSO, 1862–1910.

Letters of Queen Elizabeth and King James VI. of Scotland. Ed. John Bruce. 1849; rpt., New York: AMS Press, 1968.

Levin, Carole. *"The Heart and Stomach of a King": Elizabeth I and the Politics of Sex and Power.* Philadelphia: Univ. of Pennsylvania Press, 1994.

———. " 'We shall never have a merry world while the Queene lyveth': Gender, Monarchy, and the Power of Seditious Words." In *Dissing Elizabeth: Negative Representations of Gloriana.* Ed. Julia M. Walker. Durham, NC: Duke Univ. Press, 1998. Pp. 77–95.

Levine, Mortimer. *The Early Elizabethan Succession Question 1558–1568.* Stanford: Stanford Univ. Press, 1966.

Lewis, Jayne Elizabeth. *Mary Queen of Scots: Romance and Nation.* London: Routledge, 1998.

The Lives of Philip Howard, Earl of Arundel, and of Anne Dacres, His Wife. Ed. the Duke of Norfolk. London: Hurst and Blackett, 1857.

Lloyd, Christopher, and Simon Thurley. *Henry VIII: Images of a Tudor King.* London: Phaidon, 1990.

Loades, D. M. *Mary Tudor: A Life.* Oxford: Basil Blackwell, 1989.

———. "Philip II and the Government of England." In *Law and Government under the Tudors.* Ed. Claire Cross, David Loades, and J. J. Scarisbrick. Cambridge: Cambridge Univ. Press, 177–94.

———. *The Reign of Mary Tudor: Politics, Government, and Religion in England, 1553–1558.* London: Ernest Benn, 1979.

Lodge, Edmund. *Illustrations of British History, Biography, and Manners, in the Reigns of Henry VIII, Edward VI, Elizabeth, and James I.* 3 vols. London: G. Nichol, 1791.

Logan, Sandra. "Making History: The Rhetorical and Historical Occasion of Elizabeth Tudor's Coronation Entry." *Journal of Medieval and Early Modern Studies* 31 (2001): 251–82.

Loomis, Catherine. "Elizabeth Southwell's Manuscript Account of the Death of Queen Elizabeth [with text]." *English Literary Renaissance* 26 (1996): 482–509.

MacCaffrey, Wallace T. *Elizabeth I: War and Politics 1588–1603*. Princeton: Princeton Univ. Press, 1992.

———. *Queen Elizabeth and the Making of Policy, 1572–1588*. Princeton: Princeton Univ. Press, 1981.

MacCulloch, Diarmaid. "Bondmen under the Tudors." In *Law and Government under the Tudors*. Ed. Claire Cross, David Loades, and J. J. Scarisbrick. Cambridge: Cambridge Univ. Press, 1988. Pp. 91–109.

———. "Catholic and Puritan in Elizabethan Suffolk: A County Community Polarizes." *Archiv für Reformationsgeschichte* 72 (1981): 232–89.

———. *Suffolk and the Tudors: Politics and Religion in an English County 1500–1600*. Oxford: Clarendon Press, 1986.

Maclean, Ian. *The Renaissance Notion of Woman: A Study in the Fortunes of Scholasticism and Medical Science in European Intellectual Life*. Cambridge: Cambridge Univ. Press, 1980.

Manning, Roger B. "The Origins of the Doctrine of Sedition." *Albion* 12 (1980): 99–121.

———. *Village Revolts: Social Protest and Popular Disturbances in England, 1509–1640*. Oxford: Clarendon Press, 1988.

Manningham, John. *The Diary of John Manningham of the Middle Temple, 1602–1603*. Ed. Robert Parker Sorlien. Hanover, NH: Univ. Press of New England, 1976.

Marcus, Leah S. "Erasing the Stigma of Daughterhood: Mary I, Elizabeth I, and Henry VIII." In *Daughters and Fathers*. Ed. Linda E. Boose and Betty S. Flowers. Baltimore: Johns Hopkins Univ. Press, 1989. Pp. 400–417.

———. *Puzzling Shakespeare: Local Reading and Its Discontents*. Berkeley: Univ. of California Press, 1988.

Marotti, Arthur F. "Southwell's Remains: Catholicism and Anti-Catholicism in Early Modern England." In *Texts and Cultural Change in Early Modern England*. Ed. Cedric C. Brown and Arthur F. Marotti. New York: St. Martin's Press, 1997. Pp. 37–65.

Martin, Colin, and Geoffrey Parker. *The Spanish Armada*. London: Hamish Hamilton, 1988.

McClure, Peter, and Robin Headlam Wells. "Elizabeth I as a Second Virgin Mary." *Renaissance Studies* 4 (1990): 38–70.

McCoy, Richard C. *Alterations of State: Sacred Kingship in the English Reformation*. New York: Columbia Univ. Press, 2002.

———. *The Rites of Knighthood: The Literature and Politics of Elizabethan Chivalry*. Berkeley: Univ. of California Press, 1989.

McLaren, Anne. *Political Culture in the Reign of Elizabeth I: Queen and Commonwealth 1558–1585*. Cambridge: Cambridge Univ. Press, 1999.

———. "Prophecy and Providentialism in the Reign of Elizabeth I." In *Prophecy: The Power of Inspired Language in History 1300–2000*. Ed. Bertrand Taithe and Tim Thornton. Stroud, Gloucestershire: Sutton, 1997. Pp. 31–50.

———. "The Quest for a King: Gender, Marriage, and Succession in Elizabethan England." *Journal of British Studies* 41 (2002): 259–90.

Mears, Natalie. "Courts, Courtiers, and Culture in Tudor England." *Historical Journal* 46 (2003): 703–22.

Mikalachki, Jodi. *The Legacy of Boadicea: Gender and Nation in Early Modern England*. London: Routledge, 1998.

Millar, Oliver. *Tudor, Stuart and Early Georgian Pictures in the Collection of Her Majesty the Queen*. 2 vols. London: Phaidon, 1963.

The Mirror for Magistrates. Ed. Lily B. Campbell. 1938; rpt., New York: Barnes & Noble, 1960.

Miscellaneous State Papers from 1501 to 1726. Ed. Philip Hardwicke, Earl of York. 2 vols. London, 1778.

Montrose, Louis. "Celebration and Insinuation: Sir Philip Sidney and the Motives of Elizabethan Courtship." *Renaissance Drama*, n.s. 8 (1977): 3–35.

―――. "The Elizabethan Subject and the Spenserian Text." In *Literary Theory/Renaissance Texts*. Ed. Patricia Parker and David Quint. Baltimore: Johns Hopkins Univ. Press, 1986. Pp. 303–40.

―――. "Elizabeth hinter dem Spiegel: Die Ein-Bildung der zwei Körper der Königin" [Elizabeth through the looking-glass: Picturing the Queen's two bodies]. In *Der Körper der Königin: Geschlecht und Herrschaft in der höfischen Welt seit 1500*. Ed. Regina Schulte. Frankfurt: Campus Verlag, 2002. Pp. 67–98.

―――. "'Eliza, Queene of Shepheardes' and the Pastoral of Power." *English Literary Renaissance* 10 (1980): 153–82.

―――. "Gifts and Reasons: The Contexts of Peele's *Araygnement of Paris*." *ELH* 47 (1980): 433–61.

―――. "Idols of the Queen: Policy, Gender, and the Picturing of Elizabeth I." *Representations* 68 (Fall 1999): 106–61.

―――. "New Historicisms." In *Redrawing the Boundaries: The Transformation of English and American Literary Studies*. Ed. Stephen Greenblatt and Giles Gunn. New York: Modern Language Association, 1992. Pp. 392–418.

―――. "Of Gentlemen and Shepherds: The Politics of Elizabethan Pastoral Form." *ELH* 50 (1983): 415–59.

―――. "'The perfecte paterne of a Poete': The Poetics of Courtship in *The Shepheardes Calender*." *Texas Studies in Literature and Language* 21 (1979): 34–67.

―――. *The Purpose of Playing: Shakespeare and the Cultural Politics of the Elizabethan Theatre*. Chicago: Univ. of Chicago Press, 1996.

―――. "'Shaping Fantasies': Figurations of Gender and Power in Elizabethan Culture." *Representations* 2 (Spring 1983): 61–94.

―――. "Spenser and the Elizabethan Political Imaginary." *ELH* 69 (2002): 907–46.

―――. "Spenser's Domestic Domain: Poetry, Property, and the Early Modern Subject." In *Subject and Object in Renaissance Culture*. Ed. Margreta de Grazia, Maureen Quilligan, and Peter Stallybrass. Cambridge: Cambridge Univ. Press, 1996. Pp. 83–130.

―――. "The Work of Gender in the Discourse of Discovery." *Representations* 33 (Winter 1991): 1–41.

Morgan, Hiram. "Extradition and Treason-Trial of a Gaelic Lord: The Case of Brian O'Rourke." *Irish Jurist* 22 (1987): 285–301.

―――. "The Fall of Sir John Perrot." In *The Reign of Elizabeth I: Court and Culture in the Last Decade*. Ed. John Guy. Cambridge: Cambridge Univ. Press, 1995. Pp. 109–25.

Morgan, Victor. "The Cartographic Image of 'the Country' in Early Modern England." *Transactions of the Royal Historical Society*, 5th ser. 29 (1979): 129–54.

Mueller, Janel. "Virtue and Virtuality: Gender in the Self-Representations of Queen Elizabeth I." In *Form and Reform in Renaissance England: Essays in Honor of Barbara Kiefer Lewalski*. Ed. Amy Boesky and Mary Thomas Crane. Newark: Univ. of Delaware Press, 2000. Pp. 220–46.

Mullaney, Steven. "Mourning and Misogyny: *Hamlet, The Revenger's Tragedy*, and the Final Progress of Elizabeth I, 1600–1607." *Shakespeare Quarterly* 45 (1994): 139–62.

Nash, Jane C. *Veiled Images: Titian's Mythological Paintings for Philip II*. Cranbury, NJ: Associated Univ. Presses, 1985.

Neale, J. E. *Essays in Elizabethan History*. London: Jonathan Cape, 1958.

Nicholas, Harris. *Memoirs of the Life and Times of Sir Christopher Hatton, K. G.* London: Richard Bentley, 1847.

Nichols, John. *The Progresses and Public Processions of Queen Elizabeth.* 3 vols. 1823; rpt., New York: Burt Franklin, 1966.

————. *The Progresses, Processions, and Magnificent Festivities, of King James the First.* 4 vols. London, 1828.

Nuttall, Geoffrey F. "The English Martyrs 1535–1680: A Statistical Review." *Journal of Ecclesiastical History* 22 (1971) 191–97.

Original Letters, Illustrative of English History. Ed. Henry Ellis. 11 vols. in 4 series. London: Harding & Lepard, 1824–46.

Original letters relative to the English reformation: written during the reigns of King Henry VIII, King Edward VI, and Queen Mary: chiefly from the archives of Zurich. Ed. Hastings Robinson. 2 vols. 1846–47; rpt., New York: Johnson Reprint, 1968.

Orlin, Lena Cowen. "The Fictional Families of Elizabeth I." In *Political Rhetoric, Power, and Renaissance Women.* Ed. Carole Levin and Patricia A. Sullivan. Albany: State Univ. of New York Press, 1995. Pp., 85–110.

Osborne, Francis. *Historical memoires on the reigns of Queen Elizabeth and King James.* London, 1658.

Oxford Dictionary of National Biography. Online edition. http://www.oxforddnb.com.

Panofsky, Erwin. *Problems in Titian, Mostly Iconographic.* New York: New York Univ. Press, 1969.

Parker, Geoffrey. *The Dutch Revolt.* London: Allen Lane, 1977.

Parmenius, Stephen. *The New Found Land of Stephen Parmenius: The Life and Writings of a Hungarian Poet, Drowned on a Voyage from Newfoundland, 1583.* Ed. and trans. David B. Quinn and Neil M. Cheshire. Toronto: Univ. of Toronto Press, 1972.

Paster, Gail Kern. *The Body Embarrassed: Drama and the Disciplines of Shame in Early Modern England.* Ithaca: Cornell Univ. Press, 1993.

Pastor, Ludwig Freiherr von. *The History of the Popes from the Close of the Middle Ages, drawn from the archives of the Vatican and other original sources.* Ed. Ralph Francis Kerr. 40 vols. London: Kegan Paul, Trench, & Trubner, 1938–68.

Patterson, Annabel. *Reading between the Lines.* Madison: Univ. of Wisconsin Press, 1993.

Peck, D. C., ed. *Leicester's Commonwealth: The Copy of a Letter Written by a Master of Art of Cambridge (1584) and Related Documents.* Athens: Ohio Univ. Press, 1985.

————. "'News from Heaven and Hell': A Defamatory Narrative of the Earl of Leicester." *English Literary Renaissance* 8 (1978): 141–58.

Peele, George. *The Life and Works of George Peele.* Gen ed. George Prouty. 3 vols. New Haven: Yale Univ. Press, 1952–70.

Perry, Curtis. *The Making of Jacobean Culture: James I and the Renegotiation of Elizabethan Literary Practice.* Cambridge: Cambridge Univ. Press, 1997.

Petti, A. G. "Richard Verstegan and Catholic Martyrologies of the Later Elizabethan Period." *Recusant History* 5 (1959): 64–90.

Phillips, James Emerson. "The Background to Spenser's Attitude toward Women Rulers." *Huntington Library Quarterly* 5 (1941): 5–32.

————. *Images of a Queen: Mary Stuart in Sixteenth-Century Literature.* Berkeley: Univ. of California Press, 1964.

Plowden, Edmund. *The commentaries, or Reports of Edmund Plowden.* London: S. Brooke, 1816.

Pollen, John Hungerford. *Acts of English Martyrs Hitherto Unpublished*. London: Burns & Oates, 1891.

Prescott, Anne Lake. "The Pearl of Valois and Elizabeth I: Marguerite de Navarre's *Miroir* and Tudor England." In *Silent But for the Word: Tudor Women as Patrons, Translators, and Writers of Religious Works*. Ed. Margaret Patterson Hannay. Kent, Ohio: Kent State Univ. Press, 1985. Pp. 61–76.

Pritchard, Arnold. *Catholic Loyalism in Elizabethan England*. Chapel Hill: Univ. of North Carolina Press, 1979.

Proceedings in the Parliaments of Elizabeth I. Ed. T. E. Hartley. 3 vols. London: Leicester Univ. Press, 1981–95.

Puttenham, George. *The Arte of English Poesie*. Ed. Gladys Doidge Willcock and Alice Walker. Cambridge: Cambridge Univ. Press, 1936.

Queen Elizabeth and Some Foreigners: Being a Series of Hitherto Unpublished Letters from the Archives of the Hapsburg Family. Ed. Victor von Klarwill. Trans. T. H. Nash. New York: Brentano's Publishers, 1928.

The Quenes Maiesties Passage through the Citie of London to Westminster the Day before her Coronation. Facsimile ed. Ed. James M. Osborn. New Haven: Yale Univ. Press, 1960.

Quilligan, Maureen. "Incest and Agency: The Case of Elizabeth I." In *Generation and Degeneration: Tropes of Reproduction in Literature and History from Antiquity through Early Modern Europe*. Ed. Valeria Finucci and Kevin Brownlee. Durham: Duke Univ. Press, 2001. Pp. 209–31.

Rahter, Charles A. "A Critical Edition of Churchyard's Challenge (1593) by Thomas Churchyard with Some Notes on the Author's Life and Works." Doctoral diss. Univ. of Pennsylvania, 1958.

Ralegh, Walter. *The Discovery of the Large, Rich, and Beautiful Empire of Guiana*. Ed. Sir Robert W. Schomburgk. London: Hakluyt Society, 1848.

———. *The History of the World*. Ed. C. A. Patrides. Philadelphia: Temple Univ. Press, 1971.

———. *The Poems of Sir Walter Ralegh*. Ed. Agnes Latham. Cambridge, MA: Harvard Univ. Press, 1962.

———. *The Works of Sir Walter Ralegh, Kt*. Ed. William Oldys and Thomas Birch. 8 vols. 1829; rpt., New York: Burt Franklin, 1965.

Records of Early English Drama: Norwich, 1540–1642. Ed. David Galloway. Toronto: Univ. of Toronto Press, 1984.

Records of the English Province of the Society of Jesus. Ed. Henry Foley. 4 vols. 1877–78; rpt., New York: Johnson Reprint, 1966.

Recueil des lettres missives de Henri IV. Ed. M. Berger de Xivrey. 9 vols. Paris: Imprimerie Nationale, 1843–76.

Redworth, Glyn. "'Matters Impertinent to Women': Male and Female Monarchy under Philip and Mary." *English Historical Review* 112 (1997): 597–613.

Relations politiques des Pays-Bas et de l'Angleterre, sous le règne de Philippe II. Ed. J. M. B. C. Kervyn de Lettenhove. 11 vols. Brussels: Hayez, 1888–1900.

Richards, Judith M. "Before the 'Mountaynes Mouse': Propaganda and Public Defence before the Spanish Armada." In *England and the Spanish Armada*. Ed. Jeff Doyle and Bruce Moore. Canberra: University of New South Wales and Australian Defence Force Academy, 1990. Pp. 13–34.

———. "The English Accession of James VI: 'National' Identity, Gender and the Personal Monarchy of England." *English Historical Review* 117 (2002): 513–35.

———. "Love and a Female Monarch: The Case of Elizabeth Tudor." *Journal of British Studies* 38 (1999): 133–60.

———. "Mary Tudor as 'Sole Quene'? Gendering the Tudor Monarchy." *Historical Journal* 40 (1997): 895–924.

———. "Mary Tudor, Renaissance Queen of England." In *"High and Mighty Queens" of Early Modern England: Realities and Representations.* Ed. Carole Levin, Jo Eldridge Carney, and Debra Barrett-Graves. New York: Palgrave, 2003. Pp. 27–43.

———. "'To Promote a Woman to Beare Rule': Talking of Queens in Mid-Tudor England." *Sixteenth Century Journal* 28 (1997): 101–21.

Richardson, Lisa. "Elizabeth in Arcadia: Fulke Greville and John Hayward's Construction of Elizabeth, 1610–12." In *The Myth of Elizabeth.* Ed. Susan Doran and Thomas S. Freedman. New York: Palgrave Macmillan, 2003. Pp. 99–119.

Riggs, David. "Marlowe's Quarrel with God." In *Marlowe, History, and Sexuality: New Critical Essays on Christopher Marlowe.* Ed. Paul Whitfield White. New York: AMS Press, 1998. Pp. 15–37.

The Roanoke Voyages 1584–1590. Ed. David Beers Quinn. 2 vols. London: Hakluyt Society, 1955.

Roper, Lyndal. *Oedipus and the Devil: Witchcraft, Sexuality and Religion in Early Modern Europe.* London: Routledge, 1994.

Rosand, David. "*Ut pictor poeta*: Meaning in Titian's *Poesie*." *New Literary History* 3.3 (Spring 1972): 527–46.

Rose, Mary Beth. *Gender and Heroism in Early Modern English Literature.* Chicago: Univ. of Chicago Press, 2002.

Rosen, Barbara, ed. *Witchcraft in England, 1558–1618.* 1969; rpt., Amherst: Univ. of Massachusetts Press, 1991.

Samaha, Joel. "Gleanings from Local Criminal Court Records: Sedition amongst the 'Inarticulate' in Elizabethan Essex." *Journal of Social History* 8 (1975): 61–79.

Sander, Nicholas. *The Rise and Growth of the Anglican Schism.* Trans. David Lewis. London: Burns & Oates, 1877.

Savile, Henry, trans. *The ende of Nero and beginning of Galba: Fower bookes of the Histories of Cornelius Tacitus.* Oxford, 1591. STC 23642.

Savine, Alexander. "Bondmen under the Tudors." *Transactions of the Royal Historical Society*, 2nd ser., 17 (1903): 235–89.

Sawday, Jonathan. *The Body Emblazoned: Dissection and the Human Body in Renaissance Culture.* London: Routledge, 1995.

Saxl, Fritz. "Veritas filia temporis." In *Philosophy and History: Essays Presented to Ernst Cassirer.* Ed. Raymond Klibansky and H. J. Paton. Oxford: Clarendon Press, 1936. Pp. 196–223.

Scaligi, Paula Louise. "The Sceptre or the Distaff: The Question of Female Sovereignty, 1516–1607." *The Historian* 41 (1978): 59–75.

Schleiner, Winfried. "*Divina virago*: Queen Elizabeth as an Amazon." *Studies in Philology* 75 (1978): 163–80.

Schwartz, Kathryn. *Tough Love: Amazon Encounters in the English Renaissance.* Durham, NC: Duke Univ. Press, 2000.

Scot, Reginald. *The Discoverie of Witchcraft.* 1584. New York: Dover, 1972.

Scott-Warren, Jason. "Harington's Gossip." In *The Myth of Elizabeth.* Ed. Susan Doran and Thomas S. Freedman. New York: Palgrave Macmillan, 2003. Pp. 221–41.

———. *Sir John Harington and the Book as Gift.* Oxford: Oxford Univ. Press, 2001.

Shakespeare, William. *The Norton Shakespeare*. Ed. Stephen Greenblatt et al. New York: Norton, 1997.

Sharpe, J. A. "'Last Dying Speeches': Religion, Ideology and Public Execution in Seventeenth-Century England." *Past & Present* 107 (May 1985): 144–67.

Sharpe, Jim. "Social Strain and Social Dislocation, 1585–1603." In *The Reign of Elizabeth I: Court and Culture in the Last Decade*. Ed. John Guy. Cambridge: Cambridge Univ. Press, 1995. Pp. 192–211.

Sharpe, Kevin. "Representations and Negotiations: Texts, Images, and Authority in Early Modern England." *Historical Journal* 42 (1999): 853–81.

Shell, Marc. *Elizabeth's Glass*. Lincoln: Univ. of Nebraska Press, 1993.

Shephard, Amanda. *Gender and Authority in Sixteenth-Century England: The Knox Debate*. Keele: Ryburn, 1994.

Shuger, Debora. "The 'I' of the Beholder: Renaissance Mirrors and the Reflexive Mind." In *Renaissance Culture and the Everyday*. Ed. Patricia Fumerton and Simon Hunt. Philadelphia: Univ. of Pennsylvania Press, 1999. Pp. 21–41.

Sidney, Philip. *The Countess of Pembroke's Arcadia (The Old Arcadia)*. Ed. Katherine Duncan-Jones. Oxford: Oxford Univ. Press, 1985.

———. *Miscellaneous Prose of Sir Philip Sidney*. Ed. Katherine Duncan-Jones and Jan van Dorsten. Oxford: Clarendon Press, 1973.

Skinner, Quentin. *The Foundations of Modern Political Thought*. 2 vols. Cambridge: Cambridge Univ. Press, 1978.

Smith, A. Hassell. *County and Court: Government and Politics in Norfolk 1558–1603*. Oxford: Clarendon Press, 1974.

Smith, Sir Thomas. *De republica anglorum: A Discourse on the Commonwealth of England*. Ed. L. Alston. 1906; rpt., Shannon: Irish Univ. Press, 1972.

Smuts, R. Malcolm. "Occasional Events, Literary Texts and Historical Interpretations." In *Neo-Historicism: Studies in Renaissance Literature, History and Politics*. Ed. Robin Headlam Wells, Glenn Burgess, and Rowland Wymer. Woodbridge, Suffolk: D. S. Brewer, 2000. Pp. 179–98.

Snyder, Susan. "Guilty Sisters: Marguerite de Navarre, Elizabeth of England, and the *Miroir de l'âme pécheresse*." *Renaissance Quarterly* 50 (1997): 443–58.

Solomon, Nanette. "Positioning Women in Visual Convention: The Case of Elizabeth I." In *Attending to Women in Early Modern England*. Ed. Betty S. Travitsky and Adele F. Seeff. Newark: Univ. of Delaware Press, 1994. Pp. 54–95.

Southwell, Robert. *An Humble Supplication to Her Majestie*. Ed. R. C. Bald. Cambridge: Cambridge Univ. Pres, 1953.

Spenser, Edmund. *The Faerie Queene*. Ed. A. C. Hamilton. 2nd ed. London: Longman, 2001.

Stallybrass, Peter. "Patriarchal Territories: The Body Enclosed." In *Rewriting the Renaissance: The Discourses of Sexual Difference in Early Modern Europe*. Ed. Margaret W. Ferguson, Maureen Quilligan, and Nancy J. Vickers. Chicago: Univ. of Chicago Press, 1986. Pp. 123–42, 344–47.

Starkey, David. "Intimacy and Innovation." In *The English Court: From the Wars of the Roses to the Civil War*. Ed. David Starkey. London: Longman, 1987. Pp. 71–118.

———. "Representation through Intimacy: A Study in the Symbolism of Monarchy and Court Office in Early-Modern England." In *Symbols and Sentiments: Cross-Cultural Studies in Symbolism*. Ed. Ioan Lewis. London: Academic Press, 1977. Pp. 187–224.

Stevens, Scott Manning. "Sacred Heart and Secular Brain." In *The Body in Parts: Fantasies of Corporeality in Early Modern Europe*. Ed. David Hillman and Carla Mazzio. London: Routledge, 1997. Pp. 263–82.

Strathmann, Ernest A. *Sir Walter Ralegh: A Study in Elizabethan Skepticism*. New York: Columbia Univ. Press, 1951.

Strong, Roy. *The Cult of Elizabeth: Elizabethan Portraiture and Pageantry*. London: Thames & Hudson, 1977.

————. *The English Icon: Elizabethan and Jacobean Portraiture*. London: Routledge & Kegan Paul, 1969.

————. *Gloriana: The Portraits of Queen Elizabeth I*. London: Thames & Hudson, 1987.

————. "The Popular Celebration of the Accession Day of Queen Elizabeth I." *Journal of the Warburg and Courtauld Institutes* 21 (1958): 86–103.

————. *Portraits of Queen Elizabeth I*. Oxford: Clarendon Press, 1963.

————. *Tudor and Jacobean Portraits*. 2 vols. London: HMSO, 1969.

————. *The Tudor and Stuart Monarchy: Pageantry, Painting, Iconography*. 3 vols. Woodbridge, Suffolk: Boydell Press, 1994–98.

Strong, Roy, and J. A. Van Dorsten. *Leicester's Triumph*. Leiden: Leiden Univ. Press, 1964.

Strong, Roy, with V. J. Murrell. *Artists of the Tudor Court: The Portrait Miniature Rediscovered 1520–1620*. London: Victoria & Albert Museum, 1983.

Strype, John. *Annals of the reformation and establishment of religion, and other various occurrences in the Church of England during Queen Elizabeth's happy reign*. 4 vols. in 7 parts. 1824; rpt., New York: Burt Franklin, 1964.

Stubbs, John. *John Stubbs's Gaping Gulf with Letters and Other Relevant Documents*. Ed. Lloyd E. Berry. Charlottesville: Univ. Press of Virginia, 1968.

Suzuki, Mihoko. "Elizabeth, Gender, and the Political Imaginary of Seventeenth-Century England." In *Debating Gender in Early Modern England, 1500–1700*. Ed. Cristina Malcolmson and Mihoko Suzuki. New York: Palgrave Macmillan, 2002. Pp. 231–53.

Tanner, J. R. *Tudor Constitutional Documents, A.D. 1485–1603*. 1922; rpt., Cambridge: Cambridge Univ. Press, 1951.

Thomas, Keith. *Religion and the Decline of Magic*. New York: Charles Scribner's Sons, 1971.

Thomas Platter's Travels in England 1599. Trans. Clare Williams. London: Jonathan Cape, 1937.

Thompson, E. P. *Customs in Common*. New York: New Press, 1993.

Thurley, Simon. *The Royal Palaces of Tudor England: Architecture and Court Life 1460–1547*. New Haven: Yale Univ. Press, 1993.

Traub, Valerie. *The Renaissance of Lesbianism in Early Modern England*. Cambridge: Cambridge Univ. Press, 2002.

The Troubles of Our Catholic Forefathers Related by Themselves. Ed. John Morris. 3 vols. London: Burns & Oates, 1872–77.

Tuck, Richard. *Philosophy and Government 1572–1651*. Cambridge: Cambridge Univ. Press, 1993.

Tudor Royal Proclamations. Ed. Paul L. Hughes and James F. Larkin. 3 vols. New Haven: Yale Univ. Press, 1969.

The Two Books of Homilies Appointed to Be Read in Churches. Oxford: At the University Press, 1859.

Ungerer, Gustav. *A Spaniard in Elizabethan England: The Correspondence of Antonio Pérez's Exile*. 2 vols. London: Tamesis Books, 1974–76.

Unpublished Documents Relating to the English Martyrs. Vol. 1, *1584–1603*. Ed. John Hungerford Pollen. London: Catholic Record Society, 1908.

Van Gelderen, Martin. *The Political Thought of the Dutch Revolt 1555–1590*. Cambridge: Cambridge Univ. Press, 1992.

Van Thiel, Pieter J. J., et al. *All the Paintings of the Rijksmuseum in Amsterdam*. Amsterdam: Rijksmuseum, 1976.

Verstegan, Richard. *The Letters and Despatches of Richard Verstegan*. Ed. Anthony G. Petti. London: Catholic Record Society, 1959.

Vives, Juan Luis. *The Instruction of a Christen Woman*. Facsimile ed. In *Distaves and Dames: Renaissance Treatises for and about Women*. Ed. Diane Bornstein. Del Mar, NY: Scholars' Facsimiles and Reprints, 1978.

Walker, Julia M., ed. *Dissing Elizabeth: Negative Representations of Gloriana*. Durham, NC: Duke Univ. Press, 1998.

————. *The Elizabethan Icon, 1603–2003*. New York: Palgrave Macmillan, 2004.

————. "Reading the Tombs of Elizabeth I." *English Literary Renaissance* 26 (1996): 510–30.

Wall, Wendy. *The Imprint of Gender: Authorship and Publication in the English Renaissance*. Ithaca: Cornell Univ. Press, 1993.

Walsham, Alexandra. "'Frantick Hacket': Prophecy, Sorcery, Insanity, and the Elizabethan Puritan Movement." *Historical Journal* 41 (1998): 27–66.

————. "Miracles and the Counter-Reformation Mission to England." *Historical Journal* 46 (2003): 779–815.

————. "'A Very Deborah'? The Myth of Elizabeth I as a Providential Monarch." In *The Myth of Elizabeth*. Ed. Susan Doran and Thomas S. Freeman. Basingstoke, Hampshire: Palgrave Macmillan, 2003. Pp. 143–68.

Walter, John. "A 'Rising of the People'? The Oxfordshire Rising of 1596." *Past & Present* 107 (1985): 90–143.

Watkins, John. *Representing Elizabeth in Stuart England: Literature, History, Sovereignty*. Cambridge: Cambridge Univ. Press, 2002.

Wedel, Lupold von. "Journey through England and Scotland Made by Lupold von Wedel in the Years 1584 and 1585." Trans. Gottfried von Bülow. *Transactions of the Royal Historical Society*, n.s. 9 (1895): 223–70.

Weiner, Carol. "The Beleaguered Isle: A Study of Elizabethan and Early Jacobean Anti-Catholicism." *Past & Present* 51 (1971): 27–62.

Wernham, R. B. *Before the Armada*. New York: Norton, 1966.

Wethey, Harold E. *The Paintings of Titian*. 3 vols. London: Phaidon Press, 1975.

Whitgift, John. *A most godly and learned sermon preached at Pauls crosse the 17 of November, in the year of our Lorde 1583*. London, 1589. STC 25432.

Whitney, Geffrey. *Whitney's "Choice of Emblemes."* 1586. Facsimile ed. Ed. Henry Green. London: Lovell Reeve, 1866.

Willis, Deborah. *Malevolent Nurture: Witch-Hunting and Maternal Power in Early Modern England*. Ithaca: Cornell Univ. Press, 1995.

Wilson, Elkin Calhoun. *England's Eliza*. Cambridge, MA: Harvard Univ. Press, 1939.

Wilson, Thomas. *The State of England Anno Dom. 1600*. Ed. F. J. Fisher. Camden Miscellany, vol. 16. London: Camden Society, 1936.

Wingfield, Robert. "The *Vita Mariae Angliae Reginae* of Robert Wingfield of Brantham." Ed. and trans. Diarmaid MacCulloch. *Camden Miscellany* 28. London: Royal Historical Society, 1984. Pp. 181–301.

Womersley, David. "Sir Henry Savile's Translation of Tacitus and the Political Interpretation of Elizabethan Texts." *Review of English Studies*, n.s. 42 (1991): 313–42.

Woodall, Joanna. "An Exemplary Consort: Antonis Mor's Portrait of Mary Tudor." *Art History* 14 (1991): 192–224.

Woodbridge, Linda. *Women and the English Renaissance: Literature and the Nature of Womankind, 1540–1620*. Urbana: Univ. of Illinois Press, 1984.

Woodward, Jennifer. *The Theatre of Death: The Ritual Management of Royal Funerals in Renaissance England 1570–1625*. Woodbridge, Suffolk: Boydell Press, 1997.

Worden, Blair. *The Sound of Virtue: Philip Sidney's Arcadia and Elizabethan Politics*. New Haven: Yale Univ. Press, 1996.

Wormald, Jenny. *Mary Queen of Scots: A Study in Failure*. London: Collins & Brown, 1991.

Wotton, Henry. *The State of Christendom; or, A most Exact and Curious Discovery of Many Secret Passages, and Hidden Mysteries of the Times*. London, 1657.

Wright, Celeste Turner. "The Amazons in Elizabethan Literature." *Studies in Philology* 37 (1940): 433–56.

Wright, Pam. "A Change in Direction: The Ramifications of a Female Household, 1558–1603." In *The English Court: From the Wars of the Roses to the Civil War*. Ed. David Starkey. London: Longman, 1987. Pp. 147–72.

Yates, Frances. *Astraea: The Imperial Theme in the Sixteenth Century*. 1975; rpt., Harmondsworth: Penguin Books, 1977.

Yates, Julian. "Parasitic Geographies: Manifesting Catholic Identity in Early Modern England." In *Catholicism and Anti-Catholicism in Early Modern English Texts*. Ed. Arthur F. Marotti. New York: St. Martin's Press, 1999. Pp. 63–84.

Zeigler, Georgianna. "England's Savior: Elizabeth I in the Writings of Thomas Heywood." *Renaissance Papers* (1980): 29–37.

Index

Note: *Italicized page numbers indicate figures.*

Accession Day. *See* Queen's Accession Day
Act in Restraint of Appeals (1533), 36, 260n7
Acts of Supremacy and Uniformity (1559), 187
Adams, Simon, 287–88n4
Adler, Doris, 127, 277–78n20, 280n16
adultery, 11–13, 37
Aeneas, 159, 283n19
Ales, Alexander, 63–64
Alexander III (pope), 140
Alford, Stephen, 256n4
Alkyngton, Samuel, 171
"Allegory of the Tudor Succession": described, *58*,
    58–62, *59*, 268n9; versions of, 267n2
Allen, William Cardinal: on acts of Supremacy
    and Uniformity of, 187–88; on Armada, 74, 75,
    165–66, 171, 172; on Elizabeth, 38, 257–58n8; on
    martyrdom, 197, 208; mentioned, 231; on
    monarcholatry, 74, 106, 107; opposition to, 169;
    on Queen's Accession Day, 75; sectarian agenda
    of, 80; seminaries founded by, 84–85, 88, 195,
    273n13; suppressed pamphlet of, 195–96; on
    torture and executions, 192–93
Amazonian images: Elizabeth as, 285n30, 285n31;
    Elizabeth-Europa as, 157–58; personification of
    America and, 285n28
anecdotal evidence: approach to, 6–7; Looking
    Glass trope in, 241–47; maliciousness in, 151–52
Anglican church: appropriation and substitution
    in, 75; charges of idolatry against, 80;
    countercharge of heresy against, 183; monarch's
    dominion over, 15, 22, 24. *See also* Protestant
    Reformation
Anglo, Sydney, 112
Anglo-French marriage negotiations: "Ditchley"
    portrait and, 277–78n20; Dudley and, 109, 120;
    dynastic succession issues and, 211–13;

Elizabeth's portraits during, 121–27; end of, 137;
    as opportunity for Catholics, 88; opposition to,
    70, 121–22, 165–66, 276n9, 296–97n57; rumors
    about Elizabeth's sexuality and, 125, 127; trope
    of invasion in opposition to, 121–22, 276n9
Anglo-French Treaty of Blois (1572), 59
Anglo-Spanish conflict: anti-Elizabeth polemics
    on, 161–63; "Armada" portraits and, 145–48,
    146; as battle of good/evil, 145, 161;
    Elizabeth-Europa's triumph in, 154–55, *155*,
    157–59; Elizabeth's parliamentary speeches on,
    159–61; Elizabeth's Tilbury speech and, 148–52,
    157–58, 168, 173, 282nn10–11, 282–83n14,
    283nn15–16; Irish rebellion and, 144–45.
    See also Armada
Anjou, duke of (François): in allegorical prints of
    Low Countries, 132–36, *133*, *135*, 279n5; death
    of, 278n1, 279n9; Elizabeth's nickname for, 138,
    280n16; inept military ventures in Low Coun-
    tries, 133, 134, 279n6; in Parisian cartoon, 137–38;
    royal garter received by, 297n62; title of, 276n8.
    See also Anglo-French marriage negotiations
Anne Boleyn (queen of England): absent from
    Whitehall Privy Chamber mural, 26;
    Elizabeth's likeness of, 268n14; execution of,
    14–15, 34, 37; fall of, 63–64; Mary's hatred of, 37;
    pageant's depiction of, 39; Protestant
    Reformation role of, 62–63; women's riot
    against, 12–13, 257n5
Antichrist, identifications of, 281n23
antipapist campaign: imaginary embedded in,
    189, 209, 292n13; instructions in, 271n13;
    intensification of, 85, 87–88; pamphlets on,
    207–8; planned Armada invasion and, 168–69;
    seminary as target of, 84–85. *See also*
    executions; interrogation by torture